D0777113

NORMAN CORWIN'S LETTERS

NORMAN CORWIN'S LETTERS

EDITED BY A.J. LANGGUTH

BARRICADE BOOKS INC.

NEW YORK

Published by Barricade Books Inc.
61 Fourth Avenue
New York, NY 10003

Printed in the United States of America

Library of Congress Cataloging-in-Publication Data

Corwin, Norman Lewis, 1910-
    [Correspondence. Selections]
    Norman Corwin's letters/edited by A.J. Langguth.
    p. cm.
    ISBN 0-9623032-5-9: $22.00
    1. Corwin, Norman Lewis, 1910-   —Correspondence. 2. Authors, American—
20th century—Correspondence. 3. Radio producers and directors—United States—
Correspondence. I. Langguth, A.J. II. Title.
PS3505.O777Z48 1993
814'.52—dc20   93-15898
[B]   CIP

First Printing

To Emil, Beulah, and the memory of
Rose, Samuel and Alfred Corwin

OTHER BOOKS BY NORMAN CORWIN

They Fly Through the Air

The Plot to Overthrow Christmas

Seems Radio Is Here to Stay

Thirteen by Corwin

More by Corwin

Untitled and Other Radio Dramas

We Hold These Truths

On a Note of Triumph

Dog in the Sky

The Rivalry

The World of Carl Sandburg

Overkill and Megalove

Prayer for the 70s

Network at Fifty

Holes in a Stained Glass Window

Greater Than the Bomb

Trivializing America

CONartist
TEXT TO SELECTED CARTOONS BY PAUL CONRAD

Years of the Electric Ear

NORMAN LEWIS CORWIN was born on May 3, 1910, in Boston, Massachusetts, the third son of Samuel Corwin, whose father had come to the United States from England, and Rose Corwin, who had been born in Hungary. His brothers were Emil (1903-) and Alfred (1905-1987); the fourth child, a daughter, was named Beulah (1914-) but called "Booie."

Norman attended the James Otis Primary School and the U.S. Grant Elementary School in East Boston and, after the family moved to Winthrop, Massachusetts, went to Winthrop High School.

Emil graduated from Massachusetts Agricultural College in Amherst and Alfred from Harvard College in Cambridge. But to enter college, Norman would have been required to retake high school Latin courses and went to work instead as a reporter for the *Greenfield* (Massachusetts) *Recorder*.

EDITOR'S INTRODUCTION

Editing *Norman Corwin's Letters*, I came to see the book as a passport and each letter a visa. His letters opened the way to Norman Corwin's America, a land wittier and kinder, more gracious and literate than the places I'd left behind. I predict that as you come to the last letters, you, too, will find yourself sorry that the tour must end.

For decades, historians have called Corwin a giant of radio's Golden Age. His first national success came before he was thirty. Since then, he has known and corresponded with scores of prominent writers, actors and politicians—Carl Sandburg, Bette Davis, Ray Bradbury, Kurt Weill, Judy Holliday, Thomas Mann, Orson Welles, Charles Laughton—and broadcasters from Edward R. Murrow to Charles Kuralt and Bill Moyers.

But there has been more to his life than famous friends or the acclaim for such historic radio dramas as *We Hold These Truths* and *On a Note of Triumph*. Letters from his early days as a reporter in Massachusetts evoke a pastoral age, and they echo with youthful and uncertain notes as Corwin finds his voice.

After the Second World War, with radio in decline and professional patriots trying to silence him, Corwin moved to Los Angeles. His letters about those of his movie and television projects that were either aborted or compromised are sad because they show what has been lost. But they are also very funny. Although Corwin's temperament is famously benign, he permits himself an occasional lapse. Listen to him giving a lesson in manners to a Hollywood boor. Or reproaching an editor who has been slow in acknowledging a manuscript. Or setting straight an actor who presumed to lecture him on the character of Francisco Goya. Thirty-five years later, Corwin's box on the ear still stings.

Corwin took politics seriously. His letter to the *New York Herald-Tribune* defines an honest liberal, and from Hitler until today he has despised the right people. But he also seems to have set aside hours each day for encouraging young artists in their disciplines, urging them to persist, hold to their vision—and get paid what's coming to them.

With more established friends, Corwin's criticism falls into two categories. Asked his opinion before a work has been published or performed, he delivers judgments that are keen, direct and not necessarily tactful. You will hear a professional speaking in the language of his craft. But once a piece or picture is on display, Corwin offers what every artist wants—intelligent praise. Seldom has a gifted writer volunteered so much generous enthusiasm.

How do we happen to have letters dating back to 1927? Corwin's parents saved his early messages from Europe and the Rutland sanatorium. Once he became a reporter, he began to file carbon copies of every letter he typed. Although I am listed as editor, the book has been something of a collaboration. After Norman selected a representative sample from the 10,000 or so letters he has written, we pared the selection still further and consulted on where they might be cut. Then I called on Norman for detailed recollections of the last eight decades, filling in dates, names, circumstances. I also appreciated the careful research of R. LeRoy Bannerman's biography, *Norman Corwin and Radio: The Golden Years*. My job was staying out of the way and stitching Norman's memories together with the lightest and least visible thread.

Norman abandoned his autobiography years ago, and I hope these letters provide consolation for its loss. I've tried to edit them less for browsing than for reading straight through, as one version of his life's story.

Since the book promised to be long, paragraphs often have been cut that ask about the health or schooling of friends and their families. In each case, dots show the deletions. Whenever Corwin himself used dots in a letter, dashes have been substituted. Any parentheses are his; brackets represent editorial additions.

Corwin's return address appears when he was traveling and each time he moved to a new residence. The customary "love" or "sincerely" at the end of a letter has usually been cut.

During the past half-century, an occasional voice has protested that Norman Corwin's America has never existed, that his nation and its people were only myths. These letters prove the skeptics wrong. Throughout a long life, Corwin has celebrated a country he found splendid in its idealism and valor. We know that Norman Corwin's America exists because Jefferson, Lincoln, Thoreau and Whitman have lived there before him.

Now you will cross the border to explore an American life, eloquent and decent, that has spanned most of the twentieth century. To me, Norman Corwin's spirit would be rare in any age. He would insist that it flourishes today, as it always has, in everyone around us.

A.J. Langguth
Los Angeles, 1994

TO ROSE AND SAMUEL CORWIN / From Greenfield, Mass., July 19, 1927

Dear Ma and Pa:

On the occasion of your twenty-fifth wedding anniversary I write you as a beneficiary of your efforts to encourage all which signifies uprightness...to express my sincere and deep-felt thanks and apprecia- tion. I shall take every step in my power to assure you that your efforts have not all been in vain; to requite and account for the unpayable debts that I now owe and evermore shall owe you.

Congratulations on this day! Be mindful, on this day, that *the best is yet to be!*

TO SAMUEL CORWIN / From Greenfield, Mass., May 5, 1928

Dear Pa:

I shall always cherish your brief note of greeting. It is sincere, and animated with a spirit too strong and fine to ever be lost. It is a gift I shall always keep with me, and it is more useful than any material thing I have. In the deepest of ebon moods, re-reading this little note, hastily written as all your letters at the shop must be, will cheer me and help destroy whatever cobwebs are woven between my ears.

At this stage of my life, when I am upon the threshold of manhood, I have come to the full realization that I am blessedly fortunate in having for parents two of the most unselfish people in the world. You gave Emil and Al and me the freedom to carry out our own careers, you offered to pay the bills of educating us, you kept on plugging in the face of physical and circumstantial adversity. Home discipline was never rigorous or entirely lacking, and the foundation laid within the walls of our Bremen Street tenement is firm and sound. The high regard held by every member of the family toward each other is accountable. Nowhere outside of fiction have I ever come across three fraters who were so closely interested in each other's welfare or more proud of each other's accomplishments.

If ever I am famous, and they come to interview me, I shall be prepared. When they ask me what accounts for my success, I shall show them your letter, Ma's bakelite rose and the pictures of my fraters. By that time, however, Booie will have become a great artist and they'll be interviewing her instead.

In 1929, Emil left his reporting job at the *Springfield* (Mass.) *Republican* and recommended Norman as his replacement; the pay for a five-day week was $32.50.

TO ALFRED CORWIN / From Springfield, Undated (1930)

Dear Al:

I wrote a letter to Sherman Bowles, owner and publisher of *The Republican*, suggesting that I write a column of humor for the paper. The great oaf walked into the office, picked the letter out of the mail basket, turned on his heel and proceeded to the business office, where he immediately dispatched the following reply, scrawled in pencil on a piece of scrap paper and lacking a salutation.

"Just think of the number of young gentlemen that have worked here in the last 35 yrs. that have been humorists, that have looked at Mr. Cook [Waldo Cook was the newspaper's editor-in-chief] and kept the humor to themselves. You have worked here 18 months and have the temerity to suggest that *The Rep* should have a humorist. I am amazed. Think of the shock to our readers! It would be like putting a pole-sitting operation on top of the 1st Church. However, would be glad to have you submit samples. We might be able to use it elsewhere."

In 1929, Corwin published his first book, *So Say the Wise*, with the collaboration of a friend, Hazel Cooley. It was a collection of 1,000 quotations on various topics by such writers as H.L. Mencken and Heywood Broun. The next year, he began to conduct interviews and announce the news over radio station WBZA in Springfield, which led to a series of programs he called *Rhymes and Cadences*. On it, Corwin recited poetry, and a friend, Benjamin Kalman, played the piano.

TO ROSE CORWIN / May 1, 1931

Dear Ma:
For your birthday, three verses:

> If my wealth were a jewel,
> Each facet lighted dual,
> Each flame fed by a fuel
> Of starlight mixed with dew,
>   I'd give it now to you.

> If my wealth were a lyre
> Which all of heaven's choir
> Did specially inspire,
> Each swiftly swelling string
>   For you alone would sing.

> Alas, my slender purse is
> But filled with tiny verses
> Which toil alone imburses
> So from my pen I lift
>   What dare I call a gift.

TO BEULAH CORWIN / From Springfield, Mass., May 7, 1931

Dear Boo:

Your birthday card and your handkerchiefs arrived this morning. Thank you sincerely for them. Now that I am 21, and a voting citizen, I expect that you will write me more often. Remember, I haven't an awful lot of time left before my address starts moving around for a few months, and you won't be able to write me.

Be a good girl. Write me more than one letter each term. You haven't averaged even that much....

And after all this exhortation, thanks again! Be a good girl, study hard, and take care of your feet, and maybe on your birthday I'll buy you a movie theater or something.

Love and kisses,

TO ROSE AND SAMUEL CORWIN / May 27, 1931

> To stimulate Congressional appropriations for its new Air Force, the U.S. Army dispatched an armada of 600 warplanes to tour the main geographic areas of the country. Corwin volunteered to cover the New England leg as a reporter. It was his first flight.

Dear Ma and Pa:

I rode with the army's aerial armada on Monday, and I viewed Winthrop from an elevation of 2,000 feet. It was a thrill and an experience I shall not forget....

I enjoyed the takeoff and landing, and was without any sickening impression of height at any time during the three-and-a-half-hour journey—I was furnished with a parachute, along with an air cushion for floating if we happened to land in water. I was also outfitted with aviator's togs, a helmet, goggles and safety belt. The plane was of the fast observation type and I was seated behind the pilot, just rear of the wings. Although almost four hours in the air was a heavy dose for a beginner, I enjoyed every inch of it. More anon.

Norman and Emil left for Europe later in 1931, traveling for eight days on a Hamburg-American Line ship from New York to Le Havre. After Paris, Emil returned to his editorial job in Ohio, and Norman continued alone to Switzerland, Italy and Germany.

TO ROSE AND SAMUEL CORWIN / From Hotel Europe, Geneva, August 29, 1931

Dear Ma amd Pa:

I arrived here last night after having seen Emil off at the Gare St. Lazare in Paris. Geneva is the cleanest, neatest, most sharply chiseled city I have ever seen. It is also the most expensive.

The trip from Paris was long (nine hours) but full of incident. I struck up an acquaintance with a Chinese Frenchman, and held an intelligible conversation with him over many miles of road. Later I met a pretty blonde French girl who told me she had studied piano three years under the famous Alfred Cortot.

This afternoon for four hours I rode on the lake, as far as Thonon-les-Bains. On the return I discerned the snow-capped peak of Mont Blanc, pink and hazy in the distance. I was seeing it in one of its rare colored moods, and at a distance of about 70 kilos.

The Swiss are a pert people, not half as interesting or nice as the small town French. I was amused this morning when a Swiss cop, to whom I applied for information, admonished me for not tipping my hat. "*C'est impolitesse,*" he said.

The reason you have the honor of viewing my penmanship is that my Corona fell off a table on the train, victim of a nasty lurch. The Swiss Corona agent estimated the damage at five to six bucks, so I'm taking it to Venice for repairs.

As I write, I hear the radio in the social hall of this barely satisfactory hotel. It is an Italian station.

Milan tomorrow.

TO ROSE AND SAMUEL CORWIN / From Hotel Marino,
Milan, Italy, August 30, 1931

Dear Ma and Pa:

I arrived in Milan at three this afternoon, and before I was in my
hotel room ten minutes, the air was filled with an ominous droning that
brought me hurrying to the window. The Italian air corps was putting
on an exhibition, and I was treated to the spectacle of smoke screens
and bombs bursting in air.

The fierce nationalism of the Italians is already evident, and the
Milanese seemed to lap up the aerial war propaganda. I enclose one of
the millions of little slips which were dropped from the planes.

The ride from Geneva was the most glorious in the world. The electric trains, run so efficiently by the Swiss, took us right along the entire
western border of Lake Geneva, stopping at Lausanne, Montreux and
other resorts. I had a good look at the celebrated Castle of Chillon, in
the bargain.

It would require too much time, space and writer's cramp to attempt
to describe the beauty of the lake and mountain regions through which
I passed. The sheer magnificence of the scenery kept me jumping from
side to side of the train, and it was not until the last hour of a seven-
hour journey that the noble settings faded out.

I regret to leave Milan tomorrow after staying only one night, since
it is a very charming and interesting city. Its railroad station is the most
handsome I have ever seen.

Now for some spaghetti, some sleep, and Venice tomorrow.

TO ROSE AND SAMUEL CORWIN / From Hotel Savoia &
Principessa Jolanda, Venice, Italy, September 1, 1931

Dear Ma and Pa:

Ah, to be in Venice now that September's here. The days are sunny
with a semi-tropical toast in the air, and the nights are not so cool that
they require the wearing of hats.

Venice has a charm that entitles it to all the fame it enjoys. The
canals are indeed picturesque, and they're not (as one of the Hoffmans

reported) overly dirty. Bridges are of necessity numerous, but there is none without its individuality and quota of grace. The gondolas have been upholstered until they resemble floating living rooms. I have not yet seen a couple of lovers cruising around in one, and I've still to hear any serenading.

And speaking of love, I cannot refrain from musing on how glorious it would be if I were here with a girl that I loved. The city is simply a theater of romantic thought, and it grieves me to gaze upon vistas that have inspired canvases, and be unable to communicate, even slightly and poorly, my thoughts and emotions.

The swells at all the Lido hotels wear pajamas exclusively for dinner, for dances and shopping. On the beach, men's bathing apparel is quite abbreviated, in many cases accentuating that which permits them to wear men's bathing suits.

One of my discoveries is that the Adriatic is only slightly salty. I tasted it.

European inefficiency is again demonstrated by the failure of a Venice agency to fix my broken typewriter after holding it for a week.

I'm dying for word from you folks, and I hope there is a letter or two awaiting me at American Express in Paris.

TO ROSE AND SAMUEL CORWIN / From Post-Hotel, Garmisch, Germany, September 9, 1931

Dear Ma and Pa:

I am writing this before a window which looks out on three peaks of the rugged German Alps. A brook is babbling by the hotel. The air is clear and cold, and the peaks are streaked with snow.

The Post Hotel is easily the cleanest I have registered at since leaving Winthrop. It is, moreover, luxurious, commodious, and moderately priced. A buck a night! Streets in this town are clean enough to eat out of, and everything has an air of wholesomeness and health.

It's a goddam shame the Venetians couldn't fix my typewriter in a week's time, otherwise I'd be writing longer and more intelligent letters.

Love to all,

TO ROSE AND SAMUEL CORWIN / From Hotel Vater Arndt, Bonn Am Rhein, Germany, September 20, 1931

Dear Ma and Pa:

I have just a moment to write before I'm off for Cologne and Dusseldorf. Your correspondent is situated on a little balcony outside his hotel room, and as I am dotting my i's, I can view all manner of craft passing up and down the Rhine.

This morning I visited the birthplace of Beethoven, and viewed many of his original manuscripts, the piano and organ on which he used to play, his death mask, and a number of personal effects.

Yesterday I sailed down the Rhine from Mainz, an uninspiring city. Some interesting boats are churning the river, and across it, in Beuel, church bells are ringing. In this atmosphere I leave this letter.

When he returned to his reporting job in Springfield, Corwin was given the added assignment of delivering news nightly over WBZ-WBZA of Boston and Springfield. He did this for nearly a year until, during a visit to Winthrop in the summer of 1932, he developed lung trouble.

TO EMIL AND ALFRED CORWIN / From Winthrop, Mass., August 29, 1932

Dear Em and Al:

Inasmuch as you don't want to be kidded along, I might as well advise you that I am low with a touch of tuberculosis. The matter has been gone into thoroughly, and has had the corroboration of Boston's reputedly best lung man.

Aside from the symptom of coughing up blood and x-ray pictures showing a small lesion in my upper left lung, there are no indications. I mean that by *listening* to my lung, no sign of tubercular activity is evident.

And so I must give up work for a while. Three months at no labor. The medics say my case is very small, but that now's the time to get at it. Dr. Floyd, the expert forementioned, said that the coughing of blood was, in a sense, "a godsend" in that it apprised me of a condition of which I might otherwise have remained ignorant. Incidentally I had been planning an intensive program of writing for the fall and winter, and so I suppose I am fortunate that a little corner of the lung gave out the way it did—and when it did—

I have never loafed intensely before, and it is hard. If only someone played chess here. But soon, my regimen permitting, I'll do some writing.

Now there's no need for you gloops to feel sorry or bad about this. I have accepted the disappointing revelation with what I like to regard as philosophic calm.

Well, John Keats, D.H. Lawrence, Eugene O'Neill and me.

TO EMIL CORWIN / From Winthrop, Mass., January 31, 1933

Dear Em:

Thanks immensely for your letter. I think it is needless to express my gratitude for your splendid attitude and for your fine willingness to contribute to the funds necessary for my convalescence. I am glad to say that [my] earnings of several years of...general journalism will probably be more than sufficient for my needs....

Your impression of the locality of Rutland is in error. There *is* a Rutland, Vermont, but the place in which I shall probably spend the next three or four months is in good old Massachusetts, and not very far from Holden, where once I witnessed your performance in *Wedding Bells*....

Needless to say, the news that I must hie me to a sanitorium was a tackle from behind. I assumed I had the germ, and that my recent cold would set me back, but I didn't think it would be more than a month. Now I shall not be able to return to work until the fall, probably spending my summer at home.

But I felt sorrier for the folks than I did for myself. Pa and Ma took it quite hard—needlessly hard, I think. But forty minutes later, I was thoroughly reconciled and ready to meet the requirements for a comeback. I am now reasonably cheerful, and looking forward to the creative work which I earnestly hope may come from the excessive time and tranquillity of my imminent new life. They say O'Neill wrote his *Emperor Jones* in a sanitorium....

Pa took Longfellow with him to Springfield Sunday, packed my effects, took many of them back with him, and returned all in one day. The old boy gets spryer every day. I can remember the time when such a program would have horrified him were it suggested for even a husky person.

While in Springfield, according to my instructions, Pa called Bill Walsh and told him the news. Bill impressed upon Pa in their telephone conversation that no matter how long I need be absent—whether four months or four years, I'd always have my job waiting for me. He also asked Pa if there was anything he could do immediately for him or for me. It is hard to believe this is the same man who hired me so grudgingly a few years agone.

That the office misses me a bit may be seen in the fact that on the radio last Monday night, they announced I was ill. Apparently in answer to inquiries from My Public. As luck would have it, I wasn't listening, nor were the folks.

I am of course saddened by the interruption of a radio career that was just beginning to purr...but if I can do a decent sonnet in the next five, six or seven months, I will not have lost much time.

I am delighted that your attitude and, I trust, Al's is not one of sympathy or any such silly thing. Facts are facts, and the sooner they are faced and transformed into more favorable facts, the better....

TO EMIL CORWIN / From Rutland Sanatorium, March 14, 1933

Dear Em:

Your long letter, your enclosures are all at hand, and as usual they afforded me much pleasure. That you compared even the mood of my prelude to a work of Chopin flattered me into beaming for three days....

I am glad to be able to report that since I wrote you last, I have been up for three meals. The usual progress, when a patient has reached the point when he gets up at all, is to advance him a meal a week. This is considered very favorable. But in my case, I got up for the three within ten days.

I cannot say at this time whether my apparently rapid progress will culminate in an early dismissal from the sanatorium. There are tests to be made, and at least one x-ray and clinic. You see, they are extremely conservative here, and they are pretty certain nothing ails you before they turn you loose. If I am home by the first of June, I will be satisfied; and I will have had the added satisfaction of being housed and rested during the uncertain and dangerous spring weather of this, our good old New England.

It grieved me to learn the financial status of your and Al's firms. Half-pay; five-hour day!...If the banks do not recover, there is a fine chance I will have no resources with which to take a trip when I leave Rutland. But if that is the only deprivation in the family, all will be well. Pa is just getting by with his pay, and the fact that the folks are in Manchester for the nonce saves Sam'l a few pennies when they come in handy....

Last Sunday I got a carload of visitors from home, including Barney Zieff and Wally Bell. They brought me one of those games (shoot the ball and see how much you can score). Now the whole ward enjoys it, and it is well that they do. The boys don't get much of a kick out of continuous bed treatment, and any little diversion is a great help.

Time does anything but hang heavy on me here. For one thing, there is correspondence; another, books to review; papers and magazines to read; musical manuscripts to put in order; notes to make; a bit of creative writing, if I ever get around to it. And then I play chess. In a long series of games with Dr. Philbrick, a medico-patient in my ward, I have won 34; he, 39. This, representing several games I lost through absentmindedness, shows I am holding my own against mature chess players.

I have also come to be known as the sage of Ward E, and I am asked all manner of questions. I make replies authoritatively and pontifically, whether I know the answers or not.

TO EMIL CORWIN / From Rutland Sanatorium, March 16, 1933

Dear Em:

...You have no idea how greatly your interest in and approval of some of the things I work on, encourage and inspire me. Not that I ever want you to encourage me without merit. A critical kick in the arse is a good thing when justified. But I always had a subconscious object, in working on my best things, of exacting your approval. You have been my Audience No. 1, and I have shown and sent you my better products before submitting them to anyone else. Accept this as a tribute....

I am just finishing *New Grub Street* by George Gissing, a marvelous novel concerning the trials and tribulations of literary folk in a not-far-past London. Psychological understanding, definition of character and a facility at recording changes in people under stress of circumstances is masterly, and I take my hat off to the writer. There are not many novelists I care for. Wasserman is one....

TO EMIL CORWIN / From Sanatorium, Rutland, Mass. March 27, 1933

Dear Em:

...Recently I received from *The Republican*, to review, the *Last Poems of D.H. Lawrence*. His poetry is amazingly like that of Betty McCausland [Art Critic for the *Springfield Republican*].

I've had another clinic, and the results were at first tremendously disappointing, then not at all. The idea of the clinic was to see if I was able to go home. The chief doctor said he heard whispering louder on the left lung than it should be. Therefore I was advised to stick closer to bed, although not relinquishing any of my privileges, such as going to meals and entertainments.

It developed later, in a discussion with my own doctor, that politics played a little part in the attitude of the chief doctor. At the first clinic, he swore I had no TB, was all for discharging me at once. The other six doctors on the staff thought that my history was sufficient to diagnose my case as pulmonary tuberculosis. Finally my doctor prevailed upon the chief to let me stay under observation for a few weeks. Then the second clinic. The chief, probably realizing it would look tough for him if I were to be discharged and then return with a real case, this time found cause. But my doctor told me on the side that, if it were very important to me, I could go home now, probably without ill result. He said my stay should not be more than one or two months, and that it would fairly amount to no more than observation. Well, I had figured on staying no less time than this, from the first clinic on....

TO ALFRED CORWIN / From Rutland Sanatorium, Rutland, Mass., April 18, 1933

Dear Al:

...I hope the weather down your way has been better than it is here. Today is the eighth consecutive sunless day, and the fifth straight foggy one. Whether the altitude (as high as the top of the Empire State) has anything to do with this condition of fog, I don't know. But it's tough on most of the patients here, who seem to be affected by changes in weather.

There has been no indication of any immediate discharge, and the last official word regarding the length of my stay was from my doctor, who opined "a month or two" just about a month ago. I imagine that I will have another examination within a few weeks, and that if the sounds which were heard in my last clinic have disappeared, I'll probably go home. If they have only lessened, I suppose it will mean an extension in my stay here.

TO EMIL CORWIN / From Rutland, Mass., May 4, 1933

Dear Em:

...I'm terribly glad you like my *Credo*, because I was afraid you wouldn't. I quoted only two or three lines of it in a letter to Elspeth, and she replied: "Send me a copy of *Credo*. It sounds grand. I wish I felt things in strong lusty ways like that. I'm not exactly anaemic, but I am too damned genteel most of the time—I envy you for your ability to be savage." [Elspeth MacDuffie O'Halloran was a friend. *Credo* has been lost.] I am grateful for your criticism of my reference to feces, phallus and vulva—but I feel that the use of such words and images is justifiable in this case. They are truthful and sober. After all, the nose does distinguish between night and day, the north and south of odors. Should I rather say "distinguishes between the rose and hydrogen sulphide"? No, feces is a poetical word, phonetically deserving of a place in a line of poetry, and strong enough to convey the image I intend. As for phallus and vulva—when one contemplates the wonders of the human body, it is folly to ignore the miraculous mechanics whereby reproduction is achieved. Not the mind, or the heart, or the nose, or eyes, can do what the phallus and vulva accomplish. Do they not, as I have written, link the antipodes, and bridge creation? Is the image of their union any less beautiful than the imagery which you intimate it contrasts?

Leonardo da Vinci somewhere in his writings observes that the artist should study the ugly as well as the beautiful, for they are the same thing—one a perversion of the other. For that reason he used to invite horrible-looking, deformed mendicants into his studio, feed them, entertain them, to study their features and draw them. Yet this is the man who did the Mona Lisa and the Last Supper and things of breathless beauty....

Right now I am engaged in a bit of research which I suggested to the officials of the San[atorium], and which they liked sufficiently to place the patients at my disposal. I thought it might be a good idea to determine the percentage of cases which were incorrectly or improperly diagnosed by one or more physicians before coming to the San. So far, almost 45 percent among the men, and about half that for the women. I am interviewing each patient in the house, including the women. The facts in many cases are amazing, the whole survey revealing—and if I can get this published in a national magazine, it will raise a fine stink among the medical profession.

Imagine diagnosing TB as yellow jaundice, ulcers of the stomach, asthma, etc., etc. Delays ranging from a few months to seven years were suffered by patients improperly diagnosed, and the errors meant years of treatment and lots of dough....

Nearly time for the ward to close down. Before starting this letter, I took out my fiddle, which the folks brought me here, and joined a guitarist and a mandolinist in an hour of highly respectable jazz....

Corwin was discharged from Rutland Sanatorium after three months, with the warning that he had suffered a lesion in the apex of the left lung and should exercise reasonable caution in the future. The doctors urged him to rest at home, and it was some months before he returned to the *Springfield Republican*. From that time, Corwin found himself vulnerable to respiratory illnesses.

TO MARY Y. MUNFORD, Head of a family welfare agency in Springfield [on Corwin's beat as a reporter] / From Winthrop June 3, 1933

Dear Mary:

When I left Rutland, there was an apple tree in full bloom right outside my ward. I looked back on that tree just as we were leaving, and I thought I might miss the place. But three hours later I strolled up to the sea wall and gazed once again at my old friend the Atlantic, and I had completely forgotten my three months at Rutland, and the apple tree in full bloom....

It is magnificent to be able to stay in bed a half hour extra; to go three days without shaving; to receive friends without shooing them off at 1:30 p.m. or 7:00 p.m.; to repose practically nu on a cot on the roof; and to guzzle a bit of wine without fearing immediate discharge and disgrace....

Nor has my short sojourn home been without incident. Saturday night the family chariot burned to a crisp in the garage. It was blazing merrily when we, at dinner, were notified, and my father stood like Nero without a fiddle, watching his mobile Rome burn down. It was uninsured. How the fire started is unknown, but the firemen who extinguished it theorized a short circuit. So now we are without means of conveyance, at least for weeks, and the pater has to travel ten miles by train, subway and street car to get to his work on Commonwealth Avenue.

Then my music. I have completed a trilogy on social themes. The first piece, a prelude named *To Conquest*, I did before matriculating at the sanatorium; the second and third I did last week. These I have named *Jazz and the Machine*, and *Satire*.

This is a hodgepodge of a letter. I am going to tell you now of the parting counsel given me by the professors at Rutland. They told me that I have never had any tuberculosis in the lungs; that I did have a bit in the hilum, situated near the root of the lungs, and that my haemopt-ysis undoubtedly came from there; that whatever tubercular activity there may have been in the gland has been arrested. Nonetheless they are not enthusiastic about my return to work before the fall, preferring that I take the added precaution of being idle during the hot weather ahead....

Next week I am going to New York to visit Alfred and Emil, as well as to take care of a little business. By boat. I intend to return in time for a speaking engagement here in Winthrop the 14th. It is a meeting to be held in the garden of some aristocrat, and there will be about 150 women. I like to read poetry to women, because they seem to grasp it more easily than do the average men. I have a suspicion that many men regard poetry as sissified, just as they did music not so long back.

I may not return to Springfield until the fall. Bill Walsh, City Editor of *The Republican*, has been extremely kind to me, and has promised to take me back on the staff on whatever conditions the doctors impose....

Well now, if Dorothy Kelly is, as you say, about my age, a Radcliffe girl, a good thinker and lovable, I see no reason why you shouldn't give me her address and telephone number. Mary, it has been so long since I have fallen into love with a girl my age that the next one will seem like my first love....

TO EMIL AND ALFRED CORWIN / From Winthrop, Mass., June 23, 1933

Dear Em and Al:

Grandma [Celia Ober, Rose Corwin's mother] never went in for anything fancy, and she was buried in a crude wooden coffin with the nailheads showing. I represented Corbros at the funeral—the first, inci-dentally, which I have attended. The only thing dignified about it was the memory of Grandma, and the genuinely deep feelings of a few of the children.

There were various delays, late arrivals, panhandlers, airing of ani-mosities, an old gazonk from the *shool* [synagogue] holding out a pooshky for everybody to drop coins into, and the dramatic wailing of one Tanta Rosie.

Inasmuch as I am of a different tribe from the Obers, according to Hebrew ritual I could neither enter the house in which Grandma's body reposed, nor could I enter the cemetery during the burial service.

Grandma shared old Grandpa Joe's simplicity and straightforwardness. I don't believe either ever showed the slightest hypocrisy, or ever told a deliberate and calculating lie. They were truly of the good earth, rooted to the simple peasant traditions of the Old World, and constant in them despite their being transplanted in a new world. Their pleasures? Grandpa: pinochle, humming old Ungarische tunes, playing jokes, telling dirty stories, mending stoves. Grandma: going to the movies, receiving visits from her children, making strudel. They managed to keep eleven children alive on funds one-fiftieth as big as those by which Harry [one of five sons] with his one child, runs his house.

I doubt if either grandparent had much in the way of intellect or artistry. But I think we owe to them our heritage of a fairly liberal streak handed down to Ma; of a certain attachment to earth which shall always prevent us from being Van Putter-Putters; of a sympathy with the insensitive humdrum fellow who minds his own business and patches your stovepipes.

So Grandma, the last connection with the dim Hungarian past, who conceived and bore Ma in that older world, and for whom life resolved itself into two things, East Boston and perennial pregnancy, has gone the way. She died piecemeal, and that was a shame.

The grave is in a cemetery, the least pretentious of several in Woburn. It gave me satisfaction to know that Celia Ober is not buried in THE PRIDE OF BOSTON cemetery, a walled-in plot where reside the souls of the swanky Hebrews of Brookline, I suppose....

TO DR. KENDALL EMERSON / From 63 Mulberry Street, Springfield, Mass., October 23, 1933

Dear Dr. Emerson:

Thank you for your letter and your generous appraisal of my manuscript. On the strength of what you have said concerning the fallibility of the x-ray in revealing the earliest lesions, and concerning the occurrence of apparently reasonable error even in the hands of specialists, I feel that my article is without firm foundation. For this reason I have withheld it from *The Mercury*, after debating the issue with myself for over a week....

TO ELSPETH MacDUFFIE O'HALLORAN
From Springfield, December 7, 1933

Dear Beth:

Your letter, besides being a chronicle, is also a chart of your condition. It holds a hand to your forehead, takes your artistic pulse, then diagnoses your ailment. That is a lot for one letter.

You have often shown that you can write powerfully when you want to, and that you are concerned with truth, not mock-truths or specious brilliance.

"Lately," you write, "I have had my conscience shaken by a lot of criticism. I've read about the beauty of restraint...the chiseled phrase...the compact emotion." Whenever anybody says "restraint" to me, I ask what it means. I do not believe one should say restraint when he means discipline. The dictionary will not support the notion that they are interchangeable, and neither will art or life.

Good things ought never to be restrained. I disagree with the axiomatic "too much of a good thing." We can never have too much peace, or good government, or Beethoven. Quantity may be subject to restraint, but never quality—never spirit or style or texture. Keats, in his lush and profuse *Endymion* has written an exquisite poem but a lousy epic. As a static poem nobody can challenge its beauty; as a narrative poem it is halting and jammed with conceits. Entirely a question of quantity, not quality....

Having recovered his health, Corwin returned to his double role as reporter and newscaster and broadened his activity in radio by creating a series of poetry and music broadcasts over WBZ-WBZA, NBC affiliates.

TO GORDON SWAN, NBC Executive, Boston / May 17, 1934

Dear Gordon:

Developments of the past few days move me to write you concerning the *Rhymes and Cadences* program which [Benjamin] Kalman and I are doing out of WBZA every Tuesday at 2:30. Last Tuesday we had David Morton as our guest, and we expect to present Wilbert Snow, Robert Hillyer, Frank Prentice Rand, Walter Prichard Eaton and others, on future Tuesdays. All these men are very well known, and all but Rand have a national reputation.

Within a week, I learn that our program was recommended on the floor of a teachers' convention in Boston; that classes listened in at Holyoke Tuesday; that a library bulletin, which lists programs of cultural value, has included our spot. Also, over a period of three or four weeks, I have received many requests, by letter and by mouth, for a longer program. As I wrote George Harder, I am wondering whether WBZ considers the response I mention symptomatic of sufficient interest, active and potential, to broaden the program. I would appreciate your consideration of these requests that we go on for a half hour instead of fifteen minutes....

TO ALFRED CORWIN / June 6, 1934

Dear Al:

...You refer to my Palmer speech in your letter. I did not address this convention, because of laryngitis. But two weeks ago I did get around to addressing an audience of almost a thousand students at Central High School. The kids were packed into the auditorium so tightly that it was necessary to utilize space on the stage. Many stood in the rear and along the sides. For a half hour I talked to them informally, and read them poetry calculated to make them laugh. They interrupted my speech several times with applause, and I could see that look of pleasure and anticipation on their faces which is a sign you have your audience in hand. At the conclusion, I was applauded for about two minutes. And I was told later that the kids thought I was the best speaker they had had that year. My formula was merely to give them something they could understand, appreciate and find amusing.

No progress on the purchase of a car. I have Bernie Klein scouting for bargains for me. I'll not buy a new car, for that would demolish my lifelong savings ($600) in no time. My savings were once within a few ten-spots of $1,000, you know, but a year's idleness at Rutland and home, an appendectomy, a tonsillectomy and a few gifts of money to the folks—the day I deposit my one-thousandth dollar I'll withdraw fifty, and we'll have a celebration....

TO EMIL CORWIN / From Springfield, Mass., June 8, 1934

Dear Em:

An important thing I neglected to mention in my last letter is that I am starting on my vacation July 22. I'll probably take two weeks off with pay, and two without.

Others on the staff are working an extra day each week for twelve weeks in order to get a month with pay. I don't care to expose myself to any risks in broiling weather by working six days a week, and so I'll take my extra two weeks without pay. This will enable me to coast along at the present rate of two days off each week. I plan to apply one of these days to recreation; the other, to lucrative writing.

Next week Tuesday, I am having Roberta Swartz Chalmers of Mt. Holyoke College as guest poet on my radio program. The week after that, Wilbert Snow of Wesleyan, a poet only slightly less well known than David Morton....

I'm seriously planning to buy a used car, and today I looked at a 1929 Graham. A chap in the office wants to sell me a 1928 Pontiac in good shape for $85, and this seems the more likely buy. It has been jacked up in his garage for over a year, and its motor was always kept in the very best of repair.

I plan for a license-test Monday. I've been driving illegally for five or six years now, and it's high time I got a license. Chief reason for this sudden inspiration is that I am going to Amherst, Smith and Mt. Holyoke next day for a feature story, and I must produce a license before Bill Walsh lets me take one of the firm's cars.

Yesterday I went...to the Smith College Museum, where we saw an exhibition of [John] Marin, [Charles] Demuth, [Charles] Burchfield,

[Edward] Hopper and [George O.] Hart watercolors. I like Demuth for his remarkable cleanness and the cheerfulness of what he paints. Marin, as you perhaps have found out for yourself, is dynamic—forceful, splashy. He socks you in the eye and you like it. I like him chiefly because I think that I would paint the way he does if I could paint. "Pop" Hart's work you must know. His technique isn't as bold as Marin's and certainly not as restrained as Demuth's, but somewhere in the wide gulf between....

Back to the vacation matter: Would it be possible to delay your vacation by one week, so that we could start out together? I rather favor the idea of a short trip somewhere—Nova Scotia, Saguenay River, the gulf of the St. Lawrence, any five- or six-day boat trip. Perhaps we could take along the mater or pater, both of whom are in need of a complete change of scenery....

TO EMIL CORWIN / June 12, 1934

Dear Em:

The most important item in your letter concerns your indecision about marrying. You do not directly ask my counsel, and that is wise, because I would be a poor one to give it; but you have apparently been asking your own counsel, and losing sleep about it.

Just as well determine to be right about God or immortality, as about love and marriage. I have had the experience of being fiercely in love with a woman, and then outgrowing in a year that sincere and ardent affection. I have had the experience of starting out with a Platonic agreement not to love a girl, and then finding myself in love.

If you relish the companionship of a girl—if you are anxious to see her and loath to leave her, that is the criterion. If you are at ease with her in company, if you find delight in what she says, if her mannerisms do not irk you, if she understands and allows for your idiosyncrasies; if she is sexually stimulating three nights in a row or twice in one night; if she can cook; if she would rather walk in the woods or by the shore than go to a party or a movie; if she is not likely to reduce your efficiency and make you unhappy—then you have a gal friend....

You write that Freda "frankly asked that I lay my cards on the table." Did you *have* any cards to lay on the table? Had you talked marriage with her? If you had not, I would say Freda was pressing it a bit.

You advise *me* to marry. "Too much waiting brings in too many girls," you say. Personally, I think it is better to have a crowd of girls in your life, because the chance of getting the gal you dream about is numerically improved. As for myself, marrying is poor counsel. Just now. I am uncertain about my health, my philosophy, my talents, my likes and dislikes. I get a crush on every pretty girl I see. I'm holding off another year or two at the very least.

Of course getting married is not a death sentence. If you find after a year or so that you are not happy or compatible, there are some very fine divorce courts. I would marry with the understanding that if something unforeseen arises to disturb your relations, you would divorce. A minor variation on the companionate marriage idea....

Later in the year, Emil married Freda Feder, a Cleveland teacher, and they moved from Ohio to New York City.

TO ALFRED CORWIN / November 14, 1934

Dear Al:

I don't remember having been much busier at any time in my life than I am right now. My new job, like Emil's old one, demands from nine to eleven hours every day; I am in the midst of preparations for the first recital ever conducted on a strictly professional basis, i.e., people paying to hear me; and I am also in the midst of activity toward the end of organizing the Springfield Newspaper Guild, in which I am certain to be an officer. The constitutional committee met at my room this morning, and we drafted a line-up to submit to the first annual meeting this Friday. We are assured of a membership of twenty to begin with....

Ha cha chonya,

The concert, held in a Springfield hotel ballroom, was an evening's live version of radio's fifteen-minute *Rhymes and Cadences*, with Benjamin Kalman playing Chopin and Franck, and Corwin reading his own poetry, along with poems by Horace and D.H. Lawrence.

TO ALFRED CORWIN / From Springfield, January 4, 1935

Dear Al:

The work on the novel was grueling, quite the hardest sustained work I've ever done. It sapped my energy toward the end, and the last four chapters were written in bed. The introduction was rewritten no less than five times. Not only rewritten in draft, but in the completed copy.

I have no illusions about it. It will not win the Guild contest, your good wishes and favorable hunches notwithstanding. You will understand why it cannot win the Guild prize when you read it. [The Newspaper Guild was offering a $1,500 prize for a novel.] I hope its dedication to Emil will not be a joke on him. I hope he's not ashamed of it. But the act of dedication was no whim. To him belongs whatever credit can be taken for my tastes. I caught from him a taste for music (he took me to my first concert); a taste for literature (he first called [Heywood] Broun to my attention); a taste for hospitality (he was always exercising it on his friends); a taste for liberalism. The things I did not catch from him, unfortunately, were neatness in dress and manner, and certain common decencies. I am afraid I'll always be a shloomper and a barbarian.

Well, now Em is married. Good. Only two months ago I was thinking about him and Freda, and wishing they would get married, because I like to buy toys for kids.

I don't know just yet when I'll be down. I have a radio series starting tomorrow, a lecture January 14th, a brief radio skit to write on commission, a concert to attend in Northampton on the 8th ([Jose] Iturbi), and a few other things....

TO JOHN HOLMAN, Radio Executive, NBC, Boston
July 5, 1935

Dear John:

Out of a dinner with Professor David Morton of Amherst the other night evolved a plan whereby I could get Grantland Rice, Stephen Vincent Benet, Joseph Auslander, Madame Bianci and other nationally known figures for the *Rhymes and Cadences* program, which has intermittently for two years gone out over WBZ. Also Carlin in New York agreed to take a network shot of original, unpublished material written expressly for my program by outstanding American poets.

None of these celebrities would charge me anything for his services, and with this in mind, I'd want to make their trips to Springfield (or Boston in instances when Carlin wants something for the network) worthwhile from a standpoint of potential audiences. Hence, if there is anything open in the way of a fifteen-minute spot weekly, it might be an added inducement to my guests, and at the same time furnish WBZ with a good exclusive feature attractive to publicity. (Last spring the *New York Times* ran three-quarters of a column on an advance story of one of my programs, even though it was to go out over WBZ only.)

If a straight poetry series does not seem attractive, it might be an idea to combine the best features of *Rhymes and Cadences* with those of a flock of interviews I conducted experimentally over WMAS last year. In these I talked, without scripts and informally, to men and women outstanding in their crafts and professions—a prize-winning painter, a drama critic, an expert photographer, etc. The idea was old, the technique new. The informality of scriptless discussions, when the interviewer and his subject have their topic well in hand, creates an illusion of eavesdropping for the listener.

I hope you see enough merit in this idea to pass it on to John McNamara with your endorsement. It might pan out nicely.

Dear Jeanne:

That you have "an independent nature and a ponderous conceit" is all in your favor. It gives you something to work for. Just as one can't go deep-sea fishing without a deep sea, so one can't joust with life unless there are forces with which to contend. And with the qualities you ascribe to yourself, you won't have to worry about meeting up with antagonists and antagonism.

As for independence, I urge you to cherish it, to guard and protect it in the fortress of your mind. As for conceit, I recommend you whiff it into the nearest ashcan at the earliest opportunity. One is strong and upbuilding, the other flaccid and corrosive.

I don't mean to be philosophical this early in our acquaintance. But your thoroughly alert and witty letter nudges me into a consideration of things which I had long ago put by as Conclusions Arrived At, in a sort of mental ledger. I am forced to believe, from what you say about "an intense hatred of feeling inferior to any man" that the carburetor of your philosophy needs delicately to be adjusted. You should, first of all, nail down a conception of inferiority and an understanding of what it constitutes.

Mere prowess—a talent for juggling oranges or words, an ability to interpret Chopin, a flair for forensics or histrionics or wearing clothes, a penchant for picking fast horses or a deftness at baking angel cake—is cheap. I think you'll agree that any of these talents doesn't necessarily establish "superiority"; hence, the absence of any special ability need not imply the opposite—inferiority. By this logic you need worry no further about having "a fighting chance in a literary context." I have known many people who, save for an ability to express themselves well, are first-class asses. Even so-called "intellectuals" like Benjamin De Casseres, poets like Edgar Guest, editors like [William Randolph] Hearst and [Arthur] Brisbane, are dim-witted in comparison with any number of undistinguished but competent and reliable doctors, reporters, or brush salesmen.

Such terms as "inferior" and "superior" are so relative that they deserve to be kicked out of the main vocabulary. Was Eve inferior to Adam? Christ to Moses? Caesar to Alexander? Hugo to Zola? Is blueberry pie inferior to strawberry shortcake? Baseball to football? Lambert to Corwin? I think not. There is no single standard of measurement, and therefore no means to exercise judgment.

As for your disinclination to be surpassed by men, it is a healthy form of scrappiness and a good thing providing you don't permit it to make you unhappy. In many ways, physically, intellectually and spiritually, you may find yourself "inferior" to certain men, but I wouldn't avoid them for that reason. On the contrary, I would cultivate their acquaintance and confidence, so that you may learn something from them, and equip yourself all the better to hold your own against or outsmart them.

Don't pay the slightest attention to Sue's warning that I am wife-hunting. That occupation is reserved for aging men who fear lonely twilights, and it has nothing to do with hot-blooded young writers who regard the world as their oyster. I confess to a perennial quest for companionship and the inspiration derived therefrom; and if the logical conclusion to that quest is marriage, I suppose I'll marry some day. But I have a lot of hard work to do before then. I must win my own self-respect as a writer and thinker before I can expect to capture anybody else's, and if a person happens to be an incurable idealist, the courtship of his self-respect is an arduous and long one.

Now that I mention those adjectives, it strikes me that this is a longish letter, and that it reads more like an essay than like Exhibit 3 in the Lambert-Corwin correspondence. I have extended myself here chiefly because I want you to overlook the "charm" (a cloying quality which I associate with poseurs) and the slightly skilled-labor touch to my writing. I don't want you to be scared to write me.

I'm not, believe you me, an intellectual. I proceed by intuition and the painful method of trial and error. I go bludgeoning my way through life, always in the thick of some Fight or Cause or Movement, and nearly always getting thrown for a loss. I'm also an incurable romanticist. I still hope some day to meet a woman who can be independent without being arrogant or aloof; upright without being stiff-necked; wholesome without being holy about it; in love without permitting herself to be completely absorbed in the personality of her lover. Maybe such women are not on this earth. And maybe I've got a nerve to expect her to be interested in me when we do meet. But as I said before, I'm an incurable hoper.

The first edition is rolling, and I must get busy on a story for the second.

Please write me what you are thinking—how you feel about being alive on this curious earth—your pet hates and prejudices and your enthusiasms. I recall that when I was your age, I had an immense curiosity, a speculative mind, an eagerness limned by occasional accesses of melancholia and adolescent despair. Now I'm a lot tougher, of course. But I wish I had chronicled or recorded my thoughts in some such correspondence as this. Do that with yours, Jeanne, and I'll preserve your letters for you, so that when you are a grandmater you can show your descendants those letters and say:

"That, *mes enfants*, was when I was young and romantic, just emerging fully into a world full of sights and sounds and people and impressions. I was pretty then, and the fame of my beauty was so widespread that a young and impetuous and slightly daffy newspaperman who later led the Second American Revolution, was attracted to write me. See, here's a three-page closely typed novelette. And that is my reply. Observe how I wrote with the longhand of a schoolmarm. And now that you have inspected these documents, go upstairs to bed. Go on, scat!"

TO ALFRED CORWIN / September 20, 1935

Dear Al:

Just now bought a new silent Corona portable, which retails for $67.50, for $54.67. Got my discount through *The Republican*. This is the first writing I am doing on it. This may seem to you exorbitant spending, but I figure thisaway: The old machine, which is still in mighty fine shape, I will have cleaned, dressed and put shipshape and then give it to Booie for a gift. I'm pretty sure she'll want it. I could get

$12.50 allowance on the old one, and with the $5 it would cost me to have it overhauled, it will represent a goodly sum.

This here machine is so silent that it can be used at the most ungodly hours of the morning without disturbing the neighbors; and if I ever hope to get some work done, it will be necessary to do some pecking away at night....

Figured up the other night that between the *New York World-Tel[egram]* and Station WLW, I was able to bank $120, which otherwise might have taken me from eight months to a year to save—if at all. Hence this splurge.

Gee, this machine is so quiet it's making me sleepy.

After an audition, Corwin had been hired as an announcer for 500,000-watt WLW in Cincinnati, the nation's most powerful radio signal. Two weeks after his arrival in Cincinnati, he protested the station's policy of not broadcasting news of labor strikes. The station let him go, and he returned to the *Springfield Republican.*

TO EMIL CORWIN / November 4, 1935

Dear Em:

Thanks for the letter and clip. I'm dashing this off before getting down to work on the novel this afternoon, and enclosing a check for $30. Of this, $25 is for the loan at Winthrop, and the other $5 goes toward the $7 I owe you on the Rolls Razor. Were I sufficiently prosperous this week, I'd make it $7....

The novel is getting into difficult terrain, for I'm now treating of the publisher....Here's my first paragraph of the section devoted to him:

The main staircase in the Citadel had been built by R.F. McDonough & Co., contractors, under the surveillance of Hudson Rand, but it might have been built by Gabriel under Louis XV. Like the lord of the estate, the staircase was of the variety known as self-supporting; like his mistress, it had exuberance, gaiety and magnificent curves. Rand liked to think of it as L'escalier de Monda, and indeed it had been designed for just such use as was now being made of it—the triumphal descent of Monda Lambert, danseuse, into the midst of the imperial court.

Monda is Rand's mistress.

Now to get to Monda.

Ards bar dow.

TO EMIL CORWIN / From Springfield, Mass., January 10, 1936

Dear Em:

Heard Jose Iturbi at Smith College last Wednesday night. He sits cold as a dead herring at the pianny, and proceeds to watch the ceiling while his hands are traveling so fast that you can't see them. For the first time in my concert-going it was impossible to shut my eyes and listen to the music. His hands were too amazing, and I sat banjo-eyed watching him do some intricate tricks with Debussy and DeFalla. Equally exophthalmic was I when he marched through a Beethoven sonata which took three years off my life.

You and Freda incorporated so niftily that I have had no chance to get you a present. Have you any choice, or shall I venture my taste? And you don't mind waiting a bit until I have a chance to look around, dost?

I intended to send my novel down ahead of this, but La Neilson has been wrestling with your copy in order to make it letter-perfect. If the thing never gets to publication, I want you to own this copy, or even the original. I shall not be ashamed of it until I can do a far better novel, and the more I reread parts of it, the braver I become about asserting its right to be dedicated to you. I shall try to visit you this week, probably arriving Wednesday evening. I'll have the book with me. Please, no plans, no tickets, no parties. Just you and Al and Freda and possibly Samuel Rudd.

I've got some new compositions for piano, which I wrote as a means of relaxation when I was working on the novel. Is the pianny tuned?...

Corwin had worked on his entry for the Newspaper Guild's contest for several months, but two weeks before the deadline, he decided the novel was inadequate and destroyed the manuscript.

TO MRS. HICKOX, Chairwoman of Women's Republican Club of Springfield [which paid Corwin $100 for five talks]. From Springfield, February 23, 1936

Dear Mrs. Hickox:

I will be able to begin the series on schedule this Thursday.

I have planned tentatively to devote one discussion to general important issues—state, national and international; another to a discussion of the party as an unofficial organ of government; another to issues and candidates in the state campaigns; a third and possibly a fourth, to issues and candidates nationally; and a fifth to general consideration of political and economic forces at work in the world.

I am interested less in projecting my viewpoint than in affording the members an opportunity to examine and weigh contending ideas of a political nature, so that current events may be better understood and interpreted.

TO BERENICE MACHLIN / From Springfield, April 13, 1936

Dear Berenice:

I am going to be on your island Wednesday and Thursday of this week, and I wonder whether you might be interested in having dinner with me or attending a broadcast or playing lotto or shooting craps or hearing some music or going for a long walk or seeing a good play or posing for Acme and Wide World or reading the funnies or holding hands or skiing.

Will you drop me a note indicating whether you will be in town, and whether one night is better than another, and will you write pronto? A postcard'll be sufficient.

Emil Corwin had recommended Norman for a job in New York in the publicity department of 20th Century-Fox. He was interviewed in April and started work on June 15, 1936.

TO RUTH GERSIN / From New York, January 20, 1937

Dear Ruth:

Your words bring back to me every last memory of our strange and turbulent and delightful and rueful friendship—all our confidences, our feigned and unfeigned indifferences, our laughter, our quarrels.

There were times in the past five years when I feared that the world and I had lost the real Gersin—the sensitive, vital, brave girl who came into my life when my appendix went out of it and who brought *Cyrano* with her. That you have come back now and then has been as reassuring as Spring. Your world, I decided, was too much with you, as mine has been with me. But it is heartening to know, after your letter, that you were never lost. Only mislaid. You have put the world in its old place, and I salute you as I did of old—with a kiss and an embrace and a poem in my heart.

Yes, when you mention that afternoon on the windswept fort, those midnight promenades on the Crest, our foxing of poor Mrs. Howe, a whole pageant of memories unwinds. I recall the proms, the dark night on the roof when I confided in you the secret gnawings of my mind and you soothed me with cool and sane words; the evening when we watched the westering sun from the windows of my Paw's room; the northbound boat from New York; your sister's wedding, and the cynicism with which we profaned it; that perfectly incredible afternoon when you brought two of your good friends together and they instinctively repulsed each other; that almost fictional design for living, when you and Louise and I got along so unbeautifully; luncheon together in Boston....

And now we drop our work for a moment to look across those crammed years, enjoying the paradox that, much as our friendship wallowed in mud, it still retained its ability to go "vaulting through a vast and peakless sky." You and I have lived through a dozen relationships with others, and yet we still write letters like this to each other.

You do not advise me on the state of your health. Are you well? Do you have any remnant of that cough which was worrying you when we last met? Are you as lithe and firm as when we played ball together, or have you, like me, lost a tooth, acquired a wrinkle or two, and grown a little lean?

All hands here send their best to you. I, my Love,

TO BEULAH CORWIN / From New York, June 3, 1937

Dear Boo:

It comes to my attention, via reliable sources in Winthrop, that you have an aversion to one of nature's most remarkable creatures, the bee. I understand that several times you've retreated from the vicinity of same, fearing you'd be gobbled alive. Let me assure you that your fears are groundless, and that the bee whom you hold in such terror is more afraid of you than you of it.

Although I'm not an expert ap——apia——apiari——although I am not an expert on bees, I'm pretty certain that the bee never attacks unless attacked. I have seen pictures of men whose faces were covered with bees without any ill effects save perhaps a drop of honey here and there. Wasps and hornets are less tractable, but they too usually mind their own business if you mind yours.

The one time an insect larger than a mosquito ever stung me was once when I was playing golf in Swampscott. I am sure it was an act of God, in punishment for some language I had just been using. I had called the golf ball a goddam little pill. For this I was stung in the—may I say it—arse. It was not so much painful as insulting.

It was good seeing the folks, if only for a little while. I had a fine time in Amherst. Among people I met there was Madam Rimsky-Korsakov, niece of Tschaikowsky and cousin of R-K. She is an old lady, in her seventies, but very bright and charming. Also met Madam Bianci, niece of the poet Emily Dickinson.

This is about six times as long as any letter I received from you, and I hope you feel fit to reply before the winter of 1975. You do write a good letter, you know.

TO DAVID MORTON, Amherst College Professor, Author of "Ships in Harbour" and "Earth's Processional," among other works
From New York, August 4, 1937

Dear Dave:

...I am developing into a frank propagandist for poetry. [Joseph] Auslander's teachers at Columbia [University] last Friday got a good slice of Morton, and I have been giving credits on WQXR for some time now.

From [Arthur Davidson] Ficke this week comes a letter about his dedication to [Edna St. Vincent] Millay, which for frankness and courage is really a document. He loves the woman and is wonderfully open about it.

I promised in a recent letter to say something about that bunch of swells whom [Upton] Close, [Padraic] Colum and I addressed at Oyster Bay. They were all multimillionaires, and seemed inbred, to hear them talk, just as in the movies, about yachts and polo. At dinner we discussed poetry—they wanted to know what we were there for. None had ever heard of [Robert] Frost or E[dwin] A[rlington] Robinson or [Carl] Sandburg or [Vachel] Lindsay.

The estate was vast—far as the eye could see—and one of the rooms—I mean "rooms"—was a takeoff on Westminster Abbey. High, vaulted, like the nave of a church. Immense tapestries, seventeenth and eighteenth century paintings, an organ, everything but the tomb of a king.

I like Colum least of any of the writers I have met in New York. Uncommunicative, a little scornful, and a fanatic on the subject of Spain. Mrs. Betts, plutocrat, was defending the Loyalist regime from Colum's charge of having started the war. Colum proceeded to state, as absolute truth, the most patently ridiculous atrocity stories about the Loyalists. What they did to nuns and all that sort of thing. And there were Barbara Hutton's kinfolk arguing in behalf of "Red" Spain against little Padraic, with our poet getting more and more vindictive. At that point the organ in the Abbey got going on something, and the discourse ended.

I am going to make a life mask of you when you come down. A fairly simple though precise operation which is not at all uncomfortable to the person masked. Tomorrow night I make one of Audrey [Wurdemann, wife of Auslander]. I've already done ones of Al, Emil, and my Ma and Pa. The mask will be yours when I've finished.

TO ROSE CORWIN / From New York, January 3, 1938

Dear Ma:

Enjoyed a refreshing visit to the country over the holiday, spending New Year's eve in Westport, Ct., at the home of Dr. Louis Dublin, chief statistician for Metropolitan Life Ins. Co. I know his son, and was invited there by him. Big country home in the middle of the woods. We took a long hike in the snow, and it felt great. Al spent the weekend in Cornwall, N.Y., upstate, with his newest girl; Em & Babe stayed home quietly. But tonight they're out celebrating their anniversary at dinner and a show. 20th-Fox has a big opening of *In Old Chicago* at the Astor Thursday night, and I will be required to attend in tuxedo, etc. I am, as you know, on the air over WOR Sunday....

TO ROSE CORWIN / From New York, January 10, 1938

Dear Ma:

I know I have a bad record for last week, but you can blame it on the opening of the picture. The Corwins were well represented, with Al and me resplendent in formal dress, and celebrities falling all over each other. I handled a broadcast from the lobby, and there were such as Darryl Zanuck, Jean Hersholt, Lauritz Melchior, Will Hays, Ethel Merman, and others to speak. Details connected with the work of the opening not only kept me from keeping on schedule with these dispatches, but from answering a hundred letters which I should acknowledge.

TO ROSE CORWIN / From New York, January 11, 1938

Dear Ma:

I got a look at the unedited newsreel of *In Old Chicago* today and found I was in about six of the shots. When this is edited, there will be considerably less of me (I hope) because I am not quite movie material. I suspect Taylor is handsomer. But at any rate I may be seen hovering like a guardian devil around the vicinity of the chief goings-on. From Amherst, via Dave Morton, came evidence that my Sunday broadcast was heard and well liked. They were quite excited because I called Amherst "the unofficial poetry capital of the U.S.," and even had a stenographer taking down what I said. I understand news stories were sent out from Amherst College about it. I'll advise you if any of the finished newsreel matter has my phiz in it. Meanwhile love to all.

TO ROSE AND SAMUEL CORWIN / January 25, 1938

Dear Ma and Pa:

Well, here I go with another resolution to continue my system where I left off. My recent *Mary* program aroused the interest of a man who wants to take me under his wing as manager, and who speaks sniggeringly of salaries such as $100 a week. I intend to place myself under his management as soon as a six-months contract I have with QXR expires—it meant paying him 5 percent, but if there's any kind of $$ in it, it's worth much more than that. There may be some developments in the direction of radio in six weeks or two months, and you can be sure I'll keep you posted. Meanwhile I got a $5 raise at the office! I expected more, but not all the boys were raised, so I suppose I should be satisfied. Tomorrow nite I go to a dinner at which the tariff is $7.50 a plate. But the company pays for me! More in tomorrow's dispatch.

TO ROSE AND SAMUEL CORWIN / January 26, 1938

Dear Ma and Pa:

The magazine *Variety*, Bible of the show world, reviewed my *Mary* program today, and sed it was "clever...well written, well acted...

clicked....scripting showed plenty of imagination and capable mimicry of eleven different styles....a fine comedy possibility for the idea-weary airwaves."

All the Corwins were invited to the Kreymborgs' the other night, and Em and I went—Al being on a date and Babe not wanting to go out on accounta her figure. [Alfred] Kreymborg is the author of *Lyric America*—the book the Hadassah gave me wunst, remember?

TO DAVID MORTON / From New York, January 27, 1938

Dear Dave:

I have just listened to four 12-inch ERPI recordings by Robert Frost. As a reader he is fine on a podium, where an audience can see him as well as hear him, and get something of the spirit of the poem from the spirit of the man. But there is no such contagion from a phonograph record. His interpretation of "The Death of the Hired Man" is hurried, botched, undramatic. You don't give a damn about the hired man, or Warren, or, for that matter, Frost. Half the time you don't know who is speaking.

There is not enough time between selections. "Stopping by the Woods" is fairly well done, but its effect is spoiled when Frost runs right into the title of the next poem, "Dust of Snow." Result is, it sounds like this:

"...and miles to go before I sleep. Dust of snow."

I heard Frost read about five years ago, and thought he was very good indeed. Maybe he was, or maybe that was before my ear sharpened.

Do you suppose it would be lese majeste to suggest to Frost that he be coached on the interpretation of his own poems? If all the poets who are only so-so readers could be made into good or even fair readers, we'd be doing something. Of all I have heard anywhere, any time, there are so far only two poets who speak their poems as well as they write them—Sandburg and Morton.

See you in Amherst.

TO ROSE AND SAMUEL CORWIN / February 3, 1938

Dear Ma and Pa:

It develops now that I am to be on the same radio program Sunday with Edgar Lee Masters, one of the most famous poets and writers in modern American history. Possibly I may read one of his poems, too....

I just finished work on a new (and I think my best) piano composition. You'll hear it on the radio some day soon.

TO ROSE AND SAMUEL CORWIN / April 12, 1938

Dear Ma and Pa:

This is one of the last letters I'll be writing on this stationery, because this very afternoon I signed a contract with the Columbia Broadcasting System to serve as a director of dramatic programs. My salary is to start at $125 a week [Fox had been paying $50 per week], with automatic raises of $25 a year if my contract options are renewed at the end of each year.

I begin the job on the 25th. I will probably direct two or three programs a week to begin with, and may not be on the air myself (i.e., with my own work) until after I have been there a while. CBS maintains a small staff of directors, who handle, as I propose to do, two or three sustaining shows a week. If later on I take over any commercial shows, they will pay me extra.

We here in New York are very happy about the opportunity, but of course I am modifying my enthusiasm until I have had a chance to learn the ropes around CBS and get the feel of things. In the meantime, I'll be busy winding up things at Fox and at WQXR....

TO ESTHER MILLER / From New York, April 22, 1938

Dear Esther:

I have just come back from a walk along [Riverside] Drive, where I inspected the great engineering project on the Hudson Highway, and gave my approval to certain proposals for landscaping the area around

Grant's Tomb. There were a few minor alterations necessary, and I dismissed three steam shovels and six tractors for failing to salute as I passed.

Of course the walk along the Drive can in no way compare with the walk along the Crest [in Winthrop], which I took just about a week ago, in your excellent company. The breezes along the Drive stink of carbon monoxide, burnt oil and smoke from the great factories in Jersey across the river. The only gases mixed in the east wind off Winthrop must come from the streets of London or Liverpool.

It was swell to see you after all those years of wanting to. The only thing lacking from our farewell embrace was *enough* to embrace. I mean, more of Miller. Are you sure the Guinness Stout you are drinking *is* Guinness? Do you drink enough milk and eat enough eggs? Have you tried any of Abbott's various vitaminized oils of cod, halibut, sturgeon, barracuda, shark, smelt, haddock, flounder and gefilte fish?

I've been resting this week preparatory to going to the wars Monday, but as usual, my rest is more fatiguing than my work. I find all sorts of puttering things for myself to do. My last program on WQXR I gave on Wednesday. Albert Hirsh, a fine young pianist, played two compositions written by, guess who—me. One I laboriously set down as a musical supplement to James Weldon Johnson's ingratiating spiritual-poem "Go Down, Death." Several of my best friends and severest listeners thought it got across....[Corwin's music for Johnson's poem was later arranged and sung by the Golden Gate Quartet on a CBS broadcast.]

TO MARGERY MANSFIELD, Poet / From New York, May 14, 1938

Dear Mrs. Mansfield:

...Thanks a million for your felicitations regarding the new radio job. I have been on it three weeks, and I like it very much. Each program presents new problems, and that's what I love about the work. A challenge a day keeps the doldrums away.

TO DAVID MORTON / May 21, 1938

Dear Dopey:

...Yesterday ended my fourth week as a CBS director, and you will understand how busy I have been if you got no bulletins from me since we parted at the Greek's. It is work which I love—far more demanding that any work I have yet done; requiring immense concentration and a general sharpening of the faculties. To a person inclined, in the past, to be vague and indecisive about many things, the new work is wonderful schooling. As director I have all the decisions to make—in a hurry— and all the responsibility. The director is Boss around the studio—over actors, over sound men, over the engineer, over the script. If it's a good show, he's the one who gets the orchids; if it isn't, his are the brickbats.

Right now I am handling three shows a week: *Living History*, from 7:30 to 7:45 Wednesday nights; *Americans at Work*, from 10:30 to 11:00 Thursday nights; and *Adventures in Science*, from 7:30 to 7:45 Friday nights. All are under the Adult Education Board of CBS's wings. Of the three the *Americans at Work* has the best set of whiskers.

TO T. WELLS CHURCH / From New York, September 14, 1938

Church, along with Emil Corwin, was a publicist for the National Broadcasting Company. At Emil's prompting, Church arranged for Norman to appear on the network's prime variety show, *The Magic Key of RCA*, and later brought Corwin to the attention of CBS's program chief, William B. Lewis. In his first year at the network Corwin relied heavily on Church as adviser and friend.

Dear Ted:

...The news here is that I knocked over Bill Lewis and Dave Taylor with an audition of a show I conceived and wrote. I asked Lewis to give me a budget of $100—script unseen—to audition a program of what I called "orchestration and augmentation of verse." ...Lewis agreed; I hired a cast of twelve (at the AFRA audition rate of $7.50 per); did the best job of casting since I've been at 485; and knocked the thing together in six hours. The material was so exciting that the actors came to me separately to tell me that it was the most enjoyable work they had ever done in radio. It had swing, rhythm, tempo—whatever you want to call it....

Lewis heard the record, and in a long memorandum (carbons to [Douglas C.] Coulter and Dave Taylor) he called it "magnificent"—suggested that: (1) it be done pronto on *Workshop*; (2) it be made a series; (3) my technique be applied to a dramatization of *John Brown's Body* on the Mercury Theater spot during Orson Welles' vacation in November.

That was last week. Since that time, Taylor heard the show and told me it was good stuff. He was the last one to hear the records, apparently, for the next day they vanished and have not been found since. Incredible. Nothing has been scheduled for *Workshop* yet, and the *John Brown* suggestion pooped out. It seems Welles will not permit *John Brown* on the Mercury Theater unless he can act in it—and cannot permit himself to be directed by any outsider. So the original move to have Corwin write and direct the Mercury Theater's *John Brown* is scuttled. Now there is some talk of Welles directing and performing my adaptation, but I will not transform the Benet book into an hour script without getting paid for it...and I think $250 is a moderate fee, don't you? Chances are twenty to one Welles will not pay any such fee when he has a dozen stooges around to do his adapting for him.

I was asked for my estimate of a budget on a *Poetic License* series. On the basis of average literary rights and a cast of ten, I quoted a price of $335 per show. That seems to be beyond the reach of their current budget, so the last I heard of the series idea was Lewis's opinion that the thing might be scheduled after the first of the year.

I don't suppose you have had time to listen to my *Americans at Work* shows lately, but I know that they have been better in every way. They have just got their first rating, and the execs seem to be pleased about it. *Living History* and *Adventures in Science*, never very healthy from the standpoint of script, have bogged down and will go off the air at the end of the month. What I'll be doing after I'm relieved of those two, I don't know. *Americans* will of course keep me going, but they may wish the sober *School of the Air* (five-day-a-week) on me.

In the meantime, I'm directing the *Workshop* for the first time since *The Red Badge of Courage*, on Thursday, September 29th, from 10 to 10:30 p.m. Immediately after the end of this show, I'm directing the *Americans at Work* from 10:30 to 11, in the same studio. *Americans* will concern the songwriter, and will have an orchestra. You can imagine my rehearsal situation....The two shows will be as alike as Christ and Hitler.

And so it goes. I might report that I feel increasingly confident of my directorial powers, and become increasingly convinced that I can outwrite 99 out of 100—or maybe 101—radio writers. I am managing things with greater efficiency as time advances, and only last week I required only three hours, instead of the allotted six, to rehearse my *Americans at Work*. I feel that I'm getting better results out of my actors than most directors; and although I'm still making my lion's share of mistakes, I am fairly optimistic about the feeling that I don't make them twice....

My health up until two days ago has been simply wretched. Air conditioning in the control rooms has been so brutal that I caught a low-grade summer grippe, not enough to keep me in bed, but enough to hang on. After a month of the doldrums, I got myself x-rayed and saw three different doctors. I'm a little better now, in that my temperature has been behaving the past forty-eight hours, but I'm not yet quite off the ropes....

Corwin finally did adapt, direct and produce *John Brown's Body*, based on Stephen Vincent Benet's epic poem. It was presented on July 20, 1939, before a live audience in CBS's Broadway Playhouse. Orson Welles was not involved. Corwin was tempted to cast a prominent radio actor named John Brown, so that credits would read, "The role of John Brown was played by John Brown," but thought better of it and cast Ray Collins. For a reaction to the program see the letter to Robert Saudek dated April 16, 1989.

TO T. WELLS CHURCH / November 27, 1938

Dear Ted:

Well, it looks as though I will be kept busy for a while. Beginning tomorrow, I have a show every day except Sunday....Mr. Orson Welles, the man from Mars, will grace the opener tomorrow night.

Words Without Music (Bill Lewis's name for *Poetic License*) becomes a series next Sunday at 5 p.m. It will be a half-hour spot right after Philharmonic, until further notice. For the opener I will repeat, substantially, the Workshop program which was not heard except in a few scattered cities. (At that, it pulled 150 letters—50 from Chicago alone, the one big city that did hear it. Average mail on Workshop for the past year has been 12 letters, with the *full* net[work].)

This means, of course, that I am not going to enjoy the luxury of a day off at any time. The other day I raised a squawk about not having a full-time secretary, and if I don't get one I am just not going to do those shows. My goddam phone rings 347 times a day, and there are scores of memos and typing jobs which I have been obliged to do myself.

I don't think you will approve in the least the arrangement under which I am writing and producing *Words Without Music*, in addition to the five strip shows per week, without any extra compensation. I'm afraid that your absence from town is costing me money, for if you were here I'd never have submitted to such a deal. I mean to say that your moral support is as much a backbone to me as to Bob [Robert Trout, a newscaster who was also counseled by Church], and that without it I am not a good businessman.

Please write soon, Ted, and send me your new address and phone. I'll never have time to write you after this, and I guess all communication will have to be by phone, so you better give me a full schedule of when and where you can be reached.

TO BEULAH CORWIN / January 9, 1939

Dear Boo:

It was good to get your letter, because letters from the Bell branch of the family have been pretty rare of late—almost as rare as my letters home. [Corwin's sister had married Irving Belkowitz. Corwin truncated her new name to "Bell" in this letter.] You must forgive me for not having answered sooner, but if you knew how desperately busy I am with six shows a week—and with the prodigious amount of work that goes into that Sunday show, you would wonder that I have any time at all.

You ask about the possibility of work in radio. All I can tell you is that radio acting is a very specialized sort of work, and that there are hundreds, if not thousands, of actors and actresses who are working away at it with a discouraging lack of success. If you are anyway near good—if you can read a script without a trace of self-consciousness, if you can sound NATURAL—then you are a radio actress. But of course acting is not merely realistic interpretation of lines. Just as often as not, actresses are required to turn on the emotion—to laugh, cry, sob, get hysterical, silly, angry, etc.—and not many of them are up to it.

I assume that when you speak of radio acting, you mean doing work in New York. What about your family, if you should turn out to be an actress? You realize that only in New York would there be the volume of work, and sufficient pay to make it worthwhile.

If you are serious about acting, I would advise that you listen carefully to dramatic shows on the radio, and keep an ear tuned to the nuances of the performance. You will hear a lot of tripe, especially from local stations, and I urge you not to emulate that stuff. The best acting is to be found on the network shows, such as Orson Welles, The Columbia Workshop and my own shows.

The most important phase of this letter I have not yet touched upon is, WHY do you want to act? Are you in any way embarrassed financially, because if you are, you are silly not to let me know. There is nothing to be embarrassed about when it concerns money, because some of our very greatest and ablest people have been pinched and jobless for long stretches. Is Irv having a tough time finding work? Why doesn't he take a crack at New York, where there is a greater job turnover than in any city in the world?

TO MARY ELEANOR VAUGHAN, Program Department at WLW
in Ohio / January 31, 1939

Dear Mary:

It is not "dates with glamorous New York dames" which prevent me
from writing you, but dates with a radio audience six nights a week. I
no longer know what a date with a dame can possibly mean.

Congratulations and super-congratulations on your career with P.&
G. I think it's swell that you have had three promotions in as many
months and I hope you are headed for high places in the organization—you deserve it.

TO SARAH ROLLITS, Columbia Management
December 7, 1939

> When Corwin joined CBS, he was required to be repre-
> sented by Columbia Management, a talent agency owned
> by the network, which automatically took 20 percent of
> his earnings. The agency had submitted Corwin's name to
> Hollywood film studios without informing him.

Dear Sarah:

While I appreciate all you are attempting to do in my behalf, I
would appreciate consultation before any letters are sent out to film
companies regarding my availability for work in pictures. The truth of
the matter is that I am not now seeking picture work and do not want
to be represented as doing so. I would infinitely prefer to wait until
some company is attracted to the prospect of taking me on for certain
potentialities which they may recognize out of my radio work. It was on
this basis that Mr. Healand of Paramount first approached me and this
is how I would prefer to have it every time. Thus your letters about me
to [David O.] Selznick and RKO, while very generous in their intent,
are sources of potential embarrassment to me. I hope no other letters of
a similar nature have gone to other studios. I feel that we are in a much
stronger bargaining position when a studio comes to us than when we
solicit a studio.

I would appreciate consultation regarding any letter representing me to either film or radio markets. In this way we can avoid the possibility of mutual embarrassment.

TO CHARLES R. JACKSON / From New York, February 23, 1940

Corwin and Jackson worked in adjoining offices on the 18th floor of the CBS Building, and Corwin had dedicated to him his first published radio play, *They Fly Through the Air with the Greatest of Ease*, which had been broadcast on February 19, 1939. Jackson later wrote the novel *The Lost Weekend*.

Dear Charlie:

Your report of the extent to which my work is known and followed in Washington, and your reaffirmation of faith in my potential as a writer, helped me through a very unhappy period in my work. I have become, as you know, fed up with creative inactivity. The Sunday show [a series called *The Pursuit of Happiness*, which Corwin directed] has resolved itself into keeping the elements of a clambake from becoming a clambake. It is like wiring a jigsaw puzzle for sound, and the amount of energy burned in this thankless and uninspiring pursuit comes out of the reserve previously available to such works as you and I enjoyed together last year.

...As for your worry concerning my work: It is of no small consolation to know that it *does* concern you, and it returns me to the spirit and enthusiasm of those days when I would dash into your office six times an hour with a new verse and read it to you for your opinion. It puts me in the same frame of mind I had then—an aggressive and creative and confident frame of mind, and it is only out of such an attitude that my best work can come.

You are silly when you say, "You have the gift, the genuine article, while I only have the gift of saying true, poor or careless though the writing may often be." There are a thousand men who can write with the same sort of semi-contemptuous authority which I get into an article like "The Sovereign Word," for one man who can write quietly and truthfully and beautifully. My power is in the occasional explosive compression of my lines and images. I slash at things. I assault. Your strength is in the sheer, deep-down humanity of your people and of your writing.

...I have no doubt about you except that I think it will probably take longer in your case to be appreciated and rewarded than it would in the case of a flashier but superficial writer. The main thing is for you to keep writing. You were burning with stories during your last months here, and I hope that you will not let the fire sink low at any time.

On June 20, 1940, Corwin flew to Hollywood at the invitation of film producer Erich Pommer to work on a screen adaptation of Elmer Rice's Broadway play *Two on an Island*. On this trip, his first west of the Rockies, Corwin was the house guest of actors Charles and Elsa Laughton in Brentwood.

TO CARLY WHARTON, Theatrical Producer / June 25, 1940

Dear Carly:

This is a bulletin from Room 311, Building "G", 780 Gower Street, HOllywood 5911, Pommer Unit, office conveniently located overlooking a power house and not far from the commissary where all the cuties and babes of a George Abbott production are coming and going the day long.

I did not get a chance before I left on this eight-week safari to thank you for having recommended me for that post of war correspondent. It was swell of you to speak of me to [Ralph] Ingersoll, and I was very sorely tempted to drop everything and run to the nearest passport office. But CBS, to which I am wedded by contract for the next three years, would hear nothing of it, and the adventure was scotched before it could begin....

TO EMIL CORWIN / From Brentwood, California, July 1, 1940

Dear Em:

Thanks a million for the letter and the pictures. Never have I looked more like a rhinoceros—a rhinoceros with astigmatism....

I'm probably going to stay with the Laughtons for the remainder of my visit, since they find themselves entertained by my puns and I have been able to furnish reasonable opposition to the Ping-Pong player of the household, one Rene Rubin, secretary of the Laughtons. They live twelve miles out of town, which means quite a bit of commuting by car but I rented myself a nifty little Ford convertible, the first such job I have had since our safari into the White Mountains years back.

The Laughtons have a magnificent pool, wonderful grounds, and my quarters look out on some pretty rugged hills, just behind which lies the Pacific. The days are very toasty, the nights cool enough for double blankets....

So far I have not had time to go out on the [movie] sets much but I have been watching a number of rushes at the elbow of Erich Pommer.

Finished my Laughton script today and you'll be hearing from it in about six weeks....

TO ROSE AND SAMUEL CORWIN / From Brentwood, July 5, 1940

Dear Ma and Pa:

Just a hasty note to let you know that all is well and that I'm making reasonably satisfactory progress. The work here is leisurely compared to the pace of radio and I do believe I'm getting fat.

I have been neglecting the matter of the weekly budget for the new maid Ma promised she was going to get herself, and the check herewith enclosed is intended to be applicable to that account.

If Ma doesn't get the maid I will consider myself embezzled and will bring action through the Supreme Court of the land.

Nothing very new to report, chiefly because news moves much more slowly in Hollywood than in New York. It's the difference between doing a show every week and working on maybe two or three pictures a year....

TO ALTON COOK, Radio Critic, *New York World-Telegram*
July 19, 1940

Dear Alton:

I met an old friend of yours for the first time the other day, in the dining room of a country club, and we got together the next day and had a very fine lunch and talked about you a good part of the time. I am referring to [the comedian] Fred Allen, whom I have admired lo, these many years. It was paradoxical that all the time I've been in New York I never met him, but now we are working on adjoining lots.

The work here is tremendously absorbing, and it marks the first time I've returned to writing exclusively since leaving newspaper work. I miss the impact of people and the immediacy of interpretation which comes out of directing but, on the other hand, I am again tapping those inward circuits of expression which, as you well know, all writing is based on....

Southern California is the great portable radio belt of the country. Even on the lot they are numerous. Most people wouldn't think of taking a swim in their pools without having a portable radio on hand. I shouldn't be surprised but what the listening audience has increased greatly because of the growth in the quantity of portables, and consequently I should think the whole approach to summer radio might well be revised. A good percentage of the audience which broadcasters feel was being lost to motoring and assorted summer sports, has probably come back into the listening fold....

Corwin had recommended to CBS a young radio writer from Iowa, Perry Lafferty, who later became a network Vice President.

TO PERRY LAFFERTY / From Hollywood, August 6, 1940

Dear Perry:

I miss you too, you bastard. It was a shame I saw you so little after you came to CBS.

I'm delighted to hear of your rapid progress and have no doubt you will shortly be, if you are not already, inheritor of the slightly battered mantle of Corwin.

Don't expect too much from my Forecasts. The one I am writing is the lowest common denominator of simplicity, so don't expect any hooks or curves or fadeaway balls. It's just a guy who writes a letter to his son. [Corwin was writing *To Tim at 20*, which was broadcast on August 19, 1940, and starred Charles Laughton and Elsa Lanchester.]

TO FREDA [MRS. EMIL] CORWIN [nicknamed Babe]
From Hollywood, August 7, 1940

Dear Babe:

...I'm getting tired of singlehood. It wasn't so bad in New York, because I was so busy I didn't have time to do my sparking properly. But out here, damn it, I'm leading a civilized life, getting plenty of rest and air and sun and exercise and eating well, and there's a hell of a moon when there's any moon at all, and I get kind of lonely....

There is at the moment a general buzzing of terms and contracts and a new deal, but I have definitely decided against a long-termer on the basis of my inclination, observation, and good counsels....

TO ROSE AND SAMUEL CORWIN / From Brentwood, CA, August 16, 1940

Dear Ma and Pa:

The past week has been more like the old days. I've been almost as busy as during the hectic days in New York. The difference is that here I manage to get my quota of sleep and exercise. There is a Ping-Pong table as well as a pool at the Laughtons, and spending a Sunday at home is the equivalent of going to a resort. Especially since the Laughtons are such great fun.

Feeling that I might be outwearing my welcome, I made a move last week to look for an apartment, but they would hear none of it. They said they saw no reason why I shouldn't stay until the cold weather sets in, which means November.

About myself and Hollywood: I have turned down a long-term offer for the second time. For good and sufficient reasons. I may in the future turn down salaries three or four times my radio salary to achieve what I believe in the end will profit me both artistically and economically.

Pa has asked about the nature of my work here. Let me give you a typical day:

Up at eight, breakfast in the garden, a twelve-mile drive to work, arriving in the office about 10. I open mail, do a little work on the script, go to lunch on the studio lot. After lunch there may be a conference with the producer. We discuss points raised in the script, go over material, outline story and character development. I happen to be fortunate in working for an especially keen man [Erich Pommer] receptive to new ideas. We are frank with each other and sometimes will argue a single point for a half-hour. We find that we're 50 percent right usually, and never have the slightest unpleasantness. [The project was *Two on an Island*.]

I usually leave the studio around six or seven and drive home to dinner at the Laughtons. Once in a while we take a drive or see a picture or go to the studio after dinner for a screening. But mostly we sit around and read stuff aloud or argue about everything in the world. On a warm night we swim. One or two nights a week I stay in town for dinner or dine with friends.

TO LYN MURRAY, Composer / August 27, 1940

Dear Lyn:

I was especially glad to get your note about *Tim*. You are one of three or four guys in the inner sanctum of radio from whom a word of approval is as coveted as a fat royalty check. By telling me that the broadcast made your week, you made mine. Thanks.

Murray later wrote scores for several radio dramas of the series *26 by Corwin*.

TO WILLIAM B. LEWIS, Vice President in Charge of Programs, CBS / From RKO Studio, September 13, 1940

Dear Bill:

Okay, okay, you're absolutely right. The fact that you think I'm a great director and terrific writer shows your vacation has not in any way softened the keenness of your judgment or affected your sense of values. Lewis, I love you.

To hell with money, anyway. This morning I boiled two eggs over a fire kindled from dry, crisp ten-dollar bills. You should have heard it crackle.

I expect to be back in town within two weeks and will let you and Sarah invite me to dinner for a slight charge, and will sign Ragan's autograph book for nothing. Numerous things I want to discuss with you, about both Lewis and Corwin, and Lewis & Corwin.

My plans for the fall, providing I am not indispensable to the armed might of the nation, are gravitating toward pictures because of interest shown in me recently both here and at Paramount. But I have signed nothing, have declined another long-term offer from RKO, and am perfectly free to do what I want after October 15th. RKO has asked me to stay on through the production of *Two on an Island.* I should like you to know that as far as radio is concerned I would be interested in any good 26-week setup, even though it paid less than movie dividends, providing I could do a show that would make us all happy and self-respecting rather than rich. I mean a whopper of a prestige show, in which I might be given resources and a free hand to write and produce the best goddam show on any air. That, sir, would be worth more to me than the Hollywood lucre which, mind you, feels very nice on the inner lining of the pocket.

TO MILDRED OBER COHEN, Rose Corwin's sister
September 26, 1940

Dear Millie:

I am shocked to find a letter from you dated June 26th, which, if my memory serves right, has not been answered. For this I apologize, especially since you are by all odds my favorite aunt....

Concerning your dream-dance with Charles Boyer, I suggest you stop eating blintzes and varnishkes before going to bed. I don't want to disillusion you but did you know that Charles Boyer is a very short man and wears high heels in most of his pictures? I may not be handsome or have beautiful dark Latin eyes, but Jesus, nobody eats beans off my head.

I have been here three months and am leaving for New York tomorrow with what is familiarly known as a sigh of relief, but I expect to unsigh in about three weeks, at which time it is quite likely I will return.

P.S. Was it you who sent me the enclosed poem by Thelma Rubin? If so, I wish you would convey to Miss Rubin my hearty congratulations for a precocious bit of writing. I think she should keep on writing poems willy-nilly. The reason it took me so long to develop as a writer was that I *didn't* write poems willy-nilly. I only wrote them nilly—the willy didn't come until after I was twenty-one.

TO JOAN ALEXANDER, Actress and Friend / January 12, 1941

Joan dear:

Your letter arrived at the Chateau [Elysee] the day after I left to live in a cottage by myself high up on one of those phony mountains out here. I say phony, because a mountain has no right to be crisscrossed by roads, like some effete real estate development. Yet it is quite wonderful, except that it takes me hours each morning to thaw the very marrow of my bones, so penetrating is the night cold.

As a gazette and chronicle of your life and times in the greatest city that ever was, your letter is a notable failure because it says much too much about me and far too little about you. You brush off with a slight skiddoo your current production course, furnishing me no other description than that it is "fun and interesting." Whose work are you observing, pretty one, and how often, and does it really help you to get a sense of radio's peculiar foreshortening of time? Of its special rhythms and cadences? Of its vast wide-ranging potentials?

You mention Lafferty. A wonderful barefoot lad, he, with a touching naivete about the world of politics and economics, but a solid-enough education (greater than mine, I suspect) in other stouter things of life. He has an unusually keen ear for what radiomen call "balance," and his *Workshop* of last week showed all kinds of promise....

I wish I could be a party to your suspicion that I am going to be the greatest writer in America, but when I read such works as *The People, Yes* and certain sections of *Leaves of Grass,* and read the little bejeweled lyrics of Emily Dickinson, I could weep for the beauty and strength in them, and for the lacks of my own writing. I shall die a happy man if I have written ten lines that can move a stranger living a century hence, to feel the world more closely, or if I shall have contributed one jot of one tittle of one iota to the advancement of a universal brotherhood of man or to the establishment of a brave and clean and working peace, for all men, for all time.

I am glad you communicate with Al every now and then, for I do want some trusty lieutenant to keep a beautiful eye on the boy. I am very fond of him, as you may have gathered. He's so sensible, and I am such a mercurial ass.

The work here proceeds in a most jolly manner, with tea at four in the afternoon and a contest between my producer and me to see who can rewrite each other's rewrites faster and better. The only thing is, I am anxious to return to my own, my native land, where when the weather is mean it is stinking, rotten, low, nasty and viciously mean....[Corwin's film project, *Two on an Island,* was never made.]

Please tell Marty [the actor Martin Gabel, who was appearing on Broadway] I am glad to learn about the advance raves on his play, and that I hope it is finer in every respect than anything which will have been done in this half of the century, excepting, of course, my own.

Eh bien, alors, well then, good cess to you, bon sante, Yokohama hickydoola, and skoal.

TO ROSE AND SAMUEL CORWIN / January 13, 1941

Dear Ma and Pa:

Well, I have spent my first weekend in my cottage on the mountaintop, and am happier for it. There is no comparison between this place and the fancy Chateau Elysee, where I had to shave before sticking my face out of my room, and I couldn't bring in any foodstuffs without looking and feeling like a fugitive from an A&P store.

Now, however, I am the country squire. Yesterday was a golden, toasty, warm day. I took me a sunbath on my private sunpoach, then made me a snorter of canned grapefruit juice, a couple of boiled eggs, and dawdled and napped and read and basked and walked and had a perfectly swell time.

I have a big fireplace, and in addition to enjoying its warmth and cheer, I love the idea of throwing all my scrap paper and cast-off wrappings into it, as a huge waste basket....

The remarkable thing about this place is that it is only twelve minutes from the office, via winding, steep hill roads. Yet you'd think you were in a different country....

TO DAVIDSON TAYLOR, CBS Program Department Executive
January 16, 1941

Alfred Eisner, a young writer in Hollywood, was unaware that he was terminally ill with cancer. His sister had asked Corwin to lure him home to New York by promising him a job as Corwin's assistant at CBS, with Eisner's family reimbursing the network for his salary. Corwin had persuaded CBS to agree.

Dear Dave:

Your letter moved me on several accounts. First, for its reference to Eisner, who died thinking you and I were two of nature's finest works whereas we were being merely Supersud-white liars; second, by its reference to [Edward R.] Murrow's achievement of "personal integrity" out of that whole reeking cesspool of Europe; third, by your expression of a belief in my future.

Eisner was a rare jewel of a boy, and I find his memory lingering long after I thought I would have put it by. He was earnest, and when he said something he invariably meant it. One of his most admirable qualities, I thought, was his unwillingness to be influenced by a sense of gratitude in the exercise of his critical faculty—a keenly developed faculty, by the way. He told me one minute that he was eternally indebted to me for the "opportunity" I had presented him, and a minute later told me that he thought a new script of mine was quite dull. At the hospital, when you saw him last, he was by no means ready to surrender any point without a struggle. The night I repeated *Seems Radio* I took him along to dinner with Sir Cedric Hardwicke, and I believe his knightship paid the bill, but that didn't prevent Al from almost tearing Cedric limb from limb over the issue of whether American boys should die on the fields of Egypt, Turkey and Bulgaria to rectify the blunders of [Stanley] Baldwin, [Neville] Chamberlain and [Lord] Halifax.

Like you, I feel I did too little for the boy. His sister asked me way back, while he was still walking around, to get some photos taken of him, ostensibly for publicity purposes. I thought there would be plenty of time, so I delayed it a few days, and when I finally arranged with Mike Fish to put an order through, Eisner was leaving for the hospital. I saw him only once after we visited him together, and phoned him only twice.

There are a lot of young men dying before their time where [William L.] Shirer has just come from, and it fills me with a great sadness to think, as I always do when I arise in the morning and look out of my window on the clean and quiet country, that a lot of young kids who don't care very much for their work are getting it in the guts even as I shave and drink grapefruit juice. It doesn't make any sense, and it never has, and it never will.

This morning I was talking with Hardwicke and Bob Sisk, the latter one of this town's better producers. Hardwicke said his kid (aged ten) asked him yesterday, "Father, why do we have to kill Germans?" Sisk reported that his girl (aged nine), seeing pictures of shells costing $5,000 apiece in one of *Life*'s educational spreads asked him, "Dad, isn't this a great waste?" I was reminded of Eric Davis's story of the eight-year-old shipwrecked boy who said, "I say, thank you very much," when he was pulled onto a raft. And I thought we'd better turn over portfolios of government to children if we ever hope to get anywhere.

But it is stirring to hear of Murrow's attitude. What a stroke of luck to have a man of his stripe in that spot! He is one of the really great men in Radio, and I think he is worth eight [David] Sarnoffs, twelve sponsors, Mr. and Mrs. [Andre] Kostelanetz, and the Workshop.

What you say about your belief in my future is very warming and buoying, especially since my spirit is dampened so much by the horrible intellectual mists of this place, and I am given to great accesses of loneliness in which I find it difficult to recall ever having written a worthwhile word. I hope, by Jesus and by lesser saints, to do some decent work in my lifetime, and in the process to rise above the subterranean level in which I so often grope for reason and for understanding. I really spend too much time in a sort of bombproof cellar for the soul.

Regarding *26 by Corwin*, I now think that it would take me three weeks to a month to get a sufficient head start on that series, after winding up my picture commitments. I would like, while I am young and (so far) free of gastric ulcers and radio bladder, to see what would happen if I were turned loose for six months to write, direct and produce twenty-six shows. Maybe it would be my swan song in radio, I dunno. Maybe I would rumble like a mountain in labor, and bring forth a mouse of a rating. But I would just like to see where I stand as a man and a technician—to take a fierce fling at the objective of doing the very best kind of radio I know how to do, for the glory of CBS or of Corwin or of nobody.

I have never had the luxury of complete concentration, for all during *Words Without Music* I was directing five fifteen-minute shows a week in addition. *Pursuit...* scattered my concentration inasmuch as we all had to hold hands and run backstage to sell scripts to Barrymores and try to put on great American entertainment at the same time we were carrying budget figures around in our heads and auditioning hillbillies.

Workshop is indeed attractive, and one of the most attractive ideas about it is the prospect of again collaborating with you. But I would like to walk the plank on a series, first, which made me so completely answerable to myself that I would again make the sacrifices in my social (and sex) life which the traditional "artist" likes to think he has to make....

I see Benny [Bernard Herrmann, composer] often, and watched him record on the music stage today. He is a dear guy who upbraids movie musicians quite as impartially as radio musicians. And he has done some excellent work for [Orson] Welles. You are no doubt aware that the Hearst Enterprises are threatening the whole motion picture industry with earthquakes and blackmail if the Welles picture [*Citizen Kane*] is released. Orson is quite worried, but if the studio does anything less than back him to the hilt, it is nothing but a moral latrine....

TO ALFRED CORWIN / February 19, 1941

Dear Al:

...I will probably want to live in the country when I return to New York early in March. The place need not be quite as big as the Nyack house but I would like to have a nice location, and remoteness from traffic.

Since you will be very welcome indeed to share this place with me without any rental cost to yourself, I feel less imposing than I would otherwise in asking you to check with Quiz Marcum [a rental agent] as soon as you can, about renting such a place. I would want to take it for about six months, stretching through the summer. I will need a combination cook and maid....

The reason for all this is that CBS has offered me the *Workshop* for six months to do *26 by Corwin*. This will constitute the greatest opportunity in my career to distinguish myself as a writer-producer, and it would be folly to pass it by. But in order to produce twenty-six shows week after week and make them all on the level of *They Fly...* and *Curley* and *Seems Radio*, I will have to get a month's head start on writing....

Financially the deal is not going to be a killer-diller. I would be working for my basic CBS salary (which will be hiked the usual amount if and when my option is picked up at the end of April), plus a nominal flat fee, probably a hundred dollars, for each script. Against the expense of running such an institution [a rented house and hired help] there will be little profit all told, since by the time I am through paying for utilities and toll calls plus the upkeep of a new car and salary for a cook, I will have enough to buy a few airmail stamps maybe.

I am sending copies of this letter to Em and the folks. What I want you all to understand is that I am really tackling something around the ankles, and if I seem to go into somewhat of a retirement for the next five or six weeks between the time I leave Hollywood and the start of *26 by Corwin*, it is only because I want to make sure that a series bearing such a billing, especially on *Workshop*, should represent the very best work of which I am capable....

TO LT. COL. MAXWELL SETTON [With British forces in Egypt]
From 35 West 90th Street, New York, February 19, 1941

Dear Max:

Ever since we went different ways that night on 52nd Street, I have been wanting to write you. This is my first opportunity, for since that time I have not had as much as a single day off and have been forging along like the triphammers of hell. I wish I could say forging *ahead* but that would be rather an exaggeration.

I know my story is far less exciting and important than yours, and I blush to tell it here, but for the sake of the record you should know what has come of my encounters with Hollywood. I worked with Erich Pommer on *Two on an Island* last summer and I am here at the moment working on a picture for British War Relief. The first script ran into star trouble when Miss Ginger Rogers objected to playing a "stooge to New York City"; the second is not yet before the cameras.

Nor yet has my picture writing begun to approach the level of my radio work, and I feel this is due to the routine of overcollaboration which one has to put up with in Hollywood. I am best as a lone wolf, which radio permits me to be, and for this reason alone, I am returning to radio at the end of this month and expect to swing into some very tough but worthwhile work. It is likely I will take over the Columbia Workshop for twenty-six weeks.

I cannot wait until the war is over to hear from you the story of your life since you left America. If you are in any way a part of the brilliant British campaign in Africa, you have the admiration and gratitude of many millions of Americans including myself. Certainly it is the brightest thing that has happened since the gloom descended at Munich.

I dream of the day when the war will be successfully over and we can all get together at Laughton's new Palisades home and drink to better times. It will be good to see you under any circumstances, and I hope that until we meet again you will remain in the best of health, spirits, and company....

TO DAVIDSON TAYLOR / From Sunless California (eleven days since our favorite star has last been seen here), February 21, 1941

Dear Dave:

Your letter gave out a fine blue spark of coincidence, for I have just come from an evening of conversation with a man and his wife, both of whom are wise in the way that few human beings ever get to be—and I felt on reading your letter that it was an extension of the evening's talk, for you too are a wise and a good and important man—and in your letter you wrote mostly of a great poet and said of him, "I think he is a wise man."

And because Wisdom is a rare radium, buried under tons of shale and clay and disintegrating granite, it is wonderful to pass through a triple concentration of its rays all in one evening. I feel a little incandescent from it, and that is a good way to feel once in a while.

I felt that I had to answer your letter immediately, though it is 1:30 a.m., and the place is as cold and damp as a dog's nose. Immediately, I say, because I want the letter to reach you before I reach New York. The things one says on the eighteenth floor and in Louis & Armand's are never quite the same things one says in a letter. You can't tell a man what a wonderful guy you think he is, to his face, because that would be embarrassing. But there it is.

I think you are important to the industry and therefore to the country. You are one of the reasons why CBS is what it is, in its better moments. It comes out of the fact that you happen to be guided by a set of principles rather than the lastest Hooper Report; that you believe it is in the nature of Man to want to do good and ambitious things, and that in direct ratio to this instinct, he is distinguished from the Gorilla and and Mr. and Mrs. Hummert [Anne and Frank Hummert produced soap operas]; that when you don't like a thing you will say so, though Hell and Mr. Klauber [Executive Vice President of CBS] stand in your way; that your loyalties are durable, in a highly transitory medium; and that you are a goddam smart writer and exec.

I am, of course, happy to know that you look with favor upon the forthcoming 26, and what you say about making suggestions, I wish you would put in the form of a promise. Because even if you *didn't* want to make suggestions, I would be breaking into conferences in your office to ask what you thought of some deathless verse I had just written, or of Homer Foof as a man who could both narrate and whistle with four fingers in his mouth.

I am coming East next week to begin preparing the series, and for a month or so I want to work at it away from the madding eighteenth [floor of CBS] etage. It will be good to get back to an honest climate, where when the weather's lousy you are convinced of it, and no deception. But here, there are great heroic cloudscapes, stormy and dramatic, the way Cortez must have seen them standing silent on a peak in Darien. But it's phony, somehow, and you half expect a Goldwyn credit to appear suddenly in fancy skywriting. And meanwhile it pours and pours and the streets are impassable, and your car's a mess and your feet are wet and your bed is damp, and the sun is remembered less and less as a bringer of warmth and light. The only compensation is that those indecently healthy-looking movie people, who are only six shades lighter than Night and look as though they spend all their time at Palm Springs (which they do), in this weather are quite bleached and normal, and they melt down into the melting pot with a slight hissing sound of bubbling fat.

[Bernard] Herrmann has left for home, and by this time you have probably seen him. Before he left he played me his new symphony, and I thought the last movement was smashing. If it sounds as grand in the orchestra (and Benny is no Horowitz on the Steinway, you know) it should be greater than anything you or I have done in the last ten years, or perhaps eleven.

...I hope you weren't able to see the February *Stage*....I wrote a kidding article, full of what I thought was good-natured ribbing, but in order to fit it on one page they cut it without consulting me until it sounded pontifical and irascible....

P.S. I loved the [Robert] Frost poem, which was new to me. But Frost himself is not new. I have heard him read and he has heard me, but never have we met.

A poem like "Drumlin" and a man like its author always shame the hell out of me, because they are so simple and unaffected. I would like to do good work, not tricky virtuoso stuff—work that got the best out of me and, if that best is any good at all, could give something to somebody else. That's all I really want to do, that's all I hope to do. The world is too small and life too short not to want to spend the best part of one's waking time making both better.

As I write this a terrific bolt of lightning has struck somewhere nearby. That's better punctuation than I could imagine.

It's a wonderful evening, all told.

TO WILLIAM B. LEWIS, Vice President in Charge of Programs, CBS / From Hollywood, California, February 23, 1941

Dear Bill:

I am leaving here Tuesday, and will be in to see you Friday if the train is not held up by bandits.

I'm in a fine mood of rolling-up-sleeves, and want to do you a job that will make you proud of your protege. It will mean extremely concentrated plugging through the Summer and Fall, but after the soft work and easy money out here, that's what I want—and I am enthusiastic about the prospect of building something with you and for you.

I am certain that for the first three weeks after my return it would be much better to work away from the 18th floor and its interruptions, so I will not be needing an office and secretary until around the middle of March, at which time I trust Douglas C. [Coulter] will get his executive broom out and sweep away some of the riffraff to make room for the visiting Shriner and Potentate.

For the purposes of your plans, then, consider me back on staff March 3rd. I naturally would prefer to stick to my plan of working night and day exclusively on the Workshop scripts, but I want you to feel free to call on me for any and all help you may need on the Free Company series, because I think it is important, at this hour, to CBS and USA, both of which cover a lot of territory....

TO ROBERT ARDREY, a Writer [who later wrote *The Territorial Imperative*] / From Palisades, Rockland County, N.Y., July 9, 1941

Dear Ardrey:

You make it easy for me to fight the constant scrap that has to be fought to get, or keep, the kind of thing we both want on the air. A note like yours from a guy like you is a terrific dose of vitamin for a guy like me. I want you to know that I appreciate it down to my socks.

I hear you are writing a play down there [South Africa]. I hope it's coming along in the way you want it to come. That's an awfully fine sleep one sleeps after beating a page of script into the shape intended for it. Explains why I suffer so much insomnia.

I've taken a cottage just above Sneden's Landing, and find I can work 17.4 times faster and better than anywhere in town. It's a week-to-week grunt, involving maximum hazards of time, but so far (crossing four pairs of fingers and locking thumbs), I've had only one show out of the ten to date which I am ashamed to play back.

It's fun. Charles [Laughton] may come east, or I may go west, to do a literal job of the Book of Job. Deems Taylor today consented to compose an original score for it, and I am celebrating this with a magnum of strong tea.

Best regards to Helen [Mrs. Ardrey], and good working on the script, and again my deep and sincere appreciation for your thoughtfulness in letting me know you liked No. 8 [*Daybreak*, broadcast on June 22, 1941].

On December 15, 1941, eight days after Japanese aircraft attacked Pearl Harbor, the four major U.S. radio networks combined to broadcast *We Hold These Truths*, written and directed by Norman Corwin. The drama commemorating the 150th anniversary of the Bill of Rights, and broadcast nationwide from Los Angeles, reached half the country's population. Among the actors were James Stewart, Orson Welles, Lionel Barrymore, Edward G. Robinson and Walter Huston. The program concluded with an eight-minute talk by President Franklin D. Roosevelt broadcast live from the White House, with Leopold Stokowski in New York conducting the NBC Symphony in the national anthem.

TO KURT WEILL, Composer / From Washington, D.C., January 8, 1942

Late in 1941, Weill had proposed several ideas for Corwin to work on with him, one a musical adaptation of Corwin's play *Mary and the Fairy*. In December, he suggested that Corwin live with him and Mrs. Weill at their home in New City, New York, "where we'll probably write the whole play in a couple of months."

Dear Kurt:

This is one of the hardest letters I have ever had to write, because by it I find myself obliged to decline with warmest thanks and regrets your wonderful invitation to work with you in the country in this month of January.

I have been urged by the Office of Facts and Figures to organize, control and direct radio's first major war series [*This Is War!*]. Quite against my doctor's imprecations, I left California, where I was trying to snatch two uninterrupted breaths of fresh air—to rush to Washington in order to get this big project going. It is a series that will be broadcast every Saturday night for about thirteen weeks beginning in February over the combined networks of the country—some five hundred or more stations. Writers on the project will include (if I am lucky in lining them up) Steve Benet, Marc Connelly, Edna Millay and Carl Sandburg. If you have any time or inclination to pitch in on this I would of course be delighted to produce a Weill score to some one of our shows. It would pay—but not, of course, on a big league commercial scale....

TO JULIAN P. BOYD, Librarian, Princeton University
From Washington, D.C., January 21, 1942

Dear Mr. Boyd:

Carl Van Doren was good enough to forward to me your letter requesting the original manuscript of my forthcoming book. I have been depositing my original mss. with my brother for some time, ever since an outfit in New York shocked me one day by asking for the original of a radio play. They wanted to raise money by auctioning it off. I have not been in the habit of saving these things but thought better of it thereafter, and began turning my waste basket into a depository of archives.

I have given the original ms. of *13 by Corwin* [his first collection of plays] to my brother, Emil Corwin, and I cannot presume to be an Indian giver. I am afraid you would have to ask him for the papers and I am also afraid you will have to offer him an associate professorship at Princeton to get them. He is unconscionably sentimental about my stuff, as only a very fine brother can be, but there is no harm asking, if your interest goes to that length.

TO CARL VAN DOREN, Author of Foreword to *13 by Corwin*
From New York, February 15, 1942

Dear Carl:

I have just this minute seen the Foreword, and I am deeply moved not only by the generosity of your appraisal but by the brilliance and clarity of your discussion of the sensory aspects of radio. You have summed up in a few words what exhaustive analytical treatises have never succeeded in making plain. Your perspective is so fresh and discernment so sharp that what may have seemed obvious to you will be revelation to the radio man and listener alike. Again my profoundest gratitude for what you have said and for wanting to say it.

TO DAVID O. SELZNICK / From New York, June 24, 1942

Selznick proposed that he and Corwin work together on a series of short films that would contribute to "the war effort." They had talked together in New York before

Corwin left Manhattan to prepare for a trip to London to write, direct and produce *An American in England.*

Dear Mr. Selznick:

Two things have delayed this letter out of all proportion to my intentions: the unbelievable red tape and staggering amount of preparation in connection with the proposed London trip, and a sudden and stern dictum from my doctor to stop in my tracks and take to a resort or else. The day after wiring that optimistic chirrup to the effect that I would presently ship you some basic suggestions, I was exiled to Montauk. For a week I rested in lonely splendor, and now I am back in town, not exactly raring to go, but at least able to sleep and eat and look a thought in the eye.

First, let me say again that I think your concept is important and offers immense possibilities as an instrument of war—one whose desperate need can be calculated in terms of flesh and blood, whose urgency can be measured against current headlines. These were incentive enough; but, in addition, your idea excites the imagination as a fertile soil for new techniques and for daring and boldness in the means of reaching millions of people quickly, directly, and with something to say.

It is a truth of this war that in those countries where the people and the armies were well indoctrinated, where there was an understanding of the forces at work, where there was the least confusion, there was the most success. Unfortunately, we have to look to our principal enemy for a fierce example. The Germans have been so thoroughly indoctrinated by Nazi propaganda, so convinced and hoodwinked by the Nazi press, radio and cinema, that for all practical purposes they were, and are, a doped-up but efficient military nation. They were brought up to understand what was represented to them as the truth: the warped and diseased interpretation of the world about them, as put forth by Hitler. On the other hand, there is the case of our strongest ally, Russia—a politically conscious country, but with entirely different ideas and motives. They long ago went in for political education; they installed political commissars in the ranks of the army (and still have them there); the people were schooled to *their* understanding of the world about *them*; and as a result, they have fought with unity, energy and will.

But in the countries where confusion existed—Poland, the Lowlands, France—countries where there was no clear understanding of the true nature of the enemy, no grasp of the world since Versailles, countries where in the name of appeasement it was forbidden to attack or even to *discuss* Fascism (long the case with British, French and American radio policy before the war), in these countries the people folded up, the armies threw down their guns, the cities fell.

It happens that since 1932 everything the Germans turned out in the way of propaganda was very much to the point—to *their* point. But we have *our* point—we've had it right along—ever since 1776. Our point happens to be the truth. In this war we have chosen, as all free men would choose, the strategy of truth. But, *having* chosen this strategy, for God's sake let us stick by it and serve it and work at it and accomplish it.

To get specific: A picture glorifying the heroics of our fighting men may be the best-made and most exciting cinema in the world—but heroics is an old staple of drama. The quality of heroism, if isolated, can serve to defeat your purpose. Let me explain what I mean: An entire generation of moviegoers has been raised on it, in times of peace as well as war. Not enough new has been added. What the moviegoer should be brought to understand is not that Jack Dalton is indeed a brave pilot, which one suspects from the beginning of the picture, but why he happens to be piloting in the first place—WHY he enlisted, FOR WHAT he is fighting, what his people can expect from victory and what from defeat.

It is the short film that you're mainly interested in, and in this department I have made a few observations. The only reasonably good short I know of is one made by Warner's for the Air Corps, with Jimmy Stewart doing the narration....It was well done and cleanly put together. But for my money it failed. It said to potential flying men: "See here, boys, we give you ships and a big organization and we give you all kinds of interesting jobs, and a uniform with wings, and you will be the envy of the other boys, and the girls will go for you, and oh boy will it be fun, and besides you will be serving your country." But not a glimmer of WHY we are building a terrific air force. (I take that back—*one* glimmer—a three-second stock clip of an Axis bombing of a city.)

It is important that you see the German propaganda shorts which our Army has confiscated. I looked at them in Washington a couple of weeks ago. If you haven't already seen them, you should screen *The Will to Triumph* and *Victory in the West*....Note the strategy of the big lie in the commentary. American shorts have done nothing comparable with the strategy of the big truth.

I hope you are determined to press your project immediately and with energy. One can't afford to wait, because there just won't be any films left for any of us to make if we lose the war. The attitude you enunciated in our conversation at the Waldorf makes me confident that you share with me the sense of immediacy, and are, as I am, activated by it.

Coincidence: Just after finishing this letter I picked up the morning *Times* and came upon the enclosed article by James Aldridge. It demonstrates the main thesis of my letter: "Death is what a soldier expects, but he does not like to die unless you keep telling him sensibly what he is going to die for."...

TO ROSE AND SAMUEL CORWIN / July 2, 1942

Dear Ma and Pa:

Well, I like London. I like the British. I like my colleagues, and I like where I am staying. Moreover, I am sleeping well, and actually feel better generally than I did during the last few weeks in New York....

I am established in a room at the Savoy which outdoes for sumptuousness anything I have ever run into. It feels a little odd—London so grim and businesslike about the war, and the splendor of the rooms at the hotel. The bathroom alone is practically a club—mirrors, marble, one of those incredibly long bathtubs, super-gadgets for all kinds of little conveniences, a beautiful ivory telephone set in a niche; and in the room proper, a buzzer-set for summoning valet, waiter, maid; air conditioning; special light controls, etcetera. I am telling you this not to revel in the opulence of it all, but to dissipate whatever idea you might have that I am living in a shell hole somewhere. The Hollywood atmosphere of the Savoy is, in fact, a little irksome. I don't like tinsel and plush, but I do like a quiet and clean place in which to work and sleep, and that is what the Savoy manages to be. They have the best soundproofing of any large hotel I have ever been in, and to a guy who likes his eight hours a night, this is a great relief over the back of West 90th Street.

I had no idea London was as beautiful a city as it is. Somehow I always carried with me the impression that it was grim even in peacetime. But the charm of the place, the variety and quality of its architecture, its many wide streets, the area of [Westminster] Abbey and Big Ben—all these have given me an impression, oddly enough, even more pleasant than what I remember of Paris. Of course Paris is an old almost forgotten impression—more than ten years back—but Em would know what I mean when I speak of the grace and dignity and solidity of this old-world construction.

I cannot tell you how happy I was to find Murrow and Bob Trout and Charles Collingwood [the CBS staff in London] such immensely pleasant and likable fellows. While it is too early to discuss the shape of the series to come..., I feel at this writing that production of the series seems much less formidable a prospect than when I was trying to figure out angles in the States. And I say this only because of the apparent eagerness of the rest of the staff here to be of help.

Lest the picture be entirely rosy, I must report that my first contact with the equipment of studios and other facilities has been somewhat disappointing. By this I mean that due to the exigencies of the war, the studio space and the selection of facilities is not optimum. The BBC is working under difficulties which have certainly never confronted any of the boys at home. But none of these handicaps is going to be insurmountable to a man who did his first dramatic programs out of a glorified closet at Station WQXR. Hell's bells, I'll have all I want in the way of music and cast—except maybe my main narrator (a casting problem that worries me at the moment). Worries Murrow and me. Murrow sent a long cable to New York tonight demanding they send over a good actor. An American, not anybody else, must tell from *his* point of view how the war is being handled by the people of this island. There just doesn't happen to be a good American actor in town....

TO KATHERINE LOCKE [a young actress whom Corwin had cast in a radio play after she finished a run in Clifford Odets' *They Clash by Night*] / From London, September 9, 1942

Darling:

Your four letters,...your wonderful grab-bag assortment of blackout buttons, flashlights, peanuts, dried apricots and Hershey krinkles, and your streamlined packet with the butter and eggs and canned marmalade, have all arrived and been digested. That is more than I can say about the air programs we transmitted to America.

Easily the meatiest and best of the six was the last, by my reckoning. Before going on the air we had reports of an excellent circuit across the Atlantic....Only next noon did I learn that the first part of the program faded so badly that New York carried only the second half. That must have been like coming into a movie in time to see the last reel. Apparently the atmospherics are so freakish that reception can deteriorate or improve vastly within a few seconds....

The news of Al's induction was surprising, but not altogether unexpected. It made me a little sad to think of the family dispersing from New York.

About the *American in England* series as a whole I can only report that at this end it seemed pretty solid. The best travel piece was the first; the best looking-around piece and the weakest ideologically was the second; the third was the best handling of any subject (food); and the fourth was the most critical and constructive (women) on any one point. The fifth was a little euphemistic, but perhaps closer to the broad objectives of the series; i.e., an all-out Anglo-American friendship theme. The last, as I said before, was the best from the standpoint of guts and content. What I said in the portion you must all have missed was that from the distance of three thousand miles, and from this country, America has a very peculiar look—smug, green in the ways of war, too placid about cracking down on the dissenters and carpers and home-grown fascists, etc. It also had some definite constructive platforms, such as suggesting a radio high command for integration of the radio effort of the United Nations; the pooling of knowledge and experience in aircraft performance so that instead of national and professional pride standing in the way, the allies could acknowledge weaknesses wherever they exist and translate these weaknesses immediately into remedial production in the factories. It was full of stuff like that; and it was my great misfortune that the first half of the show should have been blanketed by severe fading. The second half was mainly the long coda of a series and, because of time considerations, was slackened down to a snail's pace. I have had not a single reaction from the States on the show, so it must have really gone plunko down the drain.

The first three weeks of the grind here were not so bad, because I did have a little margin on the series, but the second half was murder in the good old *This Is War!* tradition of all-night sessions. Murrow was a great help, indeed many of his thematic ideas were among the best developed; but the job of writing about this island as though I had covered every square inch of the place and seen thousands of people in all kinds of pursuits and activities, and of assimilating the important things to be said, was a jigsaw-puzzlement....

Got an offer from Selznick to write a screenplay about Yugoslavia, carte blanche, but it means doing it in England and hanging around for production at Denham probably, and devoting five or six months to a single project when in that period I might be turning out twenty or thirty good radio shows and maybe half a dozen decent articles. So I turned it down.

I have had remarkably little correspondence from the States, considering how bowed down I was by fan mail when at home. Got a wire from House Jameson [an actor who narrated or starred in many of Corwin's radio plays] after the first show, and a letter from Hester Sondergaard [a radio actress]. Both very nice people, with whom I have enjoyed working, and they have done the finest individual acting jobs on any of my programs....

The period of lionizing Corwin has ended, and probably will not be revived now that they know here that I have a tendency to be outspoken and critical in my radio scripts. I turned down several opportunities to broadcast over the BBC and write for local publication simply because I didn't have time....

So far I have beaten a path between the Savoy and Broadcasting House and a couple of parks, where I have been writing outdoors in good weather....

Dinner tonight with the brilliant Dr. Drummond [Britain's chief nutritional consultant], who is more responsible than anyone else for the fine nutritional job being done in Britain; and before dinner, a conference with the Australian Broadcasting Corporation re their application for permission to do my *An American in England* series there. If it is to be done on a sustaining basis I shall charge them no royalty. War effort, you know....

The weather has been beautiful lately. Apparently takes summer a long time to make up its mind here. But I am advised that the bad spell will soon enough set in. I hope that applies to the Axis too. I'd love to see a real good long sustained bad spell for those dirty bastards. At the moment all prayers are for Stalingrad to hold, and as of today the defense has been glorious.

TO ROSE AND SAMUEL CORWIN / From London, October 20, 1942

Dear Folks:

Once again, my apologies for not writing sooner. The job of gathering material for the renewal of *An American in England* upon my return, has been a big one, involving much travel and interviewing and concentrated observation. Moreover, the moment that pressure of the broadcast deadline was removed, I found myself so tired that I couldn't bring myself to write a line even when there was an occasional moment free to do so.

The New York Times Radio Editor a month ago asked me to write a piece for the Sunday section, and would you believe that it is still unwritten? I just felt too unwound to start pounding a typewriter again so soon after the end of such a hard series as the one I did from here. Only this past week have I felt sufficiently rested to ask myself to take on any extracurricular writing chores. And only last night did I bat out a piece for the British edition of *Good Housekeeping*—a piece I had promised *them* a month ago.

Lest you think I have been dawdling, indulging a disinclination to write, let me advise that since my last letter I have visited Liverpool, spent several days on a farm in Norfolk County, gone to a former summer vacation resort [Cromer] on the North Sea, been to Eton, visited a country camp for evacuee children from the city, etc. In between trips I have delivered three lectures to no less than one hundred BBC producers, and spoken to a big meeting in New York's Carnegie Hall via short-wave radio, and delivered what is known as a "postscript" to the 1:00 p.m. Sunday news on the BBC home service—considered rather a choice spot in the broadcasting week here. The latter, on a record, has been used since on the Australian Empire service, so apparently it has been getting around the world....

I am told by several people in local radio that I have had a marked influence on British techniques. They say, flatteringly enough, that the standard of British drama has noticeably improved in the past two months, and charitably ascribe this to the borrowing and modification of devices demonstrated in my plays. Be that as it may, I have never been so technique-free as in my writing of the *American in England* series. I chucked overboard all my Workshop stylization, and went in for straightforward simple story-telling....

TO ARCHIBALD MacLEISH, Poet, Librarian of Congress
From New York, February 2, 1943

Dear Archie:

I am honored and happy to have your letter, and you may be sure that I shall send the Library [of Congress] any of my manuscripts worth their postage. The only trouble is that I am a bad judge of my own work, and will have to be told whether a particular play merits preservation even in an attic trunk.

Incidentally I wish it were possible for you to find time for MacLeish radio. There was far too long an interval between *Fall of the City*, *Air-Raid* and *The States Talking*. The country is the loser. One of my oldest ambitions is to produce a MacLeish premiere. And if you wrote us a war piece it would be worth two divisions in Tunisia.

I go to the Coast Friday to do *Transatlantic Call*, a new series of exchange programs with Britain. This commitment runs through April, but if anything occurs between now and then wherein you want to draft whatever special services I have to offer, please do not hesitate to call. First things first, as they say.

TO CLAIRE TREVOR, Actress / From New York, March 25, 1943

Dear Claire:

I got out of a sickbed in Chicago to transmit that Midwest program which you loyally got out of a wellbed to receive, and as a result had my ears pinned back. Literally. Nothing was ever more eminently deserved. I poured myself onto the Century and rode a fevered ride, arriving home in time to come down with an impressive middle-ear infection. Both ears; and had I a third ear, that would have been involved too.

Mirabilu sulfa, I am over the thing now, but my ears still feel as though I were flying at 15,000 feet. All this clinical detail by way of explaining that I have had to ring off *Transatlantic Call.* Somebody else will have to finish. My doctor insists that I consolidate my recovery by a good month's rest, arguing that I've been hammering away for four years without letup, and now is an auspicious time to knock off. So in about two weeks I am going to some quiet spot on the desert—a spot as yet unselected, but whose qualifications will improve if it has no telephone. You don't know a good rancho, do you?

Claire, you are very sweet to tell me how much you like *13 by Corwin* and I love your report of the anarchy it touched off among your hidden yens and self-hypnoses. But you must not be too jealous of [Everett] Sloane, [Jeanette] Nolan and [House] Jameson [actors in Corwin radio programs]. Shall I do a play for you when I return to the lists and the listings? What would you like it to be like? Endymion or Liz? Blue and cantabile, or blonde and presto? An explosion with smokeless powder, or the curtain stirring by the half-open window? I am, when sound, arrogant enough to try any and all such.

If you liked the 13, I hope you will like my next collection—as yet unnumbered and unnamed. I have two books coming out this year, one in the summer, one in the fall. Not very patriotic, what with an imminent paper shortage. But the piece responsible for my hearing from you will be among the bric-a-brac, and as such it wears a special shining badge....

TO CLAIRE TREVOR / From Dirty Train Window, Neb.,
April 29, 1943

Dear Claire:

I have been following the Trevor legend with keen fascination. In the last fortnight various columns appearing in the New York press have announced momentously that (a) you enjoy hot baths; (b) you smoke a rare meerschaum hookah for relaxation after a hard day's work; (c) you have installed a large photomural of Tyrone Power over the west rotunda in the south wing of your new hacienda; and (d) a large natural-color portrait of Trevor is the center of the Press Photographer's Exhibition at the Radio City Museum of Science and Industry.

I did not get a chance to see this *objet d'art*, alas, but then I would far rather see the model anyway.

I am, as the above golden sunset suggests, at least heading for a rest in the west. I am bypassing L.A. to go directly to a ranch Nat Wolff [Corwin's Los Angeles agent] has picked out for me. If I like it, I'll stay there three or four weeks, then make one of my infrequent public appearances in Hollywood, probably selling peanuts at the Bowl.

It may be of mild technical interest to you to know how it happens that this note is so late an answer to your charming post-midnight longhand letter, and why it is being composed in Nebraska and Wyoming. Well, two days before leaving, I discovered that my reply to said letter had got misplaced in one of my elaborate and ingenious devices for keeping papers straight. It (my letter) was in the company of a telephone bill...an invitation to address the radio workshop at Vassar (on the subject of writing for the air, no fee, and please reply soon because we are planning our Spring program in advance); and a request from the Writer's War Board to sign a statement saying that I'm interested in world collaboration after the war....

Now for a little sun on my face. See you before very long, I hope. I'll write or phone ahead of myself.

TO ROSE CORWIN / Heading for Wyoming, April 29, 1943

Dear Ma:

Here is another one of my unoriginal birthday presents, to follow up my telegram from North Platte. I know these checks never have the glamour or excitement of a well-wrapped package, but I am such a poor picker of *objets d'art* that I get absorbed by all the wrong things in a gift shop, and invariably wind up presenting books, dictionaries, encyclopedias or floor lamps.

Now the enclosed check resembles so closely the royalty statements issued from time to time that it may not have the full effect of a birthday present. But please note the gay red-and-black designs, and the fancy spacing of your name. Also the stars indicate your rank: eight times more important than the biggest star in the world.

However, it is what you do with this check that will make all the difference between an ordinary royalty dividend and a birthday gift. In other words you must...act as my agent in buying the following things for yourself: any hat that catches your eye, any coat that catches your eye, six good books, a big box of chocolates, tickets to the best show in town, a royal dinner, and a trip to New York with Pa. Anything less than this will be construed to mean that you don't think I am the best radio writer-director who ever produced a series called *26 by Corwin*....

TO CHARLES LAUGHTON AND ELSA LANCHESTER
From Santa Ynez, CA [where Corwin was staying at an inn owned and run by Actors Ronald and Benita Colman], May 3, 1943

Dear Charles and Elsa:

Postcard country, so beautiful it's corny. Maybe Van Nest Polglase [a prominent movie art director] had something to do with it. Quiet, refayned, no drunks, no cowboys, 800 feet high, two miles from the ocean, 200 yards from Ronald & Benita Colman, 50 feet from a mountain stream.

There is a stinking goddam fog today, and that is not good for my ears, which recently had abscesses in them. If the weather continues poor, I will pick up and head for the desert.

Sorry I missed Charles at the studio. If you'll be in town in three weeks, I'll be back in Hollywood and would love to see you. If you want to gimme a ring sometime the phone is Santa Blinchiki [Santa Barbara] 92268.

TO CLAIRE TREVOR / From Palm Springs, May 9, 1943

Dear Claire:

I am a fugitive from a fogbank. The Santa Ynez mountains are a joy to behold and fun to climb, but if I wanted overcast and drizzle I could have got it in the East, where there is the best to be had. I therefore fled to the desert, manuscripts and all, and now I am happy swatting flies and baking my brow in the post-season sun.

I have tried several times to phone you, but all I was able to raise at CRestview 6-7968 were two Don't Answers, one busy signal and, the last time, a man named Gumpfert or something. Have you changed your number, or was there the slip of the pen when you postscripted the number in your last letter?...A friend of yours was at the switchboard when I placed the call to Miss Trevor the other night, and he cut in with the request that I ask you how your hop-checkers game is going. Wooster by name, for I am staying at the Casitas. I gather you were the hop-checkers queen of the pampas....

Do clear up the mystery of the secret telephone number, and write me an epigram to cheer me up, will you? I get sad every time I think of Congress, and of trusting the peace to [Hamilton] Fish, [Martin] Dies,...[John E.] Rankin [conservative Congressmen] and [Henry R.] Luce [founder of *Time* Magazine].

Trevor for Senator!

TO DAVIDSON TAYLOR / From Casitas del Monte, Palm Springs, California, May 15, 1943

Dear Dave:

This is more like it. The sun here comes up with the sun, and gray is a color they speak of in textbooks. Never have I seen such brilliant, forthright, primary sunlight daylong. I have been out in it, and am now the color of a Sicilian.

You and your bride would like this country. Hot and dry, but a breeze stirring; dragonflies by day and bats by night; hummingbirds standing still among the bougainvillaea and oleanders; Corwin standing still among the cassowaries and portmanteaux; huge sand dunes off to the east, and 11,000-foot snowcaps to the west; canyons; waterfalls; owls; frogs; loons. The town is an incarnation of Hollywood, and much to be avoided; but the Little Houses of the Mountain are two miles south of Bullock's and the Chi-Chi Club, and this is an advantage not to be dismissed.

Your letter of the 3rd was forwarded to me after I left San Ysidro. I appreciate it more than I can say, and once again thank the fates, Radio Division, for guiding me to a house of which you are a main pillar. I have thought with affection of you and Mary Elizabeth since leaving New York, and always with the glow of a double martini. There is not another man in the world who is greater tonic to my work, and I only hope that in what is to come I shall in some way justify your patience, your friendship and your faith.

I am feeling better, although the mending of the frayed mind is slower than I had hoped. The zest is returning in short takes, and now and then a lyric line runs through my head. Maybe it's progress.

TO FRANK STANTON, Director of Research and Advertising, CBS
From Casitas del Monte, May 16, 1943

Dear Frank:

Your letter caught up with me here, and I thank you for it....You may be sure I will be delighted to continue the discussion we began in Chicago, and that I look forward to seeing you when I get back. I feel strongly that the whole craft of radio will ultimately be the beneficiary of your pioneering. I, for my part, would like to know and do more toward the translation of your achievements into the object-all-sublime of end product. I am sure that, having much to learn in the matter, I should be learning it from the highest authority in yourself.

TO ORSON WELLES / From Beverly Hills Hotel, Beverly Hills, California, July 10, 1943

Dear Orson:

Before another day goes by, I want to tell you what there was no time to communicate to you during or after Thursday's clambake: First, that I was genuinely dismayed over the misunderstanding which kept you from doing what I had hardly dared hope you would have the time or willingness to do: i.e., the whole show. [Welles had complained about RKO-Radio executives' cutting of his film *The Magnificent Ambersons.* Corwin no longer recalls the details of the misunderstanding.] To this I attach special regret because I would have given a gold inlay to have you do it, as indeed I indicated to your secretary.

But more important than this, I would like for you to know how deeply I appreciated your sportsmanship in staying on through what was obviously a depressing experience for you, in a bad psychological climate. As for your generosity in proposing and saying what you said about myself in your preamble to the show, I can only tell you that it moved me very much; and that I would rather have had that come from you than from any other man in American radio—or in America, for that matter. These are my late and inadequate thanks.

I know you have been in low spirits because of recent events; but at the risk of burdening you with unwanted assurances, I should like to reiterate a confidence in you I have long entertained: that your kind of genius cannot be damaged by vicissitudes such as those you have just experienced; that Art is long and RKO-Lockheed-Fox is short; that you are at the threshold, rather than at an advanced point of your potential accomplishments.

I also think you share with me the conviction that any creative man worth a grain of riboflavin bears a responsibility to these times and to the common people of the world. I sometimes suspect that matters of billing and contract, sponsors and agencies are far less significant in the long run than we like to believe.

I hope we shall work together again under happier auspices, and that I may have the opportunity to justify and reciprocate your honesty and fellowship. My best to you always.

TO CLIFTON FADIMAN, Editor and Critic [who had written the introduction to Corwin's second collection of radio plays, *More by Corwin*] / December 15, 1943

Dear Kip:

At medium-long last Henry Holt has sent me your introduction to my book, and it is a thing of beauty and (to me) a joy forever.

You are a sweetheart to have taken this thing on in your crowded schedule. Now I will not have to wait until I'm dead to see what a master critic's appraisal of my work looks like.

For your generosity in accepting Holt's invitation you have my enduring thanks; for the generousness of your comments on my work you have not only my gratitude, but my ambition to justify increasingly what you have said.

TO KATHERINE LOCKE / From Little Verde Ranch, Victorville, California, January 18, 1944

Dear Katie:

We arrived safely, thanks to a squadron of guardian angels who must have given us fighter escort all the way from Pasadena, where I left off driving, to the Rancho El Verde where Sawyer rounded the last corner on two wheels. [Lou Sawyer was Corwin's secretary; she later married and became Lou Ashworth.]

The desert is a yummy place when the sun shines, which it hasn't to date. The local Joshua forest is very pretty, and all the mesas and verdes and yuccas and arroyos and panchos and lomas and coyotes form a pattern of rare pebecco as they stretch out toward the snow-capped peaks of the Little Farfel range.

I have had very little rest since arriving, thanks to wires from New York, and such things as having to drive fourteen miles to make a phone call in reply. If you can imagine standing in a telephone booth in the Victorville Santa Fe Railroad Station and arguing with three executives in New York from a pay station while freight trains go thundering by every forty-five seconds, you have some idea of the joys of quiet convalescence on the Mojave Desert.

It is bitterly cold here at night, and I sleep with a hot water bottle at my feet. There are better ways of keeping warm. In fact, I would rank the hot water bottle as low down as number twelve.

I am going to have to come back sooner than I anticipated, and by the same token, leave for New York sooner. My series is now scheduled to begin on March 7 instead of the 14th, and I don't know where the hell I am going to get time to prepare sufficiently all the work which must be done.

I have fallen into a deep poetic mood in the past twenty-four hours—no doubt the result of a change in climate, food, and water. The first fruits of this spirit are two lines dedicated to none other than yourself:

> I like to sit and gawk
> At Katherine Locke.

TO JOHN K. HUTCHENS, Radio Editor, *The New York Times*
From Little Verde Ranch, January 21, 1944

Dear John:

Your melancholy reflections on the dilemma of writers in the issue of the sixteenth finally reached me hard by the shadow of a Joshua tree (*yucca brevifolia*) on the fringes of the Mojave, and I read it with the greatest relish. I had missed [Arch] Oboler's fine article in the fat issue of *Variety*, and so the quotes were fresh. Your summing up of the case I think profound and important and once again I feel a sense of gratitude that you, with your great honesty and courage, are among us, bringing to this medium its first consistently mature and constructive criticism. I could not agree more emphatically with your point about the tragedy of networks having permitted the initiative in the program department to be seized by advertising agencies. Indeed I was delighted to see how closely alike we think on the subject, for in a moment of idle chatter in my forthcoming collection I make the same point about agencies— except that I go on to attack them for deliberately fostering and propagating the mediocrity and bad taste which are today about us on all sides.

I don't know when you were last on the West Coast, but it is truly the hellhole of radio. The air is ashriek with jingles, jangles, and jungles of pitter, patter, and putter concerning Muntz, who advertises himself as the automotive madman (the idea being that he sells used cars so cheaply he must be crazy); Pepsi-Cola, which hits the spot; Eastern Columbia (tick-tock, tick-tock, Eastern Columbia under the clock); Dr. Beeman's Chewing Gum (the girl with the baby voice); Rinso—white (Got it? *Get* it!), etc., etc.

Add to this the stations which are given over exclusively to evangelical pursuits, those specializing in complete race results from Tia Juana, and the usual run of jerkwater stations playing commercials interpolated with Standard, Bluebird, and Decca dance records (two per fifteen-minute slug), and you have the beginnings of an idea of what radio offers in this unhappy belt. Of radio criticism in the press of course there is none, and one is lucky indeed to be able to find out where his favorite program is in the listings.

However, I have not written this letter to bury Caesar, but to praise Hutchens. As for myself, I am resting up for another flying tackle at a series of twenty-six programs, scheduled to begin the first week in March. This has been a winter of lousy health, and my being here on the desert is not out of a zest to study the local flora and fauna. I expect to be back in New York around the middle of the month and I look forward to having a drink with you again.

TO JOAN HARRISON, Film Producer / From Little Verde Ranch, January 25, 1944

Dear Joan:

The food ain't the Savoy brand and the power system broke down this morning and it's damn near freezing every morning up here and when the wind blows off the mountains it sometimes breaks up cabanas and there was .00571 inches of snow last night and I have to drain the water out of my radiator and engine block before I put the car away for the night and refill it the next day because I cannot buy any antifreeze up here, but in spite of it all I love the place, I am feeling better, I'm getting work done, I am less cross and moody, my Ping-Pong game is sharp and there is (O joy!) no telephone.

The place seems to be booked full in advance (I had to wait a week after getting back from Dallas), but even so full isn't very much, because the jernt is small, and the neighbors mind their own business quite all the time, so I really have nobody in my hair. Meanwhile I have won the first round against CBS by getting them to agree to less than thirty-nine weeks. [*Mary and the Fairy*] has been sidetracked while I concentrate on my series opener, and poor Sawyer has been working harder than she ever did at Metro, keeping ahead of my suddenly voluminous mail. Also I knocked out a script for Wolff for Silver Theater (in one day—a piece of fluff, too). Which brings me up to date.

I hope I can stick it here for another ten days, but I may have to come in sooner. The no-telephone situation has been my ally up to now, but people are catching on to the fact that mail does get delivered here somehow....

TO DOROTHY MAGUIRE, Actress / Undated, c. October, 1944

Dear Dorothy:

In memory of our bicycle ride down Wilshire Boulevard to the La Brea Tar Pits, during which you split a seam in the front of your dress, and by way of commentary on the infatuation of young Wurtzel for Maguire, and young Maguire for T.S. Eliot, I have written the following three-part "Te Deum to D.M.":

I.
Not even I
Can understand why
A girl so ostensibly shy
Should wear, in full view of the public eye,
A dress with an open fly.

II.
To the girl who idly flirts'll
Come inevitably a Wurtzel
And he, once caught up in her mesh'll

Be eaten like a blue-plate special
But she, while chuckling at his loss'll
Turn into a dry old fossil.

III.

The psyche of Maguire is fractionally split
At least eleven different ways; *id est, comme ca,* to wit:
Two of her growl with a terrible glee as they calmly swallow men
And one of her spitefully giggles aloud as she reads *The Hollow Men*
Three of her live in a world of dreams produced by Zoltan Korda
And one of her stops the best man short at the Alabama border
One of her fell for a Baltimore swell and three for a monk at
    Fordham
But all of her die a daily death of utterly horrible boredom.

That is what comes of confiding in me that you feel your personality
is split eleven ways, and that you are bored with your routine in
Hollywood. Think of those poor sabre-toothed tigers caught in those
sticky tar pits, and soar, soar.

TO ORSON WELLES / From New York City, January 15, 1945

Welles had played Nero in a Hollywood radio production
of Corwin's *The Plot to Overthrow Christmas,* which
Corwin heard in New York. Cresta Blanca, the wine-
makers, had sponsored the program. Welles was married to
the actress Rita Hayworth; their daughter, Rebecca, was an
infant. Paul Porter, Chairman of the Federal
Communication Commission, had been active in the
Democratic presidential campaign of 1944, for which
Corwin had produced an election-eve program broadcast
over four networks.

Dear Orson:

You are much too modest about the kind of hell you raised for
Cresta Blanca, and your Nero was the most robust of the entire dynasty

(1938–?). I would have written right after the broadcast except that I was down with a blueplate special throat ailment; and the only writing I did over the holidays was my signature, on checks.

I wish you would extend my greetings and congratulations to Rita; and I don't suppose I have to tell you that the Independent Committee of the Arts and Sciences would very much like to have Rebecca on the executive board. They are starting a whole new project and feel they could use new blood.

I met Paul Porter the other night, for the first time since the election, and he spoke mellowly of the good old days of the campaign; and how he wanted to get the boys together down in the White House some one of these days so we could sit around and tell stories. According to Paul, you and I were mainly responsible for carrying Illinois and Pennsylvania; and your sore throat toward the end of the campaign was the only reason Ohio went bad. Fine lad, that Porter, and I think I shall appoint him Chairman of the FCC.

Salud and love to you all,

TO BERTHA WHITE NASON, Wife of the President of Swarthmore College / January 26, 1945

> Returning from Franklin Roosevelt's fourth inauguration in January, 1945, Corwin had fulfilled a speaking engagement at Swarthmore, reading from an unfinished manuscript of *On a Note of Triumph*, which he was preparing for the time that the Allied Forces defeated Germany.

Dear Mrs. Nason:

Yours is one of those prized letters, three of which per year suffice to keep me chained in somewhat Promethean discomfort to this squawky medium. I am especially happy that you liked my sneak preview, because it was the first time I publicly exposed the script and the idea. And the audience was exactly the kind I hope to reach on the air. I am afraid the day is still far remote when one can expect the type of audience which establishes Bob Hope sovereign over the domain of American radio, to take interest in "sharp questions ask'd." I have given up hoping against Hope. The most I can pray for is that programs such as the V-E Day script will stimulate the lively and intelligent discussion—yea controversy—which followed my reading the other night. A number of students and older people sat around until my train time and asked *me* some sharp questions, and it was nippy and healthy.

I am indebted to you also for your thoughtfulness in letting me know how the recurrence of the "conqueror" motif struck you. It is curious that you should have hit upon this, for it has already given me considerable concern. Recently I translated the radio script into a version for print, and this particular device I found embarrassing in its cumulative effect. However, the suspension of "dramatic climb" which you experienced at these moments may possibly be absorbed by the musical treatment which has been planned for these very spots. The score has already been composed and Bernard Herrmann has used a very shrewd device in the music which peculiarly accents the connotation of the word "conqueror." It is a faint wash in the strings, with a suggestion of distant taps, remote and half-heard. Through such a gentle scrim of music one would be less likely to see the same terrible outlines as that given to "colossus" in the section on the rise of the Nazi.

None of this is to suggest that your point is not well taken. Like so many other things I attempt, the proof almost always lies in the rehearsal: We must wait to see how it plays. But I am mindful of what you say and all the more suspicious of flaw because your observation is first cousin to my own.

I much enjoyed meeting your people and I hope that the script to which you listened so cordially will have occasion to be broadcast sooner than we expect. When are the Germans really going to get scared?

TO FRANK FARRARA [a Massachusetts State Prison inmate who wrote Corwin many letters, though the two never met] / From New York City, March 20, 1945

Dear Frank:

For once the reports are correct. I have been pretty much at the bottom of the hill recently, thanks to a thyroiditis condition, but I'm on the right side of the books again, with the aid of rest and penicillin. In fact I'm in such good shape now that I'm undertaking a show for CBS from San Francisco on the eve of the April 25 Conference. This promises to be a big job but I'm getting such wholehearted cooperation from all quarters that it minimizes the headaches connected with an all-out operation of this kind.

I agree with you that radio is the perfect medium for accomplishing not only penal reform, but a good many other repairs that our society seems to need. Time, talent, and public-spirited networks are, I suppose, the answer, and so far we have only two of these.

I'm sorry to hear that you haven't heard any good word on your parole. Perhaps spring in the offing will lubricate the joints and stimulate the hearts of the Board.

TO THOMAS MANN / March 27, 1945

> On April 24, 1945, two weeks before his *On a Note of Triumph* celebrated Victory in Europe, Corwin produced an international program, *Word from the People*, on the eve of the organizing Conference of the United Nations in San Francisco. Short-wave pickups were made from all the continents, and several prominent people participated, including Secretary of State Edward Stettinius, Dr. Alexander Fleming, Thomas Hart Benton, Carl Sandburg, Bruno Walter, Elmo Roper, Paul Robeson, Bette Davis and Thomas Mann.

Dear Dr. Mann:

At the suggestion of Mrs. Mann, with whom I spoke on the telephone last night, I am setting down here details of the world-wide program which CBS is planning for broadcast on the eve of the San Francisco Conference.

From 7:00 to 8:00 P.W.T., on the night of April 24 we shall present a program which for the main part will come from the lips of men and women of the United Nations. To do this we will literally contact the six continents, going to home towns and battle fronts, Pacific archipel-

NORMAN CORWIN'S LETTERS / 87

agos and mountain cities, airdromes, camps and hospitals to bring word from soldiers, farmers, workers, statesmen, artists, and scientists.

The main theme of the show is that of popular hope for the success of the Conference. We will attempt to translate its meaning in terms of the hopes of people in all walks of life; and in this direction we want to present a painter, a scientist, a composer, and a writer to tell our audience what special stake each has in the realization of a world security organization. Thus an obvious approach for the painter might be to say that when war destroys a country, it destroys not only the artist's studio and his paintings, but the artist himself. He might express the hope that the paintings of this generation will not have to be protected by sandbags from the politics of the next.

We would be honored and happy if you would consent to be one of a group including Artur Rodzinski, Dean Gildersleeve (for education), George Biddle, and Dr. Alexander Fleming, discoverer of penicillin. None of these appearances will require more than one or one and a quarter minutes of speech. Each participant introduces himself, including our Secretary of State, and Mr. Forrestal, Secretary of the Navy, both of whom are going to be on the program. Your spot would begin, "This is Thomas Mann. I am a writer..." and would proceed with your interpretation of the significance to literature of the possibilities implicit in the Conference opening at San Francisco the following day.

Though the central control for the broadcast would be San Francisco, we can easily pick you up from Hollywood, and the whole business would involve no rehearsal time—merely your presence in the studio from about 6:45 PM, P.W.T.

As the work of this program involves a coordination of pickups from a score of countries, it is important that we organize our material as early as possible. If you are willing to participate, as we keenly hope you are, would you wire me collect in care of CBS and furnish me with a text of your speech at your earliest convenience.

When Franklin Roosevelt died on April 12, 1945, Corwin wrote a brief eulogy at the request of CBS. Less than one month later, the Germans surrendered. *On a Note of*

Triumph was broadcast on May 8, with Martin Gabel narrating the hour-long program. It began:

So they've given up!

They're finally done in, and the rat is dead in an alley back of the Wilhelmstrasse.

Take a bow, G.I.

Take a bow, little guy.

The superman of tomorrow lies at the feet of you common men of this afternoon.

TO WILLIAM L. SHIRER, CBS Correspondent / May 8, 1945

The teletype to Shirer in San Francisco was to position him for a live pickup during *On a Note of Triumph*, which was being broadcast from CBS Station KNX in Hollywood. The text quoted Shirer's original transmission from Compiegne.

BILL SHIRER—CBS-SF

FOLLOWING IS TEXT OF SPOT CONCERNING YOU. NARRATOR SAYS "SHIRER, THE REPORTER, STANDS AT THE EDGE OF THE CLEARING, WATCHING THE PARTY ADVANCE TO THE ARMISTICE CAR. HIS EYES ARE ON THE FACE OF THE FUEHRER, WHO DID A LITTLE DANCE FOR THE NEWSREEL CAMERAS WHEN HE LEARNED THE GOOD NEWS OF THE DEATH OF FRANCE."...

IMMEDIATELY UPON THE CUE "GOOD NEWS OF THE DEATH OF FRANCE" YOU COME IN WITH THE FOLLOWING—

"HE GLANCES SLOWLY AROUND THE CLEARING, AND NOW, AS HIS EYES MEET OURS, YOU GRASP THE DEPTH OF HIS HATRED—REVENGEFUL, TRIUMPHANT HATE. SUDDENLY, AS THOUGH HIS FACE WERE NOT GIVING QUITE COMPLETE EXPRESSION TO HIS FEELINGS, HE THROWS HIS WHOLE BODY INTO HARMONY WITH HIS MOOD. HE SWIFTLY SNAPS HIS HANDS ON HIS HIPS, ARCHES HIS

SHOULDERS, PLANTS HIS FEET WIDE APART. IT IS A MAGNIFICENT GESTURE OF BURNING CONTEMPT OF THIS PLACE."

WILL BE ON PHONE WITH YOU LATER CONCERNING EXACT TIME OF SHOW AND APPROXIMATE TIME YOUR SPOT COMES UP. MILLION THANKS AND GREETINGS APPROPRIATE TO THE DAY. BEST. CORWIN

TO JOHN MASON BROWN / June 1, 1945

Dear John Mason Brown:

I have just come away from the only local bookstore that has sense enough to stay open after 6:00 P.M. to sell the *Saturday Review*. I was so excited by your opening paragraphs that I stood in the middle of the street, exposing myself to Beverly Hills traffic, to read it through. I cannot tell you how grateful I am, not only for your generous estimate, but that a review of my work should be incorporated in so brilliant and penetrating an essay on radio drama in general. For me your review is especially happy because I have for years been a Brown fan. Your work has seemed to me a constant epitome of what reviewing should be and I am delighted and honored that *On a Note of Triumph* not only crossed your orbit but came away shining from the experience.

TO LT. COL. PAUL HORGAN, A Playwright and Chief of Army Information Branch / July 2, 1945

Corwin recalled in 1993 getting a "mealy-mouthed response" to the following letter and that he had felt the matter "was not worth pursuing." He was told the rebroadcast of *On a Note of Triumph* had been withheld because it treated the Russians as an ally and included criticism of some U.S. newspapers.

Dear Paul:

I notice in the May 27 issue of *Stars and Stripes* (page 11) the following reference at the end of a report of *On a Note of Triumph*: "It would be a swell idea if AFRS [Armed Forces Radio Service] could get recordings of the show and re-broadcast it in this theatre for the thousands of us who were not able to hear it."

I have heard disturbing reports to the effect that somebody in AFRS, Washington, had objected to *Note of Triumph* being transcribed for playback to the troops. If so, I should like to know what specifically is found objectionable. I feel I have some small right to ask, since I have on numerous occasions been happy to grant AFRS permission to use some of my shows.

Recently I heard (unofficially) that the Harburg-Arlen song "The Eagle and Me" from *Bloomer Girl* was likewise banned. I know you will share with me the conviction that this is an old-fashioned kind of censorship and one which is dangerous in view of the objectives for which this war is being fought. I shall appreciate anything you can tell me which might serve to explain this bottleneck, because Harburg and I are naturally interested in knowing whether and why "morale" material which has been and is being heard by Army and Navy personnel in the United States is out of bounds for servicemen overseas.

TO JOHN COLLIER, Writer / November 28, 1945

Dear Mr. Collier:

At this late date I have just finished reading *Presenting Moonshine* and I want to tell you how much delight it gave me. With evangelical zeal I read many of the stories to friends and I have not had such a good time since the news that Goebbels was found burned to a turn among some garbage in the Wilhelmstrasse....

TO EMIL CORWIN / From New York, December 5, 1945

Dear Em:

...At this writing the folks are here, having come down last night for the first time in about a year. I've moved out for a week to give 'em the comfort of my place, and last night I took them to the Crisis meeting on the Atom Bomb at Madison Square Garden. Dr. Harold Urey and Julian Huxley spoke, as did Col. [Evans] Carlson and Henry Wallace. Urey was great, Wallace was remarkably disappointing. The weakest speech I ever want to hear *him* make. Freddie March read my *Set Your*

Clock, and there was a tremendous ovation. Freddie then indicated for me to take a bow, but I was sitting in the audience with Ma and Pa and Kate, and the searchlight roamed the section, looking for me. There was an increasing din, and cries of "Author! Author!"—the first time those blood-curdling cries have ever been directed my way. I rose and bowed like an Arab toward Mecca. The folks, who hadn't been listening to me carefully when I told them [previously] that I was to be represented on the program, were taken by surprise and enjoyed it....

TO THOMAS HART BENTON, Painter / December 19, 1945

Dear Mr. Benton:

I only wish your congratulatory letter on "Modern Man Is Obsolete" belonged to me. You have confused me with Norman Cousins, Editor of the *Saturday Review of Literature*—a mixup which happens quite often. I am sending your letter over to Norman this day....

It was good to hear from you, even though by mistake, and I hope that the San Francisco broadcast of last April will not be the only such enterprise in which we are associated.

At the end of 1945, Corwin was awarded the second annual One World Award, established by friends of Wendell Willkie, the Republican Presidential candidate in 1940. The award included a trip around the world, patterned on a flight by Willkie in 1942. Later recipients included New York Mayor Fiorello LaGuardia; John Huston, the film director; and Albert Einstein.

TO WILLIAM S. PALEY, President, CBS / March 5, 1946

Dear Bill:

Next to the pleasure of receiving the One World Award is the receipt of your letter.

As in the past when certain citations have come from sources outside of radio, I am fully aware of the instrument by which the cited work was done and of my deep personal debt to that instrument.

CBS is vastly more than the physical and mechanical facilities of a great network of stations—it is a spiritual core and substance—the essential quality of yourself and your associates which has made working with you not only a broad and constant challenge, but a lucky privilege.

I hope the One World trip is of service to oneness of the world; certainly if it is that, it will be of service to CBS. I am especially heartened that you believe as you do, and that your faith will accompany the project.

I look forward to seeing you before I go, and to acquainting you with setup, itinerary and objectives.

TO CLIFFORD DURR, Chairman, Federal Communication Commission / From West Los Angeles, California, March 8, 1946

Dear Mr. Durr:

I met Mrs. Durr at an ICC reception [Independent Citizens Committee of the Arts, Sciences and Professions, also known as ICCASP, headed at different times by Franklin Roosevelt's son James and by Harold Ickes, Roosevelt's Secretary of the Interior—Corwin was national Vice President]...and was dismayed to learn that you have been considering resignation from the FCC. Immediately I called on all three major ICC divisions, through their radio committees, to get going on a campaign that will do two things: keep you there, and make it a commission worthy of your ideals and performance. They are pretty much the same thing, those two—except that the business of keeping you there is the first and most urgent.

On my arrival in California a few days later I learned that the California Committee for Freedom of Radio had wired [President Harry S] Truman recommending that if the FCC chooses a chairman from within the Commission, it be you; that if one is chosen from the outside, it be me. This flatters me, and is of course impractical. But I did nothing to discourage the illusion that I might be available for the job (or equipped to do it, which is even less likely) in the outside chance that I might be nominated. Then, by God, I would have the great pleasure of telling them that they are foolish to have thought of anyone but you, and I could make a loud noise of deferring to you. So I am prepared if anything should come of it.

It may be some days before the ICC can swing into action—especially as it is new and creaky on matters like this—but in the meantime, please accept my urgent and earnest plea to stick with it. Don't quit yet. Maybe we can arouse enough citizens to make it worth your while....

TO KATHERINE LOCKE / From West Los Angeles, California, March 8, 1946

Darling:

I have spent a good deal of time at Emil's, at the Lewins', at CBS, I had dinner at the Ira Gershwins', at Yip's [E.Y. Harburg], with [the playwright Harry] Kurnitz, with Dorothy Parker, etc. I went to the Academy Award presentations to see how they do those things, and found they do them fairly dull. I played football in the park with Em and his two sons. I met Oscar Levant and found him a mildly unpleasant type. [Corwin and the pianist Oscar Levant subsequently became friends.] I had dinner with Jack Goodman, who had on his arm a very drunk little girl. I had dinner with [Broadway musical composer] Arthur and Kay Schwartz and Carly Wharton.

With your usual prophetic accuracy...you anticipated Eddie's [Edelaine Harburg] curiosity about the state of our relationship. Amiably I did like you told me, which was to give her no satisfaction whatever, and I did little entrechats and pirouettes which I learned from my distinguished career as a debater in high school, and as an argufier in post-graduate tiffs with thee, little poopshen.

There is some kind of a movement under way here to throw a testimonial dinner for me on the 27th, but nothing definite yet. The idea is to recruit members for ICC and other worthy organizations. But meantime I have reserved space on the Constellation for the 29th. This is the ship which makes it in ten hours when the weather is right....

As for you, you beautiful two-legged and blue-eyed creature who laughs at your own jokes, I hug you and kiss you with a sound roughly approximating smack, smack.

TO BILL COSTELLO, CBS Correspondent in China and Japan
From New York, June 14, 1946

Dear Bill:

No doubt you have received word from Ted Church about the trip
Lee Bland and I are making. The setup is roughly as follows:

I have received the One World Flight Award, established by the
Wendell Willkie Foundation. It provides for a flight around the world to
dramatize Willkie's concept of One World, as expressed in his book. It is
designed as a mission of cultural exchange, toward advancing good will
and understanding among peoples in general and artists in particular.

This is necessarily vague language, but translated into practical terms
it means meeting high government officers, major party leaders, representatives of labor and industry, and key people of radio, films and theater. Obviously in the limited time of our stay, we will not be able to
cover much ground unless advance arrangements can be made.

Bland, Production Supervisor at CBS in New York, is coming with
me as technical associate, bringing with him a wire recorder to take
down whatever interviews or messages may be of particular interest to
an American audience. In addition, we want to get atmospheric sounds,
music, etc., indigenous to the places visited.

The auspices of the trip are fairly high, and in a number of countries
arrangements have already been made for us to meet government
people, as well as a few kings, queens and jacks. Also I'll want to record
workers, farmers, students, and people in the street. From the enclosed
itinerary you will see that we are burning a lot of space in a short time.

We look forward with the keenest pleasure to meeting you, and will
advise you of details of our arrival as soon as we know them.

Corwin sent similar letters to other CBS correspondents
on his route. Traveling on Pan-American World Airways,
Corwin left for London on June 20, 1946 and arrived in
Honolulu on October 8th for the final leg of the trip to
Los Angeles. His itinerary over the four-month tour
included Paris, Copenhagen, Oslo, Stockholm, Warsaw,
Moscow, Prague, Rome, Cairo, Delhi, Calcutta,

Chungking, Nanking, Peiping, Shanghai, Tokyo, Manila, Sydney and Auckland.

TO KATHERINE LOCKE / From Moscow, July 19, 1946

Dear Katya,

...I am afraid the frequency and extent of communication from me is going to disappoint all hands, including your own, because there are complexities arising in each country, which sometimes make it awkward. For example, here in Moscow, my host Voks [acronym for Soviet Foreign Cultural Relations Society] insists on paying for everything. Even cables. And as my room, board, transportation and other expenses add up to enough to strain anyone's hospitality, I don't feel it right to send personal cables at their further expense....

I received a letter from Pa today, dated July 1. That means it takes nearly three weeks, even via airmail. Postal performance as well as cable stuff is still suffering from the effects of the war, and it is a wonder to me that things get through as well as they do. At home we are accustomed to having things done so efficiently that we lose sight of the problems affecting this war-devastated part of the world.

Telephoning is another thing. In London my calls to you and the folks were put through in no time. In Paris it was hours slower. Some of these countries have only special days, or hours, in which foreign calls can go through. At other times the phone exchanges are ready but the atmosphere isn't. At still other times they say they'll deliver a call at such an hour, and you wait around until it's time to go out and eat, and while you're gone the call comes through, then they cancel out when you don't answer. It was this kind of routine that had me working two full days on my call from as sophisticated a city as Stockholm....

On our best days—that is, the days in which we accomplish the most work—we come home tired. Not washed out and beaten, as after a hard broadcast, but good and tired, healthy type. In these instances the ritual is to hit the hay so that we will be fresh for the next day.

Just to give you an idea of the directions from which our activities are shaped, I was interrupted in the typing of this letter by a phone call from Mrs. Bedell Smith, wife of the U.S. Ambassador to the USSR. She invites us to come over to supper Sunday night, and to see an American movie afterward. That means canceling a previous engagement. Tonight we are dined by Voks. Last night I had the rare treat of sitting in one of those literary evenings wherein critics, editors, writers analyze and criticize a work. The only time it was ever done with a foreigner before was in the case of John Hersey and his *Bell for Adano*. It was done last night with me and *Note of Triumph*. There was stimulating give and take, with many brisk but friendly points scored by both sides. Mikhoels [a master puppeteer and Jewish, who was later murdered by the OGPU, the Russian secret police] was there, also Karaganov and Schneerson [a Soviet musicologist] and Sohklovsky.

Last week we got down on the recorder interviews with Prokofiev, Eisenstein, Kapitza [a leading Soviet physicist]. May yet see Shostakovitch. Unlikely we'll get to see Stalin or Molotov. We did get inside the Kremlin, however, to see the Palace of the Soviets and a museum of the czars in which the only thing that wasn't gold, silver or platinum, was the visiting fireman from Kansas.

I've also given an interview, made a broadcast, seen a collective farm, visited the Park of Culture & Rest, a department store, and the subway.

To Prague we go on Monday, thence Rome. By the time you get this, you'll have had later wireless word from me, so for the present, I bid you loving adieu, and bid you be sensible and not stay up late nights, and bid you hugs and kisses.

TO ROSE AND SAMUEL CORWIN, EMIL AND HIS WIFE FREDA AND SONS TOM AND BILL, ALFRED AND HIS WIFE SARITA, BEULAH AND HER HUSBAND IRVING BELKOWITZ AND SON MICHAEL AND DAUGHTER CYMA
From New Delhi, India, August 17, 1946

Dear Ma, Pa, Al, Em, Booie, Katie, Irving, Cyma, Tommy, Billy, Sarita, Freda, Michael:

For the first time this really feels like a world trip. I had been to Europe before, and had even touched on the continent of Africa, on my way home from England in 1942. But this is the first time I've put the soles of my feet on the earth of Asia, and in the process of getting from Egypt to India, I really got a sense of the vastness of the globe, and of the immensity of the desolation of huge areas of it....

New Delhi has the appearance of a trim American university town—broad streets, vast, sober-looking buildings of the government type, trees and vegetation everywhere. The Indians are altogether a fine-looking people, and their women know how to wear a long, flowing dress. One cannot, in three days, arrive at any kind of estimate of the political, social and economic complexities of this country, and here more than any other place I have visited so far, I have felt the terrible superficiality of this trip. One would require five years to understand and know India—and who but an Indian has this time to give it?

I had an interview with the Viceroy the other day—Viscount R.A. Wavell, CKG, ABC, BFM, KNX, ICCASP, UOPWA. He is the general who pushed [German Field Marshal Erwin] Rommell from Egypt to Bengasi at one point in the war, before Rommell pushed the British right back again. The poor gentleman has only one eye, and he seemed to be shy and self-conscious about it. He gabbed for about forty minutes—not for recording, as that was against his policy—and roamed over a great many subjects including, of all things, poetry. He's an anthologist by avocation, and fancies he knows a lot about verse....His favorites are [Rudyard] Kipling and [John] Masefield, so you have a picture of the man who is ruling India today in behalf of the so-called Caretaker government.

Last night Lee and I were dinner guests of the U.S. Commissioner, one George Merrill, a State Department careerist who previously served in China and other eastern posts. He lives in the fabled splendor of the east, which has been somewhat well advertised by film and story, and not since the dinner I had at Samuel Goldwyn's, the Viceroy of Beverly Hills, have I seen such fixings. It is always comforting to know that our representatives in poor countries like India are living so close to the people, and that they have a mere fifteen servants—which takes up the slack in unemployment, doesn't it—even though it may cost you and me, as taxpayers, a little more....

TO ALFRED CORWIN / From Shanghai, China, August 26, 1946

Dear Al:

So far I have had not a word from you, and I am sure that there must be six letters in your fine Emersonian hand drifting around in space like asteroids. A few minutes ago, I got a letter from Kate which had been sent to me in Moscow, returned to Washington, forwarded to New York, and remailed to me here in Shanghai....

Being in China is completely unreal to me, as have been so many other experiences and sensations on this trip. Somehow, after Egypt, Iraq and India, this seems very close to home. The restaurants here seem not at all unlike those we dine at in Chinatown, save that the food is more varied, better, and interminable. The city is full of Americans, jeeps, and English signs. I have the feeling that home is right across the bay, which is correct if you want to count 8,000 miles of the Pacific as a bay.

Oddly enough, though I have come 16,000 miles, I am not yet halfway round my scheduled trip from point of distance. The southward diversion to Manila and Australia will burn up many thousands of miles, although at a much faster clip than has been the case heretofore.

China marks the resumption of the grand reception business which left off in Rome. I dodged parties and receptions in Egypt, wanting to rest up for this part of the journey [Corwin was the guest of George Polk, the American correspondent who was later murdered in Greece]. But here I am being ushered and bowed at. The mayors of both Nanking and Shanghai want to throw me dinners, and no less than three tea parties were planned for me in the capital—to which I go tomorrow. I have asked that these be reduced or eliminated, as such affairs simply bore the ass off me, and I get no work done. There's also the likelihood that we shall be hopping a troop-carrier plane to Peking as on-the-cuff passenger-guests of the U.S. Army.

Of flying with the Army, I must confide in you here that I—astigmatic and occasionally cross-eyed, whose driving on the ground you do not implicitly trust—personally and solely PILOTED A C-45 PLANE BETWEEN THE RED SEA AND THE NILE. One afternoon we went up with a fine guy, an Army Colonel, in his cabin-plane, a twin-engined Beechcraft accommodating six passengers. The flight was solely for my benefit, to give us a look-see at the Nile valley, the desert, the Suez Canal, the Bitter Lakes, Suez itself, and the Red Sea. I sat for a while next to the Colonel, and suddenly he released the controls and said to me, "Fly it." It was easy. There was considerable groaning from Bland and our friend George Polk behind me—the passengers—as I flipped her over on her side and went into a beautiful, stately reversible loop, but I had control of her every second, and she purred in my hands. I flew until, out of the hot Egyptian desert as we headed back from the Red Sea westward (see your map) toward the country south of Helwan, we made out the Nile, lying like a thread of gold across the distant flatness. We turned north, followed the river up past Memphis, flew low and circled round the Pyramids, then cut across the plantations and drove straight through Cairo to the big airport at Payne Field.

Flight from Cairo to Karachi, India, was remarkable for the desolation of the landscape. From what I saw of Iraq and Iran, you can have your oil fields. Christ, what unmitigatedly wretched country—really geographical puke. Morbidly flat, sandy or marshy—the Euphrates and Tigris coiling hugely, with a gray-green scummy, muddy color....Probably four degrees below boiling, in that sun. On the Persian Gulf coast of Iran there was mean, forbidding mountain country—also that little tip of Saudi Arabia called Trucial Oman (see your map again) which we traversed. You can practically trace our path by drawing a very straight line from Basra, in Iraq, to Karachi in the northwestern corner of the Indian coast....

I hope to be in a position to cable you, Al, on your birthday. If not, I extend to you now as down payment on September 16th, a hale and cheery greeting and my fondest wishes for many happy returns of the day. By this time next year, I hope and trust you will be the father of another Corwin—and may he (she) be a better man (human being) than her uncle (the younger).

TO KATHERINE LOCKE / From Shanghai, August 26, 1946

Darling Katya:

What a banquet! Two letters from you in two days! The first, which you had sent directly to Shanghai, arrived only a day before the second, which had gone to Moscow and bounced back like a radar wave, and had then been re-addressed, with embroidered comments on its envelope, in your own sweet hand.

I think you reached the high-water mark of tantalization with your comment: "...we sat up talking about the radio convention to be, also the stench that has been raised by the Research Institute of which Eli Cantor is a member. He is now on my stink list—heading it. I shall keep the details for a rainy night...."

Lordy, Lordy. Never give out with such curiosity-tickling gossip unless you follow up immediately with details. Now how am I ever going to rest between here and New Caledonia, if I am wondering what the "radio convention to be" can possibly be. And the Research Institute and Eli Cantor and your stink list. Amid the throbbing of motors, the waving papayas, the whispering breezes among the pale fronds under the Southern Cross, the drip-drip of my sweat on the pavement, the high hum of the mosquito; amid the grackle-grackle of the smurge and the whimper of the frobish, and to the strains of the muted grunk, I shall wonder and wonder about the Research Institute and Eli Cantor. Never mind a rainy night in the Catskills. What about a dry hot night in Shanghai?

Interesting you mention Colter [Rule, a medical doctor who had a lame leg] in the same letter. I was thinking of him just the other day. Of how tremendous a companion he would have been....But the trip would have been awfully rugged for him unless I am too greatly underrating his ability to overcome his physical handicap. We have had to LUG heavy equipment—recorder, batteries, coils, mikes, cables, up six flights of stairs on a sizzling afternoon in Rome; have had to go thirty-six hours without sleep on a bucket-seat plane, flying over mountains, alternating between sweating and freezing; have taken chances with food; have worked hard enough to drop onto a bed and be asleep in ten seconds—and knowing me and my insomniac tendencies you have some idea of what this means.

I did not see the parade of which you speak—the Russian Army affair. But I did see the great Sports Parade in Dynamo Stadium. Tell you the details on a rainy night.

TO JOSEPH BARNES, Foreign Editor, *New York Herald Tribune*
December 16, 1946

Dear Joe:

...Let's get together for a lunch sometime and I will tell you of my interview with God (nee General [Douglas A.] MacArthur) and of his opinion of *you*. You'll never be Secretary of State in his cabinet, but I warrant you will manage to remain cheerful about life in spite of this....

Norman Corwin and Katherine Locke were married in March, 1947.

TO ROBERT HELLER, Corwin's Research Assistant at CBS and later a Network Executive / From 1851-1/2 South Beverly Glen Boulevard, Los Angeles 25, California, July 26, 1947

Dear Bob:

...The AP came back again with the offer to carry a statement from me replying to that fascist [Walter S.] Steele, but on the CBS advice you relayed, I kept my tongue. Still, I am sorry that nobody, not even [the liberal tabloid] *PM*, took up the matter of identifying Steele for what he is. He has one of the most flagrant records of fascist activity to be found in the country.

Katy is working at Fox on a picture—*The Snake Pit*—for Toler [the director Anatole Litvak]. She tells me the part is small, but she doesn't mind because Toler is such a good director and the picture (adapted by [Arthur] Laurents) is purposeful and superior.

The Thought Control Conference here was a lulu, injured somewhat by the fact that nobody expected it to be so popular and as a result hundreds of grumbling customers were turned away. It was refreshing to look out from the speakers' platform and see faces like Rudy Vallee's in the audience. I thought my own paper was among my better attempts, although alongside some of the deeply scholarly papers in the Conference, it must have seemed journalese, overbrisk and punchy....

In October, 1947, Corwin was among the Hollywood organizers of the Committee for the First Amendment to protest the investigation into the film industry by Representative J. Parnell Thomas (R-Ohio), Chairman of the House Committee on Un-American Activities. That same month, Corwin spoke at a rally held in the Shrine Auditorium in Los Angeles and supported by John Huston, Gregory Peck, Marsha Hunt, William Wyler and George Stevens, among others. Corwin also produced the West Coast segment of an American Broadcasting Company radio special, *Hollywood Fights Back*, with Judy Garland, Humphrey Bogart, Danny Kaye, Burt Lancaster, Frank Sinatra, Ava Gardner and two dozen other Hollywood figures. Well before the Committee was organized Corwin spoke forthrightly against one of the "atrocities" of the House Committee.

TO WALTER DAVENPORT, Associate Editor, *Collier's Magazine*
August 5, 1947

Dear Davvy:

It was good to get your letter. I understand and respect your position on the Hollywood Red piece, but I think the project is caught on a snag by an honest difference over a key definition.

You write "In the first place, why should the Un-American Activities Committee charge them (Robinson, Welles, Cagney, deHavilland, etc.) with being anything from Reds to Pinks? What did they do to earn such dubious distinction?" This is the crux of the matter. It is my considered conviction that the Un-American Activities Committee is the single most dangerous force in America today—more so than sporadic Red or Fascist individuals or groups who at least are obliged to operate without congressional immunity. My authority for this extreme claim comes from widespread and chronic sources of documentation, and corroborative studies of the Committee's personnel, such as your own brilliant article on Rankin in *Collier's* of December 1, 1945. To be called a Red by this Committee is usually less a ground for suspicion of subversive activity than it is a tribute to the steadfastness and effectiveness of one's fight for democratic principles. To be called a Fascist by this Committee is too rare to be of any consequence. The Committee itself is so close to being Fascist that none of its actions or pronouncements can be accepted without the deepest cynicism.

I will cite only one of the atrocities of this Committee in the way of charging people with being things. This happened just two weeks ago: The Committee called upon Walter S. Steele, Chairman of the National Security Committee of the American Coalition of Patriotic, Civic and Fraternal Societies (wow!), to name Communists and fellow travelers. Mr. Steele obliged. His qualifications as an expert witness were that he had been one of fifteen Americans to endorse an official Nazi propaganda pamphlet containing a foreword by Hitler, and that several of his co-signers were later indicted for "seditious conspiracy to overthrow the government." The "Reds" he named had earned this dubious distinction by standing for things which displeased Mr. Steele.

Since practically all of the name-calling, labeling and smearing originates with this Committee (a large section of the press being only too glad to carry the ball once it has been slipped to them by J. Parnell Thomas), it is easy to see why this Committee enjoys the abuses of its powers, and in its thirst for publicity damaging to liberals and progressives, is eager to attack wantonly anybody who doesn't admire or agree with its aims and methods.

You write, "As far as I know, none of these people accused by the Committee has attempted any court action nor done anything more definite than cry 'it ain't so.'" This is because they have no legal recourse, since testimony before the Committee is protected by congressional immunity. The press cannot be sued for merely *reporting* the minutes of the Committee or the statements of its firebrands. Occasionally, when such smear charges have originated outside the Committee, action has been taken. One such instance is Fiorello LaGuardia's suit for $100,000 damages against the National Home and Property Owners' Foundation, which called him a Communist because he opposed the elimination of rent controls. A thousand people in Hollywood just three weeks ago attended a five-day conference to investigate ways and means of doing exactly what you have commented upon—something more definite than crying "it ain't so."

I agree that this piece, or any piece appearing in *Collier's*, should be "objective" and impartial. But usually, it's just a question of which side you're impartial on. It has to be this way. Your masterpiece on [Congressman John E.] Rankin was partial to decency and enlightenment, and prejudiced, praise be, against rank Rankinism. I cannot write an objective piece on this subject, if by objectivity is meant surrendering for one moment my conviction that the witch-hunters are mainly perfect bastards and thorough villains, and that the accused are mainly decent Americans who have contributed much that is worthwhile to the culture, edification or just plain entertainment of their fellow Americans.

You asked what I think, Davvy, and I have given you a frank answer. At this stage I think our basic definitions of the position, scope and objective of the people in question, are too much at variance to attempt the job, but I do want you to know that I greatly appreciate the spirit of your letter, and that if any fractional distillation of this idea appeals to you at any time, I would be delighted to tackle it for you. [The article that Corwin suggested was not commissioned.]

In fact, any time you have a strong hunch for a piece on subjects ranging from God through radio to double-crostics and sound effects, please don't hesitate to ask me. [Henry] LaCossitt [former editor of *Collier's*], whether foolishly or otherwise, used to ask me now and then for a celebrational piece, but I hope I am more than a psalmist. Besides, there is getting to be less and less to celebrate.

TO ELIZABETH KINGSLEY, the creator of Double Crostic puzzles for the *Saturday Review*, who had included several of Corwin's texts / August 30, 1947

Dear Mrs. Kingsley:

Fan letters such as this are surely no longer rare in your mail, and I suspect they merely serve to confirm that which you already know: that you have numberless enthusiastic admirers, and that you are very hard on sleep.

What you may not know is that certain of your fans exchange Double-Crostics almost as frequently as they exchange pleasantries. For example, Ira Gershwin sent me one the other day, on no special occasion, and I responded by composing one for him. The specimens are enclosed, should you ever want a busman's holiday. Also the solutions.

I was, of course, delighted to find myself a component of Puzzle No. 41 in Book No. 20. When my wife called out the definition, I immediately responded with "Welles," but we realized that Welles was younger than the 1910 birth date indicated, so by elimination we arrived at me.

Please accept the homage of this household, and our thanks for many a puzzled hour.

TO WILLIAM F. FINESHRIBER, JR., Vice President, CBS
November 11, 1947

Dear Bill:

...It was a delight to get your letter, and to learn that all has been well with you and the family since we last had food poisoning together at the Swiss Inn. Your summer, which you report as being of "a strange sort," could not have been much stranger than ours. We have been living in a modified bandbox through the largess of my lawyer, Arnold Grant. We have made several attempts to move out and rent a house or an apartment for the better part of the indefinite year ahead...[but] when we found ourselves up against rentals ranging from a minimum of $250 a month to $650 we decided that, what the hell, come what may, we would buy us a house. So we did.

We are going to fix it up so that we can have a permanent site here, and at the same time keep our apartments in New York, subleasing one or the other as our movements demand. This is the only way such commuting as we shall probably do between New York and Hollywood in the next few years, can be relieved of one of its worst horrors—having no place to go on arrival and having to settle for some dreary hole at exorbitant rents....

Our spirits have been weighted down by the way things have been going in the world. There seems to be a new atrocity every day. The latest item in this direction, the report that thirty-three of thirty-five people cashiered from our State Department since the recent purge turn out to be Jews. If this is correct it suggests something too close to official anti-Semitism to be merely coincidental. And if the Rankins and [newspaper columnist Westbrook] Peglers have finally convinced the government that Communism and Judaism are synonymous, I can just see the expanded fields of exposition awaiting Messrs. [Parnell] Thomas and [Robert] Stripling [of the House Un-American Activities Committee].

We went to Banff in August, and had a granff time. I have never seen mountain country which shaped itself more obligingly to the convenience of the tourist or the Canadian Pacific Railway. There is a valley northwest of Banff which is laid out like a bowling alley between majestic (where have I heard that word before?) mountain peaks; the Bow River, very green and swift, roars down this valley. Kate and I followed the river to its source in the Bow Glacier above Bow River, and there, by Jesus, you actually see the river being born from the underside of an enormous all year round bona fide glacier. When we were not looking at scenery, I was lecturing at the School of Fine Arts, and it brought out all the nascent ham in me. I love it. I am an unqualified exhibitionist and I say things with such a ring of authority that few care to deny or challenge. The President of the University of Alberta and his wife sat in my class, and it was a tug of war as to who could charm the other most. Kate says I won, but then she is my loving wife.

But I started to tell you about my summer. I have taken up baseball on Sundays. There is a motley gang of actors, writers, directors, clothing manufacturers, optometrists, and petty bourgeoisie who gather every Sunday morning at Griffith Park and play softball according to the Queensbury rules. We even have a professional umpire, to whose fee each player contributes. We will not here discuss my batting average, although I can say that no better fielding has been done around first base than that which I have the pleasure to report as my own.....

TO DAVIDSON AND MARY ELIZABETH TAYLOR
November 12, 1947

Dear Dave and Mary Elizabeth:

I well remember Ponte Vedra [Florida]. I was there during the war, when the entire coast was blacked out at night due to submarines just over the horizon. Half the time the ocean was not fit to swim in, because of the oil from sunken ships. I recall about Ponte Vedra a soporific quality in the air, and sulphur in the drinking water, and a daily shower which blew up from the Bahamas punctually at three p.m. I was curious about the creek back of the club but was too lazy to explore it. I loved the place.

Kate and I both felt an admiring envy for your good sense in breaking clean from your environment to make this trip. In fact, my woman seized upon a sentence in your letter, referring to you both as a kind of rallying cry to sanity and good living. The sentence was, "We have got to know each other rather better than we have known each other since Alison was born." Kate has long maintained, with justice, that we two are too much with others; that the semi-public character of my life makes it impossible to pull back into that inner cork-lined sanctum where the sound, the fury, the obligations, the dull thudding of events, the hawking critics and salesmen, and the speeches of Senator [Robert A.] Taft merge into a faint buzz, like the noise of a second-rate fruit fly angrily charging a window pane two rooms away....

We have traveled little except in time and fortune since last I wrote you. The big adventure was buying a house on a hillside overlooking Burbank and the San Gabriel Mountains to the north. This salient into real estate represents no break with New York, which we love first and best, but merely our defiance of the inflated economy by which a man cannot live decently in this town for less than $400 a month.

Our house has a lot of grace and is as cheerful as a Mozart serenade. It sits in the middle of an acre of rolling ground and there are seven oak trees on the property, and a preserve behind us in which deer have been known to roam. Yet we are exactly eleven minutes from KNX, Paramount, Columbia and RKO; four minutes from Universal; eight minutes from Warners.

We are holding on to our apartments in New York for we don't intend to spend more time here than my film commitments require, and we will simply sublease the house when we move east....

You are quite right in assuming that my decision to take a near-sabbatical from radio next year is not predicated on any theory of change in CBS philosophy or administration. Your letter, with its assurance that you are not abandoning the creative world for the austere provinces of fact, is especially gratifying. For to me you remain the umbilicus, pardon the expression, between art and the corporation....

The local [stage presentation of] *Galileo* was sloppy, with [Charles] Laughton giving it a kind of somnambulist treatment, and the production staggering under lethal doses of cuteness and awkwardness. You may soon see for yourselves how thoroughly Charles managed to marinate whatever good meat there is in the script, for the Experimental Theatre production of *Galileo* opens around your way in the near future. [Joseph] Losey and Laughton are in New York now, working on it. It may be that they have learned things from the Hollywood run and can tighten and revise the work so that it takes on the character of straight verse drama, which was what [Bertolt] Brecht, no fool, meant it to be. I wish them every success, for it is a noble attempt, set on a noble and tragic theme; and Laughton, for all that is derisively said about him, does at least deserve a pale green campaign ribbon for having worked so tenaciously in the interest of a dramatic poem. This, at a time when other successful Hollywood characters spend their lives and energies in the breeding and racing of horses....

Kate, who is soon to appear in the east without me, since I can't get away and she has to do some business there, joins me in sending you our love.

TO ROBERT HELLER / December 1, 1947

> On November 24, 1947, fifty film executives met at the Waldorf Astoria Hotel in New York and agreed to bar from future employment writers and other film workers who refused to cooperate with investigations "of alleged subversive or disloyal elements in Hollywood."

Dear Bob:

Hollywood is a ghost town now. The action of the producers last week is the moral equivalent of the South Chicago massacre, and the corpses are strewn about. It is the most degrading thing that has ever happened in American cultural life, and represents a cowardly surrender at a time when the enemy was fleeing the battle....

TO IRVING PENN, Photographer / From Los Angeles
December 16, 1947

Dear Irving Penn:

The photograph which you so kindly sent me last June was never forwarded and might still be in a pile of old manuscripts if my wife had not discovered it on a trip to New York last week. She was so struck by your work that she immediately phoned to tell you so, and she trusts the message was relayed to you by your secretary. Mrs. Corwin brought the photo back with her and it has hit me just as hard as it did her.

It is such a wonderful photograph that I find it hard to realize I am its subject. I have had many taken of me, under all circumstances and in a great many studios, but yours is the most remarkable of the lot.

Please accept my congratulations along with my thanks, not only for this portrait to which I bear a personal relationship but for the consistently brilliant work which you have been doing right along.

TO ROBERT PRESNELL, JR., Writer, and **MARSHA HUNT**,
Actress / From 3600 Lankershim, Hollywood 28, February 15, 1948

Dear Bob and Marsha:

....I have just returned from Victorville, where I went to escape the telephone, the smog, the estimates of contractors and the suggestions of my producer. Ah, the desert. It was clear and cold, and on the morning that it rained elsewhere in the province, it snowed there. I took long walks on the desert, which the local Indians call "Mojave," and you may imagine my surprise when, upon negotiating a knoll of cactus, I looked down and saw railroad tracks running east and west as far as the eye could see! I sank to my knees and uttered fervid thankfulness to both St. Christopher and the god of walking, and then, rising, pointed my sword at an angle perpendicular to the tracks, and named the railroad SANTA FE. I chose this name because at the time I was feeling rather fe.

I returned to the white men's settlement in time to read in the local prints that Marsha, among several other characters known to have had fiscal arrangements with the government, is to receive $4,196.72 in rebates from income tax. We rejoice for her, and I should like to get the recipe from her some time.

On a more sober tack, Roberto, I want to reassure you that your reservations on the matter of sponsorship of the meeting for the Ten are valid and understandable. I don't know whether any other actors or actresses are on the list, but at this point it does not particularly matter. What matters is the fact that you and Marsha have already done much for which every liberal is grateful; that you both understand the fight and have participated in it in the past, and will undoubtedly do so again in the future, when your conscience and the timing and the degree of gravity of the issue at stake and the value of your names, meet on better grounds than the present. I do not think it is vital that you co-sponsor that meeting. It *was* vital that you fought when the cannonading was heaviest, back at the time of the hearings, and it is vital that you stand ready again for a real emergency. I think the Defense Meeting is important, but it hardly rates as an emergency.

I know Marsha is not afraid and I know you are not afraid, and that you never have been. Indeed it is the certainty of this knowledge, along with the many other attributes which would only make you both blush to name, that so greatly endears the Presnells to the Corwins.

We salute you, and wish joy to *Joy to the World* [Broadway play in which Marsha Hunt was starring]....

TO THE NEW YORK HERALD TRIBUNE / From Hollywood, California, March 6, 1943

The newspaper ran Corwin's letter on March 14, 1948, under the headline "Definition of a Liberal," with a sub-heading, "Mr. Corwin Takes Issue With 'New Yorker' Over Comment on a Certain Editorial Viewpoint."

Exactly as though it were examining a butterfly through a lorgnette, "The New Yorker" in a recent issue inspects the liberalism of the Herald Tribune for the period between Thanksgiving, 1947 and the first moon of 1948. It describes the Tribune's editorials, to use its own phrases, as having sighed over, rassled with, speculated upon, trotted out, met boldly, gulped, hawked, spat out, been vaguely troubled by, overly romantic with, too full of the great tradition of, and not quite up to the essence of liberalism.

"The New Yorker" finds that the Tribune suffered "editorial shudders" which seemed to it "strange." Itself calm and unshuddering, it then defines, in a cheery and constructive spirit, the true liberal: "The liberal holds that he is true to the republic when he is true to himself." To this is added the caution: "It may not be as cozy an attitude as it sounds." Nor as cozy a platitude, either; for the reverse is more nearly true.

The liberal more often than not holds that he is true to himself when he is true to the republic. At least the great liberals in history have functioned this way. It is the reactionary or revolutionary who begins by being true to himself, and works outward from there until he is certain that what is best for himself is best for the republic.

Rassling with the concept of the liberal as a zestful dog, "The New Yorker" further explains the type: "He greets with enthusiasm the facts of the journey, as a dog accepts a man's invitation to take a walk. And he acts in the dog's way, too, swinging wide, racing ahead, doubling back, covering many miles of territory that the man never traverses. All in the spirit of inquiry and the zest for truth."

Let not the dog-loving liberal-lover who wrote those words accuse anybody of being overly romantic. I have known hundreds of liberals of all breeds, and have yet to meet one who greeted the facts of the journey with anything more than a groan. Most liberals have a living to make, rent to pay and dependents to worry about, and in their spare time they prefer going to movies, listening to music, entertaining, being entertained, making love, eating, dancing, curling up with a good Book Find Club selection, or just sitting in a chair and looking blank. A liberal would much rather sleep in the sun than run like a dog, swing wide, pace ahead and double back. He does not relish porcupine quills in his face, and gets no joy out of the plight of D.P.'s, the lynching of Negroes, the persecution of minorities, infringements of civil liberties, smears, the broadcasts of Fulton Lewis, miscarriages of justice, foreign putsches, domestic purges, censorship, libelous attacks, or committee investigations of his liberalism. He loathes the prospect of attending board meetings and writing stern letters to Congressmen and editors and having to make speeches and contributions. He wishes the nations would shut up and settle the peace so he wouldn't have to raise his boy to be a soldier under the universal military training project.

The spirit of inquiry and zest which is supposed to inspire the dog to collect burdocks of information out of his antic chase is more likely to be a spirit of stoicism at having some fact sheet, prepared by liberals like himself (on the basis of research initiated and paid for by other liberals) dumped on his desk with every mail. These he reads dutifully and wearily, his conscience being what it is; and before he is through reading his tail is between his legs; and not to wag again until he can forget the latest invitation to take yet another walk.

Before "The New Yorker" imputes confusion and contradictions to the liberalism of an organ which, like itself, is one of the last best hopes of liberalism in this country, let it look to its own kennels. Its editorial content between Thanksgiving and January has been spotty with thoughts sighed over, rassled with, speculated upon, met boldly, hawked and spat out. This in itself is not to be condemned, since it all has been accomplished with charm, indisputable talent, and a neurotic inconsistency that at least makes for variety. One must understand that "The New Yorker's" liberalism covers a wide range, from Boyer through Liebling, White and West, to Alsop and Wilson. "The New Yorker" liberals make up one of the best dog teams in the world and we all applaud and sic them on. Only it is not polite for any one of them to say that a friendly dog in the next yard is not quite up to the essence of liberalism when he himself, the old hound, has many of the same habits.

Stuart Symington, Secretary of Air, wrote Corwin that after a hard day's work he went home "(1) to hit the refrigerator and (2) to hit the sheets," but his wife said he could do neither until he had read the above letter. He added, "Please accept the congratulations of a person who can't express himself in print."

TO ROLAND KIBBEE, Writer, and **LUCILLE KIBBEE**, Actress
From 3600 Lankershim, Hollywood 28, April 12, 1948

Dear Kib & Lucy:

I have heard the extempore account of Lucy, and I have read the letter of Kib, and I now pronounce you members of that small, tight band of travelers who know what to look for, and who understand what they see....Not since my own great flapdoodle of 1946 have I been so stimulated by anybody's trip anywhere. Kate and I listened to Lucy with what impartial observers called rapt attention, and we both devoured the letter as though it were the only tamale left between us and starvation in the interior of Yucatan....

My worries about how you two golf-happy, plane-spoiled, Chasen-fed, loved and respected crossword and poker people were going to get along under the stress of bad roads, wrong directions, savvy trouble, noise, dirt, poverty, altitudes, currencies, native telephones, manana and unpredictable chow, have now been dissipated. The breadth of your own ample curiosity, sympathy, humanity and good will is reflected in that which you have chosen to see, and in the lights by which you have seen. It was my good friend Sam'l Johnson, whom I staked to many a hot grog at the Tavern, who said "A man must carry knowledge with him if he would bring home knowledge." The crack is inscribed high over the hurrying public on the walls of the Union Station in Washington, and it is the only decent thing left in that city....

I have been brooding all week about your report on Los Estudios Churubusco. To pass a film studio without that familiar feeling of nausea from the smell of all the dead ideas inside! To work in an atmosphere not fouled by exhalations of vagueness from timid and insecure producers! To meet with, eat with, work with artists who are whole men, not walking salami cut into slices by agents, managers, stooges, censors and informers.

What you say about Churubusco, El Indio, Alazraki and Brandt almost has me telling you to move over and leave us room to park our shaving kit and douche bag. I am almost ready to toss a contemptuous bump at a dozen people and institutions up here, and ask only for a bottle of rum and some unexposed film and a good cameraman and an

English-Spanish dictionary and the freedom of my conscience and just enough cheesecake to decorate the background of Zapata or who-have-you. Tempt us some more, amigo, tell us it's not just a first quick rapturous impression, tell us they're shooting films with better than a Brownie, tell us those guys really aren't kidding, and the whole story is not just a vision seen through a cloud of marijuana.

Kate and I were discussing the Kibbees after Lucy's whirlwind visits to us on her sick leave from La Ciudad last week. We agreed that not the least magnificent of your qualities is your vitality—not in the sense of your Wheaties and a tennis forearm, but in the sense of being spiritually alive and eager, with a capacity for newness and change, and a love for people and a passion for justice which is, after all, what distinguishes a man from an ape.

Life on this side of the Rio is just as dull as it is exciting on your side. The trials of The Ten begin in Washington today; here Wallace meetings are being picketed and attacked. [Henry A. Wallace, Vice President from 1941 through 1944, was running for President on the Progressive Party ticket.] Charlie Feldman has seen a preview of *The Iron Curtain*, and tells me it is the most exciting picture he has ever seen. "It's absolutely based on facts," he assured me solemnly. "Darryl Zanuck says so himself." Dore Schary has summoned all good Democrats to come to the aid of the Jackson Day dinner, writing in a form letter something to the effect that "no sensible man is fooled by Henry Wallace." You are hardly missing anything on the local scene, unless it is the crispy, tangy challenge of a cool game of Guggenheim. This, however, can hold until you get back....

TO MARK HANNA, Agent / April 16, 1948

Dear Mark:

A pleasure, as always, to hear from you, especially when your letters are accompanied by reinforcements in excess of $1.50.

I am floored by the MGM dividend. Not by the small pickings, but by the fact that the album sold at all. [Corwin's album was a recording of his early script, *Between Americans*. He had not been involved in its production.] It is such a slovenly botch that I naturally assumed no customer with the sense it takes to find his way to a record store would be fool enough to buy the album and bring it home. I wouldn't have it in the house. I burned my copy. Did you ever burn records in a fireplace? It's good sport. Seems there is a sort of shellac between the laminations of compressed soot, or whatever it is, that goes into the discs, and this burns with a fat, oily, carboniferous flame. Jolly. Records by Ted Collins, or featuring the voices of Fulton Lewis or H.V. Kaltenborn, seem to make the best fires....

TO JACK GOODMAN, Editor, Simon and Schuster / June 7, 1948

Dear Jack:

Last April I sent you the finished draft of *The Perilous Journey of Jones*, and I have not heard from you since.

Were you anybody but yourself, I would think this indicated a fairly pointed unfriendliness, but I cannot imagine such a possibility.

I know that if you thought the script abominable, or just measly, or merely so-so, you would not hesitate to tell me.

I also know that if you were enthusiastic about it you would wire or telephone me, or perhaps control your passion to the extent of writing a letter and sending it by airmail, a form of communication highly thought of and in wide practice.

But silence is what I would expect only if I, freshly graduated from South Dakota Agricultural College, had sent an unsolicited manuscript on animal husbandry to a man named Chombliss whom I had never met and never hope to meet, at McGraw-Hill.

I do not expect silence from the man who fell at my side, drunk, as we stormed San Juan Hill. Nor from the man who rode his sloop through the great hurricane of '39 flamming the futtocks across the top-mast crosstree, lashing himself to the halyards on the capstan for'd, and holding the port buntlines and clew garnets together with his teeth. I do not expect silence from a man who has lulled me with legs of turkey and fine talk in his own home; who has come in out of the snow as I worked late in my room overlooking the park, and talked to me of epic poems and sybaritic women and the decay of our civilization.

Goodman: In the name of those lusty days, in the name of the clear memory of [Goodman's bulldog] George, who snored through my readings, in the name of the shining big sea waters off Rowayton's rocky shores, in the name of that brave summer afternoon when together we established a fathead (Fred Schwade) on the beach of Marshall Field's estate, show me cause why, in the light of your delinquency, you should not be adjudged a prick.

The book was published as *Dog in the Sky* in 1952.

TO ROBERT HELLER / June 10, 1948

Dear Bob:

Much has happened since I got your letter, including the loss of two friends who were of the earth's salt. They were Dr. Leon Muldavin, whom I don't think you know—a magnificent progressive—and George Polk. Both were gold ingots, and their dying rests heavy on my heart.

I trust [you have seen] a copy of a letter from Polk to the Foreign Editor of *Newsweek*, a carbon of which George mailed me...some months before his murder. It is one of the truest measures of his fierce honesty and courage.

Our generation moves grandly toward middle age and worse things: [Carl] Mundt and [Richard] Nixon; Abdullah; [Ernest] Bevin; [Juan] Peron; the State Department. Rockwell [Kent] gives up his dairy and Polk his ghost. The American people will of course elect a [Robert A.] Taft or a [Harold] Stassen or a [Thomas E.] Dewey or an [Arthur] Vandenberg. And if Ike is nominated he will accept, and if he accepts he will be elected, together with his avowed non-segregationism and a foreign policy mightily lak that of [John Foster] Dulles. No wonder I have come increasingly to admire animals, as against their masters. Take my cat, for example.

The misanthropic tone is not to indicate that I sit in shadows and brood. I have adjusted philosophically to the degeneration of our times, and in fact permit myself release in pleasures I have ordinarily denied myself. Such as working for weeks at a time in the desert, which grows more enchanting with each visit; playing baseball on Sundays; weeding and watering our acre of busily growing stuff; and seeing a little of the country.

I have just finished my second screenplay in four months, and both came smoothly and ahead of schedule. I work at home, which is pleasant, and in the sun, which is faithful most of the time, and punctual always. I also find time, for the good of my soul, to chair meetings such as the local Peace Conference, and to toss off an occasional paper....

TO DAVIDSON AND MARY ELIZABETH TAYLOR
June 14, 1948

Dear Dave and Mary Elizabeth:

The spring has passed in a succession of golden days and macabre events, and it is a year since I have seen any of you. Worse, I have never seen Alison *awake*. This is silly, for after all I am the first person ever to send her an overseas cable. According to the protocol in such matters, a first-cable-sender is entitled to avuncular privileges, such as seeing the baby awake, holding her on his lap, and feeding her buttons and paper clips which ordinarily she would pick up off the floor.

In many ways the past year has been the strangest in my life. I have almost kept my vow of last June to lie fairly fallow for this long. Though I have been working like a unionized beaver, and have made more money for less labor than in any corresponding period, I have not toted nearly the load to which I am accustomed; so that compared to life in the salt mines of New York, this has been a vacation on the Riviera.

But I no sooner take recess from the inexorable deadline, and from the world of the world, than all hell breaks loose. The peace staggers; the Herrmanns break up; 4,000 feet of snow fall on your city; drought withers California; [Czech statesman Jan] Masaryk jumps out of a window; *Variety* reports there is nothing left to pioneer in radio; the Middle East seethes like bicarb in oil of vitriol; [President Harry] Truman attacks modern art as the work of lazy slops; [Truman] Capote takes over the novel. I can see now that I never should have left the city, and that it was a mistake for me to entrust the support of the great globe itself to Atlas.

Though in the past year I compose music no better than before and paint even less well, I have at least caught up on some of the reading which I have had to neglect in the past. I read all of Shaw, for one—a romp and a joy—and several novels and essays and books of science (the most fun being an old elementary textbook on physiography by Salisbury which answered a lot of questions about earth, sky and water which I had always wondered about); and Katherine Anne Porter and S.J. Perelman, etc., etc.

As for the year's writing: a novelette-fantasy for S&S [Simon and Schuster], which will not come out until the late spring of 1949; three full screenplays; two political-type papers; a letter to the *Herald-Tribune*; and a sharp note to the subscription department of *'48* asking them to either send me their magazine as contracted for, or refund my money.

Last week I was admitted to the presence of God, in the form of an interview with L.B. Mayer. He offered me *Raintree County* to adapt for the screen—Metro's most expensive current property—along with the flattering unction that I was the only man in America who could do it. I then went home and read the book—all 1,060 pages of it. And I would like to ask Mary Elizabeth, who came from Indiana with a banjo on her knee, whether the late [Ross] Lockridge, Jr., spoke the truth about Indianans. Even before I have her answer, however, I am pretty certain I will turn the offer down. Not that the book is not good and juicy and could make a fine movie, but because I am tired of working for indecisive producers, who blow hot and cold and change their whores in midstream.

TO ABEL GREEN, Editor, *Variety* / October 1, 1948

Dear Abel:

I have just returned from France myself, to find your charming Cadeau de Paris. Many thanks, and I must say that the little fowl is a most apt symbol of the city, since nowhere else in the world is a cock so free to make alliances.

I have for you a little Cadeau de Gdansk, in the form of a limerick I wrote to celebrate the passage of the One World Commission through the Baltic port of that name, on 25 August last [Corwin had been to Europe as a member of the LaGuardia Memorial Commission]:

A cautious young maiden of Gdansk
Who suffered from very hot gpansk
    Simply covered her belly
    With vaginal jelly
As she wished to leave nothing to gchansk.

TO OSCAR DYSTEL / October 1, 1948

Dear Oscar:

New York looks good on you, and you wear the new job like a Powers model. [Dystel had lately moved from Editor of *Coronet* Magazine to *Collier's*.]

Please remember that if time, tide or The Chief take you out this way, our electronically controlled latchstring is out for you. We have an excellent view, some imported liquor, and several back copies of *Coronet*, to make you happy.

My wife and I, speaking as one—with her voice, as usual, dominating—send you our very best regards.

TO BERNARD ROGERS, Composer / November 13, 1948

> *The Warrior*, Rogers' one-act opera based on a Corwin radio play, won the Alice M. Ditson Award for a new American short opera, and was staged by the Metropolitan Opera under the terms of the award.

Dear Bernard:

We were late getting back from Europe, hence the regrettable delay in writing you. It was the first holiday for Kate and me since we got married in March of '47, and the holiday ended the minute we disembarked from a fine Polish liner at Gdynia. We attended the Congress of Intellectuals for Peace at Wroclaw, though how I pass as an intellectual is of course open to scrutiny. And we rushed around a circuit that included Warsaw, Prague, Rome and Paris. All too fast, too exciting, depressing, tiring and transitory....

It begins to look less and less as though I will be back at CBS with anything like the old assortment of fast balls, slow balls and curves. The company has gone the way of all flesh peddlers, and is now slightly more "commercial" than NBC. I am not yet ready to surrender the artistic freedom I hitherto enjoyed, for a mess of subsidiary rights "participation" which they are generously offering. Oh, a long and a disgusting story, and I won't burden you with it here....

TO PAUL DENIS, Columnist, *New York Post*
November 16, 1948

Dear Paul:

They take their time about forwarding mail from New York, as I have just received your wonderful column on the [Arch] Oboler interview. I can only bless you for the truth and courage of the piece, which incidentally confirmed something I had just written...to the effect that the end result of radio ratings, through the use made of them, is to set rigid standards of conformity, to justify and perpetuate sameness and mediocrity, to discourage the daring and audacity that vitalize the creative worker, and to lower, ultimately, the level of our arts....

TO FLEET ADMIRAL CHESTER W. NIMITZ / July 13, 1949

Admiral Nimitz had appeared in Corwin's production of *Citizen of the World*, presented by the recently organized CBS Documentary Unit, on July 7, 1949. On the 12th the Admiral wrote Corwin that he and Mrs. Nimitz had enjoyed the "impressive" broadcast, and that he thought it "did a good job for the UN and for international thinking generally."

Dear Admiral Nimitz:

I am deeply indebted to you, both for your stirring contribution to the broadcast, and for your generous letter. The entire Columbia Broadcasting System joins me in this sentiment.

I can say without the slightest exaggeration that your presence on this broadcast and the profound significance of your words to the concept of peace through international cooperation, were together the single most important element of the program. What you did, among other things, was to give fighter escort to the basic philosophy of world citizenship, a credo which has had hard sledding in the long uphill struggle for a free world.

My deepest personal thanks for your patient cooperation and for your thoughtfulness in letting me know that you and Mrs. Nimitz felt the way you did about the broadcast.

TO ROCKWELL KENT, Painter, and **SALLY KENT**
From 104 East 56th Street, August 2, 1949

> The Kents lived at Ausable Forks in the Lake Placid area of upstate New York.

Dear Rockwell and Sally:

That is a wonderful invitation, and we already feel better about Summer and Life, just thinking about it. But I am wet-nursing a whole flock of big UN projects for September-October, and I am dizzy not only with the heat but the running-around. I commute oftener than before to Lake Success, and right at the moment I am trying to convince [Conductor] Serge Koussevitzky that even if the acoustics of the Assembly Hall of the U.N. are lousy, he should still give the concert I persuaded him to conduct for the greater glory of mankind.

These, and sundry other fussings about, make it seem unlikely that we could get up before late in the month. At that time I will be hot on the last pages of my upcoming hour-long show (September 11) and it may be that I will need to flee to an incommunicado corner of the world. Your very generous offer of seclusion in an upstairs room, or maybe in the deep freeze, may be just what I need. May I dream about the last week in August?...

TO DR. HARLOW SHAPLEY, Astronomer, Director of Harvard Observatory / October 4, 1949

Dear Harlow:

Thanks for your letter of 26th September. I am sending, under separate cover, a copy of the as-broadcast script of *Could Be.* I am sorry that you must see it in this form rather than hear it because this, like so many other of my pieces, is meant to be heard, not seen. However, you have a famous imagination, and I am sure you will be able to fill in some of the pace, sound, music and atmospherics which give the program a certain power and impact. I wish you would let me know next time you are in New York and I will arrange for you to hear a playback. The mail response was quite heartening and apparently the program, for all its UNRRA [United Nations Relief and Rehabilitation Agency] pie-in-the-sky, had a constructively emotional effect on its audience.

TO KATHERINE CORWIN / From New York, May 21, 1950

Darling:

It was good to talk to you and to hear you sounding so chipper, even though not as chipper as if I were with you. My chipperiness was more or less used up the first week, and now I am back calling on reserve, even as you....

Audrey Wood [play agent] took me to dinner and then to see *The Enchanted*—the Giraudoux play which George Kaufman directed, starring (guess who) his wife Miss McGrath. A charming, witty and pointless play without structure but full of fine lines. Kaufman directed it as though it were a Princeton Dramatic Club farce, and only [Brooks] Atkinson was sharp enough to see through his shallowness. The other critics, no doubt influenced by their mistake in panning Giraudoux's *Madwoman*, were most respectful to everything about it.

Have been to Jack Goodman's twice. He returns to anagrams each time like a ghost to the scene of a murder, and is murdered all over again. Last night he had help from two experts, in addition to which I was off form, and I very nearly got beaten before a gallery of watchers. However, at the last moment I changed his RAVAGING to REAGGRAVATING (under a rule by which all re- forms could be used on verbs) and changed ZIRCON to ECONOMIZER, and pulled out ahead. The banner still flies for you, my dove, in the form of my undershirt, which is draped tastefully on the back of the sunlamp. Neat, that's me. Lovely, that's you. And I am king of the anagrammers below 59th Street. Thou art my queen. And Stinky is the cat that can look at us both.

Had another dinner at Mabel's, and there were charades. Norman Plechette [a gynecologist] is a fine guy, I like him more every time I see him, and his wife Marge is a fine broth of a woman.

Wrote some limericks for the general edification of the assembled:

The pederasts have a colleague in
A lover of flowers named Egan
    When going around
    The gardens, he found
The asses of astors intriguin'.

A fibrous young man named Bill Harwood
Was born in the forest of Sherwood;
    His butt was of walnut,
    His scrotum was *all* nut
And his phallus was made out of firwood.

An editor's wife went to get
The counsel of Dr. Plechette
    He searched for an heir
    But found nothing there
And wrote on her abdomen "Stet."

People have told me I am good at these things, and even suggested that I write for a living. That may be true, but in the present instance I write for a-lovin', and you is my ever-bloomin' iceplant.

TO ANNE VOSKOVEC, whose husband the Czech actor George Voskovec, was detained at Ellis Island. / June 10, 1950

Dear Anne:

Your letter, as well as a letter written by George on Ellis Island, was forwarded to me here in California, hence there has been a delay in my reply. I dispatched a note this morning to Victor Jacobs asking whether there is anything I can do from this end, and assuring him that if George is a security risk, I will eat my hat, coat and coat-tree at one sitting.

About royalties on *Curley*—if the theater's very life is at stake, I not only want you to stop thinking about percentages coming to me, but I want you to take whatever royalties may have accrued, or which may accrue in future, and plow them into the operational budget of the theater. [Corwin's radio play *My Client Curley* had been adapted for the French stage, and Corwin intended to join the French Authors Society to protect his interest in French productions of his work.]

As for the French Society des Auteurs, I am glad to sign the enclosed papers, but I'll be goddamned if I will send them either the original or a copy of my birth certificate. (A *copy* is not legal in this country—why should it be in France?) What a nerve these bastards have! I wonder whether they ask Bernard Shaw or Arthur Miller or Lillian Hellman for their birth certificates. In my case if they are curious, tell them I have no birth certificate because I was not born—I am the reincarnation of a sixteenth-century horse thief of New South Wales, and before that, in an earlier life, I was a cassowary.

Please do not feel too upset and outraged over the Ellis Island matter. Strange things are happening, and the times get weirder and weirder. If you want fully to illuminate the picture, get hold of a book at Paris Brentano, entitled *The Devil in Massachusetts*. It is a wonderfully documented and recounted story of the Salem witch trials in the 1690's, and it has a deadly parallel in contemporary life, with the exception that the Salem tragedy was over and done with in a single year, and there was exoneration for the surviving witches. You must read it to understand all these things.

Kate sends her love, and we both wish you all good things, and want to know how best we can help.

TO DORE SCHARY, Head of Production, MGM / June 28, 1950

Dear Dore:

The self-announced Messiah of Smyrna whose name I promised you was Sabbatai Zevi (sometimes spelled Sebi), son of a poulterer. At twenty-four, having been up to then an obscure no-talent with less than average ability, he declared he was the Redeemer. The will-to-believe of an abjectly poor and depressed community did the rest for him. Women, impressed by his gleaming dark eyes and Pinza voice, carried on like bobby-soxers; men analyzed his cabalistic double-talk as though he were T.S. Eliot. Before long the pious elders crowned him King of the Jews.

Apparently there was a ceremony at his coronation in which he was "married" to the Torah. He affected a white mantle after this, and carried a sacred silver fan. Couriers came and went, his fame spread throughout the then world (1666), and Zebi began signing decrees as "I, The Lord, Your God, Sabbatai Zebi."

The Grand Vizier got worried about Z's rising popularity, arrested him, and gave him his choice between a martyr's death, and conversion to Mohammedanism along with the job of janitor in the Seraglio. This showed more humor on the part of the Vizier than was customary, since zealots of the time who got in the hair of the authorities were usually skinned alive, or boiled in a mixture of Dad's Old Fashioned Root Beer and sulphuric acid.) In any case, Zevi quickly chose Islam and the janitorship.

This, however, did not discourage his followers. They figured that there was a parable and precedent in the fact that Moses had lived for a time at Pharaoh's court and worn Egyptian clothes, hence Zevi's backsliding was taken as proof of his divine mission.

As I said, I am ashamed of the whole episode and intend to see that it does not happen again.

I, The Sun God, Ra,

N.C.

TO SECRETARY, NATIONAL COUNCIL OF AMERICAN-SOVIET FRIENDSHIP, INC. / July 1, 1950

Dear Sir:

When I agreed to be a sponsor of the National Council, I was motivated by the belief that American-Soviet friendship was the key to world peace and progress. I am still of that belief. But I have been disturbed by a long series of your releases, in which it seems to me that only unilateral criticism has been made.

In the past I believe you honestly and effectively served the cause of good will and understanding between the countries, but as tensions increased and American-Soviet friendship deteriorated, it seemed to me that although you were often critical of American policy, you have not leveled any similar criticism of Soviet policy, even when the latter took expression transcending the merits of any given issue. I refer, for example, to the act of decorating the fliers who, rightly or wrongly, shot down the American plane over the Baltic.

The hostility of such an act is what I am talking about, for I feel that such an exquisite gesture of vindictiveness should, among other aspects of the incident, have been noticed by and commented upon by your organization. It was not.

Now comes the shocking affair in Korea. Personally, I have a single rule of judgment in these matters. Whoever militarily *invades* is an aggressor, is a felon, is culpable. The invasion was clearly of South, not North Korea. The capital that was stormed and captured was Seoul, not Pyongyang. Had the situation been exactly reversed, I would condemn the South for invading the North.

I had hoped the Soviet position would be unhesitatingly in support of the UN's cease-fire order; that the USSR would bring to bear its influence and prestige, if nothing more, to stop in its tracks a shooting war that might well be explosive in a world made tinder-dry by fear, suspicion and hate.

The Soviet statement is to me powerfully disappointing. Whether the U.S. was or is, as it charges, guilty of prior or current aggression, seems to me beside the point. What about the *fighting*? I see no condemnation of that, no suggestion about peaceful settlement, no constructive recommendations. This then is an aspect of Soviet policy whose rightness I think a Council dedicated to rapprochement might well consider and challenge as it has done innumerable American statements and policies.

Though I have not been a contributing member, and have never attended a meeting of the Council's business, I continued my support as a sponsor because I believed in your sincerity, and in the wisdom of a long-range goal of amity and understanding between the US and the USSR—a goal upon which the safety of civilization itself depends. I believed strongly enough in this goal to continue sponsorship long after you were attacked by the usual witch-hunters as a subversive organization, and even after I began to be disturbed by what I considered your tendency toward one-sidedness and non-mutuality.

I do not think you are serving the cause of friendship, hence of peace, in this way. In fact I think you are injuring the cause by a parochialism which I believe to be as misguided as it is no doubt well-intentioned.

It may be that this view is of no interest to you, in which case you will obviously not be concerned whether I stay on or resign as a sponsor. But unless a reasonable and satisfactory explanation is forthcoming, I have no choice but to do the latter.

TO ROBERT PRESNELL, JR. AND MARSHA HUNT
August 20, 1950

Dear Bob and Marsha:

It is not true that Alexander died of syphilis. He died after swilling a great quantity of Macedonian hooch one night, and then reeling into a swimming pool. Not that he drowned; he caught virus pneumonia.

As for Napoleon, I agree it would have been much better if he had won at Waterloo. English cooking would have been vastly improved, for one thing. Buonaparte would never have parted with the Louisiana Territory, and Leon Blum would have been the Senator from the State, not Huey Long. French perfumes would be very cheap in the South, and the infiltration of superior whores across the Maginot-Dixon line would have rendered unnecessary the War Between the States....

I don't envy you your apartment-hunting. Why didn't you let us know? Maybe 104 East 56th Street is not big or elegant enough for you two scions of wealthy, corrupt, reactionary families, but it has a hell of a location and is cool in the summer. It was free as little as three weeks ago, but was snapped up by an unpublished author and his pregnant wife.

My own dear bride has done a wonderful job in a film named *Sound of Fury*. I am hard at work on [*Document*] *A/777*, which has a good possibility of being produced by Dore himself, if it is produced at all. By "at all" I mean the world we are living in.

We have seen a good deal of the Loseys. Joe's not-yet-to-be-released picture with Van Heflin and Evelyn Keyes, *The Prowler*, is not only the best thing he has done, but one of the best anybody has done in the last year. Better, for my money, than *The Lawless*.

We send you our love and kisses, in due relationship, and urge you not to feel badly about the earthquake which swallowed up all of Magnolia Boulevard between Van Nuys and Laurel [location of Presnell and Hunt's California house]. I am sure that you were prudent enough to be insured, and the fact that the Frigidaire came through miraculously unscathed indicates to me that the event was not a total loss....

TO BEN GRAUER, NBC Announcer / September 3, 1950

Jean Muir, an actress on the radio serial *The Aldrich Family* was fired from the cast by its sponsor, General Foods, after protests from a group called The Joint Committee Against Communism.

Dear Ben:

By this time it should be clear to the smearees listed in *Red Channels* and various other shitpiles, that the time for action arrived long ago, and that the Muir incident is distinguished only by the stupidity with which General Foods, on the one hand, and Miss Muir on the other, acted with respect to public relations. Both Jello and NBC, those bastions of Americanism, could have been much smarter; they could have been more hermetic about their blacklist, like [the advertising agency] BBDO, ABC, etc., who don't get into those scrapes simply because they got prophylaxis some time back. The issue is a naked, bold, economic lynching—a blacklisting so black-and-white, if you don't mind the color scheme, that at last the besieged liberal has some ammunition if he cares to fire.

One could hope for more coordination in New York. I think that every last smearee should be contacted and should pool his resources and his action in some quick, decisive, aggressive counter-campaign. I understand a committee of publishers has been formulating some kind of program.

Though I am no lawyer, and the matter certainly should be referred to one, I have an idea that in clear-cut cases such as Muir, involving both Constitutional and industrial principles of free expression and freedom to work, some complaint might be brought before the Federal

Communications Commission. This should be studied immediately. Paul Porter, who was once FCC Chairman, would be the best man to contact on this.

I understand there are both state and federal laws prohibiting black-listing, and that the individual is entitled to some protection under legislation affecting conspiracy in restraint of trade. If this is not being studied by some lawyer (is it too much to ask *Mr.* Muir—that is to say, Mr. Jaffe, a lawyer—to move his ass on this question?), then every liberal in this country is being gypped, or gypping himself.

In your telephone call, you mentioned that some element quite outside the pariah caste should be brought in to intercede or take action in behalf of the smearee. I think you are perhaps naive to think that the Brahmins are available. All of them have been running so fast that not even the smell of their beshitted pants lingers in the air. The few good men, the incorruptible ones, are themselves coming more and more under attack. I notice for example that John Hersey, who has been pure and free of affiliations of any kind, and who never opened his trap on any specific issue, was attacked by some drip in Congress for having written *Hiroshima.* He also made one of the *Counterattack* issues for having put his name to an Author's League statement on the Hollywood Ten.

I think the fight has to be tough, and direct, and that it is useless to try to pretty it up by engaging a Republican gentleman or a fancy corporation lawyer.

I wish you would write and tell me what came of your meeting with the NBC brass. I am really out of touch with things here, since the local press is chronically skimpy on all but the more lurid and sensational news, and I am working so extremely hard that I rarely read the news magazines or eastern papers.

TO WILLIAM BENTON, U.S. Senator / October 17, 1950

Benton, a former Vice President of the University of Chicago, was promoting a form of subscription radio that would have no commercial advertising.

Dear Bill Benton:

Your welcome letter makes me realize what a pity it is that we, who, as you say, have been working toward the same goals, were never in the same backfield. This was pure mischance, for I have known and admired your work in and out of office since I first entered network radio in 1936, and I would have counted it a privilege to have been part of your fight at any time.

You speak of having "failed" in the quest for that goal. I do not allow that, since it was radio and its operators who failed, not you or I. I think our consciences are entitled to peace on that score. I certainly am rooting on your side, and if there is anything I can ever do to assist, directly or indirectly, you have but to sound the alarm.

I hope you found [Robert] Hutchins' *Listener* article as salutary as I did. He's a great man, as are you. I am delighted to have your letter.

TO ROBERT MURPHY MALIN, Executive Director, American Civil Liberties Union / October 25, 1950

Dear Mr. Malin:

I am delighted to learn that the ACLU is proceeding with an investigation of blacklisting.

Concerning my listing in *Red Channels*, I can give you the following information:

1. I am cited as toastmaster of an American Youth for Democracy dinner in San Francisco on November 11, 1945. I was in New York on that date.

2. I am listed as participating in a carnival-bazaar at New York City Center. I did not even attend, let alone participate.

3. I am listed as a panel speaker in the Scientific and Cultural Conference held at the Waldorf. Though I sponsored the event, I was unable to attend, let alone appear on the speaking program.

4. No attempt whatever was made to verify any of the "data" with me, nor, as your letter asks, was I invited "to explain or refute the listing."

5. To date the listing has had no appreciable effect on my work, but this, I believe, is because radio stations and personnel, being pretty well

familiar with my programs on American and international affairs for ten consecutive years, recognized in my case, as in others, the utter trashiness of Fitzpatrick's slander. [Theodore Fitzpatrick was publisher of *Red Channels: The Report of Communist Influence in Radio and Television* and *Counterattack*, publications that supported the black-listing of suspected Communists.] I am under no illusions, however, that were I sponsored by a General Foods, this listing might not have damaged me. It just so happened that I have never been interested in sponsorship.

TO SAM ZOLOTOW, Theater Reporter, *The New York Times*
November 18, 1950

Dear Sam:

...This is the Age of Adaptations. Television drama is one big quivering, quaking mass of adaptations from the stage and screen, and the effect on original writing in the country is toxic. I am just waiting for Marc Blitzstein to do an adaptation of Lillian Hellman's adaptation of *Montserrat*. If it succeeds, perhaps [Betty] Comden and [Adolph] Green will adapt it for Arthur Freed as a Metro musical.

TO ROBERT PRESNELL AND MARSHA HUNT, From 3600 Lankershim Blvd. (Note change of address: By the time you get this we will have fought our way back into the house, thru the barricades of garbage left by our tenant.) / February 13, 1951

Dear Bob and Marsha:

...I am disqualified from commenting on your script [*Michaela*] beyond a certain point, for it has [a T.S.] Eliot quality about it, and I am so pissed off against that worthy for his ideas that I am inclined to go off the shallow end in my hostility. I don't mean that you two think alike—not you, mon brave—you are a human being and an artist through whose veins courses plasma, not sacramental 7-Up, and your thinking is on the side of the unconservatives. But I am disturbed by the resemblance, to a degree, of a certain intellectualism. I can see your lip curling in cold contempt as I pull out this stop, but you must bear in mind that I am a brutish and instinctive writer who gets lost quickly in the maze of metaphysics. I have an ally in Voltaire, who said:

> When he to whom one speaks does not understand, and
> he who speaks himself does not understand, this is
> Metaphysics.

I will tell you my favorite and unfavorite Presnelliana from what you have sent me, and you will note that I stop at street corners rather than survey the county, that I pick out lines rather than climb into the ring with your ideas.

I think you do a disservice to the harmonies and the modulations of your poetry when you permit newspaper phrases like "mass suicide" and "nuclear extinction" to membership in the club. I know you are shooting for a blend of heightened language with colloquialism, but I feel that in such places the blend is imperfect....

And as an old sinner myself, who is still serving time in Parnassus Penitentiary for some premeditated alliteration back before the war, I counsel you not to twang like so:

> Not for a kindless, caitiff, Cain-bred race
> Condoning dissidents with death.

No, Robert. I don't *care* if Shakespeare did it....It is not what you and I, who live in the time of Sean O'Casey and [Carl] Sandburg, knowingly and deliberately do.

I love your theosophical disquisitions:

> Save us all and wear God's medals on your hands and feet
> And His prickly cluster round your head.
> Or aren't you bucking for the ribbon of Resurrection?

That's your fourth verse drama, the Pulitzer Prize one, shining through this early one. I like:

> Out of the slime came mind.

It is economical and athletic, which cannot be said for enough of your lines, which I feel are spendthrift and sedentary....It's easy to be picky with someone else's verse; the trick is to write it one's self. You are doing that, and I cheer you on. Were I a few blocks away, I would wrestle with you for the solid prizes of your poetry; I would argue each phrase. But you are surely surrounded by friendly critics better than I, and you are your own best. Send me more. Write more....

TO SHEILA SIBLEY, Australian Journalist [whom Corwin met in 1946 during his One World trip] / April 17, 1951

Dear Sheila:

...I left CBS two years ago on a matter of principle. They wrote a new contract in which they asked merely 50 percent (!) of the subsidiary sales of any of my material originally produced for them. This meant that, if I sold a broadcast to films (as I have done several times), they were entitled to half the loot. Not me, I told them, and sent back their contract. Just in time, too. The network, in common with all U.S. radio and TV, has become so venal and avaricious that there is no longer any time for quality programs. CBS canceled its symphony broadcasts, School of the Air, its Documentary Unit, its Invitation to Music; NBC kicked around *its* symphony so badly that [Conductor Arturo] Toscanini got fed up and quit. And so forth. So I removed to the high ground of the United Nations, where I am Chief of Special Projects. A nicer group of people I have never met north of Australia; and if the organization were not constantly teetering on the edge of a cliff it would be unalloyed joy to be part of it..

About America, and principally New York: I think you should come by all means. Either now or later, but inevitably. I am almost ready to guarantee, in answer to your specific query on the point, that you will never find New York as compelling and irresistible as Paris. There is only one Paris, and I am beginning to believe that, spiritually, there are several New Yorks. A deadly, poisonous conformity has overpowered American culture, and penetrated even to the core of the hitherto unassailable New York. It is a great, sprawling, energetic city—crowded, noisy and miasmic with the fumes of what you auslanders call petrol. Only a short time ago it was the intellectual hub of the universe, and its theater was a puissant and cher thing. But the cold war hysteria, the witch hunts, the rise of Deweyism, McCarthyism, the lynching of liberals, the rabid press, the "loyalty" oaths, the indictment of people on "conjecture," all this has tended to grind thought down to a low plateau, and to reduce the spirit of American letters to what may soon become an all-time low.

You ask how expensive New York is these days. Damned expensive. One cannot get a meal in a decent restaurant for under $2; most average $3 for dinner. Telephone calls have just been raised from 5 to 10 cents; subway fares were raised 100% last year; a man's haircut, which used to cost 50 cents a few years back, now costs $1.25....A room in a midtown hotel costs anywhere from $150 to $250 a month. You can live for less, but not too comfortably. The best bet is to find some gal who would share the expenses of a small apartment. But prices of everything are quite high.

I am in Hollywood, where living is just as expensive, on a leave of absence from the UN. I took the leave in order to work on two film scripts—one of which is even now before the cameras. It was an exciting and profitable excursion...from the production of programs dealing with the world and its dreadful chronic yaws. The picture has to do only and entirely with people—characters and their development—and it was, for me, a needed and tonic change of pace....

TO KURT BERNHARDT, Film Director / June 8, 1951

Dear Kurt:

Herr Direktor, I give you New York. It stinks. It is a network of monoxide canyons, and the humidity takes me back to Calcutta. The people are hurried and worried. Restaurants are crowded and expensive. Dust blows. No man would dare be seen with an open collar, or wearing laceless shoes.

The UN building rises like a matchbox, and from my corner of it I gaze out over the East River toward a vista of unmodified shit—the handsomest feature of it being the big Pepsi Cola plant and a haven for garbage scows. Give me the Seine. Give me the Tiber. Give me even the Los Angeles River.

I miss your noble face and your worried brow. By now I assume you are despairing of *The Blue Veil*. [Corwin wrote the screenplay for *The Blue Veil*, which Bernhardt ultimately directed.] Don't. I have word from no less than Joan Crawford, who read it on the train, that it *has* to be a fine picture. Who gave her the script? I promised her a look at the UN when we were all wrestling with that tub of lox, *Sudden Fear*, in your atelier that Sunday. So now she's going to see Trygve Lie, no less. Do as much for you, Pappy, any time you want. [Corwin had arranged for Joan Crawford to meet with Trygve Lie, the Secretary General of the United Nations.]

TO JUDY HOLLIDAY, Actress / July 15, 1951

Dear Judy:

The Fairy [of *Mary and the Fairy*] comes from a long line of curious phenomena in Eire, but has no accent from the old country. As you will see, she is far removed from the delightful people you played in *Born Yesterday* and *Adam's Rib*, but I believe she has ingratiating qualities of her own.

I still have some work I want to do on a couple of characters, but this is relatively minor—principally Mary.

Jean Arthur was once going to do this, before something or other traumatized her. She had learned the play by heart, and did it all from memory one night, for [Broadway producer Alfred] DeLiagre and me. But this is already folklore of the theater, and you must have heard about it by now. I fled in disgust to the assembly halls of the United Nations, and lost interest in the play until it occurred to me one day that you might possibly be interested, even though you are ensconced on Olympus, where I trust you shall always be.

There has been some talk of making this a play with music, and for a while, way back, Frank Loesser was intrigued by it, but that was before he took off after Rogers & Hammerstein....

TO JERRY WALD AND NORMAN KRASNA, Film Producers of *The Blue Veil* / September 24, 1951

Dear Jerry and Norman:

I enclose Alice Hughes' syndicated column of September 15. As I understand Alice is the sister of Howard Hughes, you better damn well read it carefully, memorize it, and have the text set to music by Sibelius.

[Alice Hughes—no sister of Howard Hughes—had written a syndicated column praising Corwin's screenplay of The Blue Veil.]

The line "What a pot of money it should make!" together with the eloquence of the exclamation mark, sounds to me like the kind of war-cry that looks so pretty in a trade ad.

After you have fondly stroked the clipping, will you send it back to me for the archives?...

I trust and hope you are having horrible anguish over script and story problems without my skill and talent, and also that you will remember your promise to let me know when the *B.V.* is screened again, so I can invite my ailing agent (mental infirmity, of course) and my other two friends.

You are still my favorite cartel. Love and kisses.

TO JERRY WALD AND NORMAN KRASNA
October 5, 1951

Dear Norman and Jerry:

Attached is my baptismal certificate. A statement from God is on the way, but will of course have to be certified by a notary public....[Wald and Krasna had asked for material to defend Corwin against an attempt to blacklist him for his political views.]

A body of impressive data is being assembled for shipment to you as soon as the job of editing it down to two hours, is finished. I feel you should have this to reinforce yourself against any crackpots. You are no doubt aware of the new trend in crackpottism: death threats. I suppose you know that the manager of the Boston Braves received several death warnings from Brooklyn, for having beaten the Dodgers 3 out of 4 in the last week of the pennant race.

Anyway I am glad *you* are not playing the Yankees, and am most pleased to see that you are in no mood to be pushed around....Neither am I. As has been shown in enough instances to indicate a pattern, a tough answer turneth away rats.

TO EDELAINE HARBURG, Wife of Lyricist E.Y. ("Yip") Harburg
November 19, 1951

Dear Edelaine:

...Both my wife, who can speak for herself at the rate of about 20,000 words an hour, and I feel stricken that we have not communicated to you by some kind of language in the last McCarthyiad. Truth is, Katherine is now the mistress of a hillside manor, a maid, an orchard of fifteen fruit trees, a menagerie of two cats, and a patch of ivy geranium; and between care and administration of the foregoing and her new and triumphant accomplishment of becoming a licensed automobile operator, she is so busy that I have to make an appointment if I want to sleep with her, let alone speak to her.

As for me, I write even less than she—not because I am busy, which I am, but because I am also lazy about correspondence. All correspondence. An insurance policy held by the State of Massachusetts on my charmed life has just lapsed for no more romantic reason than that I carried the premium notice around with me for three months, always intending to get off a check on the morrow.

I was in New York twice this past year, and both times for long enough to do some very hard work, get a haircut, loathe the city volubly, and buy a ticket home on the soonest DC-6....

Anyway, we miss seeing you and Yipper. However, it is of palpable comfort for us to know that you still exist, and have up to this time found exile unnecessary. I have a feeling that gradually all of the artists and intellectuals will move out of the country and leave it all to Arthur Schlesinger, Jr., Arthur Godfrey, and Coca Cola....

TO EDWARD R. MURROW / December 26, 1951

Dear Ed:

I bought Kate a new outsize TV machine for Christmas, and the first program we watched on it was yours. [Murrow had begun a new television series, *See It Now.*] All instruments, human and inanimate, should have as good a baptism. We had not seen the earlier sessions, so this was our introduction. We watched silently for about 1:55 into the program, and Kate turned to me with a big grin and said: "Class."

That it is, and that it has. Up to you, only Garroway has had a penetrating sense of the dimensions of the medium, but you have gone beyond all precursors with a stride as wide as the continent you have shrunk before the very eye. It is already a monument in the strange landscape that is TV.

I cannot remember a half hour that has made the belly of a cathode tube so powerfully absorbing every second of the way. If anything, your material was so attractive and compelling that it seemed almost a pity to hurry away from it so quickly. I take it the impression of haste was peculiar to this special show, in which you had to cover so much ground. There was one detail that has nothing to do with you or Friendly: In the Alcoa commercials there is a still life that is supposed to represent aluminum in some state or other. From our living room, 2,463 miles west of you, it looked like a dead fish that had been mangled on the way to the morgue. Small point.

The concept of the show is smashing, and your presence and appearance give it an authority and strength no one else in this country of 165 millions could duplicate. Congratulations to you and your cohorts. And our love to Janet and that superman jr., Casey.

TO HERBERT MOSS, President, Gotham Recording, and
MOLLA MOSS, Painter [in whose Manhattan apartment Corwin was a frequent guest] / December 30, 1951

Dear Herb and Molla:

Good gray Norman sits in Herb's good gray sweater, looking beyond the horizon of his typewriter at a perfect jewel of a clock and wondering how soon he can get out of the third person and back to normal. You guys are just wonderful and thoughtful and kind, and I thank you from my knishes.

I look well in the sweater, as I do in all of Herb's clothes (his tie brought me many unaccustomed compliments for taste, and one of his shirts so inflamed a wench that I had to fight her off), but the little clock is so cute that Kate wanted (a) to make a wristwatch of it, (2) to eat it, (c) to sleep with it. I finally compromised with her by letting her tell time by it....

The most exciting thing that has happened since I returned was today's rainstorm, which was so violent that it ripped out three years of planting I had done on a cliff behind the house. Where in New York can you come to grips with nature in such an exhilarating way?...

TO SHEILA SIBLEY / December 30, 1951

Dear Sheila:

Your good letter arrived just under the wire for the full flavor of its Christmas greetings....When are you going to have your baby? It is an exciting and happy event—or should be—with or without its sire around. In the case of the father, whom you describe as a French intellectual, I can only say he is a poor advertisement for both France and intellectualism, if he walked away from Sibley under *any* circumstances. Has the man no *eyes?*

I trust your move to England will be in time to insure your child's British citizenship. I am more or less an Anglophile—to the extent that I consider the English one of the few civilized people left to the world. They have a sense of humor, a sense of culture, and a sense of freedom. All three of these qualities are on the wane in my dearly beloved America, which is rapidly becoming a quagmire of singing commercials. The new indoor sport, replacing bridge and canasta, is the investigating committee. One's loyalty is now checked as often as one's auto tires. The art museum is slowly giving way to *Life* Magazine, and the symphony concert to jalopy derbies. Television is moronizing the masses. Books and films suffer progressively. Radio is dead. *Requiescat in pace,* dear poetry of space! Decline, corruption, decay all round us—and the men of moral vigor are exiled and dispossessed. But enough! It is the winter of discontent, and there is a rumor that spring comes even to boreal parts.

What have I been doing? An occasional broadcast for the UN—if you were in England you'd have heard them, since the BBC carries them all; an occasional movie; an occasional pass at personal writing—a play in progress....My first film credit is an affair called *The Blue Veil,* based on a French specimen of the same name. Has Jane Wyman, Charles Laughton and a good cast. Long and lachrymose but has quality, I think. Wish you would cast your beautiful eyes on it and let me know how it strikes a striking writer from Australia. It should be in its first run in Paris now; in London I believe it is in its second run.

What of *your* writing? You know how strongly I have felt about the heft and twang of your style. I would not like to see it given up to detective stories forever—though these can have class, too. Playwriting is another thing, a brutal branch of the craft, and too dependent on an assembly line of producers, directors, scenic designers and electricians to be entirely satisfactory to the writer who cares....

TO JUDY HOLLIDAY / 3 Jan 51—no, 52

The actress had been blacklisted for alleged Communist sympathies.

Dear Judy:

I am distressed to hear that the goons are still at it. More than distressed—infuriated! If only one could meet the bastards in some arena! Even the Christian martyrs had a chance to kick a lion in the nose before being clawed by the mighty paw. But they are not lions, these fascists, they are amoeba, and it's like fighting amoebic dysentery. Go sue the City Health Department.

Except on economic grounds, loss of TV and radio at this juncture is not the biggest catastrophe, considering the gutter level of the general political and esthetic standards. I wrote them off as long as four years ago, prior to *Red Channels*. Now here is a modest proposal: If, God and Miss Liberty forbid, movies should be cut off from you—a thought so horrendous I shall bury it in the back yard with the gophers—then why don't you come on in on *Mary and the Fairy* not only as its star but an equity holder? I alone hold the play rights, whereas Charlie Feldman [head of Famous Artists Agency] has a 50 percent bite on the movie rights. In other words, if you want to go along with the play, I would like to set up a deal whereby you will have an extraordinary share of the loot. I will hold the piece in trust for you for a reasonable time—say forty or fifty years....

TO LOUISE MACE, Film Critic, *Springfield Republican*
February 13, 1952

Dear Louise:

Some friends sent me your review of *The Blue Veil*, and it was as refreshing as a visit to Springfield in the spring. As always, you write with the poise, civility, discernment and intelligence one associates only with qualified critics—the classic prototypes who are today so far from us in time, and so few in numbers.

God, how I get nostalgic sometimes for the decency, the honesty, the straightforwardness that was around us in those dear, dim days on the *S.R.* I was spoiled, I am afraid, by the integrity of Waldo Cook, the guilelessness of Madeleine Ball, the solid American stuff of the Regals and Jenckes and Eddie Fields. I thought I would find these people everywhere. I thought the world outside of that sweet river city would afford us many a critic as even-minded, with as cool a judgment and so few axes to grind, as Louise Mace. It was not to be.

We have come to a time of evil, of corruption, of hysteria, of the ascendancy of the materialist values until the dollar is not just a god but God Almighty. That people like you stand fast in this time is one of the things that help me to keep the faith.

Of *The Blue Veil*, which was my first film credit, and which represented the best I could do with a sentimental and lachrymose premise, I can only say that I am indebted to it because I learned from it; also perhaps because it resulted in Academy Award nominations for two of its actors. But my eye is not toward the screen. It looks to the printed page, and to the theater, which are still relatively free....

TO ALEXANDER KNOX, Actor / February 13, 1952

Dear Alex:

A joy to get your letter, and to learn from it, as well as from Emil, that you are in good spirits, in Rome, in an assignment, and in a mood to write for yourself.,... [Emil Corwin was working for the Food and Agriculture Organization in Rome.]

It is four years since I have been in Rome, and I long for it. I wish you would tell [Roberto] Rossellini that I am still indebted to him for the afternoon in 1946 when, after lunch, he took me with Sergio

Amidei [writer of the screenplay] to a projection room and showed me *Open City* [directed by Rossellini]. I think he's a great man, and I congratulate him on his escape from Romanoff's.

You missed the wrath of God on Laurel Canyon during the recent floods. It was closed to traffic, and I believe your house was one of the few that floated only a few yards off its foundation instead of moving down to Sunset Boulevard....

TO NORMAN KRASNA / March 23, 1952

Dear Norman:

I feel you are entitled to this news item: Yesterday I bumped into Tennessee Williams. We had met only once, ten years ago. He studied me for a moment trying to remember; then, grasping my hand, he cried heartily, "Well, well, Norman Krasna! How *are* you?"

I repeat the question.

Krasna replied by asking Corwin whether he was happy and proud to be Krasna.

TO NORMAN KRASNA / May 4, 1952

Dear Norman:

Of course I am proud and happy to be Norman Krasna, especially since this increases my worldly goods, plunges me into partnership with Jerry Wald, and gives me certain attractive privileges not unrelated to Droit de Seigneur.

And since I am Krasna, it is silly for me not to be living in that fine big house on Monovale. I don't want to rush you, but I would like to start moving in around May 15th.

TO MAURICE AND JENNY LOCKE, Katherine Corwin's parents May 29, 1952

Dear Maurice and Jenny:

That is as handsome a pair of pajamas as the Aga Khan wears, and it looks so much better than most of my suits that I am tempted to wear it out on the street. You are very sweet and good to remember my birthday, which was celebrated on this end by the fact that Kate, for a whole day, threw only *wooden* objects at me instead of metal and porcelain, as is her custom....

Your family is doing quite beautifully, including the one which Katherine is so smugly concealing inside her....

Sammy [the Lockes' son] was here all too briefly. He seemed to flash in and out of the place, stopping on our hillside only long enough to have an argument with Kate. It was good to see him on this side of the country, though, and I hope he will return soon—as indeed we hope you too will be able to visit us before long. [The Lockes were living in Milwaukee.]...

TO GERALD KEAN, Producer, United Nations Radio
June 15, 1952

Dear Gerry:

...Just a fast note amid heavy duties to tell you that I will definitely be among you around mid-July. Among other things that will take me East is the Golden Wedding Anniversary of my folks.

Tell that beautiful bride of yours that our good mutual friend Katherine is with child. While she gets pregnant, I get an ulcer—showing which of the two makes better use of the midsection.

TO LOU ASHWORTH / September 25, 1952

Corwin's former secretary was working for Simon and Schuster, where an artist named Gergely had requested a delay in producing drawings for Corwin's *Dog in the Sky*.

Dear Lou:

...Believe me, I love you and I love Jack and I love S&S, and if anybody could appease me you could, but I'm a mongoose's asshole if I can understand the key element in your valiant brief of 23 September.

You say a month and a half is not an undue length of time for Gergely. That might be true if he were starting from scratch, but it was my impression that the sketches were completed before we even had galleys, and that all that was indicated were minor revisions.

Furthermore, six weeks is a powerful long time. I believe Michelangelo painted half the Sistine Chapel and did the sketches for three book jackets and a calendar in six weeks. I definitely know that France fell in only ten days, and Tobruk in one....

I have no wish to pursue the matter further or harass anybody. Only I shall not conceal my disappointment at what I believe to be a definitely injurious six-week delay....

TO EDWARD R. MURROW / October 13, 1952

Dear Ed:

Perhaps we had what is known in Lower Aramaic as chutzpah to have elected you a reference without asking your leave. [When the Corwins wished to adopt a child, they gave Murrow as a reference.] But when Kate and I were filling out the forms, and it came to parties who might be called on for an estimate of our fitness to rear a child, we decided that as long as we were surveying the landscape of our friends, we might as well shoot for the peak of Everest. Certainly that is what you represent in stature and eminence, and in the heights of our affection.

Your letter to the adoption bureau indicates this was not taken amiss by you, in spite of the pressure of your work, the limits on your time, and the boldness of our act. We are as deeply touched as we are grateful. And one day Tony, for whom we are already quite mad, will thank you too....

Kate, who is big with the one we expect in January, sends her blessings, along with mine, to you, Janet and the phenomenal Casey.

TO ROSE AND SAMUEL CORWIN / January 7, 1953

Dear Folks:

Things are humming around this house, what with the two kids, two nurses, and an occasional maid to do the heavy housecleaning. Also the gardener twice a week—what a hell of a payroll! But as soon as Kate gets on her feet this should be easier.

Kate is coming along beautifully, and looks better than at any time since I've known her. I never had any idea how important children are to a woman's sense of fulfillment. She is happy no end. And the kids are just right—complete opposites—Tony very blonde, very calm, Diana very brunette, very lively....

Em phoned from Santiago de Chile on New Year's Day and it was the biggest thrill I've had since the days in 1946 when I spoke to you all from Cairo, Australia, etc....

TO BERNARD ROGERS / February 7, 1953

Dear Bernard:

I think it wonderful that [John] Hersey is willing to release *The Wall* as the basic for an opera, and I am flattered to be invited to do the libretto for you. Nothing could make me happier than to work on it; but a month ago I took a commission to write a play for Hume Cronyn, and this will absorb the greater part of 1953. I would not want to see you wait, for, as you say, it's a necessary theme.

I am happy to hear about the commissions, and your Fulbright Grant. I envy the orbit of freedom in which you move. As you must by now have guessed, the medium in which I won my battle stars is now in a zone of perpetual twilight, having been eclipsed by TV; and the impact of my liberal ideology on the hatemongers was such that I am to all intents and purposes exiled from the airwaves. The Wall indeed....

By the way, I published a new book last month: *Dog in the Sky*, Simon and Schuster. A light satiric fantasy which has been favorably compared with Swift and Twain—an outrageous disservice to both those hallowed names....

TO ROSE AND SAMUEL CORWIN / March 12, 1953

Dear Folks:

...The big news here is that on the 10th, Tony legally became ours. Under California law, an adopted child does not permanently belong to the parents until six months have elapsed from the time of bringing him into the home. This is in order to permit the adoption agencies of the county time to investigate; also, to allow the parents time to make up their minds, in case they want to change plans, or in the event the child was found to be sickly or retarded. We are happy to say that we certainly did not want to change our minds, and neither did Tony, who beamed and chuckled all the way through the formalities in court. Now that he is officially and legally our own, and no one can take him away from us, his birth certificate is changed permanently, and it reads ANTHONY CORWIN.

The boy is so sunny and bright that we keep pinching ourselves to make sure it's true. He is crazy about Diane, too, who is just about the sharpest little lady we have ever seen. She has big eyes, like Kate, Ma's exquisite profile, my smile, and a whole series of expressions that range from Billy Corwin to Pa to Kate's father to Al and back to Ma. She is very strong, active, and a loudmouth. Although there are six months between them, and allowances must be made for that, Tony is easily the possessor of the best conduct star. The day we took him down to court, awakening him from a sound sleep, driving for miles, waiting in court, making a necessary errand, and driving the long way back—a matter of several hours in which he had to sit up and be toted around, he was the model of good humor, wreathed in smiles, always ready to interpret everything as a game.

Diane is making quite a variety of sounds and tries hard to talk even at her tender age of ten weeks. Kate is working like ten women...but she loves it so much that she's thriving on it.

TO EDELAINE HARBURG / March 22, 1953

Dearest Lady Astor:

Now that all my favorites came through in the Academy Awards, and I don't have to worry for another twenty-five years about De Mille not being honored as a great soul (ass-soul), I can relax to the point of attempting to answer your missive of recent date, in which you bring up the question of whether the bagel came before the lox. [Cecil B. De Mille's *The Greatest Show on Earth* had won the Motion Picture Academy's award as Best Picture of 1952.] I urge you not to waste your time on metaphysical problems of this sort, for no man knoweth, and I would go so far as to say that not even Arthur Schlesinger, Jr., could guarantee unequivocally that a departed spirit can communicate with an investigating committee from the great beyond.

It is good to hear from you, and to read your long, flowing, silken, sassy strophes, full as usual of exquisite misinformation. I gather from the third anagram from the bottom of page 1, that Ypr ["Yip" Harburg] is looking for a great idea for a musical. How foolish of him to beat around Bushwick Avenue, when a mere three thousand miles away sits a man of great fecundity and no commitments to speak of, who has been known to create twenty-six different and original ideas, strung together like knackwursts of dramatic art, in twenty-six weeks. I am the primer on the pump, notwithstanding the estimate of a few thousand enemies that I am but a loose washer. They are journeymen plumbers, and mostly right-wing Methodists, who speak this way of me.

You ask for pictures of our young ones. I have stepped down as the family's official photographer after having—honest to God—taken some movies of Diane upside down. You have to stand on your head to watch them. Anyway, we're hiring a professional photographer next week, and I'm putting away my Argoflex forever.

Speaking of photography, I saw CinemaScope last week. You walk twice around the screen and you've gone a mile. A close-up looks like a planet about to collide with the earth. Marilyn Monroe's pubic hair looked like the hawsers that keep the *Queen Elizabeth* in berth. The sound is magnificent, and the dialogue that comes through the speakers stereophonically is the best-engineered merde that ever was siphoned down a sewer.

I miss you all....My presence here, however, is in a good cause: I am enjoying, with mein frau, two rare pippins. Tony is pure joy, wid golden hair and a smile that would melt tungsten, and a bellylaff that does your kishke good to hear, and there's not a neurotic ganglion in him. Diane has developed the most pixy smile east of Gloccamora, and she has big blue eyes like her mater, and a noble profile like her gallant father. She also shares my aversion to hard liquor, and so was taken off cow's milk today and put on soy juice....

I pass Bentley Drive every now and then, and you will be interested to know that your old house has been torn down, and a White Tower Hamburger joint built in its place. Sunset Boulevard between Sepulveda and Beverly Hills looks like the Far Rockaway branch of the Southern State Parkway on a Sunday afternoon in midsummer. But our little hilltop is pristine. You can still get poison oak within a short climb, and my cats chase lizards through the underbrush. Next week, we expect the Watusi to come down in their annual trek for salt.

Many kooshen to you, and I hope you read me a good fortune out of a cup of farfel soup.

TO WILLIAM GORDON, Head of Public Relations, Universal Pictures / July 31, 1953

> Gordon had protested when his studio bowed to blacklist pressures and dropped a project called *The Holy Grail.* Corwin had worked briefly on the screenplay.

Dear Bill:

If The Holy Grail is worth seeking for, so is a good friend. I feel that I have one in you, though I don't know what, beyond my lifelong attempt to put my pen to the service of my country and poor old mankind, can have deserved your friendship.

I want you to know, as I leave the precincts on something less than a note of triumph, that it was rewarding to be on the same lot with you; and that the blow which I have received—for it is one—has entirely lost its sting in the knowledge that you are who you are. You have taken your stand on the battle-weary ground of reason and decency, and for that I as a friend and compatriot, am forever in your debt.

TO HUME CRONYN / September 23, 1953

> Cronyn, married to actress Jessica Tandy, had proposed that Corwin adapt Eric Knight's story *The Flying York-shireman* for the stage. Knight's widow and a man named Collins retained power of approval over the result, however.

Dear Hume:

Distressed to hear about Jessie's struggle with Meniere's Disease, but I'm glad she's restored to balance. I am always intrigued by the names of rare afflictions, but I wish they wouldn't happen to my friends. My favorite nomenclature in pathology is a thing called Zenker's Degeneration.

...I hope to be filling your ruminative hours with considerations of Sam and Mully. I am steaming along strongly, and should have the first draft of Acts 1 and 2 finished by the month's end. The last act, by its nature, is going to be slower travel. And when the draft is completed, then begins the polishing process. I am a dogged revisionist, with an unbroken record of never having been satisfied with a work from my hand, not even by those thumping big broadcasts which you, among others, received so kindly.

You could help all right, but only if you were here. I am working at a pace which would be thrown off by hiatuses of correspondence. Come on out and we'll drive up to Death Valley, and at the end of one week you'll have a play in hand, a deep tan, and a long-range theatrical scheme that should make art *and* good money. It's an idea I have been incubating for a long while, and I wish it were possible for us to discuss it before you "plunge," as you put it, into a repertory adventure. Ars Gratia Artis is really a misapplied concept; I have never believed that it must be kept in separate quarters from Art Gratia Pecuniae. Lots of good men bridged the two, and you strike me as an eminently good man.

The agenda of this note is to say cheers, to coax you to come out here, and to report swift and encouraging progress on the scaffolding and lower terraces of the "Yorkshireman." Of no less hearty timbre are Kate's and my loving good wishes to you and Jess.

TO JUDITH CHASE CHURCHILL [who had written to ask Corwin what he would most like to own] / October 14, 1953

Dear Miss Churchill:

Since your proposition "What I'd Most Like to Own" implies material rather than spiritual possession, and since you have made house rules in answering the question which allow for "a tall order quite out of this world," then I must divide my cupidity into two parts:

1. I would most like to own the Library of Congress; or

2. The mineral and geologic exhibit at the American Museum of Natural History;

or both.

Though this ambition possibly casts a shadow on my sense of public spirit, since I would be placing public trusts under my ownership, it goes without saying that I would immediately return the properties to the Government and the Museum as a donation prompted by a high sense of citizenship; so you see, the whole business would cancel out. Still, it would be nice to own both for about fifteen minutes.

TO LEO MISHKIN, Film Critic, *New York Daily Telegraph*
November 14, 1953

Dear Leo:

...I have studied your rebuttal of my rebuttal, and have come to the conclusion that I am too hard on TV and you are too soft. I don't think it's as good as you claim or as bad as I accused it of being. The thing to remember, when you make comparisons of TV writing with the earlier radio counterpart, is that radio had no precursor or competitors in its particular aural medium, whereas TV is made essentially in the image of movies—an earlier *visual* medium—and its techniques, except for being instantaneous and electronic, are fundamentally the same. I think the writers you champion are doing perhaps the best that can be done within the limitations of the screen, but at their whitest hot, I say again with possibly tiresome persistence, I think they are no better, and almost always not as good, as film writing at *its* best....

TV is a medium of fits and starts—it brings you a funny fifteen-minutes of Martin and Lewis or a side-splitting skit by Red Buttons, but there is no Olympian sweep of a Chaplin or Keaton. To change my metaphor, consider TV as you would a motorcycle. Perhaps it is the best motorcycle within the power of man to fabricate; but it still isn't a motor car. For a fast and perhaps refreshing spin in a Harley-Davidson, I'll tune in Felix Jackson or my old favorite Fred Coe; but for a ride in a Cadillac, give me Fred Zinneman. It's a difference of dimension, of scope. There's nothing wrong with Beethoven's Rasoumovsky Quartets—they're about the best of their kind—but they are by their very nature lesser works than the Symphonies.

And now to other points: I wasn't praising Goody Ace's TV writing, but his radio writing, so we are apparently agreed on at least that point. As for my embracing the Hollywood yardstick for measuring talent— God forbid! My argument rests on the fact that if Segal, Jackson et al.

were all that hot, and have given us, as you claim, "immensely more exciting, more stirring" product "than anything even [William] Wyler, [Fred] Zinneman, [John] Ford or [Joseph] Mankiewicz have given us on film," this lewd picture business would have grabbed them long ago, because it *needs* great directors, looks for them very hard, and makes offers of the huge nature that I cited—the six-figure fee.

Hollywood, for all its faults and fatuities, doesn't deliberately assign dull directors to pictures. It takes the best it can get, and when it can't get the Zinnemans it settles for the Irving Rapps. But how, in the name of all that we hold sacrosanct, including your sixteen-foot cruiser, can you say that TV has exceeded the best product of these four men? Name me any TV program greater than *The Informer*, *All About Eve*, *High Noon* and *Roman Holiday*—to name only a few of the exceptional product of these men.

But as I said before—pish and posh for our little differences, and hurrah that they have renewed our converse. I feel all such minor disputations are extremely little, especially when, as happened to me between the last paragraph and this one, I lifted the receiver of my ringing telephone and was told that my dear friend Felix Ferry has just died in Europe. [Felix Ferry was a literary agent who once represented Corwin.] Life is so frail, so short! So get that cruiser! And have fun writing the column! And enjoy the blessings of a Doctor in the family, and of a Judy who is besieged on the telephone.

End of page, end of letter, but not the end of our love to you and Bea.

TO JACK GOODMAN, Simon and Schuster / February 6, 1954

Goodman had written Corwin about the sexual attractions of Angora goats.

Dear Jack:

You are not the only one who has sown wild goats. The very thing you find praiseworthy in the Angora, I cannot stand. You say they hold still. That's just the trouble. They hold still because they are essentially frigid. Once, in a moment of passion, I cried out to a shapely Angora, "Tell me you love me!" Not a twitch from her. I think she was blandly chewing cud at the moment, although from where I was situated I could not be sure.

Sheep on the other hand are appreciative. Their attitude is never casual, and some of them form lasting attachments.

I know you are impetuous, and the story you tell of your services to the Imam bears this out. But as a friend I hope you will not let any idle fascination for some goat cloud your judgment. Have such liaisons if you wish, but I implore you to be discreet about it. Because if you should get a goat enceinte, you are in for some kidding. —Love (fraternal),

TO ROBERT PRESNELL AND MARSHA HUNT,
310 West 79th Street, New York 24, New York / February 15, 1954

Dear Bob and Marsha:

...I miss you both in this cold and troubled city. Yesterday I bumped into a mild and pleasant boy named Orson Bean, a comedian, who solemnly reported that he sanitarily conceals the *New York Post* before entering a radio studio or advertising agency. The atrocity stories multiply, the persecution quickens, and only Jack Gould and Ed Murrow and John Crosby continue to write like free men.

Some good plays in town. *Tea and Sympathy*, slick and Ibsenian in construction, with all of Kazan's Greek cunning plainly showing; *The Immoralists*, a powerful piece—tragic in the Greek, not Kazanian, sense. I agree with [Brooks] Atkinson, the only one of the executioners to spare it, that it is excellent theater. *Oh Men Oh Women* has only one good act. *Picnic* is a cheap bore. *Pennypacker* would die of asphyxiation without a marvelous caricature of a minister by Glenn Anders. I have no idea why Jack Houseman went to the trouble of producing *Coriolanus*. I hear the new Eliot, *The Confidential Clerk*, is a bore. Read the *T.S. Eliot Myth* by Russell Hope Robbins for the pleasure of seeing the panjandrum reduced to a spot of gristle and pomade.

TO KATHERINE CORWIN, New York / March 26, 1954

Darling:

Thanks for the 8mm film and the marvelous color shot of our babies. I gaze at it by the hour, and it gladdens my heart. So do Em and Babe, who wish they had more little ones. Tony is really handsome, and that pixy Diane, with that warm and pretty mouth and the humor playing about it! I have to fight down the impulse to get on the next plane and come back to you all before nightfall of this very day....

This is a difficult period for me because of the vacuum in work—to say nothing of my absence from you—and I am trying to keep my humor high and my head clear. The Lincoln Douglas project is stymied until we get a Lincoln. Our latest try has been for Louis Calhern; he's interested but naturally wants to see a script. He is on the coast; nothing will be decided until I arrive back in Hollywood and go to see him. I have been thinking of other Lincolns, since Calhern is far from the ideal casting, as far as I am concerned. I yesterday did considerable brooding about alternatives, and came up with a few: Michael Rennie (tall, handsome, a good actor, gaunt enough to make an impressively physical Lincoln); Wendell Corey, who has a lot of the simple and American in him; Michael Redgrave; Gregory Peck; Rex Harrison; Alan Napier; Royal Dano. The list runs down rapidly after Peck. Gene Lockhart could play Douglas; also Eddie [Edward G.] Robinson. Even Edward Arnold, who has the florid style that Douglas used—and the "jolly face" that Lincoln alluded to so wryly at one point....

Saw two plays within the last week—*The Burning Glass*, about a scientist who has an invention that could wreck the world. A dreary and pompous and heavy-handed melodrama that deserves to close as soon as it will after the Theater Guild's subscription clientele runs out in a week's time. Cedric Hardwicke should be analyzed to find out why he ever would lend himself to such a play. Then the other night I saw *The Golden Apple*, John LaTouche's lyrics to music by Jerome Moross. It got rave notices from almost everybody except Atkinson and the *New Yorker*. I found it disappointing except for ten or fifteen minutes of the first act. Yet it is a smash hit at the Phoenix, and may come uptown.

I mentioned the indecision that plagues me. Last week I actually spent a whole day digging again into the Roman period for a theme, so I could get started on a verse play. Then seeing the LaTouche piece made me realize that I could well make use of my faculty for rhyme. There is the Andrews offer, too; the uncertainty of Cronyn's plans; and the elusive Lincoln-Douglas business. A producer (who has to date offered me no option money) on Monday is going to deliver to me a literal translation of what he describes as the best of Giraudoux's plays—an old one which has never been produced here—to see if I would be interested in adapting it. On Tuesday I am going to see Billy Rose, at my request, to suggest a plan for a revue. Buzz, buzz, bumble, bumble, the wheel goes round, talk, negotiations, figures, meetings, and still no writing.

And I think of you up there on the hill every time a soft breeze blows or the sun shines—especially every time I see the pictures up on my dresser....

TO HUME CRONYN / April 16, 1954

Dear Hume:

I certainly am solidly outvoted, and I can only assume that I lack both talent and judgment with respect to comedy-fantasy, and that my two sets of highly approving auditors, one on each coast, were giggly simpletons.

The vigor of the reaction from Mrs. Lindtner and Collins, to say nothing of the negative views of yourself, Jessie and Leah, make it ringingly unanimous, and I accept the verdict regretfully—but, I must confess, with the ludicrously persistent feeling that the play is not only better than you all think, but that it represents perhaps the only kind of structure that can validate, in today's world, this curiously dated story whose magic, I am afraid, has worn a little thin with the years. Magic and charm there still is in it, and always will be, but whether these properties can be stretched over the distance of an evening in the theater or on the screen and still keep, is a question I must now refer back to you, Lindtner and Collins. I will say for myself that I did not even attempt to do this: I made it the story of Sam Small flying solo in 1954, not 1934—a Sam who remains the same as he always was but changes the New World.

But enough of what I did and didn't do. The hard fact is that the Owners, as the contract calls them, hate it, and I will not attempt to swim upstream against such active dislike. I think I could make some progress against even the dead weight of indifference, but the Owner attitude you report is paralyzing, and I have no choice but to go on to my next project.

As a last word, I feel obliged to add, for friendship's sake, my morbid and cautionary prophecy that, considering Mrs. Lindtner's confused state of mind as to whether Sam was to turn up as a musical or as a Gallic Yorkshireman a la Giraudoux, it will be a long, long trail to the script that will please you all. I hope for your sake that I am as wrong about this as I seem to have been about the rest—but faith is a beautiful thing, and you have it, and I sincerely and earnestly wish you the best.

My crowning disappointment is that it should have been you, of all people, whom I had to disappoint. Rather a hundred Selznicks, a thousand Goldwyns. It was a privilege for me to have been associated with you however briefly and unsuccessfully, and to know you that little better. You are creative and fecund, a superb artist and a rare man. I am sorry that my little world of Sam Small has fallen from your orbit and now lies dead. Long live its successors....

Although the Small project was abandoned, the Cronyns later appeared in the Westinghouse Group W television series, *Norman Corwin Presents*.

TO DORE SCHARY From 3600 Lankershim, Hollywood 28, California, / April 21, 1954

Dear Dore:

I was going through some old papers the other day, and I found the original manuscript of a fine undersea yarn by a writer who has since gone places. [Schary had written a script called *The Human Angle*, which Corwin adapted for radio in 1941.] I thought you might like to have it for the archives.

It occurs to me in connection with below-sea-level fiction, that no studio has ever really taken advantage of the immense interest in the sort of thing that made *The Sea Around Us* such a smash best-seller. Since that book, the adventures of those French divers in recovering an ancient Greek wine ship have made exciting reading (their book, if you haven't read it, is a sizzler); but nothing has yet been done on film except some poor low-wattage documentary footage shown on ONMIBUS, where it belonged.

It seems to me that the bump of wonder raised by oceanography in general could and should be hitched to drama—and I don't mean just fights with sharks and octopi. We've had enough pictures about atomic scientists—how about a genius who knows the great waters, for a change? I'm sure that romance at sea—even on a scientific expedition, can be as diverting as the landlubbing type. I'll never forget the good time I had seeing an expedition-type story integrated so beautifully in *King Solomon's Mine.*

TO PHYLLIS KIRK, Actress / June 12, 1954

Dear Phyl:

...From London to Moab [Utah] is travelin', ma'am, and I want to hear no complaints from you about the dust or the flies. For I am in love with the desert, a love that is hopeless in view of the steady and relentless encroachment on its domain by airdromes, cement factories, 7-Up billboards, trailer camps, oil wells, gambling dives, diners, and uranium prospectors. Now all that is left to me is the Gobi, the long swells of the Pacific, and whatever just deserts I can lay claim to.

I was strongly tempted to set out for Moab, for the double objective of (1) seeing Dana Andrews, for whom I have just finished a screenplay, and who is now shooting up there with the U-I colony; and (2) seeing the country. But I hear that the place is so crowded with geologists and second units that a kangaroo rat has no place to burrow....

TO RICHARD WALTON / September 24, 1954

Dear Dick:

...I got out of New York fast. It is a cancer. Social man is the only animal who warps his ecology in this way. Bees and ants, for all their totalitarianism, know when to leave a hill or hive for another, when the apartment building should be condemned, when to amalgamate, and when the old queen should be kicked out.

Give me the hills, even if they are wrapped in fire, as at present. There's been a big brush fire in the mountains to the north and west of us here, and at night one could see a sharp, short profile of flame hanging, ghostly, in the sky some twenty-five miles distant. I expected to hear something choral, possibly Wagnerian, at any moment, but all that floated up to our little amphitheater in the hills was the incessant intestinal growl of the Diesel trucks that have taken over the freeway around the clock.

Don't speak to me of my plays until I write a good one. I am in a low frame about my recent writing, and am ready to chew carpets as well as pencils.

TO MARIANNE RONEY, Caedmon Records / October 5, 1954

Dear Marianne:

...I hope for the sake of dear Caedmon and dear Barbara and dear you and what is left of our culture, that the Faulkner record is superb and sells madly. But I am mystified by the fact that you cast authors to read their own works. Only a few can do this well—Sandburg, chiefly; John Hall Wheelock, Dylan Thomas, Vachel Lindsay, and Corwin, to mix the quick and the dead. I hope your Sitwell readings are better than those I heard him give with his sister in Beverly Hills two years ago. MacLeish was fine when I heard him last—almost made the varsity team. But I heard Steve Benet read from *John Brown*, and I have a disc of Robert Frost treating his own poems abusively, and I was once on a program with Edgar Lee Masters in which he coughed his way through [a reading of his poem *Silence*], and Padraic Colum was on my old WQXR program—and they all would have done better in the hands of [Frank] Silvera [actor].

Is it for its historic value that Faulkner reads Faulkner? Then I have no quarrel. But if your first concern is The Spoken Word, let me ask you this: If Shakespeare were alive, but had a cleft palate or a whistling denture, or had the difficulty of a Chinese with his r's and l's, or a voice like Lionel Stander or even (God forbid) like Arthur Godfrey's, would you have him do an album of the Sonnets for Caedmon?

I hope I have put you on the defensive, if only as reprisal for the insinuation that I don't know a kobold from a female. I do, and *vive la différence*, and since you are *both*, *vive* you all! Ah, Marianne, you speak cruelly of my gendered allusions when you complain that they "spatter" my letters, and the effect of this is to drive me back toward the walls of the monastery. *Spatter?* Not illuminate? Coruscate? Just old dreary spatter?

A fine time to be thanking you for the *Hearing Poetry* disc, which arrived yesterday and which should have been the lead sentence here. I haven't heard it yet, but I look forward to recapturing the pleasure it gave me when I caught it on WNYC one afternoon....

TO MILDRED COHEN / February 23, 1955

Milly me love:

Tony came to me the other day (age 32 months) and reported that "a nail bit me." I asked him where this happened, and he conducted me through several rooms to a carpet, where a loose tack had indeed nipped his stockinged foot.

Diane, six months younger, has a vocabulary ranging from 300 to 500 words larger than mine, but the two she uses most often in relation to me are "Be quiet!" This she commands whenever I try to sing. Already she has a critical faculty, inherited from Kate.

TO MARIANNE RONEY, who had sent Corwin material relating to the life of Vincent Van Gogh / Undated (c. August, 1955), Hollywood, California

Querido Majahuatl:

You are the slow neutron of generosity, and when you hit a compact mass of material like Van Gogh, there is a handsome shower of facts and suggestions. Great gods and little fissions, where do you find the time and energy? Is it not enough to run Caedmon and its rarefied stable of talent; juggle the books to the satisfaction of the Revenue Department and Mrs. Winthrop Stuyvesant Caedmon, widow of Hercule Caedmon, founder of Caedmon Publishers and principal stockholder; maintain cordial relations with T.S. Eliot; live mysteriously in Jackson Heights; stabilize one Peter; keep in your head several languages at once; be in the right about Orff and Ixtaccihautl; laugh at clavicord bums; enjoy a virus or two; flap off to Cuba; and scold the Marlowe of radio—without descending into the bowels of the library to do the work of Metro's sluggish Research Department? Bless you for that energy and goodness anyway, but in the name of the posterity that will saint you for your daring catalogue, do get enough rest between 4th Avenue and your opium den in Jackson Heights....

Don't confuse the film in work with a literary project. We are going to be far less scholarly than the least of the scholarly works—but perhaps more human and basic and true. There will be the usual telescoping of events in order to bring the picture under twelve hours in length, but if I have anything to do with it, not a scintilla of truth will be avoided or euphemized or dusted with talc.

My tools are, so far, the letters to Theo, Rappard and Bernard; Meier-Graefe (see his ending for one of the worst examples of pathetic fallacy—the colors, each with a Capitalized name, come down out of his paintings and stand around Vincent's bier on the billiard table in the cafe in Auvers); Nordenfalk's wonderfully clean and dry and economical book; the de la Faille catalogue; and various items of Gauguiniana. My able associate and dialogue writer is Vincent Van Gogh.

Enough. I put in a twenty-hour day yesterday, and the coming week is steeper than K-2....

TO EDWARD R. MURROW / October 13, 1955

Dear Ed:

I had lunch together with Bob Lee and Jerry Lawrence, co-authors of *Inherit the Wind.* As usually happens in all informed and intelligent conversations, your name and works came up, and both men confessed that it had long been an ambition of theirs to meet you; yes, even to have lunch with you. I told them that you are a spectacularly busy man, and that although I am a charter member of the Murrow-is-God Club, I have no special influence on your social calendar. But these are two first-rate citizens and very talented playwrights, and I think that if you could find time to see them, you would not be altogether unrewarded. They will both be in New York after October 26, so any time after that date would be appreciated.

TO EMIL CORWIN / April 20, 1956

Dear Em:

The off-Broadway production of *Mary and the Fairy* annoyed me very much, since it was all handled through my publisher, and I knew nothing about it. I would certainly never have permitted a stage adaptation had I known, especially one which was going to advertise in the New York dailies. I raised hell through my agent, but fortunately the show closed after five performances, so I hope not too much damage was done.

Things are going along well here, and our kids are thriving. Specimen of conversation overheard a couple of days ago: TONY: Diane hit me. DIANE: Did you saw me do it? TONY: Yes, I saw you did it....

TO RICHARD WALTON / May 1, 1956

Dear Maitre:

...Your letter of April 13 represents you as "toying with" the idea of coming to L.A. Have you got beyond the toy stage? You must not fail to include us in your itinerary of historic sights. We have added a swimming pool to our property since you were last here, and I have been waiting for five months for an opportunity to use it....I hope when you come down here you will bring with you hot and dry winds, so that this feature—so typical of decadent Hollywood—can be put to use....

Ever hear from [Bernard] Herrmann? We have been out of touch for about two years. He seems to have graduated to a higher echelon of society that includes Stokowski and various other longhairs. We are plebeian, and that's the way I prefer it.

I have just finished writing a screenplay of the life of Vincent Van Gogh, and I feel in my bones that you will like it. For once, it tells the story pretty much as it was lived, with no crap or cheesecake or violations of fact and spirit.

We are delighted to have your letter, and to know that you still coruscate among the decadents of that gambling hell in which you live. [Walton was living in Reno.]

TO HERBERT MOSS / June 15, 1956

Dear Herb:

I may be going East late this month or early in July, so as not to miss the crisp coolness of a New York summer, and the vagrant thought passed through the concrete shield that is my mind, that if the Junior Modern Museum which is your lovely home is idle around this time, perhaps we could make a deal. I can offer minerals: a priceless ruby from the twat of an idol recovered from the hold of a sunken Tyrrhenian frigate in the Aegean....

I will understand perfectly if your home is given over to visiting Gotham sales representatives, to a Foamflex convention or, possibly, to yourselves. In this case I will sleep in the park, on a bench within sight line of your roof, so that we can communicate by flashing mirrors in the sun....

TO HERBERT MOSS / June 28, 1956

Dear Herb:

What a generous telegram! It appears now that I will be in the city only from July 23 through 28 and will fly back to the coast on the 29th. I thought you might like to know this so that you can make proper arrangements with the valet, the cook, the bearer, the houseboy, the chauffeur, the string quartet, the laundress, and the hot and cold running maids whom you always place at my disposal.

I would also appreciate your clearing the living room so that I may practice certain golf shots. As you see, I will be of no trouble to you whatever.

TO HERBERT BLOCK, Cartoonist / August 8, 1956

Dear Herb:

I am sending you under separate cover copies of two of my books....Remember your end of the deal: an original Herblock. You are being cheated, but by a devoted, nay, slavish, fan.

I hope you had a happy vacation, and that you are refreshed for the wars. God knows you are worth fifty armored divisions. I am speaking of present-day armor, which includes atomic warheads.

TO MARTIN GABEL / August 23, 1956

> Corwin had drawn on the Lincoln-Douglas debates for a stage play, *The Rivalry*. Henry Fonda read the role of Lincoln at the home of George Brandt, who had an option to produce the play.

Dear Martin:

By God's dignity, man, how can you have thought I was mad at you, or even irritated? The farthest thing from my mind was pique at any phase of your relationship—all too distant, for my taste—to the Debates. On the contrary I am nothing but indebted to you for your willingness to participate in the Fonda evening—a willingness I suspect was based on an older school tie than that which you have with Fonda or Brandt.

If there was any edge to my teeth in that letter (a copy of which I do not have), it was the sense of frustration that the definitive Douglas—you—had not already been nailed down. It would be the same as if, having finished *On a Note of Triumph* for a special occasion, I beseeched you to narrate it, only to find that you were committed to *Omnibus* and *You Are There* for an indefinite period.

As for my allusion to the successful things of mine you've done on radio, I blush to think you could possibly have construed it to intimate any obligation due me. The shoe is on the other foot: It is I who was, and am, in your debt. All I intended to convey by the reference was the historic precedent for my being in my right mind and on sound ground when I came to you with the proposition to do this or that script....

Gabel later appeared as Stephen A. Douglas in both the national and Broadway productions.

TO ARCHER WINSTEN, Film Critic, *New York Post*
October 8, 1956

Corwin's screenplay for *Lust for Life* starring Kirk Douglas as Vincent Van Gogh received the Film Critics Circle Award and an Academy Award nomination for best screenplay adapted from another medium. Anthony Quinn won the Academy Award as best supporting actor of 1956 for his portrayal of Paul Gaugin.

Dear Mr. Winsten:

Now I'm *glad* you left my name out of those credits, because it has given me the reward of a refreshing exchange with you.

Please don't bother about any rectification—your review of the film was so glorious that I'm settling for that fine print mention in the standard box.

I am not surprised at your report of a violent enemy of mine fulminating about the picture, particularly since he's an art critic. To date the film has not had even diplomatic recognition from any art journal I know of—after all, these organs are full of experts and connoisseurs; the elite; they *own* art; and along comes a fat, rich, gross major studio with the brashness to compete with them in the interpretation of an artist's life and the reproduction of his paintings. It's an invasion of their precincts, and they resent it.

I long ago resigned myself to the fact that any craftsman who stands in the public eye (as I did when in radio), is bound to collect enemies. I was, and am, loathed by blackshirts, reds, extreme intellectuals, Whitman-haters, and those who celebrate joyously every anniversary of FDR's death. I am also despised by a few of the commercial boys, because I survived for ten years in radio without ever having or needing a sponsor....

I have stopped trying to figure what makes my enemies tick—why, for example, Bernard De Voto went on for eight pages in *Harper's* viciously attacking the very same work that John Mason Brown gave an all-out rave to in a cover piece of the *Saturday Review*—why some people think I am a scoundrel, a threat to America, while on the other hand I got fan letters from Admiral Nimitz and the Secretary of Air under Truman. Since it's impossible to figure, I've stopped trying, and I just go on from project to project trying to do the best I can with each....

Incidentally, I note with pleasure that the Van Gogh film is doing excellent business. It has you and your colleagues to thank for that. In giving it your understanding and support you have given morale not only to myself and others on the picture, but to all who will explore deeper waters in the future. Again my thanks.

TO HAZEL COOLEY SPILLER / October 16, 1956

A friend from Springfield, she had collaborated with Corwin on *So Say the Wise*.

Dear Hazel:

How kind you are to have written me so warmly about *Lust for Life*. And how loyal, to have gone to see it so early in the run. From all I hear, it is playing to capacity on every performance, and people are standing in line to see it. Of course the house is small, but if it can keep running that strongly over a period of months, it adds up to a moderately strong run in a big house....

By the way, did you see the *Nation's* review of *Lust for Life*? A pitiful, mixed-up little belch of a review, in which Mr. Hatch alluded to Kirk Douglas as playing Van Gogh like a demented grocery clerk. I worry for that little magazine—it has hard enough going as it is, without alienating readers who, on seeing the picture and matching it against Hatch's comment, will think that the critic's post has been taken over by the grocery clerk's younger brother, a shipping clerk. I'd rather see an intelligent hostile review than an unintelligent dud....

TO DR. WILLIAM B. OBER, First cousin of Corwin
June 18, 1957

> Dr. Ober had sent a reprint of his article from a medical journal.

Dear Dr. Ober:

We would like very much to make a feature-length Cinemascope feature picture, starring Kim Novak and possibly Audrey Hepburn, based upon your story entitled "Ectopic Ovarian Decidua Without Pregnancy." We feel this has the basis for a suspenseful, taut melodrama, making use of a scientific background, yet affording an excellent love story. Certainly the sexual elements are deftly handled.

It is our feeling that the public may not quite understand the motivation for the response to progesterone elaborated by the syncytictrophoblast, but we have a writer under contract, M.M. Lemp, who has written many successful Westerns, and we have full confidence that he could adapt your story faithfully, without departing from the spirit or atmosphere, yet at the same time keeping intact the wonderful by-play between the mesenohyme of the urogenital ridge, and its derivatives.

If you are interested, we shall have our representative in Hackensack contact your agent or barrister. Rest assured that with Miss Novak or Miss Hepburn (Mrs. Mel Ferrer, gravida 0, para 0, errors 2) or even Joan Crawford (gravida 400) in the cast, the picture would have strong commercial pull, and we would be keen to tackle it. I see it in color, of course. It could clean out the Academy Awards like a good curettage.

Sincerely, A.J. Parameceum, Pres.

TO ROSE CORWIN / August 25, 1957

Dear Ma:

...Diane the other day was speculating on where babies come from. She decided that most of them came from the Farmer's Market. Asked if she came from there too, she replied, "No, I come from a toy shop, where I used to dance all night with the dolls."...

TO GENERAL FRANK McCARTHY, Producer, 20th Century-Fox
September 13, 1957

Dear Frank:

I have a charming letter from General [George] Marshall, the concluding line of which reads: "Please remember me warmly to Frank
McCarthy when next you see him."

I did not know, when I dropped that note of thanks to you, that
within a few days you would be a General yourself. My warm congratulations go to you, and I think the Army should be felicitated too....

TO DONALD CAMERON, Senator in the Canadian Parliament,
Director of the Banff School of Fine Arts of the University of Alberta
[where Corwin sometimes lectured] / January 11, 1958

Dear Donald:

I feel privileged to have a copy of your address to the Senate on
December 3rd. I quite share with the Hon. Messrs. Connolly and
Macdonald the view that it was brilliant; but I would add to it, the
word courageous. Sometimes just belting out a simple statistic requires
courage, in that it exposes the wild folly of an attitude or practice. Such
a statistic is your reference to the fact that the federal contribution to
education was .013 percent of the amount spent on defense!

Brilliant also was your inclusion of education *as* a measure of
defense. And your address took on added dignity and luster with every
word out of the mouth of John T. Haig. What a windbag! He even supported your position, while trying to ridicule it, when he reflected that
at the Dominion-Provincial Conference he heard discussion of roads,
bridges, dams, sewage schemes and enterprises, but not one word about
education. Did he think he was strengthening his case with that argument?

I quite agree, also, with everything you have to say on J. Foster Dull,
and your appraisal of the situation. All I can add to your letter is a
fervid and enthusiastic "Hear, hear!"...

TO ANTHONY FRANCIOSA, Actor / From Residence Palace
Hotel, Via Archimede 69, Rome, April 26, 1958

Corwin had gone to Italy to write a screenplay on the life
of Francisco Goya, to be played by Franciosa.

Dear Tony:

I was happy to see you the other day, and delighted to hear about
your enthusiasm for the Spanish music you had found, but by the time
you left I was very much disturbed. I think you were too. The cause of
the disturbance rests on a mistake I committed in telling you the outline of events beyond the script you had read; the important thing is
not what caused it, but the symptoms of misapprehension revealed in
your reaction.

I respect any thinking actor whose interest is in the best possible
result. But the existence of that interest does not automatically make his
point of view always sound, particularly in the case of a problem which
is vastly complicated by considerations of history, politics, language, art,
religion, mores, and the strictures of chronology.

Your first reaction to the first pages you received two weeks ago, was
that all the major characters seemed crystal clear to you except that of
Goya. Precisely. In the three hundred-odd biographies written of this
man, Goya remains to us a far greater enigma than any other important
figure of his century. His art to this day is, to a large extent, enig-
matic—it remains sheer guesswork for critics and biographers, as to its
meaning. Even the simplest head of a dog, among his House of the
Deaf paintings, is baffling to us. But if I understood you properly, you
seemed to feel that we should dig this man as soon and clearly as we do
the Queen, Godoy, the King and Alba. We should spell him out, so that
the audience is able to say, "1,2,3, and a,b,c, and now we know he is a
certain type, so we can all settle down now and see how he Wins Girl
and Loses Girl and Finds Girl."

I told you, at that time, that it was impossible and unfair to judge a
character's development at the halfway mark of a story whose trajectory
is certainly not usual or expected any more than Goya's life was. You
rested your case for the moment, in agreement with this premise.

However, the other day in my hotel, when I began to outline the third fourth of the story development, you recoiled in seeming dismay. I had volunteered this brief outline in the hope that it would not only give you some assurance about where we were going, but perhaps even enthusiasm. Granting that an oral outline is even less rewarding than a written one, and all synopses are awful, your reaction struck me as unthinking and unjustified. For you seemed to take a bookkeeper's position, counting your total scenes and big moments, against those of Alba and Godoy, and failing to appreciate that a character can develop and evolve even through indirection, involution, regression and pathology. Goya was vain, ambitious, jealous, finally embittered. This is how he is being drawn in *The Naked Maja*. One does not develop all these qualities full blown by page 40.

Tony, I urge you not to make yourself arbiter of how you think Goya should react to a given stimulus, such as, say, his deafness. Your idea is that he should rage—that he should throw vases and smash them against a wall in order to test his hearing. That is all right for Stanley Kowalski, but not necessarily for Francisco Goya. Beethoven too was an angry deaf man, but there are ways and ways of expressing anger. He jammed his hat down on his head instead of taking it off respectfully when the coach of a Prince passed him on a road. On his deathbed he shook his fist at a lightning storm. How much more magnificent are such gestures than smashing furniture, which any drunken bum can do when angry. I mentioned Kazanism to you when you bellowed out an enactment of how you thought Goya would behave. I yield to nobody in my awed respect for Gadge, but he does tend to break the china when in doubt. It has become his weakest mannerism, not a strength.

The other day you repeated your suggestion of a prologue in which Goya would climb a slippery pole from the top of which he could look down on the poverty of his origins, and look ahead on the horizon toward the big city—Madrid—the goal. This would be worth consideration if we had at our disposal five hours, but as it is, the problems of getting everything vital into less than three hours is already murderous.

But more than that, you are proposing something which fits your own subjective feeling about who Goya is and what he should do. I do not think I am trespassing on Koster's precincts—and I feel I would have his concurrence when I say that it would be unfortunate to shape Goya around the image of Franciosa rather than Franciosa around the image of Goya. I am sure you too will agree with this. [Henry Koster was the film's director.]

The question, then, is Whose Image? Again, unless I am sadly mistaken, the Image must be one arrived at by the usual committee—a committee consisting of producer, director, composite biographies, cumulative research, technical advice, and the assimilative power of the writer or writers. If every actor, even one as highly intelligent and responsible as yourself, were, on this picture, to braid the character to fit *his* impression of how a man would behave under certain stress, total anarchy would result.

As I said before, I was at fault the other day in trying to describe an outline; you are not to be held responsible for my tactical follies. But that is done. I have taken the time out to write this because of the high esteem in which I hold you, and because I think it might be helpful to the production as a whole if you were disabused of unfounded suspicions and mistaken impressions.

The fact remains that I am the writer of record at the moment, and that no page of the script has been written without the deepest and most searching consultation and consideration. Much work has yet to be done, and the expected and inevitable flaws of the first complete draft will be attended to at the proper time. But it will profit us all, including yourself, if you understand that the script involves people you have never met, a period you have never been steeped in, a country you have never lived in, a malady that has never plagued you, an aristocracy you have never lived among, atrocities you have never witnessed, and a Duchess you have never laid.

This does not mean that you may not have splendid ideas about each—but in the open market of creation, my ideas are probably every bit as valid as yours; and, considering the day-and-night study and concern which I am obliged to bring to it, probably more instructed.

I write this in the most friendly spirit conceivable, short of engraving it on the back of a million-lire note. I do not intend it as the start of a correspondence or controversy, for there is no time for that even if it were desirable; and no acknowledgment beyond a casual Yours Received sometime or other, is required. Peace be with you.

After Corwin left Rome, *The Naked Maja* was rewritten by an Italian screenwriter. Corwin, aghast at the result, fought unsuccessfully to have his name removed from the film.

TO E.Y. HARBURG / July 17, 1958

Dear Yip:

...Forgive the haste of this meager note, but I am dictating this as I run down Ventura Boulevard, with my secretary right behind me.

She is the Olympic champion in the two-mile cross-country event, and so is in better form than I. In fact, I expect her to overtake me within the next half mile, at which point she will be dictating to me.

Anyway, the hugs and kisses of yours and Edlee for Kate and me are reciprocated, and the tapes will be gone into with my usual thoroughgoing and methodical confusion.

TO BILL STOUT, KNX, Los Angeles / September 11, 1958

Dear Mr. Stout:

As an old hand at the documentary in radio's pleistocene age, I come to this letter with some partisan interest in the form. But with or without that interest, I would be on my feet cheering for the achievement of yourself and your associates, in last night's telecast.

Thou Shalt Not Kill [a documentary on capital punishment] is a towering achievement. Its excellences are so many that it would only tire us both to catalogue them; but even this generalization will not let me go without singling out the resourcefulness, comprehensiveness, clarity, dignity and humanity of the program.

I have many times before this wanted to drop you an applause card for this or that telecast. Now at last I am carried past the barrier of procrastination; and I am happy that, in offering you my very sincere congratulations for your (as usual) impeccable performance, I am able to include so many others. Please do me the kindness of extending my congratulations to Irwin Rosten and Dan Gingold and to all the others who had to do with this moving and civilized production.

And please add my vote to the tally of those agreeing with KNXT's and your editorial position.

TO HOBE MORRISON / October 12, 1958

Dear Hobe:

Did you ever get the tape of the Christmas show?

I neglected to tell you the reason I stuck that archive-type identification on the box: I have a feeling that some time after we have passed from the jungle, say in seventy or eighty years, somebody digging around for Christmas literature will discover *The Plot [to Overthrow Christmas]*, and its two or three extant original editions may have some value. At that time your son, or grandson, might be amused to know that old Hobe was the only nut besides the author to have a copy of the actual show. It's the only piece of mine I feel that way about.

I have not yet recovered from the capitulation of the Braves. Say something nice to tide me over to the start of the next season. I hate the Yankees implacably, but even I had to admire the uphill push. Except I could not bear to watch the TV tube after [Eddie] Mathews struck out for the eleventh time.

TO DONNA WORKMAN, Chicago Executive
November 25, 1958

> Corwin staged a tribute to Carl Sandburg, then eighty-one, at Royce Hall on the campus of the University of California at Los Angeles. Clearances were required for the many Hollywood actors who took part.

Dear Donna:

This is late and little because I am worn to a frazzle. The *Sandburg Tribute* took what little reserve of starch I had left in me, right out. The supreme fathead who engaged me, a blunderer from the start, was a millstone around my neck. I had to bail him out of serious trouble just a week before the event. At one point it was touch and go whether the thing would go on. This fellow had failed to get the proper clearances, after assuring me and everybody else that he had taken care of this long ago. I had to stop the forward progress of the production and get him off the hook with the Theater Authority and Screen Actors Guild.

But I hope Carl has told you something about the evening. Dr. Frank Baxter got himself into trouble as M.C. now and then by trying to ad-lib between carefully prepared continuity, but the mass and momentum of the program carried right through him *and* the few weak readings out of the thirty-odd people I had up on that stage.

There are tapes of the show, and while they cannot begin to communicate the very special quality of the evening—the lights, the look of the vast stage when it slowly filled up with devotees, etc.—it still is considerably better than this hurried and bare description.

My film work has gone apace. I worked harder on the Tribute than on the screenplay—and now the opening of *The Rivalry* on Broadway looms. Rehearsals start in about three weeks.

Did I tell you Carl was great on his portion of the program? You'll have to hear it to believe. Best I've ever seen him.

As for the contretemps you mention, small matter. Art is long, and attractive women are both short and par for the course. It does more honor to [Carl's] years than that whole evening at Royce Hall.

TO CARL SANDBURG / December 16, 1958

> The poet had stayed at a guesthouse on Corwin's grounds that Sandburg named "Hacienda The World."

Dear Carl:

You will recall that during your tyrannical reign over the domain of Hacienda The World, we discussed the matter of your representation. It seemed to me that you were being constantly undersold. I am still smarting over the inequity of your $3,500 fee on the [Milton] Berle show, for an appearance that took you clear across the country and demanded three full days of rehearsal. The price tag should have been closer to $7,500.

Again, I do not think that Sandburg should entertain an offer of $2,500 to write an article based on a jet flight across the country. Even I, who have not Sandburg's genius, Pulitzer awards, credits or uniqueness, have been paid $2,000 for a single page in Collier's. And in those days, the dollar was worth a dollar.

At the time we first chewed over this matter, I suggested an agent who has my unqualified respect, to say nothing of affection. I can speak with added objectivity since she is not my own representative. Her name is Mrs. Lucy Kroll. Among her clients is Helen Hayes, whose affairs she has handled with singular skill. She not only has sound literary judgment, but an awareness of the market which I am afraid your present representatives may not fully possess. I mean nothing derogatory to your present management—but let's face it, Mickey Mantle has a better batting average than, say, Peewee Reese.

For example, I think that your Berle appearance should have been followed by a rash of other offers. I don't know whether any more such appearances would even interest you, but the fact is that "offers" are not unilateral; they are most often stimulated by the suggestion or planting of an idea by an agent in the right places. Moreover, there are certain shows that you should never be seen on. Berle's is not one of them, and I won't mention the others, just in case this letter falls into the hands of the enemy. But Lucy would know which is which; and knowing it, would exploit that knowledge by demanding and getting the fees which are your due.

I have told Lucy that I am writing you about her, and have also warned her that you are the world's most delinquent correspondent. But in this matter your delinquency might cost you moola of the realm. I have suggested that Mrs. Kroll drop you a line, so you will be hearing from her directly. Incidentally it may interest you to know how she looks on the prospect of handling you. A letter from her of recent date says, "If there is anything I can do, let me know, as it would be a happy achievement in my career if I could, in any way, serve this great man with all my heart and dedication."

The town is still buzzing about the *Tribute*, and the mail is still coming in. The enclosed is from one Fritz Blocki. I have written him warning that you never answer mail.

The tapes have just come from UCLA, after much wrangling as to who owns and controls the material. I threatened them with the back of my hand unless they straightway dubbed copies for you and me, and they promised they would send you one. I listened to them the other night and I must say I have never heard you in such magnificent form. Naturally I am going to claim all the credit for this, as it was our fried eggs, the inspiration of my mineral specimens, and the stern discipline I imposed on you which produced the happy result.

The planning of a commercial evening based on the formula of the *Tribute* is even now going forward, and tonight I meet with a millionaire producer who is hot to undertake it. More of this later....

TO BEULAH BELKOWITZ / January 26, 1959

Dear Boo:

I don't generally take down the conversations of others except when I am reporting, but I couldn't resist a phone call to Tony the other day. A friend of his named Eddie, also six years old, had rung him. I picked up the extension in the guesthouse, thinking the call might be for me, and was edified by what I heard. Here's the verbatim transcript as I jotted it down. There was plenty of time to jot.

TONY: Hello?

EDDIE: Hello.

TONY: Hello.

    (long pause)

EDDIE: Are you still there?

TONY: Yes.

    (long pause)

TONY: Who is this?

EDDIE: Eddie.

    (long pause)

TONY: Why did you call me up?

EDDIE: Oh, just to say Hi.

    (long pause)

TONY: I wonder why you just wanted to say Hi.

EDDIE: Oh, I just wanted to.

TONY: Oh.
   (long pause)
EDDIE: Well, goodbye—I think I'll call you tomorrow.
TONY: Okay. Goodbye.
EDDIE: Goodbye.

Well, I think I'll write you tomorrow.
Love from all,

TO HOBE MORRISON / March 1, 1959

The Rivalry opened on Broadway in February, 1959, and
ran for eighty-one performances.

Dear Hobe:

...You are much too modest about the readability of your columns in
hardbacks. [Henry] Simon may or may not think such a book would be
commercial, but nobody can deny their attractiveness to the intelligent
reader, especially to the aficionado of theater. In any case I have written
Simon a letter, a carbon of which travels with this. Don't wait on protocol—if he doesn't call before the week is out, call him. He is a very
sweet guy, mild and a little professorial, urbane, soft spoken, with a
quick sense of humor and no little perception about his business and
almost everybody else's. He is also married to one of the most beautiful
women outside of showbiz—an offbeat beauty somewhere along the
wavelength of Leonardo. This has nothing to do with the price of your
book, but merely relates to the ornamental decor, should you ever be
invited to dinner at Henry's.

So *The Rivalry* has folded, and your pages tell me the producers
dropped $65,000. I reached first base, but got picked off the bag. I
think the figure of 65G represents some padding, or transfer of expenses
from one production to another, since they were less than 50G behind
before they had a couple of weeks in the black—but this is merely academic, as to whether the cornice dropped ten feet or eleven feet on my
head. I was not exactly enraptured by the footwork of Arthur Cantor et

als., but what did enrapture me was Whitney Bolton's summing up in his notice in the *Morning Telegraph* of 2/10/59.

> One sits there entranced by three jewel-like performances, able direction and historical words that we now know altered the shape and course of our nation. But then comes that coarse and reluctant moment which unfortunately has become a critic's untidy duty: will it take with the public?
>
> I am going to avoid this duty I have never believed in and always hated. It is not my province to forecast business at a ticket window. Not truly. That is the province of a ticket broker. I say to you I was fascinated, I was held, I genuinely thrilled to three magnificent performances—like it enormously—The Bijou is the place for you, an American, to go.

Again that terrible, ages-old dichotomy between what will do business, and what should do business. Now comes the institution of the Theater Party, and it rules Broadway with a golden scepter. For all the shortcomings of *The Rivalry*, I feel it deserved to reach second base—to run let's say twenty weeks. Twenty weeks! In the cultural center of the Western Hemisphere, ringed and crisscrossed by colleges and universities. The city that is supposed to have the country's highest IQ!

But I have long suspected our beloved old whore, Manhattan. Before either you or I were signing our names to writing, New York let down the old *World*, as Boston did its *Transcript*. It will not buy more than five hundred copies of the best book of contemporary poetry published. It watched *PM* struggle and languish. The center of liberal thought! Down went the *Compass*, down went the *Star*. *The Nation* and *New Republic* sell more copies in the provinces than they do to the population of the city.

Why does Bolton "hate" his obligation—if it is one—of forecasting business? Because, I suppose, it has been hateful from way back. If he hates forecasting he must also hate the accounting of business; i.e., the ratings, the box office returns. Hateful, perhaps, but necessary and inevitable. Yet I wonder whether we are the victims of misplaced emphases. The *premium* is almost always put on salability. How often have you heard that a product is great because it is bound "to go" on the market (like, say, hula hoops or silly putty, which made millions). Why not the reverse emphasis—that the product should go because it is great? Like *Moby Dick*, which was great but didn't go (in Melville's lifetime), or a new and exciting concerto for which the composer (Micky Rosza tells me) gets $50 if it is performed by the New York Philharmonic.

But what the hell, this is an old topic chewed to tatters at a thousand bull sessions in which both of us have engaged over the years. Except that in my case, it strikes home regularly. Not that my work is great or suffering from neglect or that I cannot make a living at it—but that I am committed to a limited audience, as in the days of the Columbia Workshop vs. Bob Hope....

TO CAROLINE ROGERS, Associate Editor, *Reader's Digest*
March 21, 1959

Dear Caroline:

I am pleased beyond measure by your report on the play [*The Rivalry*]. All the more because I had to fly back to California the morning after it opened—before the reviews were even out—and I have not been back to check on the performances from that day to this. And actors being actors, one feels uneasy about letting them carry on too long without a checkup; it's like leaving small children in a room filled with breakable *objets d'art* (the author always considers his work to be d'art). In any case, your generous and most welcome comments gratified me on that score almost as much by the sheer pleasure of hearing from you....

If you should happen to be in the neighborhood of a film named *The Naked Maja*, which bears my name as co-author of the screenplay, kindly do me the favor of not seeing it. This is the film on Goya that I was toiling at when I dropped you a line from Rome. The producers took such liberties with the script (their contractual privilege, as usual) that I am fighting to get my name off it. Such vulgarization has not occurred in the field of painting since someone cut up a Cezanne still life of three apples, because he could only afford one apple....

TO HOBE MORRISON / April 1, 1959

Dear Hobe:

I lament the fact that the pressure of getting *The Rivalry* on the stage prevented me from at least having some knackwurst and sauerkraut with you at the Blue Ribbon. But then it is always tough fraternizing with a critic who may be obliged to crack you over the pate very shortly. Not that it would put a strain on *you*, because you would pan your own grandmother if she produced a bad musical, but the strain of wondering whether my poise was showing, would be enough to make me less than debonair.

It seems only last week that I got your letter written in your own scholarly hand by lamplight at Brooks Atkinson's hacienda, but that is only because things have been so crowded I've lost sense of time. Joel Schenker told me he saw you a couple of times, and that my name crept into the conversation on its belly, and I had a great yen to see you and gas about old times (I'm approaching that age now), but there was always some part of the roof falling in on the production, or something that had to be written, or some actor to whom I had to play a cross between Erich Fromm, Polonius, Elbert Hubbard and the man who cleans out the lavatory. [Cheryl Crawford and Joel Schenker co-produced *The Rivalry*.]

The season will be running down soon, and you will have less excuse than ever for staying in that rat racetrack when you could be out here researching the progress of Little Theatre in the original home of No Theatre.

Come on out: The smog is variable but the sunshine constant. Ninety today, and I hear you have snow back there. Poor Hobe, having to take shelter against the cold at one opening after another.

Here's a closing, with my usual affectionate regards, and my constant advice: Don't take any wooden acting.

TO PAUL PORTER AND KATHLEEN WINSOR
April 3, 1959

Porter, Chairman of the FCC, and his wife, the author of *Forever Amber*, had asked Corwin for a critique of a play she had written.

Dear Paul—and Kathleen:

Work pressure has been so great that it was not until this week that I could concentrate on *America, With Love*. I am glad I waited until I could read it quietly and with full concentration, for it both demands and rewards that.

I think it is a splendid piece of writing in many ways. It moved me as few manuscripts have done. It is funny and sad and poignant and penetrating. It is, of course, in the tradition of *Our Town*—not a bad tradition—and I particularly like the two Cassys, one commenting on the other. The little Cassy is one of the most winning characters ever encountered on land or sea, and I was enchanted by her throughout—fell quite in love with her. Ruby and Frank and Russ and Jack and Peggy and Cassy's mother and father and brother, all enlisted and held my interest.

But I am sure you know yourselves, there are a few things wide and short of target. Perhaps there are too many people in this vivid and vital cross-section of life. Some of them suffer for lack of room to develop. Vivian seems to me so briefly sketched as to be a mere indication; likewise Shorty. And Ruby commits the cardinal dramaturgical sin of disappearing suddenly, on Cassy's matter-of-fact say-so, on page 125. You can't—or shouldn't—interest an audience in a character, and then drop her suddenly without further reference. To the audience it will seem as though the author did not know what to do with her, or got tired of her, or didn't care to resolve her story.

And then, with the exception of Cassy's father, the men in the play are uniformly disagreeable. Frank is mean; Shorty violent; Jack cruel to his wife, then hysterical in grief, then lecherous for the new woman; the Ivan why THE Ivan? is a bully. Only Russ and the nameless boy are nice.

But these are easily adjustable matters. What is in my opinion less easily adjusted, is the structural looseness of the work. It seems to have a rather arbitrary development, the arbitrariness of which is most clearly exemplified by the dropping of Ruby. I know what Kathleen had in mind—this is exactly how people *do* drift in and out of our ken, and it is part of the tragicomedy of human existence that people sometimes swim past us like fish under a glass-bottomed boat, and are irretrievably gone. But unfortunately what would be right and proper in a novel, will not always hold in the precincts of a play. The audience would feel cheated if somebody it has watched sympathetically from the first moment when Frank pulls her into the vacant lot, just vanishes into the wings.

Other things: Frank plays the sax too much. It is not bad on paper, but that sax would drive you crazy in the theater if it went on so long.

The kid stuff is authentic and funny and gloriously compounded, but in a script as overlong as this one, it does not consistently pull its share of the weight, and would have to be thinned out.

In my view the chief problem this play faces is the physical difficulty of production. It would require absolute genius in design, lighting and direction. The script is a deliberate and skillfully created chaos out of which the interpreters must bring a deliberate and skillful order.

Perhaps the hardest nut to crack will be getting a producer interested. For all the delight and sweetness and sadness of the script, it is a hard one to read. Partly this is due to the way the script is typed—lines running together with character designations, rather than the latter in the middle of the page and the speeches below. But still more of a disadvantage is the fact that (alas, alas) relatively few producers have the imagination to see what it can be—to see the forest as well as the trees.

In fine, I would say that *America, With Love*, has distinct possibilities in the hands of devoted and qualified people, but that it would have to be developed and refined further. The most rewarding attributes, at least to my mind, are its display of Kathleen's power, and her capacity for easy, fluent, crackling stage dialogue; her warmth; the clear pipeline she has to the wells of sympathy; the fearlessness with which she tackles a mural canvas that would terrify most playwrights; and the lifelike posture and vividness of most of her characters.

Whether *America, With Love* is the play with which Kathleen should make her Broadway debut, I don't know. There are some high snow-capped ranges between the present script and its ultimate production. But one thing I am confident of: She should write for the theater. For her first play, I would like to see a canvas of smaller proportions. Sometimes two people can create a world more dramatically than twenty. Look at Adam and Eve—and they had only two props—an apple and a snake.

TO DORIS WARNER VIDOR / June 8, 1959

Corwin wrote on the death of her husband, the film director Charles Vidor.

Dear Doris:

Words are poor ambassadors of our feeling for you in this hour, but surely you know what that feeling is. Charles was that rare combination of artist and citizen, highly articulate and talented as each, whose principles were not dulled by disuse after he reached professional and worldly success. He deserved that success, enjoyed it, and made his audiences and friends beneficiaries of it.

Along with his vast charm, Charles had a supreme knack for telling off satraps and pompous people—a skill at deflation which is badly needed in this world, and has been somewhat in eclipse since the passing of men like Bernard Shaw. We heard Charles demolish a famous lady diplomat [Clare Boothe Luce] in the Hornblow living room one night—and also read his brilliant and electrical retort to a producer's nagging memorandum in that *Life* article on the Hemingway picture. On both of these occasions, as at other times, he was a personal hero to us.

Though we saw him all too little in these last years, we shall miss him with a special keenness, not just because he was a fighter for the good things, and a luminous person, but for all the warm and strong things that were in his nature. And the love and admiration we bear for you is further cause for our attachment to his memory. None of these shall fade.

TO CARL SANDBURG / Eastland Hotel, Portland, Maine,
September 21, 1959

> Corwin had adapted Sandburg's work for a stage produc-
> tion called *The World of Carl Sandburg*. Bette Davis and
> her husband, Gary Merrill, were taking the play on a
> national tour.

Dear Carl:

For your archives, as well as for the Sandburg Room at the
University of Illinois, I enclose half a dozen baggage labels of the kind
that will be plastered over the luggage of Bette Davis, Gary Merrill,
myself, electricians, sound men, stagehands and others who travel with
the show. This is your certificate of baptism in the theater.

This communique, issued from the trenches, is to alert you to an
invitation from Wyoming. On October 18th or 25th (your availability
being the deciding factor between the two dates) a massive bronze head
of Lincoln is going to be unveiled above the Lincoln Highway near
Laramie. It has been sculpted by an old friend of mine, Professor Robert
Russin, who may be counted among the legion of your worshippers.
Knowing I have been associated with you in assorted crimes across the
years, he asked if I would put in a good word for your presence on the
occasion of the dedication, as principal speaker. Your fare would of
course be paid, and if you cared to address the culture vultures of the
University there would be a fee for that.

The strategy in Russin's mind was for me to soften you up, and for
Senator O'Mahoney of Wyoming to follow up with a call. The Senator,
who claims he knows you, will call whether or not I soften you up; and
I have advised Russin that it takes a tougher ore-crusher than I am to
soften C.S. on anything involving anything. But I told him I would
pass along the word, which I am sure as hell doing, am I not? If you can
make either date, please flash me the word, and I will relay it and there
will be a big time in Laramie.

To *The World of Carl Sandburg*: As you know, we are using
"Elizabeth Umpstead." [In Sandburg's poem Elizabeth Umpstead
describes herself bitterly as "the most beautiful nigger girl in northern

Indiana."] But there is not the slightest chance of our being able to keep it in the program in the South. Even Washington, D.C. is questionable. Would you consider making any changes in the poem for that part of the world, or will you take a chance on it if we will?

Wait till you see Gary do "Sliphorn Jazz." Yah yah loo loo.

TO MR. HORACE CASSELBERRY / November 27, 1959

Dear Mr. Casselberry:

Years since I heard from you—and—shame on me—months since I got your kind letter. It is good to know that my old critics have not all faded away, and I very much appreciate your thoughtfulness in writing.

In regard to *The Naked Maja*, there is very little I can say without launching into a twenty-page diatribe. I made every effort to have my name taken off the picture but was unsuccessful. Whole scenes and characterizations were altered without my permission—indeed, without my knowledge, after I had returned to the United States from Italy where the film was produced. I can only say regretfully that the film was a travesty of a great artist, and I am sorry I was not able to disassociate myself from it.

TO DR. WILLIAM B. OBER / November 27, 1959

Dear Bill:

...You have a magic pen. You must be tired by now of hearing me harp on the need for you to broaden out into the literary world. I feel that if you lived out here, or if circumstances were such that I saw you once a week, I would get you to do it....

I am sorry you feel ill-disposed toward Brooks Atkinson. I think he is a giant by comparison with Walter Kerr. Atkinson was wonderful critically to *The Rivalry*, but apart from this personal reason for liking him, I have felt that over the years his style has been literate, his sympathies liberal, and his heart compassionate.

The Sandburg tour has been spotty in the extreme. It played to packed houses and glorious reviews in Philadelphia, strikebound Pittsburgh, and Toronto, but has been playing to half-empty houses elsewhere in the provinces. Davis is worried that she has ceased to be a draw, and combined with the fatigue of touring, yearns to get out. It is a hard road to hoe, this concert theatre racket.

It is still too early to say whether we will be going into New York next season. It all depends on Bette and other factors beyond my control. As it is, Gary Merrill must be replaced by Cameron Mitchell after the holidays, and this chore is going to take me back East for a spell....

I invented an epitaph for a very arrogant friend of mine, who has made a career of telling people to go to hell. I told him the other day that when he is cremated, there should be three words inscribed on his burial urn: "Kiss my ashes."

Kate—who is almost as madly in love with your Rhoda as I am—sends kisses to her and the babies.

Write me a sample chapter.

TO BETTE DAVIS / December 9, 1959

Dear Bette:

Thanks for the letters, and the Chicago reviews. You know that impudent saying, We cried all the way to the bank? That's how we are taking the Chicago press, and how you should take it. Carl phoned me from Flat Rock last night and said that the ovations for you on the last two performances were tumultuous. It was apparently our most profitable week to date. So fuck Miss Cassidy, to use an elegant term in vogue among churchmen and statesmen. [Claudia Cassidy, a Chicago critic, had panned *The World of Carl Sandburg.*]

Not that the critics who love us are all sound and honorable, and those who don't like us, corrupt and degraded, but we know in our bones what we have and who we are and what we are doing, and by "we" I mean you and Gary and Clark and myself. [Clark Allen, a singer, was the third member of the cast.]

Advance reports on the six weeks following layoff are as optimistic as the early weeks were gloomy; we have been offered three weeks at the Huntington Hartford in Hollywood, four in San Francisco, and another three or four in Chicago. All with excellent guarantees. Hollywood is home; San Francisco is so pleasant it can't be considered the road; as for Chicago, I have no frame of reference, and you do, having played there.

This letter is rushed, but I wanted to get it off to you before you board the choochoo for these parts and are incommunicado in a compartment for three days. Yankee, come home!

TO EDELAINE HARBURG / February 8, 1960

Dear Eddie:

That mysterious voice you heard on the telephone that night in New York; i.e., I, called you back at a later time only to be rebuffed by a No Answer. I had hoped to come to dinner with you, as I always like to see how the natives live, especially the working class, but the long arm of a drunken performer called me away to my touring gypsy band in Miami, and I had to flah down there. Bette D[avis], that walking tranquilizer, was in a bit of a flapdoodle because her co-star was taking a nip here and there and everywhere, and I had to go down and exercise the moral suasion of Alcoholics Anonymous.

My daughter, who yesterday lost her first baby incisor, came home in a rage from a visit to her young cousin. "Complaints, complaints," she cried, "they were all pronouncing complaints!" Was she sore on Debbie and her mother both? "Yes! The only one I feel sorry for is *Sidney!*" "Why do you feel sorry for Sidney?" "Because I didn't say hello to him when he came in." This followed by tears.

So you are coming to Cal? When, when? My Sandburg tsimmis opens at the Huntington Hartford March 1 for a three-week run. Any chance you will be here during that time?

The Story of Ruth, which I writ, has just finished being shot. Did you know that Ruth held up a bank in Moab to furnish funds for a Yemenite actors' studio? Not even many Bible scholars know this.

It is time for another Amphojel.

TO STANLEY KRAMER, Film Director **/** March 25, 1960

Dear Stanley:

I was late getting to see *On the Beach*. In it, as in all your work, you have achieved that rare and happy mutuality of art and conscience, where each serves as fighter escort to the other. And they go together with your courageous and exemplary citizenship offscreen.

On all scores I congratulate and applaud you.

TO FRANZ WAXMAN, Composer / May 6, 1960

Dear Franz:

Sam Engel has told me that you have composed a beautiful melody for the choral or solo singing of the words from Ruth's "Whither thou goest" speech, to be used in the film over the montage of the trek across the desert. [Waxman had written the score for Corwin's script, *The Story of Ruth*.]

I was disappointed—I might even say shocked—to learn of it, because I thought the idea of a sung cue had been abandoned. My disappointment is based on a powerful conviction that no matter how beautiful or attractive the melody, the singing of words at *any* time in the picture—and particularly at this point—violates style as well as good taste.

In fact, the more beautiful and successful the melody the worse for us, because it will only enlarge the mistake in proportion to its conspicuousness and importance as music....

The whole concept of the "Whither thou goest" scene was to make this famous speech occur naturally within the context of what had gone before. Both in the writing and direction great care was taken not to appear self-conscious of the famousness of the lines. In the acting and photography *no italics are used;* the lines are delivered with a beautiful and touching simplicity. But the effect of taking these words and having them SUNG in reprise by disembodied voices, enormously italicizes the speech. It says to the audience: "What Ruth has just said is so great, so sublime, so noble and famous, that we are going to sing a Hosanna to it. Ruth's words have been heard by God, and He approves of them so much that he has assigned an arranger and a chorus of angels to echo her words in the setting of a beautiful melody."

Whose voices are those? Obviously they must be angels. If not, they are the hired singers of 20th Century-Fox. Neither angels nor professional singers should play Ruth's words back to the audience. Once is enough for such a speech. Any more than that is like matzos with a fig-newton filling, in the wilderness.

Already in the picture there is a heavy program of mysticism. If we add to this the sudden appearance of unidentified voices on the sound track singing Ruth's words, we are laying on even thicker the extraneous spirituality we have tried to avoid. Its inappropriateness would be to compare similar moments in other films where exceptionally famous lines occur.

In *Helen of Troy*, did a chorus sing "Hers was the face that launched a thousand ships," after the line was spoken?

In *Hamlet* did voices sing "To be or not" after Hamlet's soliloquy?

In *Julius Caesar*, did a chorus sing, "Friends, Romans, countrymen," after Marc Anthony's speech?

In any previous Biblical picture, has a famous line by Christ, Moses or David been reprised in song?....

TO GROUCHO MARX / May 31, 1960

Dear Groucho:

Herewith a tape of *The Undecided Molecule* show for your archives.

Also, attached, a clipping from a Santa Barbara newspaper which you might want for your zany file, or which you might want to take out and study should you feel the need to be depressed.

May fortune smile on all your endeavors, and the Revenue Department smile on all your fortunes.

TO MARIANNE RONEY [who had sent the Corwins several Eskimo sculptures] / June 7, 1960

Dear M:

Came yesterday a magnificent Eskimo hauling what appears to be a dead wolf over his right shoulder. He has a long, scowling expression and deeply brooding eyes; obviously he has been reached by civilization.

You know my weakness. I am mad for these figures. Whoever got the inspiration to harvest and market this sculpture is a friend of man, and I honor Serena Roney for her part in the scheme.

Myself, I am no friend of man this month. The allergy season is upon me, and to make certain that I flounder in a raging sea of allergens, the winds of April have been whipping dust into San Fernando Valley. Last night I drove over Beverly Glen, and from the ridge at

Mulholland I looked down into the valley and lo, there was a weird El Greco light that was neither day nor night, neither haze nor smog, but only a peculiar dust-filled atmosphere. Dante's list was incomplete: There is an inferno of ragweed and all the torment-type pollens, where no antihistamines are available. To this hell are consigned men of fifty who create nothing but complaints that they aren't creating.

Last week I was in Yosemite for the first time. It was still off-season; one could find a cabin on the valley floor, even without having wired reservations. The snows were just melting and the falls were full and thunderous. Thoreau and Muir were right, of course. But in their day the dazzling blue of the sky over the Sierra was not sliced by the vapor trails of military jets.

Ruth is finished. I will say nothing about it. It is by no means as bad as the Goya picture but also by no means as good as the Van Gogh. *Sandburg* is cleaning up in San Francisco after four glorious weeks at the Huntington Hartford here in Hollywood. Makes up for some of those miserable pickings in the East. On the 23rd the tour stops and does not go forward again until October, when we are tentatively booked to go into the Lyceum.

Between now and then I hope to start on some writing for myself. If not there will be a serious rupture in diplomatic relations between me & me. But between you & me, no change, I trust: Naught but the best thoughts; accompanied this time by my delighted thanks, and accompanied always by my love.

P.S. The Eskimo sits looking down at me from a shelf in my study, and when I pace, as often I do, the angle changes on him so that now he looks like a little Buddha and then like one of the Ramses figures from around Luxor way, and then, especially back-view, like one of the exquisitely fat-assed pre-Columbian sculptures—but mostly he looks like himself, a brawny, well-biceped, blubber-ballasted primitive whose women shampoo their hair in nice, foamy piss. The world needs more of them. I have never heard of a war between Esquimaux.

TO RABBI DAVID MAX EICHHORN / July 10, 1960

Rabbi Eichhorn, a friend of Corwin from the Springfield days, had written a letter criticizing Corwin's screenplay for the 20th Century-Fox film, *The Story of Ruth*.

Dear Dave:

Thank you for writing.

You rest your criticism on an abstraction, which I quote:

> *The Story of Ruth* could have been a truly great movie if it had succeeded in reflecting the profound kinship with all humanity felt by the writer of the Biblical Book of Ruth.

What is the profound kinship with all humanity? The love of a young widow for her mother-in-law, and the love of an aging farmer for an attractive kinswoman? Wherein is the "profound" kinship with all humanity?

All humanity includes Moabites. What about Ruth's kinship with the people she forswore? "Thy people shall be my people" is at bottom a rejection of Ruth's own people. Where are the mighty overtones of universal truth, the profundities that might have made the movie great if only they had been reflected?

Dummelow [a Biblical commentary] quotes a Biblical authority as saying: "The Book of Ruth presents us with a simple story of domestic life—much as has happened, and is happening over and over again in this world—the familiar story of a daughter's affection and a young wife's happiness." I am aware that this innocent story was the vehicle of liberal protest against Ezra's narrow nationalism. But I am confused as to the basis of your objection. On the one hand you define the Bible story as "a liberal's protest"; on the other you say it "breathes sweetness and light"; then you charge the picture with distorting "the spirit of the Biblical story."

Obviously you feel the distortion is of the spirit of sweetness and light, not of the social-protest aspect, for the picture not only honors but amplifies the original author's "liberal protest" against narrow nationalism. I attempted merely to combine the sociological objective with the love story.

You say: "There is not the slightest indication in the Biblical story that Ruth was received by most of the Jews in any other but the most kindly and friendly spirit." I note that you are careful to say "most" and not "all" Jews received her cordially. Boaz in the Bible tells Ruth, "Have I not charged the young men that they shall not touch thee?" Why would he say that if most of the young men in the wheatfield (let alone the city) had received her kindly.

Yes, the Biblical story does breathe sweetness and light. So much so that this charming idyll has been largely dismissed by generations of lay readers as pretty but dull, charming but vapid. I bristle as much as you do at such a characterization of this lovely story, but the facts are hard and they support me. Not long ago I addressed one thousand Jewish women at a luncheon. I asked how many were familiar with the Biblical Book of Ruth. Six raised their hands.

You speak abstractly of "the spirit of the Biblical story." You don't have to be a dramatist or producer to appreciate that if the spirit is one of sweetness and light alone, there is no play, no movie. There is a poem, an idyll, but not a work for stage or screen....

You chide the film for not having reflected a profound kinship with all humanity. There are probably a dozen reasons why the film could not be truly great, but the reason you suggest is not one of them. I believe that a story in which narrow nationalism, xenophobia, suspicion and hostility are overcome by steadfast love, faith in God, and the workings of a highly conceived Judaic justice, is more akin to the humanity you speak of, than the "simple story of domestic life" that Dummelow's scholar mentions, or the sweetness and light you feel has been distorted.

I disagree with your notion that people go to see a Biblical movie believing it will be scrupulously accurate. I think they go hoping to be entertained, enthralled, moved or edified. If the pictorial reproduction is scrupulously accurate, all the better. I personally wish it to be; wherever there is substance that yields to scholarship I insist on it; but unfortunately there is little such substance in the Book of Ruth.

I warmly appreciate the interest and regard that prompted you to write, and the frankness of your very welcome point of view. However, I am afraid that when you accuse me of distorting the spirit of the Bible, you are being to interdramatization what Ezra was to intermarriage—a nationalist. I say this, of course, in the friendliest spirit.

With warmest regards as always, I am, Sincerely,

TO KATHERINE CORWIN / From Ogunquit, Maine, September 7, 1960

Darling:

We reopened in the local playhouse last night, before a half-filled house. I do not count it a blessing that Elliot Norton, the best of Boston's drama critics, was in the audience. The good news is that Leif Erickson was in some ways an improvement over his two predecessors, Gary [Merrill] and Barry [Sullivan].

Jim Clavell, who wants me to direct his stage play, is here in Ogunquit, and I work with him on revisions in my spare time. [James Clavell's later novels included *Shogun*. His play, *White Alice*, was never produced.]

After the performance there was a cast and crew party at Bette's [Bette Davis's] place. A torrent of dirty stories, and much merriment. I was challenged to write a half dozen limericks on the names of people present, including Clavell. The party was hale but not rowdy, nobody got drunk, and bawdy limericks were a reasonable requirement. I attach nine out of the dozen I wrote on short order.

For Clark Allen—
> There was a young singer named Clark
> Who thought a distinguishing mark
> Of class was to speak
> With accented chic,
> Like, "Kindly disrobe and let's fark."

For our electrician, Paul—
> An electrical gaffer named Paul

Was blessed with a third and fourth ball.
    Whenever he screwed
    He got so confused
He couldn't keep track of them all.

For Jim Clavell—
    A writer by name of Clavell
    Attached to his dingus a bell
        He tiptoed by day
        In the quietest way
    But his nights were as noisy as hell.

For Bette—
    Our passionate yen for Miss Davis
    Is based on the hope that she'll crave us.
        If we had our way,
        We'd get in the hay,
    And then, O God help us and save us!

For Irving Sudrow—
    A wild Angeleno named Sud
    Lay down with a maid in the mud;
        Instead of soft cries
        And languorous sighs,
    He shouted, "O shit and O crud!"

Leif Erickson—
    A cynical actor named Leif
    Once disguised his tool as a fife;
        The least of his tunes
        Were wonderful boons
    To his utterly transported wife.

A friend of Bette's, named Gibbs—
    A curious fellow named Gibbs

Just loved to kiss girls on the ribs
 And such was his passion
 The girls set a fashion
Of bosom-enveloping bibs.

Another friend, named Lane—
 A lascivious lecher named Lane
 Was the scandal of Ogunquit, Maine:
  He molested a goose
  (Who it's true was quite loose)
 And knocked up a Canadian crane.

After Ogunquit, the tour starts. Grunt, grunt.

TO AGGIE GREY / October 5, 1960

Corwin had gone to Apia, Western Samoa, with composer
Lyn Murray to research a project on Robert Louis
Stevenson, who was buried on Vaea Mountain. They
stayed at the hotel owned by Aggie Grey, who was consid-
ered to be the model for James Michener's Bloody Mary in
Tales of the South Pacific.

Dear Aggie:
 Talofa. I suppose you will have some trouble remembering me, what
with the procession of adventurers and desperate characters through
Apia around the year. I am Norman Corwin, still slightly out of breath
from climbing Vaea. The enclosed clipping from the *Los Angeles Times,*
showing how much of a flap we made when Lyn Murray and I headed
for Upolu, should help to remind you of us....
 A few days after I got back from Apia, my little boy fell ill, and we
called in the pediatrician who has attended both our children almost
since they were born. He happened to see one of the Samoan war clubs I
bought at Allen's store, and his face lit up. "Where did you get that?" he
asked. When I told him that I had been to Upolu and stayed at Aggie

Grey's, he all but embraced me....He is Dr. Eugene Gettelman, who claims that he launched you in the hamburger business. Small world.

I suppose you know that your picture is in the current issue of *Holiday* magazine, the de luxe travel publication of this land. I would send it along with this letter, except that I want to hold it as blackmail, or rather as a hostage, to make sure that you reply to this letter....

Neither Murray nor I have yet had a chance to get cracking on the Stevenson musical, but it is high on the agenda for the first part of '61. [The Stevenson project was not realized.] In the meantime, I hope we shall hear from you, or see you if you come up this way. We have not forgotten a minute of our week in Apia, including Lefaga but mainly centering around Aggie's precincts; nor are we ever likely to forget it. A tribute to you.

Please write when you have a moment, and tell me how things go with you....

TO EDELAINE HARBURG / October 22, 1960

Dear Edelaine:

Your letter is the bluest note I've ever heard from you, and I know why. You are worried that Nixon won't make it. Such a good man. So useful. He makes me feel better, just to look at him. For example, the other night I had indigestion and had reached an impasse. Then I tuned in the debate, saw Nixon's face, and threw up. A wonderful relief.

You are late getting to the mainland, if by so doing you had hoped to see *The World of Carl Sandburg*. It closed after four weeks, proving once again that what the country as a whole takes to its bosom, New York rejects. It is the biggest hick town in America, and it's not a case of sour grapes or sauerbraten but the little old truth. What other city has made the Theater Party a bigger institution than the Catholic Church?

As for the Sandburg show, save for the increment that ain't, and whatever small considerations of track record and prestige are involved, I am peculiarly undisappointed. I had come to loathe the piece, having had my nose in it for an unconscionably long time. I had to direct no less than four different men in the Gary Merrill role, and each time it was over and over and over with the same material. I felt like a teacher who stands still while generations of chilluns pass through his little red schoolhouse....

Speaking of chilluns, ours are glorious. Tony, eight, plays chess with dash, puts model planes together like a scion of the Boeings, and draws like a cross between LeCorbusier and Miro. Diane does art work that could possibly rescue that kooky Guggenheim illustrated ramp; also ballet and kibitzing at chess.

I go east in three or four weeks to direct a play for Roger Stevens. Something called *White Alice* by someone named Jas Clavell. If you and Ypres are back at the old multiple dessert counter, I propose a summit meeting. Summit later than it should be, but better late than, etc....

TO RICHARD LINKROUM / December 2, 1960

> Linkroum, Corwin's associate at CBS, had moved to NBC, where he urged the network's executives to hire Corwin as a writer and producer but found the blacklist still in force.

Dear Dick:

...Never for a minute did I doubt your good faith, nor do I now. The situation is morally somewhat like what has been going on lately in New Orleans, where righteous white mothers have been cursing and ranting against priests and ministers because a little colored girl might be in the same classrooms with their corruptible kids. We understand the madness, we despise and pity it; but it goes on, and while it lasts the White Mothers will feel wholesome and upright and noble, perfectly convinced they are acting for the good of their state, their country and their God. As we both know, that feeling can never make them right; and so it is with the White Fathers of your network.

TO DR. STERLING M. McMURRIN / February 1, 1961

Dear Sterling:

Congratulations on the appointment [President John F. Kennedy had appointed Professor McMurrin of the University of Utah as U.S. Commissioner of Education.] It is wonderful to see the country placed in the hands of friends who are also scholars and gentlemen. Between

Ed Murrow and yourself, both partes infidelibus and fidelibus will be well taken care of.

I am happy for the Administration, the states, the people, and Education. All are lucky to have you....

Warmest best wishes to you and Natalie.

TO MERCEDES McCAMBRIDGE, Actress / February 16, 1961

Dear Mercedes:

Please revise your present estimate of Kate and me as barbarians for not having earlier sent you a message of thanks for your inscribed copy of *The Two of Us*. The hit-and-run character of your dropping it off prevented us from thanking you then and there.

I have delayed writing you until now because I wanted to read it first—a logical and plausible condition, you must admit. But I was so swamped with work that I did not get to the book until last weekend, and then I read it straight through with complete fascination.

...I suffered with you on that dreadful airplane; itched sympathetically when you were invaded by les pus on shipboard (made me think of the gift robe that Medea sent to Jason's wife—surely the properties of wrapping its wearer in flames is not much worse than lying under a bedbug-infested blanket!). And the old witch with the septic needle! I tell you, it is at times a harrowing account.

I identified with quite a few of your experiences. The very first trip I made to Europe was a third-class affair; and while it was spared bedbugs and threats of quarantine, it was a nightmare on several other levels. I spent most of my time in romantic Venice, in the British-American hospital; I sprayed fountain-pen ink on my only suit; broke my eyeglasses; dropped my Corona portable on a train, tried to get it fixed, found the repair man had sent it off to another city, had to wait around in a dreary place until it returned—not fixed, of course. Believe me, travel abroad is for those who can afford it. First class or army service—there is no really reliable middle zone.

Anyway we are delighted to have *The Two of Us* in our library. I shall keep it lying face up on some surface, for the picture on the jacket is pure joie de vivre—cool, refreshing, gay and sexy, all at once....

TO HOBE MORRISON / March 30, 1961

Dear Hobe:

...Your last letter to me is perhaps the best traveled piece of mail in history. Ever since I got it last June (!!!) I have carried it in a folder marked CURRENT, which contains only that correspondence which I intend to answer before the week is out....

The past year has not been dedicated to anything epic....A near-miss on directing a play for Roger Stevens (sets half-built by Meilziner, a cast all set to go on a script by James Clavell, when David Wayne defected after agreeing to play); two screenplays marinated in antiquity (currently *The King Must Die* for 20th-Fox—the Theseus legend as souped up by Mary Renault); the slow accumulation of material for two books I have in mind (riding two snails at once); and the usual quota of chores for good causes—panels, symposia, meetings of the Board of such outcroppings as the UCLA Theater Group; submission to the drafts of PTA Meetings because my next-door neighbor is the Jean D'Arc of this movement, and I like peace in my neighborhood; service on the Documentary Committee of the Academy; lectures at the University of Utah and UCLA (my revenge for never having made the grades requisite to *enter* a college); shepherding the latter-day career of Carl Sandburg; and so on and on and on, through the interstices of family and community life.

Not long ago I moderated a panel on *The Critic and the Artist*, and thought of you a hundred times before, during and after. A fair battery: Arthur Knight, Dick Williams, Larry Tubelle, James Powers, Ray Bradbury, Michael Gordon, Peppi Schildkraut, Rod Serling, Jack Lemmon. Little patches of fur and globs of gore were evenly distributed over the scene by the end of the session, and nothing was changed. But it's better than sitting at home reading [John] O'Hara or the philosophy of Ayn Rand.

Are you still a neighbor of Brooks Atkinson? Lucky man, you are. Why must he happen only once in a century of the *Times*? And cannot he be coaxed from retirement? We need him more than he needs rest. It is unfair to ask Morrison to carry the load alone.

By being east, and so stubbornly resisting the attractions of this part of the world, you have missed one of the most degrading political campaigns in the history of the West. By this I mean the war of the trade ads for Academy nominations. The propaganda barrage in behalf of *The Alamo* makes the East-West thing seem like a discussion of weather at a Hokinson tea party. Obscene. The composer of every little fart of a song has carried on as though he wrote *Aida*.

For about ten minutes back there, I thought we were on the verge of another Rooseveltian Golden Age. I mean, when a POET gets up at an inaugural, and the Foist Lady digs the ballet and modern painting, and men who can read and spell are appointed to cabinet posts. Even I, old New Deal minnesinger, was summoned by the new Lorenzo di Medici, Mr. Frank Sinatra, to write an Invocation for the snowbound Gala. I did; it was read to empty seats by Freddie March. I later heard that the President's father, Old Joe, was much taken by the words. Remind me to retire that particular invocation.

I am fidgeting, and have been for years, to do a piece of theater that approaches language without embarrassment. Save for [Christopher] Fry, who is somewhat precious and, in his imagery too often effete, no writer in English that *I* know of, is attempting anything that comes close to being Verse Drama. It is a term in bad odor, even. From Fry it seems tolerable; from [Jean] Anouilh, perfectly acceptable, because it is an import and one expects a certain exoticism to go with the foreign stamps on the wrapping. But let an American raise his sights, and POW! Yet as I say this, I think of the glad hand accorded Archie MacLeish for *JB*, and the relative success of [Robinson] Jeffers with *Medea*. Perhaps I am thinking of the movie critics. Dare one dust a few grains of poetic powder over a domestic film script, and Bosley Crowther will have your bowels out to dry like so much copra in Yap. Unless, of course, the poetry is in French, as in the somewhat arty-farty opening sequence of an otherwise formidable film, *Hiroshima Mon Amour*.

But here I am grousing when I should be exchanging personal intelligence, like the fact that when I was attending my cactus garden back of the house—a quixotic pride of mine—I last week managed to achieve what for two years I had somehow avoided by instinct—a quiverful of sharp spines in my ass. All I had to do was back into the fiercest stand of opuntia, and I did it.

Having an eight-year-old boy has led me into the happy second childhood of telescopes, microscopes and such gismos. Last week I got a beautiful view of the crescent Venus. Plainly written across the south polar region was VOTE FOR THE ALAMO.

I ramble, sir, and that is no thing to do after such a long hiatus. Let's make it shorter and shorter. You are one of the few aristocrats left. Warmest best ever and aye.

TO CARL SANDBURG / April 20, 1961

Dear Carl:

I have just finished reading [Sandburg's poem] *Timesweep*, and I am so rocked by it that I have to put my thoughts and comments down right now before they cool off. It is as cosmic in its way as Einstein's formulas; you have wiretapped the mysteries, and no jury will find against you.

All the sciences come up and report for duty and are duly registered and sent away to mind their considerable businesses. Your great verse on page 2

> The wind carves sand into shapes
> And releases them for fresh designs,
> Wind and ice are patient beyond telling
> Ice takes mountains and tips them over etc.

says everything there is to say about loess and aeolian deposits and glaciology; your "earthworms grinding limestone into loam" will stand for a fat manual on the majestic decomposition that goes on all the time in the earth's mantle; and damned if you don't have equally compact treatises on ornithology, entomology, oceanography, diastrophism, astronomy and even lepidopterology. You could put those ologies out of business if you decided to keep up this pace.

It is really an incredible Yosemite of a poem for beauty and strength and serenity and the evidence of God's hand. And it also has quiet little purls and cataracts of humor as in

> tumble bugs engaged in solemn causes

and it is terrible too as in

why have I prized my skills as a killer?

(incidentally the "my" is mistyped "b" in my copy). Also I believe there is a typo in the line of page 4:

Am I first over all, I the genius homo?

It *could* be genius, of course, but I suspect you wrote "genus."

This piece is the official anthem of the science of Natural History; the Class Song of Zoology; and one of the few tunes that could be arranged for a chorus of stars, as indicated in the book of Job where the stars sing together.

I have a couple of picky little notes no bigger than a wart on the ass of an electron. Your line

The pink nipples of the earth in springtime

bothers me because only the nipples of the *daughters* of the earth are pink; it seems to me most of the earth's own mammillae are green, or the rich brown color of loam. The line makes me see the pink nipples of virgins rather than the brown (sometimes almost black) nipples of a big bearing woman, multipara from way back; or it connotes big fat sows with an inverted Sierra of coarse pink nipples; or a cow with tumescent udder.

On page 14 you say

the splinters of an arc of northern lights

and again I am jogged momentarily out of my transport, by a word. Most of the northern lights I have seen were drape-like—flowing, subtle, with an aery gelatinous quality, and never a suggestion of the shard or the angular and sharp appendage or protuberance suggested by the image of a splinter. Also, can one say that an arc has a splinter? A tangent may sideswipe it or shatter into splinters, but an arc can't help having grace—it was born with it.

One more notion and I am done: In the marvelous passage on 17 beginning "deep roots moving in lush soil" you can to the Gobi and Mojave with

Tangled and winding roots in desert wastes rising into
cactus and the joshua tree to bring a hush on the air etc.

I miss the music of the word "yucca" where it might fit the melody. The Joshua tree is a yucca (yucca brevifolia and damn proud of it) and I have always had a soft spot in my left ear for the sound of the word and its connotation of Spaniards in armor crossing the hot desert and stopping to name flora as they went on their way to finding the big puddle of the Pacific.

A giant constellation of a poem, Carl. You ain't what's wrong with the spiral galaxy in which we live....

TO DOLORES RUBIN, Script Supervisor / May 3, 1961

Dear Loll:

You leave Literary America abandoned and bereft by taking yourself to the Mediterranean basin. Sandburg has asked for you again. When you get to Athens you must look up Homer. Only the fact that he is blind gives me any hope that he will let you go....

TO EDELAINE HARBURG / May 15, 1961

Sweet Edelaine:

You must never write on both sides of the paper, silly. It makes your letters very hard to frame unless the frame has windows on both sides and is kept revolving like a vertical barbecue.

Telling me of the atrocities of critics is like carrying coals to Goldfarb (changed his name to Newcastle when he struck it rich). I have long been a student of this branch of perversion, and have in my private museum several lampshades made out of the skins of poets, to say nothing of the bladder of a playwright which was used by a critic's child as a floating toy in a swimming pool. Have you never read Nicholas Slonimsky's *A Lexicon of Musical Invective?* It is the definitive report on the collective Eichmanns of criticism from Beethoven onward, and a single reading will immunize you for life against any lasting hurt from a critic. I commend it to you and Yip.

As for [Cyril] Ritchard, I have never liked the man or his work since the night I heard him on a Mike Wallace interview, telling how he and his friends used to sit out on their front lawn, enjoying drinks and canapes in the cool of the evening, while the Battle of Britain went on in the air miles overhead. He spoke of this with a relish and glowing nostalgia for the English countryside and his warm and good friends, and the thrilling spectacle of planes getting shot down—rather splendid sight, you know—for which they had "box seats" or some such nauseating phrase. In the same breath he told Wallace that he had no use for *The Diary of Anne Frank*, which had not long before that, won the Pulitzer Prize on Broadway. Why? Because the theatah is for Entertainment. People don't want to go to a Theatah and feel bedly. I for one have had my quota of Ritchard and his glutinous pomposity. A director who cannot understand "In Olympus it is your virtue, down here it is your problem," has no business directing that work.

But then Yip seems to have an affinity for pinhead directors and producers. Windust, Merrick, and now Ritchard. Maybe he has a neurosis that loves trouble. One of these days he must come to ME to direct a show....Just think what it would mean: We would crown a loving acquaintance of forty-six years by a joint enterprise that would leave us exhausted, lacerated, not speaking to each other, cross-filing law suits for libel and defamation, but SUCCESSFUL! Artistically, I mean. You don't expect to make MONYEH out of art, do you?

You ask about my kinder. They are glorious and beautiful. Did I tell you that I got an angry note from Diane reading, "I hate you! Love, Diane." Not long ago the following conversation took place between Kate and Tony while driving:

TONY: I don't like Paul.
KATE: Why?
TONY: He says things like, "Aw, fuck."
KATE: (startled) That's a very offensive word.
TONY: What does it mean?
KATE: (unprepared; stalling) What does *what* mean?
TONY: Offensive.

Now how about Rod [Gorney, her son] and a woman for same? I cannot play my award-winning Fixit role with the subject so far removed. Legend has it that Rod occasionally makes trips to the Los Angeles Metropolitan District, but never, according to the names registered in our guest book and the records kept by the CIA, have we had the honor of so much as a telephone call from the doctor. You have to admit this handicaps me slightly toward making a *shidduch* [Yiddish for a romantic match] (I know the phonetic spelling is *shittuch*, but life is difficult enough as it is); and usually the ravening long-waisted beauty wants to *meet* the man to whom I am marrying her off.

Though Rod has dropped us, I am very pleased that his parents haven't. And in consideration of our old and tender bonds (E, F and some municipal) I warrant that I will perform such services out of sentimental motives, topped off by a nominal exercise of my droit de seigneur, especially if she has long legs and a firm pair of melons.

It is a pleasure to do business with you Harburgs, but I am kept in a constant state of confusion and tension by the fact that you never give me optional or alternate addresses, so that I don't know whether this priceless letter will enjoy viewership in Chilmark, or deadlettership in Washington.

Katherine, who is five weeks past an hysterectomy and doing well, joins me in sending love.

TO HERBERT MITGANG / May 20, 1961

Dear Herb:

Shock and chill are the right words about Gertz's death. [Mitchell Gertz had been literary agent for both Corwin and Mitgang, who worked at CBS before he moved to *The New York Times*.] I had no knowledge that he was ill; he had been taken to the hospital after a heart attack, and was there two or three days before he died.

...I went to the funeral. It was incongruous. Not that death makes much congruity at any time, especially when it is untimely; but that genial, cigar-loving, verbose and gently schmaltz-given man who so looked to his friends and his children for the warmth and affection without which he took no pleasure from his deal-making, this type fellow seemed miscast in a horribly splendid casket.

It was in a chapel on Santa Monica in Westwood that the services were held. The rabbi made a long and quite good and moving address, for Mitch was a trustee of his synagogue and they were long friends. But when for the first time in his oration he actually mentioned Mitch's name, his voice was smothered by the roar of a diesel truck pounding past the building. Proper billing is difficult even in death, it would seem. At the end of the service, I got caught in a line of people who paraded past the casket. I should have known better than to look on his face for the last time. The art of the mortician had composed his face in a smile he never knew or used, or would have chosen to effect in all his fifty years. Thus death vies with the cigarette commercials on TV: It is kind to the T-zone; it relaxes.

I did not know Mitch all that well; he handled only one deal for me, though he had gone to bat several times in my behalf; we had maybe a dozen or fifteen meetings only, in the few years I knew him. Yet I left that chapel choked and chilled and angry with the stinginess of the lease we all have on life, considering the vasty eternities that preceded and will follow us, and in a suppressed rage against the subhumanity of the undertakers, who by the way have a powerful lobby in California.

I certainly did not mean for this to be a grim letter, particularly as none of the above reflects the genuine pleasure I had in hearing from you. I had meant for two weeks—more—to report my delight in seeing your name on the *Sandburg at Gettysburg* show. I watched it at Carl's side in a viewing room at KNX-TV, along with George Stevens and a few people from his unit. The minute it was over I asked Carl how he had worked with you, and he told me you had composed the questions. That went a long way toward explaining the brilliance of the show: one of the truly great all-time TV documentaries.

About *The Return* [Mitgang's novel, which had just been published]. I stubbornly cling to my belief in the novel as the basis of an extraordinarily strong picture. It must be shot in Italy and Sicily. It has everything that I, for one, feel should be in a contemporary film—people, countryside, issues, conflict, heart and meaning. It has bitterness and sweetness and toughness and exaltation. Whoever represents it, now that Mitch has gone, should understand and love it and want to fight for it....

TO CAROLINE ROGERS / July 2, 1961

Dear Caroline:

I cannot believe weeks have passed since I got your letter. I have been madly involved in the usual too-many things at once. Narrating an oratorio with symphony orchestra was perhaps the most exotic of these activities, although introducing Eleanor Roosevelt at a luncheon was not exactly routine in my life either.

You raise some profound questions in your good letter: whether I really like it out here... and whether I am *needed*. The answer is that I like all of the physical natural things: lots of sunshine, profuse green growth, and the nearness to the desert, the mountains, the ocean. Smog is man-made, and can be unmade, and there are ponderous and slow efforts in that direction; but as for whether I am "needed"—ah, Caroline, no man is indispensable to his art or to his time! Radio needed me, but is dead; TV programming needs me, but the manipulators of the medium, and those who control it, do not have the time of day for me...nor I for them. It takes two to tango on TV as anywhere else. If you've been reading the testimony of show people before the FCC hearings, you will realize that I could never put up with the cowardice and venality of so many of the men in charge. One fellow reported that he could not use the name of Lincoln in a TV dramatization of the Andersonville Trial, because the program was sponsored by Chrysler, and the Lincoln is a competitor!...

TO ROBERT HELLER / August 30, 1961

Dear Bob:

Long time no see each other's postmarks. And long time is too long. How are you? Jeannie? The boy? Now and then some traveler returns from some bourne bearing news of you, and I am glad to say it has all been good.

Good, too, has been life on this side, save for my mother's illnesses (fractured hip and other ailments), Kate's need for surgery (happily recovered), and normal quotas of attrition and annoyance.

Thanks to a good run of work at a good rate over the past two years, I am in the mood as well as the position to do some of the things I've had to postpone from year to year: I'm tackling a book of my *own* writing for a change (as distinguished from *The World of Carl Sandburg* which Harcourt, Brace & World is publishing as a hardback this fall); and I have just finished the umptieth and final revision of *Mary and the Fairy*—a stage version, three acts long, which bears hardly any resemblance to its original radio prototype: Now it involves a scientist with a conscience, in a comedy-fantasy that makes an amusing commentary on the decay of romanticism, and tickles the paps of a few sacred cows. I despair of Broadway, which is now the joint property of David Merrick, the musical comedy profession, and the Theater Party organizations. The only hope for M & F is off-Broadway, or possibly London or maybe even Cienega Boulevard. I'd like for you to read the play, but I have a notion that you're up to your ass in TV scripts and I will not saddle you with still another ms. Should you see ahead of you a little clear sky, then I'd send it along, but not unless.

I wish there were some good excuse for me to pick up and go off to London, where I have not spent more than forty-eight hours since 1942, lo, a whole era ago. Now is an optimum time for me; I have earned the license to leave agents and producers behind me here, though I am much less sanguine about leaving my family. I'd like to take 'em with me for a year.

Of interest to you, I'm sure, is the fact that I am committed to do the opening program (hour's length) of the big F.D.R. series that ABC-TV is preparing for mid-1962. It is heartening to think that Roosevelt is not so much a swear word now as he was ten years ago, and that he rates a TV series as well as Churchill. I have not yet begun work, since the ABC boys will not be through gathering film for another month or two; and when I do get cracking, I expect to finish the job in less than six weeks. Should there be anything in your part of Her Majesty's realm that you think would be of mutual attraction, do send me word of it. I should like to think that British TV and theater have more vitality, minute by minute and line by line, than is to be found on Broadway and Madison Avenue; any less would be a bigger loss to Albion than the thirteen colonies....

TO MAX AND BERTHA BAND / September 5, 1961

Corwin had been invited to present an award to Max
Band, painter, during a California State Hadassah
Convention.

Dear Max and Bertha:

You are wrong. Absolutely wrong. Your notion that I am only a
friend in May but not September, that I am just a fair-weather
Hadassah Convention friend, is erroneous. You were wrong to have
burned my book after ripping out the inscription and trampling on it;
wrong to have written those bitter pages about me in your Memoirs;
wrong to have done that savage caricature of me and posted it on a wall
above the sign reading DEFENSE DE URINER.

No doubt my silence and incommunicability have seemed an act of
unfriendly aloofness, but the fact of the matter is that I am LOOF, not
aloof; I have been scurrying about like some demented ant, carrying
bits of desiccated leaves and grains of sand and trying to make some
kind of order out of them, and provision for the hungry ants that live
under my roof.

Kate and I think of you both often. We miss you and hope you will
not withdraw diplomatic recognition even though the expiration date of
normal friendly patience has been passed....

TO HARRY GOLDEN, Writer / October 17, 1961

Dear Harry:

Your Sandburg book is here and has been gobbled up the way kid
actors eat breakfast food in the TV commercials.

You have done it again. The breeziness, wit, charm, energy and
humanity of the first three books are back together in this one, like an
expert acrobatic team that can perform wonders on any platform,
indoors or out. And not the least triumph of your short-short technique, which I call the Golden Capsule, is the way it assimilates biography, like some powerful enzyme that can digest anything. Though
you are at pains to disclaim any pass at formal biography, the total effect

could not be improved by a scholarly work of seven volumes, at least not in communicating the essence of the man, which is after all the heart of any such undertaking.

I can tell you, as a mountain climber who knows the main faces of Everest and has had the mountain as a guest in his home for the better part of a month, that you have done a masterful job of surveying the massif, and that your picture of the peak is clear and sharp. It should delight everyone but Edmund Wilson and the ghosts of Willie Hearst and Billy Sunday.

TO GREER GARSON, Actress / December 9, 1961

Dear Greer:

Having lost your telephone number, I tried to reach you through your impenetrable organization of secretaries and palace guards, and was given stories that you were (1) in Dallas, (2) in New York, (3) in London, (4) in Bel Air, and (5) in the hearts of your countrymen. Only about this last am I certain; and surest of all that you are in *this* countryman's heart. As you know, I have never forgiven you for marrying another. The fact that my proposal would have come at least eleven years too late, and that the bigamy laws of California and Texas are rather prim, are mere technicalities.

Enough of this outpouring of passion, and to the business at hand. You will recall, if you try hard, that following the premiere of *Flower Drum Song*, I spoke to you concerning a play that I have been invited to direct for the Dallas Theater Center. I told you it was about Cardinal Wolsey; you remarked that he had no wife (he had a mistress and a natural son, but why instruct you before thousands?) and I remarked there was Ann Boleyn. Ah yes, you said, those luminous eyes brightening, so there was. I said I would get the play to you. A presentable copy has just arrived from Dallas. Here it is.

Greer, my dear sovereign Greer, you must do Ann Boleyn. As an act of noblesse oblige for Dallas and God. Do not weigh or measure the sides; Anne's is not as big a part as Wolsey's though it is next in size. It will be a glory for the theater, which is itself the glory of Dallas; it will do your soul good to speak noble lines in a beautiful play; it will be a mere local stop from your doorstep in Dallas; and I am sure that Paul Baker will arrange to seat your husband and inner retinue in the royal box. I am also sure that a date can be fixed to accommodate you. Aprilish is my own and Paul Baker's first choice.

My telephone number is STate 4-9602. Say yes.

The actress had starred in *Scandal at Scourie*, a film Corwin wrote for MGM. Neither she nor Corwin did the play discussed in the letter.

TO LILLIAN MILLER, family friend / December 19, 1961

Dear Lillian:

I got back from a stay in Utah to find your letter of the 12th with its shocking news of Sam's [her husband's] passing. My sympathy is of deep understanding, since just a few weeks ago my beloved mother died....

The world is never the same after a loved one has gone. It may be bright and have color, and life goes on being treasurable, but never quite in the same way.

I'm glad you're staying busy. That is the best balm for the hurt. Keep on, and know that you have love.

Rose Corwin died of an aneurism on October 23, 1961.

TO TED REARDON, JR., Aide to President John F. Kennedy
January 4, 1962

Dear Mr. Reardon:

I take the liberty of writing you, knowing that Bill Gordon of Beverly Hills has had some correspondence with you, and wrote you recently from his bed in St. John's Hospital, Santa Monica.

Bill has what appears to be terminal cancer. He knows it.

No man in the country has been a better or more loyal Democrat. His services to innumerable campaigns have been resourceful, unstinting, tireless and effective—always within a context of great personal modesty and integrity. He has never once asked for any favor or reward. He has been in JFK's corner for years, ever since he met him on a junket to a film festival in Argentina years back.

I realize it is asking a great deal of a burdened White House, but I know that a letter to Bill signed by the President, would brighten the last days of a noble American. Simply for the President to take note of Bill's illness and wish him a speedy recovery, would do the trick.

Naturally Bill Gordon has no idea I am writing you. Whether or not such a letter is possible, I ask you to treat in confidence this request.

TO TED REARDON, JR. / January 30, 1962

Dear Mr. Reardon:

God bless you and JFK. If you could have seen the joy that Bill Gordon got from the President's letter, your joint kindness and humanity would have felt rewarded. Bill is still in orbit. He told me that receipt of the letter gave him the biggest thrill in his life, and he meant it.

I cannot thank you enough.

TO ROBERT HELLER / March 17, 1962

Dear Bob:

I am startled to find that three weeks have passed since I received your good letter. But the explanation is as simple as it is dull: I have been down with a digestive ailment that has been giving me hell for the past three months. Since I got your letter I have been through an exhaustive x-ray diagnostic routine—several days of it—and I am glad to report that all findings were negative. In any case, the combination of this nagging complaint and fearsome work load (the relationship of the two being highly unmysterious) has kept me from normal habits, normal correspondence and even normal amenities....

Next May I will be 52. For the last dozen years I have worked mostly in the area of adaptation. Even the Lincoln-Douglas play was of that order: After all, I was merely condensing, arranging, adapting and dramatizing a big fat stenographic record. I like to think I did it artistically and well, but that is beside the point: It was not Original. The same, in spades, for the Sandburg show. The same for the film *Lust for Life*.

While *Story of Ruth* was practically an original, the question remains: original *what?* Essentially an original variation on a theme—somebody else's theme.

I have become increasingly conscious of the clatter of the wheels of time's chariot. I have found myself rejecting offers to direct plays in this last year—something I would never have dreamed of doing in previous years. I resent the time required to present someone else's work, to correct its flaws, improve its merits, be psychoanalyst and chambermaid to sundry idiots and neurotics in the cast, and sweat out the thousand details of sound, lighting, sets, etc. etc. It comes under the convenient heading of All That Jazz.

If I am a writer, if I can think, if I am friend of the Phrase, if I have a conscience, then goddam it I should be writing for myself, by myself, even of myself. I have no wish to be Susskind or Hub Robinson. If this is a big switch, then maybe it has been too long coming. If this is the voice of indigestion, then maybe it's an ill gas that blows no good.

TO DR. WILLIAM B. OBER / March 18, 1962

Dear Bill:

Thanks for that wonderful Hallmark card. I didn't know they handled that brand of Ronald Searle zaniness; I thought they were much stuffier.

Sorry to hear about Rhoda's mother's troubles. Let's face it, age is man's greatest enemy, not death or the A-bomb. Kate's father is deteriorating pitifully: heart, failing memory, eccentric behavior, reversion to infantile patterns, etc. All the charms of atherosclerosis and its allies.

You will have to revise your notions about Thoreau by reading him again. No testimony based on a reading at age sixteen will stand up. I disagree with you that he retreated from the world around him. At one point he says that he preferred not to run berserk against society, preferring that society run berserk against him, because society, and not he, was the desperate party. When have our lives ever been as desperate as society? Have WE annihilated millions, have WE concocted monumental inhumanities? Have WE devised vicious religions, did WE build slums?

I think of Thoreau as therapy against the lunacies and tensions around us. I rate him vastly higher as a writer than you are willing to do. The dull life you ascribe to him I think was the most exciting possible: a life within one's self, radiating outward. He had a kind of radium in him, powerful enough to have influenced history. Gandhi and others were inspired by his *Essay on Civil Disobedience*, and happily acknowledged their debt....Never has a man said Fuck You to the grossness of the world, with greater style, wit and staying power. Read him again, dear Bill. You are a descendant who walks in the projection of his spirit, and it hurts me to hear you speak ill of your father, whom you hardly know.

I am very happy about Norman Ober's talent. It is all you say, and all I say. Certainly not measurable by *Bungalow Nine*, which has soft and gauche areas, but by the promise inherent in this evidence of his good eye and ear. Couldn't happen to a nicer guy. As for you, I will never accept the limitations you clap down on your writing. Who asks that you resemble anyone else in the capacity to write convincing dialogue, or in your feeling for people or understanding of motivation? It is your uniqueness, not your resemblance to others, that is the valuable essence. You have a sharp, incisive, acidulous style and a dissenter's makeup. You are a maverick. All to the good. The paper on choriocarcinoma is important, but the book on your time, your life, the cast of characters with whom you have come in contact all your life, is even more important. Assign yourself to write five pages a week. It will be there before you know it....

Thanks for the continuing arrival of *MD*. And how do you like this oil-impregnated paper? It was standing on a shelf, absorbing some 3-in-1 oil from a leaky can by slow osmosis. It now has a greasy parchment quality, and maybe we have discovered something the Chinese overlooked.

TO HOBE MORRISON / March 18, 1962

Dear Hobe:

...You mention—half-jokingly—the idea of collaborating on a book of reminiscences. It is not a bad idea, and I will buy out the joke-half of the suggestion. Between us we might do an *Aubrey's Brief Lives* (which

Rose Ober at the time of her marriage.

Samuel Corwin.

Norman at age 16.

Reporter (and movie critic), age 20.

Norman and Emil improvise a citizen's arrest for drunk and disorderly conduct.

Mock dispute between Norman and brother Al over right of way, Greenfield, c. 1928.

Norman as a writer who finds himself rejected along with his manuscript, age 17.

Norman in Paris, 1931.

Norman, Emil and Alfred. Winthrop, 1926.

...oet Edgar Lee Masters autographing scripts of Corwin's adaptation of *Spoon River Anthology* for the ...st of the twentieth of the *Words Without Music* series, broadcast over CBS on May 14, 1939. Left ...right around Masters, Ed Latimer, Rosalind Gould, Cliff Carpenter, Arnold Moss, Everett Sloane, ...ene Winston, Dwight Weist, Lou Krugman, Stella Reynolds, unidentified boy, Jean Colbert, Luis ...an Rooten and Corwin.

Corwin directing *The Odyssey of Runyon Jones*, in the *26 by Corwin* series, June 8, 1941.

...ehearsing sound technicians for *Anatomy of Sound* in the *26 by Corwin* series, September 7, 1941.

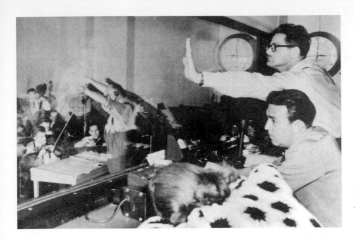

Directing *On a Note of Triumph* or V-E Day, 1945.

Rehearsal of *Wolfe*, in the *Columbia presents Corwin* series, June 13, 1944. Left to right, Charles Laughton, production aide Charles Lewin, Corwin, composer-conductor Bernard Herrmann.

With Robert Montgomery and William B. Lewis, CBS program chief, *This Is War!* series, 1942.

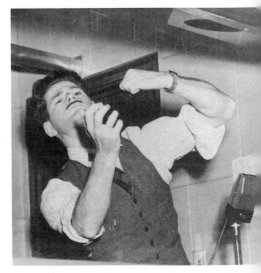

Signalling for percussive sound effect.

The company of *We Hold These Truths*, the first four network broadcast in radio history. Standing, left to right, Orson Welles, Rudy Vallee, production aide Sterling Tracy, composer Bernard Herrmann, Edward G. Robinson, Bob Burns, Jimmy Stewart, Corwin, Walter Brennan, Edward Arnold. Seated, Lionel Barrymore, Marjorie Main, Walter Huston.

Working on a script at Jones Beach.

Last-minute revision during rehearsal of a program in the *Pursuit of Happiness* series, 1939 With Burgess Meredith and Franchot Tone.

Election eve show, 1944. Column on left, Tallulah Bankhead, Irving Berlin, unidentified, Claudette Colbert, Linda Darnell, (partly hidden) Walter Huston, Groucho Marx, Jane Wyman. Right column, Constance Bennett, Mrs. Berlin, Harry Carey, Keenan Wynn, Rita Hayworth, Danny Kaye, Paul Muni.

Claire Trevor, at time of letters, 1943.

With Robert Young, star of *Passport for Adams*, 1943.

Being congratulated by the widow of Wendell Willkie at the One World Award presentation in New York. William S. Paley looks on

Speaking at a dinner in his honor at the Beverly-Wilshire Florentine Room, on the eve of his departure on the One World Flight, 1946. Left to right, Ona Masson, Edward G. Robinson, Paul Robeson, Robert Young, Charles Laughton.

Interviewing townspeople of Lavunio, Italy.

At military airport in Cairo, Egypt, with Colonel Sandy McNown and George Polk, CBS journalist who less than a year later was assassinated by a political faction in Greece.

The national radio systems of Australia and New Zealand gave prominence to Corwin's visit to those countries on his One World Flight journey. This, in four colors, was the cover of the *ABC Weekly* of September 22, 1946.

Interviewing Eduard Benes, President of Czechoslovakia, in the Presidential Palace, Prague.

Mayor Ma Chao Chun of Nanking, at Corwin's left, and members of the city government sit for a picture after an official reception.

A break in the schedule near the Forbidden City, Peiping.

Interviewing workers in a power plant outside Warsaw, Poland.

Press conference at LaGuardia Airport in New York on completion of his One World Flight.

With Fiorello LaGuardia, Mayor of New York, who succeeded Corwin as winner of the One World Award, 1947.

Daughter Diane, age 9.

Son Tony, age 9.

Katherine Locke, actress of stage and film, at the time of marriage.

Diane, art instructor, 1991.

Tony, artist, woodworker, 1992.

Fredric March, Emil and Norman, during a break in the rehearsal of *Untitled*, April 18, 1944.

Beulah Corwin (Belkowitz), Alfred Corwin and his daughters Consuelo and Vanessa, c. 1955.

Alfred Corwin in 1942.

Emil Corwin in 1989.

Unlikely chorus in a Beverly Hills living room, c. 1959. Standing left to right: Nunally Johnson, Ira Gershwin, Robert Benchley, Marc Connelly, Groucho Marx, Danny Kaye; seated, Corwin and Abe Burrows.

With Gregory Peck and Peter Lorre, in broadcast of Committee for the First Amendment over ABC, 1947.

As a guest on Fred Allen's program, NBC, 1944.

With Dore Schary, head of production at MGM, and Eleanor Roosevelt at the United Nations, c. 1951.

Corwin and Frank Sinatra after receiving Newspaper Guild Front Page Awards, Madison Square Garden, 1945.

Directing Orson Welles in *God and Uranium*, August 14, 1945

Dr. William B. Ober, author, pathologist, musicologist.

With David Ben-Gurion, Prime Minister of Israel, in Los Angeles, 1967. David Wolper listens in.

Three Normans: Lear, Cousins, Corwin, c. 1989.

Bette Davis in Corwin's production of *The World of Carl Sandburg*—"The pointing finger is best at pointing . . . "

Group gathered to fete Carl Sandburg two days before Corwin's Royce Hall production honoring the poet. Standing left to right, Clifford Odets, Robert Nathan, Ray Bradbury, Dr. Joseph Kaplan, Prof. Frank Baxter, Leonard Karzmar, Lion Feuchtwanger, Allan Nevins, George Stevens, Corwin, Joe Schoenfeld. Seated, Groucho Marx, Georgianna Hardy, Sandburg, Marta Feuchtwanger. November 21, 1958.

Reception by the Society for the Preservation of Radio Drama, Variety and Comedy, University of California at Northridge, 1978.

Partial cast and staff of the 55th anniversary of *The Plot to Overthrow Christmas*, broadcast from the auditorium of the Thousand Oaks Library on December 3, 1993. Left to right, Peggy Webber, producer; Martin Halperin, engineer; Corwin, who directed; William Windom, behind mike stand; Norman Lloyd; Marvin Kaplan; Samantha Eggar; David Warner; Kathleen Freeman.

With James Earl Jones at rehearsal of *Bill of Rights: 200*, on the 50th anniversary of the four-network broadcast of '41. December 15, 1991.

Norman and Emil in California, 1993

see, by the way) that would cast brimstone, honey, gall, guts and gore, and possibly a little light, on the media through which we have passed....

Too bad about the cooling of Oriana Atkinson because you don't like her book. I can never understand this in artists. Even as warm and generous a soul as Van Gogh destroyed his friendship with a fellow painter (and he didn't have many friends to spare) when a murky early painting did not bring the expected cheers. One has a right to be disappointed, even hurt for an hour; but great God, if the criticism is honest, one can ask nothing more. It is the *dis*honest criticism that offends me—the man who has an ax to grind, or looks at a work through the political lens of his publisher or his wife or himself; or who sheathes a jealousy or envy or personal pique. I have run up against such critics in no less than the late Benny DeVoto and a fatuous ass named Phillip Hamburger, whose style conforms with his name. An honest panning never rankles; in fact I have been beholden to some. The other is merde....

TO DR. WILLIAM B. OBER / May 10, 1962

Dear Bill:

I would have replied much sooner to your good letter of last month, but for the fact that I upped and bought me a passage on a Norwegian freighter, for Panama. I needed a rest very badly, and got it aboard ship, though I squandered my gain by flying back. I recommend a good freighter above any form of travel known by man. Wonderful freedom, wide empty spaces on the decks, too few passengers (limit: 12) to bore or annoy one, and food that is not gussied up for epicures.

Panama is a hot and steaming, dowdy little country, but the Canal is a glorious achievement, and I greatly enjoyed our trip through it. I turned about at Cristobal and drove across the isthmus. Stayed at El Panama Hilton, which boasts a Casino where all the zombies, native and American, gather to crank the slot machines and play 21 and roll dice. Pukable.

Thanks for sending me your reprint of the "Embryonal Carcinoma, Hermaphrodite division." I like your eminently readable opening paragraph. Too bad more scientific papers are not written, or at least introduced, with this good humor and charm.

Enclosed for a spare hour is a first draft of five pieces among the twenty-six that will eventually make up a book I have been asked to do by World Publishing, called *Overkill and Megalove*. I am much beholden to you for the *Times* article on Teller's silence when asked about Oppenheimer, and I also appreciate your indignation. I may do a poem around this. By a coincidence, I had already roughed out a piece on another one of Teller's beauties—his moon program. It is enclosed....

TO MILDRED ALBERG, Film Producer / June 1, 1962

Dear Millie:

...Thank you thank you for the [Herman] Kahn book. Already I have taken the text for a sermon from one of his pages—the place where he describes how a Doomsday Machine costing only $10 billion could be built for the express purpose of blowing up the world (including ourselves), as an "ideal" deterrent to the Russkis. I have done a parody on Kubla Khan, the first five lines of which go:

> In Xanadu did Herman Kahn
> A fearful atom bomb decree
> Whence Alpha radiation ran
> Through fallouts measureless to man
> Down to a poisoned sea.

It is Good News that you are coming out here in June. By that time the foggy foggy dews should be over and the weather pleasant. And we can talk of cabbages and king-sized idiots like the men who man the networks....

TO WILLIAM TARG, Editor, World Publishing / June 22, 1962

Dear Bill:

Here is half the book [*Overkill and Megalove*]. Two more pieces are in work, not as ready to see as the attached. This may be stronger stuff than you bargained for, but I don't think you scare easily. It is very late not to be speaking out.

If you find a concentration of fire on Dr. T. [Edward Teller], that is because I think he is easily the most menacing influence against the future of us all. He has made public statements that nuclear warfare can be fought "humanely" (!); he has pooh-poohed the danger of fallout from tests, as less harmful than an extra ounce of weight, less harmful than wearing pants, less harmful than the radiation from a wristwatch, and so on. He has made speeches to the effect that the world is not ready for nuclear disarmament "or any other kind of disarmament." He has defied the urgings of 9,000 scientists around the world, toward calming the waters, and is for bigger and fiercer bombs.

You remember my having mentioned the Idea of a Primer—A is for Atom, C is for Cosmonaut, etc. I have kept to this notion to the extent of an alphabetical progression in the titles, but I don't think we want to labor this; a somewhat oversized initial capital letter with each title will get across the Primer idea without any resort to a subtitle or anything of that kind.

As for the title itself, I have not given it much thought, for I prefer to concentrate on the pieces. I am not too worried about the use of OVERKILL in other books. Might not do any harm to get the word broken in; certainly the MEGALOVE part of it would take it away from the others. Incidentally I hope you like the piece of that name. I read it to a few people in my living room the other night and they carried on like I was Moses. But then I had paid for the liquor.

TO WILLIAM O. DOUGLAS, Justice, Supreme Court
July 16, 1962

In introducing Douglas to an audience in Beverly Hills, Corwin alluded to his native city of Yakima. Douglas responded that since the name of the city was often mispronounced, and Corwin had got it right, he was entitled to the traditional reward of a necktie.

Dear Mr. Douglas:
The Yakima tie has arrived and is the first trophy in my life that I can wear.

Not even the fact that I did not work very hard for it, diminishes the pleasure I take both in owning it and contemplating its source.

TO EDELAINE AND E.Y. HARBURG / October 17, 1962

Dear Eddie and Yip:

...I am living in my little thatched house by the side of Walden Pond, on a diet of grass and weeds, having learned this from my old vegetarian friend Nebuchadnezzar.

I want you to know this is a literary family. Tony came home from school the other day with a composition entitled "Why I Must Not Talk in Class," for me to read and sign. His father, on the other hand, is sending you *his* compositions for *you* to read, sign, and return. Find, enclosed, unless some crook with excellent taste has rifled the envelope looking for first edition material that he can sell as hot goods to the Huntington Library.

The pieces are from a book to be called *Overkill and Megalove* which World Publishing has scheduled for spring publication, always allowing that there will be any paper or people left by then. Tell me frankly what you think and why you believe they are great.

Had dinner at Sy and Maxine's the other night and they are the sodium-free salt of the earth. We spoke of you fondly, like.

Fuck the New York Yankees.

TO MILDRED ALBERG / November 26, 1962

Dear Millie:

...The flight to L.A. was eventful in a wry way. Do you recall my plaint that no attractive woman ever sat beside me in an airplane (N.Y. to London excepted)? Well, an intense thirty-five-year-old blonde with a British accent invited herself to sit next to me (after I had carefully maneuvered to get a row of three seats all to myself—my ideal seating arrangement) and she poured out the blackest tale of woe and anguish since Job's Curse. Replete with a hostile mother, a cruel and sexually perverted husband, her psychological problems, her monumental loneliness. She covered my hand with hers for emphases, also my right knee. I finally told her that I was racing a deadline, that I really MUST finish a piece of writing before the plane reached L.A., and she had the goodness to retire graciously to her own seat.

I can only assume that the Fates, ordinarily silent to minor complaints, overheard my grousing about the-next-seat-to-mine, and decided to play a joke....

TO WILLIAM TARG, Editor, World Publishing Company
December 4, 1962

Dear Bill:

Bibliophile in the Nursery is an Alp in the range. I am a bad judge of both books and men, if you did not have enormous fun doing it....

I got great pleasure and learned a lot from the book. Just to find out there is a Chittenango, N.Y., was an excellent start; and I especially enjoyed your...passage on taking children to bookstores—its influence on me will translate into action as soon as Tony is over the croup.

Incidentally, [Charles L.] Dodgson is not the only author who canceled an edition of 2,000 copies and paid for it. Your humble servant did just that on one of the three Henry Holt books; only, unlike Dodgson, I did not salvage any of the copies—had them chopped up— and forked over about $4,000 for the privilege. [Dissatisfied with some of the pages he had written, Corwin destroyed copies of one book after it had gone to press before he could make revisions.]

My kids are awed by the book and your inscription—only the second ever addressed to them by an author outside the family. The first was Sandburg, whom they however do not regard as an "author" because he lived under the same roof with them for a month, hence qualifies as a member of the family. You too can change your status by a residence of this minimal length, an invitation you have had now for some time. Both kids are working up letters of appreciation to you. It is nice to contemplate that their appreciation will itself appreciate with the years.

I see a picture of JFK pinning $50,000 on Dr. Teller in today's press. The unfailing formula for glory and riches is to be an object of my contempt....

TO MOLLA AND HERBERT MOSS / December 21, 1962

Dear Molla and Herb:

You have no idea how you brightened the season. *Kama Kala* is the essence of altruism in this cold world—shows you how to give your neighbor a leg up. Kate and I have worked out a schedule of possession of the book—she has it on Mondays, Wednesdays and Fridays, I have it on Tuesdays and Thursdays, and alternate weekends. Wednesday matinees we look at it together.

It is really a beautiful book, appealing both to my esthetic and prurient natures, and removing any last shadow of doubt as to which side I favor in the current Sino-Indian difficulties. We appreciate not only the munificence of this gift, but the really very dear and warm propagandistic purpose insinuated in your kindness, which is, in effect, Get thee hence and love. And how more securely could you place yourselves in our fond awareness, than to guarantee that we shall think of you every time we look at the book?...

Things are going well, considering "well" to mean important things like health and domestic concord....Tony is golden as ever, Diane went on point in her ballet education yesterday—a very big event for her—and today she is hostess to a dozen contemporaries for her birthday, to the celebration of which I am indentured as operator of the movie projector and tape recorder. I shall of course be consumed with jealousy at receiving no presents myself—I mean model airplanes and blocks and stuff. I already *have* an erector set, which *Kama Kala* will help exercise, just thinking about it.

As for the Gazette: I have just returned page proofs to World Publishing, toward a book of poems (!!!) which they are publishing in February; my two shows for the FDR series, to be done on ABC-TV sometime in '63, turned out well; I am writing a screenplay for a comedy, at the behest of an independent producer, and also working on a Paul Gaugin project, and wishing every moment that I had Molla as technical adviser.

I had an interesting ten days of lousy weather in London, cleverly escaping in time to avoid the killer smog....While in London I visited, for the first time...the British Museum. Mamma mia, what antiquities! I spent a couple of hours just digging the Elgin Marbles. And of course I went back to the Tate and basked in the light of the Turners, for which I am quite mad. Remind me to spare both of these museums in the event of a nuclear war. My book, incidentally, treats of the thermonuclear age. It will have the distinction of being liked by neither Left nor Right, ignored by the large Middle, and bought by nobody besides my two brothers, who have been loyal to me through all manner of vicissitudes.

Katherine has just looked up from a page of Indian temple sculptures to ask that I convey to you her unqualified love, together with assurances that she has not changed her attitude one whit concerning the fact that I occasionally leave a sock on the floor, which in her code is tantamount to beating your wife and abandoning your children. Nevertheless I love her; after all, it was she who first introduced me to those patrons of art and health food, the Mosses we adore.

TO WILLIAM TARG / January 6, 1963

Dear Bill:

You are correct in assuming that I would not want you to shield me from any brickbats, and I can assure you there will be quite a variety of them. Indeed if the Kirkus review were the worst we shall have, I would gladly settle for it. For we must never forget that [*Overkill and Megalove*] deals very forthrightly with the huge and threatening obscenity called Peace. *Playboy* and *Eros* may circulate profitably, but beware of that lewd and tasteless thing, disarmament.

I have rarely read a paragraph more compactly ambivalent than the Kirkus report. The words overblown, bombastic, bad taste and weakness are cheek and jowl with powerful, strength, word-skill, splendid rhetoric, precision, energy, commendable, direct and real. That's traveling.

Dear Bill, since *O & M* attacks, it shall in turn be attacked. Such is the calculated risk of anybody who speaks for his conscience. Even some who might want to like it all-out, will be afraid to; its "genuine anger," as our first critic puts it, may frighten some whom we would expect to be friendly. How ironic, to be less frightened by a bomb than by a poem!

I had a nice letter from [Carey] McWilliams. You mention a fee of $100. If that fee is payable to me, I request that it be turned back to the magazine [*The Nation*], for it has always had a struggle to stay alive, and is a beacon of courage in the killer fog....

P.S. Minor request: no photo of my phiz in regular advertising. It will hurt sales.

TO LEILA HADLEY, Author / January 6, 1963

Dear Leila:

Your letter crackles with good cheer and accomplishment. Just naming off your kids sounds like the opening of a gay madrigal....

With characteristic modesty you ask when my book is due, without in the slightest way referring to your own. When is IT due? I am eager to buy it on all counts, including the prospect of seeing your face again on a jacket. It's all right with me if they use the [Philip] Halsman portrait again. I am strong for a wallpaper design of that portrait....

My book is due some time in February, and will be called *Overkill and Megalove*, a mouthful. It is the toughest stuff I have ever written....

Fellow author, a hug.

TO SIR LINDSAY WELLINGTON / January 21, 1963

Dear Lindsay:

I am very pleased with Her Majesty's Government over the promptness with which it takes up my recommendations. When at our luncheon in the Savile Club last November I asked why Britain had been delinquent in conferring on you the knighthood that has been so eminently your due for so many years, I had no idea we were overheard. That is what I call efficiency!

I am of course delighted, as must be your many friends in many lands —including [Bernard] Herrmann, who was the first to tell me the good news. Very hearty congratulations.

Wear your knighthood in peace, good health, and the happiness that comes of the knowledge of good works done greatly.

TO GOODMAN ACE, Creator and Star of *Easy Aces*
March 25, 1963

Dear Goody:

It was wonderful to see you at Sardi's, and I shall never forget your passage with the cab driver to whom you confessed you married a Watusi.

For the lack of a pen or pencil (the distinguishing mark of a writer being the absence of these implements on his person at all times), I was unable to give you my home phone number. It is STate 4-9602. The phone company wants me to say it is 784-9602, but fuck 'em; let them speak numbers to each other; I prefer the stateliness of a Prefix. Except in prefixing a basketball game or something like that.

Please *use* that number, preferably from out here, where it will cost you less and please us more.

TO THE REVEREND NORMAN CORWIN / May 5, 1963

> The clergyman, of Boston, Massachusetts, had received unfriendly mail meant for Corwin.

Dear Mr. Corwin:

Hail, Norman Corwin. Mr. [Eason] Monroe took the liberty of sending your letter on to me, and I take the further liberty of writing to apologize at this remove of time and distance, for being the cause, however innocently, of some inconvenience to you. It is further proof, if any were needed, that not even the most inoffensive bystander is safe in any crossfire between dragons like me and the self-appointed St. Georges of the body politic....

You are only the second Norman Corwin who has come to my knowledge, the other having been, like both of us, from the Greater Boston area. He was city clerk of Somerville; one night he came up to me in Tremont Temple or some such hall after I had made a speech, and introduced himself and a young son, also named as we are—which makes four! Unhappily the elder Somerville Corwin (middle initial was

E.) died two or three years ago, but there are at least three of us left, and perhaps we should form a Society.

It is good to know that you too care about civil liberties. That they are as usual beleaguered is only par for the course of human events.

TO NORMAN OBER, Writer / May 10, 1963

Dear Norman:

Yes, there was a privately published edition of *Seems Radio Is Here to Stay* [an early Corwin broadcast] put out by CBS in 1939 or '40, and distributed only to clients, VIPs and people in high places in Washington. It is a very fancy job of printing, with engraved illustrations, two colors, and typographical fangles. I think I may have an extra one buried in my files somewhere. If so, it is yours.

Pa Corwin flew out here the other day to spend some time with us. He is eighty-six now, has less gray hair than I, is spryer, and has a sounder philosophy. I don't know what the moral is, but there must be one....

STEPHANIE DINKINS, Photographer [formerly Corwin's Research Assistant at United Nations Radio] / May 27, 1963

Dear Stephanie:

Your marvelous letter from Gupis arrived in a week's time, duly registered, and I signed for it with a flourish. If ever I was vindicated in my long and lonesome serenade urging you to write the travel book of all travel books since [Marco] Polo, it is now, with this latest batch of harassments and pleasures added to all that has gone before. The Bangkok experience, contrasting so sharply with your earlier visit, will make your whole Sikkim episode that much more colorful and engrossing. The stripping routine before Buddha, keeping a wary eye out for stray lamas, is just the kind of incident that makes a book a bestseller from Bangor to Bangkok.

And the Churu incident! Incredible! And Gilgit and Gupis! I am encouraged by your own words: "so exotic and delightful that I am going to write it all down." I shall hold you to those words. "All" means all.

Yes, your letter from Gupis is the first I've ever received that was borne by runners over any part of the route, and it joins in the treasurable archives of my mail, a boxful dumped over a cliff by a bored mailman...the mail was recovered seven weeks later, all bleached by the sun, but unharmed.

Thanks to your foot-and-airborne letter, I now know where to address you. I had earlier sent two letters, in one of which I registered my delight on finding a genuine Dinkins photograph on the *COVER* of MD! It's the dear old lady with the leafy headgear—a vast improvement over Dior.

By the way, did you know that your letter carried an acutely historical stamp? Did you read the very small print on the stamp of the map of West Pakistan? I put a magnifying glass to it and found it said, "JAMMU & KASHMIR (FINAL STATUS NOT YET DETERMINED"). Not an overprint—part of the stamp proper. Never saw anything like it....

Stay out of drafts, wars and harems, and keep well.

TO RUDY VALLEE (then appearing in *How to Succeed in Business Without Really Trying*) / September 16, 1963

Dear Rudy:

I got around late to *How to Succeed* last week, and it was a delight to see you in action. You were great, as expected. I was strongly tempted to go back and say hello afterward but I hesitated because you looked a bit tired. Besides the pleasure of shaking the hand again, I was dying to know what Morse did or said that broke you up in Act II, and for which you, when the chance came, laughingly said to him under your breath, "You son of a bitch." Me big lip reader.

Incidentally, not long ago I picked up a two-year-old issue of *Esquire* and found in it a transcript of an interview with you. It was so sharp, clean, pungent and astringent that I wanted to write you a fan letter then and there. But by waiting, I can now kill two birds with one broadside....

RALPH SCHOENSTEIN / October 11, 1963

Dear Ralph:

Well, Koufax is up there with Odysseus and Jason and Einstein. I hope you are now more than ever awed by the fact that I had dinner with him once. He signed a very soiled baseball for my eleven-year-old boy Tony, and I have taken over custody of that baseball and encased it in glass, and two policemen stand guard over it night and day....

Delighted to learn that you liked my little history paper [*The Rivalry*]. What a headache it was to do, from start to finish; but it had its rewards too. Marty Gabel was nothing less than incandescent in it. A curious thing, but the two best roles Marty has ever had are, according to him, the narrator's chair in *Note of Triumph* and Douglas in *The Rivalry*. Just worked out that way; I write well for the cello, apparently.

TO RUDY VALLEE / October 20, 1963

Dear Rudy:

Your good letter was here when I returned from the mountains....I am mortified to confess that, as a consequence of the insulating effect of having my nose up against a grindstone, I did not even know *My Time* was on the market! That's how provincial a man gets out here. But I make haste to remedy this ignorance, and shall go get the book.

Much of the grindstone, incidentally, involves a similar project—my memoirs. A publisher with a big heart and lots of courage urged me to undertake it, flourished some money in my face, and I persuaded myself that I have a story to tell, and the technique to tell it with.

Your contretemps with [Frank] Loesser strikes harmonies in my own experience....Why are there always ten shits for every man?

I missed the national company here, so I have no basis for comparison between you and [Willard] Waterman—but how could there be any comparison? As far as I'm concerned, you are incomparable in that role....

When are you coming out here again? If we don't meet here, then I hope you'll have dinner with me on your side of the divide.

TO RALPH SCHOENSTEIN / December 30, 1963

Dear Ralph:

I am thrilled. I just read your batch of pieces, published and unpublished, and there was actually one which did not come up to the Schoenstein standard. You have no idea how exciting it is to find that sometimes the ball falls inside the park for a triple, instead of clearing the fence....

The piece that puts you in the class with Shakespeare, who now and then wrote a less-than-perfect play, is, for my money, "Get Your Prestige off the Block." If it's a home run like the others, then it's an inside-the-park one. I just felt it ran out of gas, but it could possibly be I who did. In any case, you have spoiled me, and continue to do so with every piece you send along. Hence the news when man turns around and takes a nip of dog.

It reminds me of a comment by Paul Nettl on Mozart's Piano Concerto No. 13 in C Major: "Many critics carp at this concerto as being superficial, and make a cult of comparing it with some of Mozart's later, more serious works. It takes examples by Mozart to belittle Mozart!" (Exclamation point Nettl's.)

I gave all the pieces to Kate to read, and she spontaneously—without prompting or coaching from me—compared you with Mark Twain. Since Twain scores two points higher than Jesus on my poll of inspiring men, this is praise....

See you in Nineveh.

TO ROBERT M. HUTCHINS / February 25, 1964

Dear Bob:

The selection board of the Robert O. Anderson Award in the Humanities has asked me among others to submit a nomination for its $30,000 award, the qualifications being "outstanding accomplishments toward clarification of the individual's role in life and his relationship to society."

I know of nobody on the American scene who deserves it more than you, and I should like to submit your name. But I would prefer to have your permission to do so, since I don't think it cricket to enter a man's name in what comes down to a competition, without his approval. I hope you say yes. The selection board consists of Frederick Burkhardt, William DeVane, Lord Franks, Henry Allen Moe and Alvin Eurich.

Warmest best to you as always—and why don't we have a dinner when you are down here?

> Hutchins, former president of the University of Chicago, was president of the Center for the Study of Democratic Institutions in Santa Barbara, California. He gave Corwin permission and won the award.

TO CAROLINE ROGERS / February 25, 1964

Dear Caroline:

I have developed, by a kind of sclerosis of the amenities, into the world's worst correspondent. All the more shocking to me, since my intentions remain as good as ever. It was my earnest intention long LONG before now to tell you how dreadfully sorry I was to hear of the fire in that apartment of yours. Really, Caroline, there are easier ways of getting rid of my books! Allow me to replace them, as soon as I can get hold of these now deeply out-of-print items.

I hope you are back in the apartment again, and that the hotel routine is behind you. No more smoking in bed, now. Remember the Surgeon General's report and the fire ordinances.

TO DORIS VIDOR ROSE, who had just married Broadway Producer Billy Rose / March 4, 1964

Dear Doris:

Just as I was about to rouse my ailing chassis to mail you two United Nations scripts, each accompanied by a letter of explanation, comes news that you have taken unto yourself a new Pharaoh, and a mighty man is he. Were I in better physical shape, I would drink champagne to you both; as it is, I effervesce with good wishes and prayers for your happiness, scaling upwards to joy....

TO MILDRED ALBERG / June 6, 1964

Dear Millie:

I have read the contract [for a project, *The Wily Wilby*, based on a story by St. Clair McKelway], and I have a few comments to make on it:

...I find "libel" and "slander" indemnities a bore. I know a good lawyer always puts them in for his client, and a good writer always takes them out for himself. I never permit such a clause in my contracts, not even with major studios.

In all my previous contracts, and there have been many, I have never seen anything like Paragraph 7, in which the employer declares the right, if he elects, to serve as a collection agency and a sort of punitive expedition for the Guild. Since the monies alluded to have long ago been paid and the dues thereof properly assigned, this is wholly academic anyway, and its inclusion in the contract is in my view redundant and excessive. I should like it struck out on general principles....

TO MORT AND LINDA JANKLOW / June 18, 1964

Corwin wrote on the birth of their daughter. Janklow, a New York attorney, later became a literary agent.

Dear Linda and Mort:

Angela Janklow makes a beautiful sound, like the ringing of bells, and I am sure that in good time, and in the likeness of her mater, she will be a beautiful belle herself.

My love to all three of you,

TO CHARLES AND ANN SHIRLEY LEDERER, Screenwriter and Actress Wife / January 3, 1965

Dear Charles and Ann:

Thank you for that wonderful evening and the chance to renew acquaintance with my four friends and all my enemies.

There is really only one thing lacking to make those memorable parties of yours push the needle over to 10 on the Richter Scale: I don't see enough of you. Charles, who is one of my favorite people in the known world, greeted me like the President of Uruguay at a Pan American Conference; and Ann, whom I love with the devotion of a faithful sheepdog, glided across the east wing and extended her lovely hand, which I kissed hungrily, and outside of that I never saw either of you, and was left to the lame resort of watching all those pretty young Italian starlets dance with young men who were, every one, less deserving than Charles and I.

But thanks anyway, and do have a beautiful year, seeing as how you are beautiful people and I am crazy about you both.

TO LOU ASHWORTH / January 22, 1965

Corwin wrote the opening and closing programs of a thirteen-part television series on FDR, broadcast over ABC-TV.

Dear Lou:

...Bless little Polly for finding the FDR program with her junior divining rod. But if she cried, "It's by Norman Corwin," she must have caught it at the end, for that is where my credit came. Yet you speak of enjoying the show, and because I am terribly clever, I have figured out that you watched the body of the show without knowing who wrote it, and were apprised of this jeweled knowledge by Miss Polly.

Yes, I wrote the opening and closing shows of the series. The first was written as an hour, and naturally chopped into two half-hour pieces by ABC because that is the only way they could screw it up, not having produced it themselves and so being unable to piss in the beer as any red-blooded network prefers to do. Nevertheless, thanks to no gifts of mine but to the indestructible and immortal smile and voice of that man, the show was all right, and I need not count it among the mournful numbers of my past....

TO ESTHER ZIEFF / March 7, 1965

Dear Esther:

My father told me the sad news about Barney today. Nobody can feel this loss as keenly as you and Ruth, but there are many including myself who share your bereavement. And I with a special sense of loss, since Barney [Zieff] was the best friend of my school days, and shared with me the bold adventure (for kids of our years and means) of traveling together. He was a happy companion, and what we both lacked in funds was more than compensated for by the richness of the experience. I always felt an enormous quality of loyalty and dignity in Barney, and an inexhaustible capacity for giving and receiving affection. As we get older we lose friends and loved ones, and try to be philosophical about it. But the passing of Barney is a hard test of that philosophy. Kate joins me in our warmest condolences, and in sending you our love.

TO AL PRIESS, Editor, Festival of World TV Classics
March 8, 1965

Dear Al Preiss:

Some time ago you asked me to write a piece for you, and offered to pay for it. I knew you could not afford the kind of fee I get for this sort of thing, and so I told you I would gladly contribute the piece. I then took time out of an extremely heavy work schedule to write it.

You did not have the courtesy even to acknowledge receipt of it. It takes philosophy to try to understand this kind of behavior, and it sure as hell teaches me never to do a favor for the likes of you.

TO MRS. EDWARD R. MURROW / March 19, 1965

Dear Janet:

Charlotte Ramsay has told us of her letter from you. We are praying very very hard for that miracle to happen.

We were of course warmed and gratified by Ed's extraordinary honor from the Queen, although I long felt it should have come ten or fifteen years ago. [Queen Elizabeth II had made Murrow an Honorary Knight Commander of the British Empire.] But I suppose one should not quibble too hard with a gesture from a sovereign that, quite by itself, is enough to make a man immortal. Ed is a monarch in his own right. We think of him daily, and continue to hope. If there were therapy in the pressure of all the wishes of those who love and honor him, there would be no question. Kate joins me in sending you love and in yearning for better news.

TO ANTHONY QUINN / March 27, 1965

> Quinn, an Academy Award winner as supporting actor in *Lust for Life*, had been nominated in the best actor category for *Zorba the Greek*.

Dear Tony:

Whether or not it's another Oscar, *Zorba* is a glory, both to you and the whole medium. I am hopeful [Rex] Harrison and [Peter] O'Toole will knock each other off. The former had two years to rehearse, and the latter is fine, but there is not the rich range and testicular power of Zorba.

The *New York Times* interview of March 21 was what one should be. The quotes sounded accurate, for a change....

My love to you and Yolanda. I will be among those rooting hard for you on the night of the awards.

TO LEE GRANT, Actress / April 22, 1965

Dear Lee:

Good Lord, whatever led you to believe I had spent a "ghastly evening" at 490 [West End Avenue (her address)]? I liked your friends, your daughter is more fun than an Italian movie, and I raptly admire you. If you must know the awful, dreary, sub-prosaic and genuinely ghastly truth, I had dined in lonely splendor on tainted Lobster Cantonese before running up to W.E.A., and it was well that I left your company when I did. And *that* was why, not the yak of your colleagues, which I enjoyed.

I watched you with my usual slavish attention on a *For the People* show out here last week, and as usual you were superior to your surroundings and the script and the direction. But the pleasure of watching you was eclipsed by my anger over the credit given you at the end. It was far too small for your stature, to say nothing of the performance. Don't tell me you pay ten percent to an agent for *that* kind of representation.

I'm glad you like *O & M* [*Overkill and Megalove*]. I had hoped its substance and tenor and pointing finger would all be mildly ridiculous and obsolescent by now, but every fresh escalation blowing in from the rice paddies makes it, alas, graver and grimmer and truer every day.

Be happy. I mean, considering Alabama and Saigon. Reasonably happy.

TO JANET MURROW / May 3, 1965

Dear Janet:

Kate and I were out at the beach on a gray, misty day when the news came, and suddenly the ocean was emptier than ever, and the sky grayer. This is not the first testimony you will have had, nor the last, of the sense of deep personal loss; I felt it in every last person to whom I spoke, people who had never met Ed, only heard him, or saw him on the tube.

I am sure that what went on in Los Angeles must have been repeated and duplicated in cities all over the country: editorials in print and on the air, columns, playbacks of *Hear It Now*, eulogies, reminiscences.

Yesterday a young man on the ABC station spent two hours playing the albums and talking about Ed's influence on him, recalling that he was Ed's announcer briefly at one of the political conventions years back, and how extraordinarily kind and generous Ed was to him, an unknown; how Ed had remembered his difficult name months later, in a chance meeting. I watched *An Hour with Murrow*, and relived the glory to America of Ed's immortal [Senator Joseph] McCarthy broadcast, and it brought so much back in a rush of nostalgia; and of course Kate and I cried on the closed circuit speech, when Ed himself was affected. And I called Charlotte right after the telecast, and we commiserated with each other. And at a point during the hour program, we said to our twelve-year-old boy who was watching it with us, "There is the man who made it possible for us to adopt you, Tony," as it was a letter of reference from Ed to the Adoptation Bureau that, we feel, swung the balance of their consideration in our favor. Tony was thrilled and moved, and we told him that Ed's letter will be his when he gets older.

There are not many like Ed in the world, and there never have been, and none of us who had the privilege of knowing him will ever quite get over the fact that he has gone. He was so great a figure that condolences properly must go not so much to you and Casey, as to America and a world that had such need of him.

TO STEPHANIE DINKINS / May 16, 1965

Dear Stephanie:

...I am not persuaded by your argument about accepting payment on a commission only if your pictures are liked....You are incapable of turning in inferior work; your standards prevent that. My point is that if the *Geographic* asked you to do something for them, and you went places and spent time and shot film, they must pay you whether or not the results please an editor, or a majority of editors. Judgment is not an exact science; editors have the right, nay, the duty to discriminate; but an agreement is an agreement, and work must be paid for. Otherwise you do a disservice to your fellow photographers. How would it be if all the picture magazines floated on a cushion of speculation? They make enough money as it is—and the artists, as usual, make too little.

But I must not labor this. On to small intelligence: I am, and have been for the last two and a half weeks, living on the beach at Malibu, to get away from the pollens of the Valley. Glorious; right on the water; I sleep to the pounding of the surf....

Thanks for that mural display of stamps on the envelope. You are my philatelic right hand, and I kiss it.

TO BERNARD ASBELL, Writer / May 19, 1965

Dear Bernie:

...Thanks for your kind words about *Overkill*. I am flattered that your fifteen-year-old boy stayed with it; most fifty-five-year-olds complain that it is too cerebral for them. And I am flattered that you presided over a reading out-loud of passages from *On a Note of Triumph*. It is more ironic than ever, with the rattling of heavy hardware so loud in the humid countries these days.

I look forward to receiving your new book, and only wish I had one to trade you at the moment, but that is at least a year off. What a grand feeling it is, the first time you have a finished book in your hand. Something like that first kiss, except that the book is less likely to lead to complications.

I write from Malibu, where I fled to escape the pollens of the Valley. The ocean is at my door, and the sound of surf is with me day and night. What a great invention is an ocean. It is the only thing that man has not yet been able to pollute on any large scale, and on that cheering thought I leave you with high salutations.

TO ST. CLAIR McKELWAY, Writer

> Corwin had hoped to incorporate McKelway's *Boogie Woogie Ballads* in a stage production to star Anthony Quinn. He had also written a screenplay for Mildred Alberg, the producer, based on a story by McKelway called *Wilby*. Others much later filmed it as *Hot Millions*.

Dear St. Clair:

I regret having to report two pop-ups to the infield. The project for which I wanted your marvelous *Boogie Woogie* pieces, collapsed of natural causes. By that I mean the producers could not pin down Tony Quinn for longer than six weeks; and after our meeting in New York, Tony went through a whole series of inspirations—it should be a film—no, a TV spectacular—no, a play—no, an LP. I am not at my best emulating a chameleon, especially under time pressure, and so the whole thing declined and fell. I regard as the only tangible gains, my meeting with you at the Hilton, and my knowledge of the Ballads, which I still want to use in some form.

I suppose Milly Alberg has kept you informed on *Wilby*. The screenplay which you liked so much, and concerning which you generously wrote me, was apparently too simple-minded for the money people. Milly wanted changes with which I could not agree, so I passed up my equity. Cute things like having the computing machine fire Wilby's wife, and complications involving the wife's pregnancy (!) At least these were the noble concepts that preoccupied the second or third of a succession of rewrite men, four months ago. What has happened since then I do not know, and am afraid to ask.

There's no biz like showbiz....

TO ROBERT COHN, Producer / July 4th + 2, 1965

Dear Bob:

Attached, a message from Peggy Arnold, who tells me that she *likes* that little pot you have developed from fancy eating. I took the liberty of giving her your home telephone number.

Always helpful.

Of all the famous figures in American history who could make a great movie, the worst is perhaps the best. Just as the devil holds copyright to the best tunes, he also has access to the most colorful characters; and in a day when the anti-hero enjoys unprecedented popularity (as in *Hud*, *The Hustlers*, *Street Car*, *The Face in the Crowd*, *Long Hot Summer*, etc.) and the hero tends to be something of a square (extreme example, *Batman*), there commends himself as a leading candidate for immortalization in a rousing film, one Benedict Arnold.

Arnold is the worst of many villains in our 190 years as a nation (and there have been some perfect horrors)—a man who, because of the enormity of his crime, comes down to us as the very symbol of treachery. To this day his name appears with surprising frequency in books, magazines, newspaper articles. (He is even in a cookbook, represented by a recipe for Eggs Benedict Arnold.)

But what sets Arnold apart from most other anti-heroes is that he was a genuine hero before he became the opposite, and he played both roles to the hilt. It is unanimously conceded that if Arnold had been killed instead of wounded in the Battle of Saratoga he would ever since have been revered as a Revolutionary hero second only to George Washington; there would be cities and streets and parks named after him, and bronze plaques all over the Northeast, and a military academy or two. As it is, there is a tourist attraction on the maps of Maine, known as Arnold's Trail.

Incredible is the only word to describe much about the man, and about most of what happened to him and around him and because of him. In an ordinary melodrama, one is under constraint not to over-state, exaggerate, flirt with the improbable and deal in the implausible. One must not write the sort of scene to which a producer says, "Do you really expect an audience to *believe* this?" But history annihilates all these cautions. Truth being inherently stranger than fiction, it has no need to blush. For this reason, no critic carped over "improbabilities" in *Lawrence of Arabia* or *Becket*. The same would go for a film on Arnold, except that in his case, the action and drama would be heightened fifty-fold over either of the above-named biographies.

To begin with, Arnold was a powerful and absorbing character. Son of a drinking father, a "charity" scholar, at first a timid, stammering boy, he became, perhaps through the mechanics of overcompensation, fiercely brave, brashly outspoken, and contemptuously disdainful of physical hardship and danger. He developed extraordinary and contradictory qual-ities, many of them admirable: He was gallant, yet tough; charming, yet scrappy; aristocratic in tastes and outlook, yet happiest when among his foot-soldiers and sharing their trials; money-greedy, yet generous, some-times paying soldiers out of his own pocket when Congress was late with the payroll (and often not getting reimbursed); adored by the ranks, but hated by all but two or three generals; absolutely fearless, yet unable to execute one of his own soldiers who had murdered another in a drunken stupor. He was a man of winning ways and incontestable stature; as ardent a patriot at the beginning as he was heinous a traitor at the end.

Of guts Arnold had more than his share, and it took him into some pretty hairy situations, such as setting out to conquer Ticonderoga (and succeeding—perhaps in spite of, rather than because of, the collaboration of Ethan Allen); attacking the walled city of Quebec at four in the morning, in the teeth of a raging blizzard; organizing a fleet of landlubbers to take on an armada of the world's foremost naval power; leading a reckless charge against British raiders at Danbury; being pinned under a fallen horse, yet killing a Tory soldier who attacked him in this position; challenging to a duel, a tribunal which reprimanded him; disobeying orders of his commanding general by leading a charge against British troops at Saratoga, and thereby winning the pivotal battle of the entire war.

Arnold was a great man with the ladies, attractive enough in spite of a game, twice-wounded leg, to have won for a wife the belle of Philadelphia and toast of two armies—Peggy Shippen. Thanks to her endowments, no dramatic license would be required to make her photogenic; all sides, and particularly the American high command, agreed that she was a rare beauty.

Everything Arnold did he did in a big way, including his treason. He negotiated for months with the British, and held out for better and bigger terms. He was ready to deliver to the enemy no mere plan of fortifications, but the fortress of West Point itself, with all its arms, emplacements and men. Worse than that, he almost succeeded in turning over no less than George Washington—the same Washington who had signed letters to Arnold with the rare term (for him) "Affectionately—"

Down to the wire, the betrayal of West Point unfolded like a plot in a taut, bristling spy drama. On the very morning that the plot was discovered (by a fluke), there were expected at Arnold's headquarters for breakfast an incredible constellation of figures: George Washington, LaFayette, and Alexander Hamilton. These men showed up, only to find Arnold had fled shortly before; they proceeded to the quarters of Mrs. Arnold, and were greeted by the mad scene from *MacBeth*: Peggy Arnold, either with genuine or feigned hysterics, shrieked at Washington and LaFayette, accusing them of having come to murder her children. They calmed her, convinced of her innocence, and treated her with astonishing courtesy and kindness. (Not until *1926* (!) was it discovered through a probing study of documents, that Peggy was in on the treason, and may even have inspired Arnold to undertake it.)

Arnold's escape on a British warship was by no means the end of the man. He came back to taunt and haunt and harass his former countrymen, leading British troops in successful actions in Connecticut and Virginia—in the latter arena, to the acute embarrassment of Thomas Jefferson, then Governor of Virginia.

Obviously a man constituted as Arnold was, with such a colorful career as both hero and villain, surrounded as he was by so many remarkable people, and moving almost constantly in an atmosphere of danger, conflict and intrigue, presents an embarrassment of riches to the making of a film. But there was a similar embarrassment in the materials of *Lawrence of Arabia* and other successful historical films. Actually Arnold's story, notwithstanding its mural size and vivid colors, is a vastly less complex canvas than that of Lawrence, for with Arnold the alignments of power and the issues at stake were bolder and clearer; Arnold is all man and Peggy is all woman; the villain-hero does not die on a motorcycle; and while there are no deserts, there are forests and beaches and lakes and rivers and walled cities and women and brass and steel and cannon.

There is a way through this complexity, as there was through *Tom Jones* and other period dramas recently brought to life. The way lies through film techniques as modern as tomorrow's headlines, telling the story through a man who was close to Arnold from the start to the end of his fabulous career—at least to that part of it that took place on American soil; a man who at first resented him, then learned in turn to respect him, love him, and hate him; a man who, because of Arnold, ultimately stands in peril of his life.

Arnold, as a picture, would by its very nature transcend the bounds of an action-adventure story; it would trump action-for-the-sake-of-action, and go beyond tension or suspense for their own sakes; for overriding these staples would be a fresh, even unprecedented view of America's birth struggle; and implicit, though certainly not preached, would be the moral that in national affairs, no less than in personal matters, elements of envy and pique and false pride and money-hunger can be as destructive as an invading army.

If ever there was a time to make this picture, it is today, when too many people both in this country and abroad, have forgotten what America is all about. [The film was not made.]

TO LIBRARIAN, PRINCETON UNIVERSITY
August 17, 1965

Dear Sir:

On June 15th I wrote requesting Xerox copies of a dozen letters of my correspondence with Carl Van Doren, which I donated to the Princeton Library in 1951, at the request of Mr. Julian Boyd.

Two months have passed, and I have received no acknowledgment of my letter. I assume this is the result of some inadvertence, and is not standard procedure. I would appreciate a response.

TO ALEXANDER P. CLARK, Curator of Manuscripts, Princeton University Library / August 26, 1965

Dear Mr. Clark:

Thank you for your letter of August 20th. It is of course distressing to learn of the disappearance of the Van Doren letters, since besides his stature as an artist, he was a personal friend whose memory I cherish.

Perhaps it may be helpful in your search for the missing file to have the photocopy attached to this note. It is a letter I received from Julian Boyd, dated February 13, 1951, acknowledging receipt of my Van Doren letters by the library. I am afraid I took better care of Mr. Boyd's letter than the library took of Mr. Van Doren's. In any case this pinpoints the time and subject, and I hope it gives you a clue to work on.

The letters were subsequently located.

TO STEPHANIE DINKINS / September 7, 1965

Dear Stephanie:

Is five days too short to expect a letter to be delivered via airmail to Paris? I hope not; if it is, I have taken the precaution to add forwarding instructions on the envelope.

NORMAN CORWIN'S LETTERS / 239

I have been thinking of you every time there was fresh news from the Kashmir—and all of it *bad* fresh news. I know your special feeling for some of the Moslems you have met, and if I remember correctly, your travels did take you to Rawalpindi, which is in the headlines as a target for a raid. Will this sick old world EVER learn? Must people forever resort to arms as a way of settling disputes? It is sickening.

Also sickening, though on a far less astronomic scale, is the attitude of the *Geographic* toward submissions. It is shocking to hold up a writer/photographer for a whole year, while they are ponderously making up their ponderous minds. I have become disenchanted with the *Geographic* since subscribing for the first time a few years ago (and keeping up my subscription). I find them giving damn near a whole issue to the wonders of Walt Disney and Disneyland—a sickening taffy-pull in praise of that monumental geographical feature, Mr. Disney. It read like a house organ for Disney's enterprises. And every so often they go into an elaborate spread on the nation's latest military hardware. I'm interested in faroff places like Lanzarotte and Tristan de Cunha and Gupis, not in the firepower of the latest Cobra or Copperhead or Stingray. I'm interested in beetles, not battles; God knows we have daily and Sunday newspapers and TV to fill us in on *that*....

TO LEWIS MILESTONE, Film Director / October 24, 1965

He had been invited to speak at the Aspen (Colorado) Film Festival and asked Corwin to write his remarks.

Dear Millie:

Try this on for size.

I am not a registered ghost, so if you are hissed, don't say who wrote it. Say you found it in a cereal box....

It used to be that immortality was the reward only of works so great that posterity couldn't keep its hands off them, and had to take them out and look at them every now and then. But today all the films ever made are immortal, since TV has its hands on them and looks at them every night of the week.

This amounts to low-grade nonfat immortality because it is indiscriminate. It is like a director taking the trouble to live a good life so that he can go to heaven when he dies, and finding, when he gets there, that the population consists of critics, producers, agents, tax men, gardeners, and Jack Warner.

The film festival is today one of the last refuges of respectable immortality, since it is at least selective. That is why I am delighted to be represented at a good festival, either by any one of my immortal pictures, or by my mortal self. An invitation to participate in a festival is still an honor, and will remain so until such time as we have a late-late Festival on every channel right after the 1 a.m. newscast, Mondays through Fridays.

TO DR. AND MRS. BERNARD KLEIN / November 18, 1965

Dr. Klein, Corwin's second cousin, lived in Springfield, Massachusetts, when Corwin was a reporter there.

Dear Bernie and May:

It is ridiculous. I think of you a thousand times in the course of a year, and write you once. How sad it is, and yet how natural, that people drift in time and space. There is no insulation as thick as one's own family, and the concerns that surround it—being the father of two young ones, both just entering their teens, has put and kept me in an orbit, a happy orbit, and the older spheres retreat. But not the memory of them. Not the Friday night dinners, and the great warmth and love that I felt in your home; not the memory of that beautiful girl, Louise [Radding], to whom you introduced me, and I too young to appreciate her; not the bonds that meant so much to me in those lean years of my servitude on *The Republican*—at $32.10 a week!...

I am happy to say that all is reasonably well here; Emil is in Washington with the Department of Health and Welfare, fighting its anti-smoking crusade; Al is in New York in public relations; Beulah's family is of course all grown, and Pa Corwin is still rising at 5:30 a.m. daily, driving a car, and corresponding furiously with his far-flung empire of friends and relations.

I hope this finds you well and snug and happy, and in charge of Medicare for all New England. We all send you love, but especially myself, who know you best and longest.

TO ROD SERLING / December 26, 1965

Dear Rod:

For a reader to feel as you do about the book [*Overkill and Megalove*] is gratifying; when the reader is you, I am done honor; and when the honor is set in a marvelous letter, it sublimates into treasure. What few treasures I own are prized, and your letter is now one of them. I say this without even a chemical trace of hyperbole.

Altogether this has been a Serling Christmas here. First, that Kohinoor of a letter. Next, *The Night of the Meek*, whose Henry Corwin, I persuaded my gullible kids, was named for their old Dad, an aging Jew. And then, distributed broadside among my friends as required reading toward holiday cheer, *B.C. Strikes Back*, with your charming introduction. Among your other awesome achievements I admire your knowing Johnny Hart, and am even more impressed by his asking you to preface those priceless cartoons. To me it is as though Einstein had asked me to write a foreword to his theory of relativity. Tell Hart he has another abject devotee at this address; nay, four. Daily.

Let us meet in the New Year. Which year, by the way, I have charged to bring you more of the blessings you have brought to yourself, upon which bounty I invoke additional blessings of my own and God's, though not of course in that order of billing.

TO ALBERT AND DAVID MAYSLES / January 4, 1966

Dear Al and Dave:

Many thanks for the copy of *In Cold Blood*, which looks as though it might push the Bible for total sales. I think it's exciting that you should be doing a film on Capote; can't wait to see it.

Remember that next-door-neighbor family you shot for *Life*? Turns out to be the King Family. Their towering pine tree just fell across my privet hedge. Small world. [James Conkling and Donna King, of the singing King Family, lived next door to Corwin.]

Let's see more of you guys out here; in the meantime, best of luck on the Capote. And have a great 66.

TO STEPHANIE DINKINS / January 20, 1966

Dear Stephanie:

A shameful delinquency on my part, for I am now two letters behind you, upsetting the meticulously balanced debit-and-credit over the last fifteen years! But by this stroke I reduce by half my arrears. (Sounds like the fruits of dieting.)

What has kept me from writing has also kept me from just about every other civilized activity, including haircuts and days off. As chairman of the documentary awards committee of the Motion Picture Academy, I have screenings twice and sometimes three times a week; as director of my own play [*The Hyphen*], scheduled to open in Utah March 24, I rehearse three nights a week. In addition to which I am still hacking away at my autobiography. (Did I tell you that a section of this book running 450 pages, which took me four months to write, is so wrong in conception and execution that I am boiling it down to about thirty-five pages?) [Corwin had been writing an autobiography, later abandoned, to be called *Re Me*.] That this can happen to an "experienced" writer, after all the reading and writing he has done in his curious life, is a commentary on the craft we both share. It makes the *Geographic*'s cuts in the Lanzarote story seem a little little.

I am of course not happy to hear of the Nat Geog's chintzy attitude about payment. Why is it that those who can most afford to be generous, are least likely to be? Nevertheless it is a big and good credit for you, and they all count....

TO ALLEN NEVINS, Historian / February 3, 1966

Dear Allen:

The attached map will crowd nobody for honors in cartography, but it has all the salient information. I assume you know the main ship channels from the Pasadena to the Golden State to the Ventura Freeways; once you're on the Ventura, it is quite simple.

We very much look forward to having you and Mrs. Nevins with us on the 16th. Should there be any questions, the telephone number at that bottom of the legend on the map is ready with all kinds of research data.

TO ED LUDLUM, Director / February 25, 1966

Dear Ed Ludlum:

My request of some weeks ago, for the return of some script material, has gone unacknowledged.

I congratulate you on being able to afford the luxury of alienating people friendly to your career. That indicates the security of arrival, which is the goal of every artist.

TO STEPHANIE DINKINS / April 11, 1966

Dear Stephanie:

...It went well in Utah. My casting difficulties turned out to be disguised blessings—I am very thankful now that the original pair defected. They were replaced by William Shatner and an actress who gave the play vastly more verve and style than the others could have done. The audiences loved it, and so did the press. [The original cast had been Philip Pine and Vera Miles, who was replaced by Joan Payne.]

We worked hard, but in a joyous context—the play is a comedy, the University people were overjoyed with it, Shatner felt it was the best role he had ever played. There was respect and affection all the way around, and the month spent up at Salt Lake felt more like a holiday than a work session. We even had time to take off to one of the several magnificent skiing resorts within thirty or forty-five minutes from the city, and altho I did not ski, I enjoyed the superb gondola ride to a mountaintop from which, on a clear day, one can see Gupis.

At the prodding of Shatner, I went motorcycling one day (a so-called tote goat, not a full motorcycle) and we rode on rutty dirt roads in the mountains above the city. I fancied I found the secret of maintaining a high enough speed to avoid the kidney-slamming roughness of the road, and was breezing along at an authoritative clip when the t-goat bucked and went over on its side, and I plowed into a cubic yard of red earth. I scraped elbow and knee and sprained a finger, but what is that when the play was well received?....

DR. WILLIAM B. OBER / May 21, 1966

Dear Bill:

I am constantly being refreshed by evidences of cross-fertilization in literature. One of my favorite quotes out of anywhere has been Herman Melville's comment on Ralph Waldo Emerson:

> I could readily see in Emerson, notwithstanding his merit, a gaping flaw. It was the insinuation that had he lived in those days when the world was made, he might have offered some valuable suggestions.

Imagine my start, on reading in the book of *Star Names* that you so kindly sent me, to find accredited to King Alfonso X, known as El Sabio, 13th Century, the following remark:

> Had I been present at the Creation, I would have given some useful hints for the better ordering of the universe.

That is my thought for today.

TO LEONARD BERNSTEIN / June 20, 1966

Dear Leonard:

Greetings across the years, and with them, accumulated congratulations on all you have done and are doing.

Question: Do you have an address on Eve Eisner, sister of Al? I want to return to her a hallowed file of letters that includes, incidentally, one from yourself to Al.

This whole province is looking forward to the UCLA production of *Candide*. The Group is strong on acting; I hope it can do proper honor to the score.

Bernstein had written a short composition in memory of Alfred Eisner. See Corwin's letter to Davidson Taylor, January 16, 1941.

TO MARIANNE RONEY MANTELL / July 13, 1966

Dear M:

A culture buff picked up your [Caedmon Records] catalog from my desk, walked off with it, and has not returned it, so I am without this source of reference. Do mail me another. I assume you prefer to cast Lincoln [for a recording] from the names therein on the grounds that you have dealt with them in the past and are secure in their ability and reliability. I also assume you are not averse to a Lincoln outside of the catalog, if none can be found within.

I have directed two of the more familiar Lincolns: [Raymond] Massey and Richard Boone, and I recommend neither for Kobold [the Caedmon logo]. The first is a whining bore, the second hardly worth the trial. Royal Dano I have seen only as a young Lincoln, and he was good enough at it. [Henry] Fonda, who played Lincoln in the film, is monotony incarnate when you cannot see him speak the lines, and sometimes when you can....Fritz Weaver is intelligent and flexible but perhaps too authoritative, shading to pompous. I say perhaps because I have not seen much of his work—ask someone who has. [Christopher] Plummer, whom I thought fairly tedious in *Royal Hunt of the Sun,* has at least the ganglions of an actor; it is a question of whether one could get him to be simple enough. John Anderson, who played Lincoln in the California Arts Commission's production of *The Rivalry,* is first class, perhaps the best of all these, but you may be after a bigger name. I had hoped that by now Caedmon discs were selling on their own intrinsic high merits rather than on names, but you know best about all this.

I take it you have not yet read *The Rivalry.* Stop counting your millions for long enough to do so. It is only slightly longer than this letter. It has the uncommon asset, in this hour, of sharp topicality. Watts, Chicago, Omaha, and God knows where next.

TO HERB BLOCK / July 14, 1966

Dear Herb:

One of the nicest things to happen in this country since Lincoln and Jefferson were enshrined in Washington, is the exercise of good taste on the part of the government in getting you to design the Bill of Rights stamp. You honor the choice as much as it honors you, and the casting is impeccable. Now you are immortal in philately *too*.

And now for a message from the petitioner: If you are not too weary of filling such requests, would you sign your name at the bottom of these three clusters of The Stamp and return them to me in the enclosed envelope?

I hope this letter finds you healthy and hearty and enjoying life, and that you will not for too long continue to be absent from these parts. You are needed here for morale against the encroachment of actors upon politics. The precedent is dreadful—think of Mr. [John Wilkes] Booth. [Ronald Reagan, the actor, was running for the governorship of California.]

TO ROBERT M. HUTCHINS / July 18, 1966

Corwin had taken part in a symposium at the UCLA Conference Center at Lake Arrowhead, California. He attacked biologists for their research in biological warfare. When panel members responded angrily, Corwin's one supporter was Jonas Salk.

Dear Bob:

You are kind to let me know you like the paper on "The New Biology." It was fun to write and deliver, and you would have been amused by the acerbity with which some of the impaneled scientists responded. "Mr. Corwin," said one of them, "would have denigrated the biological researches of Pasteur." "Not so," I answered,"Pasteur's program was to prevent disease, not promote it." Another resented the fact that I, a layman from the arts, had dared to sit in judgment on any aspect of science. "I would suggest a body of scientists sit in judgment on the humane contributions of television to society, and see what they would find!" he said triumphantly. "They would probably find," I replied, "that *The Beverly Hillbillies*, bad as it is, cannot quite be equated with the hydrogen bomb as a social hazard."

"In the old days of Dickens that you seem to yearn for," said another, "they would hang an eight-year-old child for stealing a loaf of bread!" "Today," I answered, "eight-year-old children are cremated in napalm for doing nothing."

And so it went, my colleagues on the panel getting madder by the minute. I will never be invited back to the forums of that group, but I *have* been invited to the Center by you, and that is reward enough for any layman.

By all means let me know when Linus Pauling is back on his mended leg. And in the meantime, great thanks for your welcome letter.

TO ERIK BARNOUW, Professor of Communications at Columbia University / September 6, 1966

Dear Erik:

I have edited the attached transcript after having first recovered from the shock of seeing, in black and white, how dreadfully brecciated are so many of my spoken sentences. [Barnouw had conducted an oral history interview with Corwin and sent him the transcript.] My syntax at times should be awarded the Purple Heart. And how I did skip around and backtrack and fill in! I have done my best to bring some sense of order to the shambles without altering the conversational texture.

I have been reading my eyes bloodshot on historic material for a movie, but I did get a chance to go off to Lake Arrowhead for a UCLA Conference, where Jonas Salk and I found ourselves paired in a weekend-long fencing duel with a pair of scientists. Salk is a great person—he has the quiet strength and the simplicity and depth of the rare ones, and I had some wonderful long talks with him. I also had the good fortune to meet Ansel Adams, the photographer—one of the vanishing giants of the order of Sandburg, Frost, and Frank Lloyd Wright—a natural, made in America....

TO MORT JANKLOW / September 30, 1966

Dear Mort:

Thanks to your expert briefing I was able to walk into a typewriter shop and casually drop terms that persuaded the shopkeeper I must be either Tom Watson, Jr., or a scout for Smith-Corona. You were princely to advise me so fully and clearly, and I am indebted to you for the education. [Corwin had admired Janklow's typewriter and writing paper and had written for guidance.]

Thanks too for passing on Peter Stone's witty comment. I look forward to meeting him, for I have enjoyed his pictures, and heard much good earburn about him from witnesses whose testimony can be trusted. Of course his name is a double exposure, literally Stone Stone, considering the etymology of Peter. Perhaps his mother watched Simone Simon while gravida.

All is well here, if you except the punishment I am taking from Jefferson's memoirs. It is my luck to have truck with subjects that require a wing of a library each. Lincoln, and the American Revolution, and the Bill of Rights, and the United Nations, and now TJ. The Princeton University Press is in its twenty-second year of collecting the papers of Jefferson, and has so far completed only seventeen volumes of the projected sixty. The seventeen arrived last week, and I have been reading them. Those are not bags under my eyes, but portmanteaux.

I don't know if you and Linda share Doris' quasi-religious bigotry respecting the Dodgers, but I am sure that Koufax's win last night, in which he struck out thirteen and raised his season total to three hundred plus, has further discouraged pogroms in America. I am a little nervous, however, that the California electorate, never Athenian in its collected wisdom, may vote for Reagan under the impression that he is the excellent relief pitcher, Phil Regan.

On this solemn thought, which I hope does not come too soon after you have eaten, I close with renewed thanks and assurances of my esteem and my love to you both.

TO ARNOLD M. GRANT, Corporate Lawyer / October 6, 1966

Dear Arnie:

Another very long letter, but it poses such a crucial problem that I hope you will be able to read it at some leisure, and with patience. First, though, let me say that it was good to hear your and Bess's voices the other night, and to know that you are well and have survived the election in Georgia which nominated [Lester] Maddox. I have not yet recovered.

Your letter of the 4th reached me today [Grant was engaged by 20th Century-Fox to produce a film on Thomas Jefferson, to be written by Corwin], and I am now flying distress signals because of a meaty paragraph that has conked me on the head. It comes on page 2, and reads as follows:

> ...We will not do the job if Jefferson dominates to the point that it becomes his story rather than his times. In telling the story of the latter, he is the focal point but our hero is the nation. This is the feeling that came out of Marat/Sade. This, despite the love story told around the male and female Rhett and Scarlett, was the essence of Gone with the Wind, which told the story of the Civil War, its times and issues. The history of the times dominated and came through around these people. The people did not push the times into the background.

I am alarmed by this because it completely reverses not only what I thought was our understanding on approach, but the orientation of everything I have so far done and projected. Perhaps your concern that Jefferson does not entirely swallow up the nation, is a matter of *degree* rather than one of principle; but I fear your feeling is stronger than that.

It was my understanding that Jefferson *would* indeed dominate to the point that it becomes his story against the background of the times; that *he*, and not an abstraction, becomes the hero; that through him, as a symbol, the American experiment in democracy is heroized.

There are extreme difficulties, in my view insuperable, in making a viable picture of "the story of the birth of America," a picture in which the hero is the nation. This is because the American Revolution, on any level—political, economic or military—is vastly complex. The common conception of the Revolution militarily is that it consisted of the battles of Lexington, Bunker Hill, Trenton, Saratoga and Yorktown, and that all were American victories either in fact or spirit. But the truth is infinitely more involved than that—there were unsuccessful and humiliating campaigns in Canada, Washington was chased out of Long Island and then New York, we were clobbered at Valcour Island, Oriskany, Brandywine, Charleston and Camden; sent running from Ticonderoga; even Jefferson was embarrassed by Benedict Arnold's depredations in Virginia; and during all this time Congress was bumbling and fumbling and getting in the way of Washington as much as it was helping him. And let's not forget that the French, on land and sea, had much to do with our final victory, and so did the threat of an attack by Spain on England's flank.

Economically, the famous taxation "tyrannies" of England are by today's standards quaint and poignant. I cannot see how a modern audience will be deeply moved by a measly stamp tax, and a tax on tea, when we are today taxed beyond the wildest imaginings of anyone in that century—huge, confiscatory, crushing taxes not only on the rich but the poor—and whether the taxes are imposed by local or state or federal authorities, it comes to the same thing—a nagging burden.

I have seen the Boston Tea Party dramatized on the screen more than once, and each time it has seemed to me like a boisterous Hallowe'en party, more a beatnik riot than an Act of Liberty. When England demanded that the Port of Boston pay for the destroyed tea, which was a perfectly understandable though politically tactless move, one would have thought that the Huns had raped every woman in the Colonies.

I am not arguing that England was saintly and we were hot-headed; the Intolerable Acts and the Restraining Acts were incentive enough to rebellion; but the liberty we fought for in the American Revolution, was many degrees removed from the quality of liberty that was at issue in the Civil War, and in both World Wars. Modern audiences are accustomed to such heinous tyrannies and violent cruelties, such ghastly violations of liberty, that those for which we fought in 1776 must seem pale by comparison. *What was different and ennobling about our*

Revolution was the CONCEPT of liberty projected into the future, a concept made all the more remarkable by the fact that nobody in the world had come up with it before, and by the additional fact that it was propounded at a time when the world was largely ruled by benighted monarchies.

That *concept* was the work of a God-sent body of men, but when you examine the record closely you will find that the credit narrows down to a handful—and leading them all was our boy Jefferson. It was HIS mind, HIS pen, HIS passion, HIS enlightenment that created the Declaration of Independence. The others helped rewrite it, but rewriting an idea or a document is a hell of a lot simpler than creating it. And Jefferson did not come by those ideas overnight. He prepared for his role, and *was* prepared for it, by all that had gone before—his upbringing, schooling, law practice, his dry runs in the *Summary View of the Rights of British America,* and various libertarian works before he was called in to pitch at Philadelphia in 1776.

Jefferson led; the nation followed. But by the *time* he led, blood had been flowing for some while. You cannot really tell a *BIRTH* OF A NATION starring Jefferson, because he was not one of the prime movers in the sense that Sam Adams and Patrick Henry were; Jefferson was a mere law student, listening in the hallway, when Henry made his "If this be treason" speech. Properly Jefferson's contribution was the birth of a *creed* rather than of a nation; and God knows creating a creed is the greater of the two acts. Many nations have been born (Guyana, Tanzania, Pakistan, Czechoslovakia and Jordan, for example) but few have achieved glory though a creed. Pericles gave such glory to Athens, and Jefferson to America.

Another consideration: The complications of telling "the story of the founding of a nation and a form of government" are compounded by the huge gap between the first bloodshed at Concord in 1775, and the first compact toward a new form of government—the ratification of the Constitution in 1789—a stretch of fourteen years. And of course there developed a titanic struggle immediately *after* the form of government was worked out—a struggle led by Hamilton on the one side and Jefferson on the other. It makes fascinating history, but as a picture it would be bewilderingly labyrinthine.

One last thought on this phase of the subject, and this time a crass commercial one: If our emphasis is on the causes leading to the Revolutionary War, and the war itself, it means a picture given over largely to flogging a British enemy. At this juncture in world and cinema affairs, I gravely question whether the British, on whom we rely for no small percentage of our gross, will flock to see themselves in the role of heavy. I don't mean that we need send England a valentine, and we will certainly make clear whom we fought in the war, and why; it is just a question of emphasis. I believe we are going after far more lasting issues in this picture, issues which are still abroad in the country and the world; and in *these* contests all the world, including the Britain of today, is deeply interested.

I submit, Arnie, that the story we want to tell must be told in human terms, through a living, identifiable protagonist in whom we become interested—AND OFF WHOM PEOPLE AND EVENTS BOUNCE—or we will bog down....

Jefferson must not only dominate the picture, he must dominate the country. And he *did* dominate the country. He was the leading American but one, of his entire era, and when that one—[Benjamin] Franklin—died, Jefferson led alone. I feel we need have not the slightest qualm in pledging our picture, a reasonable amount of our fortunes, and our sacred honor, to making a picture in which Jefferson dominates from the first to last frame. One need have no worry about the nation getting lost in the interstices. That is impossible. But at moments we must tell America to *get* lost; when in Paris, for example, Jefferson takes up with Mrs. Cosway; or earlier, in Virginia, when he brings his bride through a snowstorm at midnight, on horseback, to a little honeymoon cottage on the top of his little mountain. That is personal business upon which the nation has no right to intrude. But because of such business, we'll care more about the nation—for *Jefferson's* caring.

If I have not by this time wearied you, I should like further to pursue the role of His Majesty's Loyal Opposition, and argue against your point concerning *Marat/Sade* and *Gone With the Wind*. I did not get the feeling that the nation was the hero in *Marat/Sade*. In my view there was *no* hero. The nation of Marat's time was a seething anarchy; the Revolution itself had stopped being a hero with the first victim railroaded to the guillotine. If there was any hero at all, it was the dim, ghostly, offstage abstraction of humanity, expressed fitfully through Charlotte Corday, cynically through Sade, and passionately through two or three of the more articulate lunatics. But La France came out smelling like carrion....

Re *Gone With the Wind*, either my memory or yours is at fault. I remember it as an elaborate love story to which the times and issues of the Civil War were remarkably secondary except for massive production sequences common to any historic canvas of a war. In fact I remember being very much annoyed because I felt Selznick utterly missed the basic issue of the war. An opening title referred to "the war between two nations," implying that the Confederacy was an established, running, legitimate nation at the time of Sumter or at any other time. But that was the whole *point* of the war—we were *one* nation, and a half of it was trying to break away. I remember no understanding whatever of the basic issues of the war in *Gone With the Wind*. My own modest little *Rivalry* is a college course in history compared to what anyone could learn from that film, about causes, effects and issues. The march through Georgia was fine, with all those crool Yankees pillaging and burning, but where was Andersonville, which belongs with Auschwitz among the worst atrocities of history.

The reason for this strenuous letter, is that I am deeply concerned lest I totally misapprehended our understanding. If you hold fast to the compass-bearing of your quoted paragraph, then I seriously question not only whether I can do it, but whether anybody can. I am concerned, after your letter, as I was not concerned before, that all I have written and blocked-out up to now may disappoint you, no matter how much you might be attracted to its technique. On the other hand, it could be that I am unwarrantedly apprehensive, and that in your paragraph you were ruminating and contemplating rather than laying down hard and fast guidelines. But should the latter be in fact the case, then I would with earnest sincerity urge you to put a restraining order on my work. I say this with every filament of affection intact, because one cannot quarrel with, let alone be vexed by a validly divergent point of view. You can appreciate that I would feel unhappy about going forward on, and accepting payment for, any approach which did not meet with your sanction; for after all the project is your dream, and exists only because of your personal puissance. For another thing, under the sub-dominant Jefferson approach, such retooling would be necessary, that I could never make the November 30 deadline; as it is, going full steam ahead on the present approach, it is very dubious whether a first draft will be complete by November 1st as you hope; the reason for this you will understand immediately on seeing how much is poured into how little space—a crowded canvas, but one that, I hope and trust, has breathing room and some grace and humor....

TO MRS. FLORA SCHREIBER / October 30, 1966

> A writer, she had written to ask for details about the time a pilot had approached Corwin in mid-Atlantic.

Dear Mrs. Schreiber:

It was the Navigator of a TWA flight to Rome. Time: 1 a.m., mid-Atlantic Greenwich time; place: the fore cabin. Most of the passengers were asleep, and the lights dim, but he could make out my name, which was pinned to the back of the seat in the fashion of first-class air travel. (Tourist passengers have no names.) The Navigator stopped, and, seeing I was awake, asked if I were by any chance *Norman* Corwin. When I confessed to the charge, he went right into a recital of lines from the apotheosis that concludes *On a Note of Triumph*, a program I wrote for CBS to be aired on the night of victory in Europe, a cool eighteen years earlier. He did not recite the whole thing, just the opening of the passage which starts, "Lord God of trajectory and blast," and then one of the concluding lines, which is, "Post proofs that brotherhood is not so wild a dream as those who profit from postponing it, pretend." He said he had heard the program and bought the book which S & S published following the broadcast, and he had memorized parts of it. Also he owned a recording of the broadcast, and played it, he said, at least once a year so his children would not forget that particular lesson of the past.

You ask whether he remembered the lines because of identification with them, or because of the quality of the lines. I think it was a little of both—the latter, I presume to think, because of a certain relish with which he lingered on the phrases.

Coming, as it did, right after the conclusion of a depressingly bad in-flight movie, it salvaged the truncated night for me.

TO ED WEYL, Film Executive, 20th Century-Fox
November 11, 1966

Dear Ed:

I have two historic items for you, separated by a little over two hundred years:

1. Jefferson, while Minister to France, on one occasion placed an order for 72 bottles of Frontignac wine, 36 bottles of Cyprus, and 212 of Malvoisie de Madeire.

2. Corwin, while Minister to 20th Century-Fox, waited patiently from June to November, for Office 37 in the New Writers Building to become available. For several months it was assigned to Abby Mann, and lay sealed, untouched by human hands, because Mr. Mann never used it. Then one day late in October, after I had carried my appeal all the way to Justice Weyl, it was opened! Not to me, but to Mr. Larry Forrester. I took this philosophically, and kept on in the arrangement whereby I am separated from my secretary, who shares her office with another.

But now I hear that Mr. Forrester is leaving in a week's time. I would like to renew my bid for his chambers.

The request is not based on decor or size of office, simply on the situation that requires either my secretary or myself to go in and out of doors each time it is necessary for us to convey anything to each other. I don't mind a shift from a toasty interior to what can be a chilly outside, but it is hard on Miss Fasken, who may have to do this twenty or more times a day.

I'll appreciate anything you can do, and in any case shall toast you in Malvoisie the minute I can lay my hands on any.

With best regards,

Corwin got the office.

TO BARRA GRANT, Writer and Actress / November 14, 1966

Dear Hermione:

I am glad you have been keeping company with Shakespeare. [The daughter of Arnold and Bess Myerson Grant, she had expressed an interest in Shakespeare's women characters.] The tragedy of our education is that we are brought to the treasure chest of our great language too late, then we spend too little time with it, and once we have put it away with our schoolbooks, we never look back at it again. Perhaps in the course of an average adult life, the average American will see five or six Shakespearean productions, of which half are truncated versions on TV, hamburgerized by commercials. How many of us turn to that fat volume of the *Collected Plays* for the sheer pleasure of reading them? No, we are too busy reading how many corpses lie on the ground in the Mekong Delta, or the syndicated columns of William Buckley.

Your nostalgia for this "remembered Eden" is misplaced, unless you mean the greenery and the allegedly blue skies and the scentless flowers. The electorate of God's country out here has just distinguished itself by injecting a tenth-rate actor, a Birchite by leaning and a fascist by nature, into national circulation—not only is he governor of the country's most populous state, but he is already being spoken of as presidential timber. How you can feel nostalgia for the Gomorrah that created Reagan, is beyond my capacity to imagine—save that I know he did not figure in your figure of speech.

Meanwhile, I am lost in Jeffersoniana, which is not the worst fate that can befall a man who loves his country. The work is hard and getting harder, but it will have been worth it all if the picture is ever made, and made with integrity....

Your vibrant presence is of course much missed. But the Commissary's—and my—loss, is Shakespeare's gain, and I am not going to quarrel with that.

Kate joins me in sending much love,

TO GARSON KANIN, Playwright and Author
December 14, 1966

Dear Gar:

I did not want to dip into the Maugham book until I had put pressing deadlines behind me, so that I could enjoy a full meal rather than scattered hors d'oeuvres, from time to time, and I am glad I waited. It is solidly enjoyable and awesomely instructive to any writer who worries about discipline (envying Maugham) and about the importance of immediate note-taking before the memory has cooled (envying Kanin). [Kanin had recently published a book of remembrances of W. Somerset Maugham.]

You are a dear fellow to have remembered Kate and me, and we treasure your inscription as we treasure you.

I quarrel amiably with the Beaton photo of you on the jacket flap. It has the distinction of an Assyrian bas-relief, but your left eye is focused on left field, which is neutral territory. The portrait unavoidably lacks the charm of your full-face, which in poise has such a marvelous blend of healthy iniquitousness, and the humor with which to put it into practice as well as into print.

Kate and I unite in sending our love to you and Ruth....[Mrs. Kanin was the actress Ruth Gordon.]

TO MIRRON ALEXANDROFF, President, Columbia College of Communications / January 13, 1967

He invited Corwin to receive an honorary degree of Doctor of Letters at the June commencement.

Dear President Alexandroff:

I am honored and moved by your generous letter, which is made all the more treasurable to me, for having come from the same hand as the eloquent statement of Columbia's objectives opposite your portrait in the brochure. You speak with clarity and force, and it is heartening to know there are still people who care about rehabilitating dignity in a world that is so tragically undone.

I look forward to the exercises of next June with redoubled pleasure. As for delivering an address, I wish to be neither forward nor shy; you must exercise your own wishes and judgment in the matter, for then if I do speak, you will have only yourself to blame, and if I don't you will be entitled to the credit of having, like a good general, protected the flank of your exercises. Either way, it will be a pleasure to be among you, loud or silent.

With every good wish, I am,

Corwin did speak at the commencement.

TO DR. WILLIAM B. OBER / January 26, 1967

Dear Billy:
...May I celebrate the passing Ides of January with a new limerick....

There was a skin surgeon of Taft
Who sewed a man's fore to his aft
The case was the sort
That wound up in court
And he was convicted of graft.

Ober uber alles. Love to Rhoda,

TO ARCHIBALD MacLEISH [who was being honored at a poetry festival in Florida] / February 28, 1967

Dear Archie:
I allow myself the familiarity of calling you Archie after twenty years because this privilege, like the capacity to ride a bicycle, is hard to unlearn.

I greet you across these strange decades, with the special pleasure that comes of maintaining, over such a spread of time, and with the greatest of ease, an affectionate esteem and admiration. Too often the heroes of one's formative days crumble from the defect of clay feet. Not you. Your step has been elastic always. I can never forget, and indeed occasionally refresh myself on, the beauty and thrust of your work. It will continue to inspire writers as it inspired me, long after both of us have left this vale of warring isms and escalations.

With every kind wish and a toast to the good years behind and ahead, I am,

TO ELLIOTT SANGER, Chairman of the Board, WQXR
March 17, 1967

> Sanger had been the station's general manager when WQXR booked Corwin's Poetic License Series.

Dear Elliott:

It is seldom that a man can put his finger on a moment of his life and say, "At that instant, everything changed." When our paths crossed thirty years ago, my life took another course.

God knows where I would be or what would have happened to me, had it not been for your generosity in giving what must have been the benefit of many doubts, to a brash young publicity flack from across town. When in later years I came across scripts of my WQXR shows, and listened to recordings of a few of them, my awe at your original kindness and patience increased dramatically and retroactively....

You stood at the very beginning, as you have done ever after, for all that was creative and good in radio. If there was anything useful in my own contributions to that once glorious medium, it was shaped in the matrix of WQXR, which in turn was molded by yourself.

From this you will perhaps believe and understand the emotion with which I greet and salute you at this hour of your retirement from the chairmanship of the board. Be sure that my esteem, gratitude and affectionate regard go with you always.

TO BARNET RUDER / April 22, 1967

Dear Barney:

Last night for the first time I met Henry Miller at a dinner party, and the first thing he did was to inquire about you. He said that you had befriended him in New York at a time when nobody had recognized him; that he was and continues to be grateful for the help and encouragement you gave him when he most sorely needed it. He regretted immensely that he had not heard from or about you in many years, and did not even know if you were still in New York. I assured him that you were, told him I see you occasionally and that we exchange a letter now and then.

I took the liberty of asking for his address to transmit to you, since I did not know your address offhand. He would love to hear from you—he was warm and genuine in his esteem, and the very fact that he instantly connected your name with mine because you had told him about me in those days, is an index itself of the regard and affection in which he holds you. Auld acquaintances should not be lost. Have you ever read of the wonderful way in which old Dr. Benjamin Rush brought John Adams and Thomas Jefferson together by correspondence—years after they had been estranged by politics? That is what started the immortal correspondence between the two old warriors. Neither you nor Miller is *that* old, nor am I; but there is no good excuse for such friendships to peter out....

Merry Passover to you, and all good things....

TO KATHERINE CORWIN / The Hilton, Tel Aviv, July 6, 1967

At the request of Samuel Bronston, the Film Producer, Corwin had flown to Madrid and then on to Tel Aviv with Bronston. On June 5, 1967, Israel had launched a preemptive strike against Egypt, Syria and Jordan, and Bronston hoped to make a film about that Six-Day action.

Darling:

...Before I tell you what has developed vis-a-vis the picture, let me fill you in on my four-plus days in Israel so far, and describe a little of the local scene. Tel Aviv is a sprawling, unique city, white and gray and buff, stretched out along a sandy shore. Almost impudently, there are a half dozen high-rise buildings, twenty to forty stories high, scattered about the city. The Hilton is one. When I am in my room, the sound of surf is always with me. Also the sound of the air-conditioning system.

In the short time I have been here, I have been to Jerusalem, Bethlehem (until lately in Jordanian hands); I have stood before the Wailing Wall, and of course touched it; I have been to Nazareth and Haifa and the Sea of Galilee and Safad, and down across the Negev Desert to the port city of Eilat on the Gulf of Aqaba—the denial of access to which by [Egyptian leader Gamal Abdel] Nasser, touched off the war....

But the highlight of my visit so far was a trip into Syria—the occupied portion, to see the demobilization of reserves who fought in the armored division which smashed through Syrian fortifications and penetrated beyond the town of Quneitra. This is the force that caused the big squawk at the UN, where the Syrians claimed they broke the original cease-fire agreement. The whole approach across the Jordan (about five feet wide here) was up sharply rising ground, all fortified with bunkers and pillboxes. The fighting here was particularly bitter, and Israeli losses relatively high. But they cleared out the Syrian defenses—there were overturned and burned-out Syrian tanks and trucks for miles into the high plateau. In the distance were the snow-covered mountains of Lebanon.

The weather was much cooler than in the lower valleys from which we had come. All around were markers indicating live mine fields. We drove past Arab houses, past Arabs looking on with seeming unconcern, drove through and past Quneitra, to hilly terrain outside the city. Suddenly, at right angles to the main roads, was an avenue of Israeli flags—the star of David, blue on white, snapping in the stiff breeze.

There were about two hundred people, mostly relatives of the men in the force, some of them parents whose boys had died in the fighting, and they formed a kind of reviewing stand, in whose front row we were privileged to sit. At a given signal over a loud-speaker system, smoke bombs were set off in the distant hills—white, black, magenta smoke drifted across the scene. And through this curtain of smoke, distantly, on the brow of the rolling hills, emerged tanks, half-tracks, armored trucks, crawling over the ridges, and descending in a dozen files toward the reviewing stand. Then when they had approached within about two hundred yards they stopped, and the entire force stood in their vehicles, at attention.

Now there were a series of announcements—the names and ranks of the dead were read out, and as each name came over the P.A. system, a soldier touched one of forty-nine upturned helmets which lay in a file on the ground, and each of these sprang into a flame which kept forking and billowing into the wind for as long as the ceremony lasted. Other announcements followed, and then the entire force passed in parade. The whole complement was being *discharged*—sent back to their families and jobs, so soon after the shooting. Not the equipment, but the men. That's how secure they feel their strength is on that front. Nevertheless there were outposts on the top of each hill to make sure the Syrians didn't try to start anything during the procession. I read later in a newspaper, back in Tel Aviv, that there had been exchange of fire three miles north of Quneitra, but we did not hear it. All we did hear was the firing of some rocket salvos by some of the tanks—in salute.

It was thrilling to perceive before me one of the sharpest units of this incredible army. Wonderful faces, wonderful boys—none of the robot, crew-cut types—some wore hair longer than Tony's, and the dress was motley and often baggy. But tough, in great physical trim....I also met the commanders—one of them had clobbered the Jordanians on the Jerusalem front, and *then* moved over to the Syrian front.

The people are confident and of course much much relieved over the course of events. Last night I had dinner with Mariassa and her mother at their apartment. Mariassa still walks with a cane; Bat-Miriam has those bright, burning poet's eyes, keen as a cheetah's; we had a good two hours and then I had to run off to keep an appointment with [Israeli leader Moshe] Dayan's right-hand man—a fellow named Moishe Pearlman, who, when told by Grant and Bronston that I was to do their script, burst with excitement. He said he had been a fan of mine; he was once Director of Israel's radio, and had wanted to bring me over ten years ago. Brilliant man with a British accent.

Now as to developments on the picture: I wrote a nine-page prospectus as to what the picture should say and how it should say it, and I handed it to Bronston. He had misplaced his glasses, and asked me to read it aloud, which I did. When I finished I looked up and his eyes had filled with tears. He could not speak for a minute and went into the bathroom, where he stayed for some minutes. When he emerged he said it was THE picture to be made. This was IT. Maybe he cries easily; I did not think it was all that moving or all that good; but it is pleasant for me that Sam thinks so.

Immediately Sam spoke of wanting me to spend several months of every year in Madrid; he wants me to be part of his operation. Knowing movies, knowing the sudden romances and the equally sudden end to the romances, I am counting on nothing, not even on this picture, which in any event would involve very hard work. But if there is even a 10 percent or 20 percent chance that things *do* work out, and that his enthusiasm persists beyond next shabbas, then it is worth, even at this early hour, thinking about whether and how we might operate so that part of each year is spent in Spain, with all that has to offer in the way of easy access to Paris and London.

All, as I say, is premature at this moment: Nothing is settled, especially not terms; I don't even know if or when I will be back in California before I get down to work on the Israel script, IF I do. I do know that Sam would like for me to spend a few days as his guest in Madrid, to show me his studio, his layout, his personnel. So by the time you get this, I may have left Tel Aviv for Madrid. In the event of any emergency, which I hope the God of the Israelites will forbid, I suppose I could be reached person-to-person thru Bronston in Madrid, who is damn near as well known there as [Spanish Dictator Francisco] Franco. Pfui....

I don't know when again I will have a chance to write, but will certainly take advantage of the first opportunity. Love to the kiddies and you,

TO MRS. CARL SANDBURG / July 24, 1967

Dear Paula:

There are few men of whom it can properly be said, "They belong to the ages." Most belong to their own crowded hour, and are forgotten in the next, and the ages could not care less. But Carl is one of the fixed immortals, and has as much chance of being forgotten as Lincoln.

The blow of the news—a hard one, even though Carl was crowding ninety—was lightened for me when, in one of the many television tributes to him, you were quoted as saying that the end came peacefully and beautifully.

It was a privilege to share some of Carl's days, and a joy to be able to bring his works to many audiences across the years. I share with you and the family, and with his legion of friends and admirers, rich and happy memories of a rare, great man.

You must please let me know if at any time I can be of service to yourself and the world of Carl Sandburg, a very definite planet in eternal orbit. I would, as in the past, take pleasure in the association.

With my condolences and affectionate regards,

TO DIANE BAKER, Actress / September 8, 1967

Dear Diane:

I have just returned from a week in the photogenic uplands of Arizona, and I find your very welcome letter. Since you too have great scenic beauty, it was a kind of felicitous extension of the trip.

You say nothing of your stay in Majorca so I will have to wait until we meet to be briefed on the subject. In the meantime I must deposit with you a single moment, a fleeting glory, of the Arizona cyclorama. I was driving from Jerome, which sits high in Spanish style above quite Spanish country, to Sedona, whose setting alone makes up for many of God's mistakes. To the west, in a tumult of broken clouds left over from a day of intermittent thunderstorms, the sun was setting theatrically. Off to the east, against a neutral, darkening sky, a rain shower caught the sun and glowed like a luminous ruby shaft ascending from the earth. It was empyrean, first class. While I was not so greedy as to want it to last forever, I wished it would go on for another forty seconds at least. It obliged.

What a busy girl you are, and how wonderful that you can swing from Krakatoa to Elizabeth The Queen like a limberly lass on a flying trapeze! I am pleased to note that you plan "a lonely rest" for a week or so after your labors in Madrid, and before you go on to London. Few of us have the talent to relax: I am not among the favored, and I envy you....

TO BARNET RUDER / September 10, 1967

Dear Barney:

I don't know whether you have the slightest interest in attending the Sandburg Memorial Service, an invitation to which came in the mail. But if you have, I enclose it. I will not be able to make it myself, since I'll be on my way to Chapel Hill, North Carolina, where for five weeks I will be writer-in-residence at the University of North Carolina. Should you have any occasion to write, I'll be staying at the Carolina Inn in Chapel Hill.

I see where Henry Miller has just married a nineteen year-old girl. I am now at the age when I can appreciate the heroism of that act.

We all send love.

TO TONY CORWIN / From 14145 Greenleaf Street, Sherman Oaks, California 91403, September 11, 1967

Dear Tony:

It was good to speak to you yesterday, and I was very pleased by your general tone and attitude toward the school. You seemed to acknowledge that it was going to be hard work, but were braced for it, and cheerful about it.

We did not have a chance, on the telephone, to tell you any of the details of the return trip. Do you remember all that work that the gas station people in Sedona did on the muffler assembly? Well, on the second day after we left for home, out in the middle of some of the most extreme desert in America, the whole thing collapsed again. The brand new muffler that I had bought in Sedona scraped along the road, and was damaged. Once again Mom and I learned how generous and helpful people can be on the highway. A young fellow, about twenty-four, and his old father, who reminded me much of your own Grandpa Corwin, stopped, and immediately offered to help. The young man crawled under the car, and with a wrench fixed the pieces back in place in less time than it is taking me to write this letter. In the meantime I luckily ran into a man who had a radio in his car. He was connected with some kind of manufacturing plant back a few miles on the road; he radio'd, and they sent out a huge repair truck—twice as big as the

Auto Club salvage truck that came to our help on the road in Utah. Within two minutes there were *two* men under the car—the fellow who had stopped voluntarily, and the mechanic who had responded to the radio call.

Would you believe that neither would accept money? The mechanic said, "Shucks, the plant pays me $6.50 per hour, why should I take money from you?" It was of course enormously heartening to find this kind of generosity from perfect strangers. It sort of gives you a good feeling about the human race. Just the spirit of *helping....*

TO HAL KANTER, Writer, Producer / From Chapel Hill, North Carolina, October 16, 1967

Dear Hal:

Crime does pay. When delinquency can result in as marvelous a letter as yours of 2 October, it is a study that should be added to the curriculum of every university. After a short formal period of delinquency, I shall propose it to the authorities here.

Your CHUCK CONNORS AND CHUCK REAGAN TOO has swept the campus, having been relayed with proper credit, to three classes. [Chuck Connors, the actor, was being mentioned as a Republican political candidate.] Out here it requires a little build-up to explain Connors, for people lucky enough never to have seen him on TV.

I thought you might be amused to read the text of a public lecture I gave the other night. I figured it was about time someone put in a good word for sex. The local paper has a blind proofreader, which adds to the general quaintness.

Off to Madrid (spelled Mqdr8d).

TO KATHERINE CORWIN / From The Carolina Inn, Chapel Hill, North Carolina, October 17, 1967

Darling:

The kids called today! They both sounded wonderful—happy, buoyant, confident. They said they loved the school. If this is true and they are doing better at their studies than they did at Buckley (and they seemed to think there was a good chance of this), then it is worth a hundred times over, the loneliness created by their absence, the expense, and the dropped muffler assemblies on desert roads.

I was immensely lifted by their call, which shows you what a little recognition from your own children will do for one's spirit. I wrote them immediately and said that you and I were delighted that they were so pleased with V.V.—and that I hoped to be able to come up with you on Thanksgiving....[The Corwin children had been attending the Buckley School in the San Fernando Valley before they transferred to Verde Valley School in Sedona, Arizona.]

Enclosed, a compliment for you from Roy Madsen; and a reply from Fred Friendly's *secretary!* This is a form of incivility and pompousness that I cannot abide. Fred Unfriendly. Frig him. No matter.

Off to Boston on Thursday. Love and kisses.

TO TONY AND DIANE CORWIN / From Sherman Oaks, November 19, 1967

Dear Tony and Diane:

Mom and I look forward to being with you this week. We are flying up on Wednesday—I'm not sure just when we will get into Sedona....As you know, all the parents are coming, with the aim of spending a few days....

There is a favor I ask of you. This time, when you greet Mom, *RUN TO HER* if the greeting is outside, as it was on her last visit. If you greet her at the Rondee, or at the school, SMILE. I think she was taken aback by your greeting on her last visit. She did not complain to me, but I sensed it when I asked her for details of the visit. Mom doesn't know I am writing this to you, and perhaps she would be angry with me if she did know, but I felt I should, to avoid any possibility of a repetition of your cold greeting to her last month.

I know you both love Mom. I know *all* kids your age would rather that their parents get lost when it comes to their presence among kids your own age. I know you did not mean to hurt Mom, because at all other times—or most other times—you are very considerate of her feelings, and go out of your way to please her. I need not tell you how

much she—as well as I—love you both. You know all that. But sometimes just a little extra consideration, just a little change in your expression, in your tone of voice, can make a very great difference.

Your letter and postcards have been most welcome. Your last letters,
Diane, were wonderfully well written, and you defended your point of
view in the matter of certain aspects of Mom's visit, with great articu-
lateness. I have no comment to make on the merits of your arguments,
because that is between you and Mom. But it was splendid of you to
put it down on paper.

I hope we'll all have a happy reunion in that wonderful country, and
that it will add up to FUN. Perhaps, if we are going to have time
together as a family—time off from school, that is—you might want to
suggest something special—a side trip to Jerome. Perhaps. Maybe we
could get Mom to climb onto a horse. I got her to play a game of pool
with me last week, and I'm going to get her started bowling. She already
plays a good Ping-Pong.

TO MIRRON ALEXANDROFF / December 6, 1967

Dear Mike:

It was grand to get your letter, and to learn that things are humming
at the College. How I wish there were ten of you, to fill the presidencies
of nine more colleges and universities. This has been my year for academia—Regents Lecturer at the [University of California] at Santa
Barbara in May; writer-in-residence at the University of North Carolina
in September-October; and now, Trained Seal in drama at the San
Diego State Fine Arts Festival, December 1 to 10. A wanton year—
mostly good fun for me—but in the course of it, I came to appreciate
even more keenly the uniqueness of Mirron Alexandroff.

Last night I was moderator of a panel consisting of Andy Warhol, a
far-out composer named Lou Harrison, and myself. There were two
hundred standees—people sitting on the floor in the aisles—all having
come out to see and hear Warhol. He is nearly as mute as a man can be;
he was surrounded by a coterie of inarticulate slobs; he had no ideas on
nothin', except that he felt we should all be machines; we should all like
one another. He has done a series of "Death" works, showing corpses
sliced up in auto accidents, mangled in machinery, crushed from falls.

"Any war dead in your Death Series?" I asked him. No answer. A dull stare. Finally, "Well—uh—ung—a symbol or two—maybe." This is a hero? A pinup boy for the hundreds of young people who crowded that auditorium?...

TO TONY CORWIN / February 14, 1968

Dear Tonio:

It feels good to have Diane home for a few days, and it would feel even better if you were home too. But we shall wait until after your Mexico trip, which should in itself be very exciting.

Diane told us of your being disturbed about fantasy thoughts about myself and mom. All children have those thoughts sooner or later—and the more imaginative the child, the more likely to have them. They are unpleasant and even scary sometimes, but they are nothing to be disturbed about, and they pass away like other growing pains. When I was about fourteen, I began to get such thoughts, and I had them off and on, and at first they vexed me terribly, but after a little experience I realized they are almost par for the course for any sensitive person; and later in life, I found this was also scientific opinion.

Above all, Tonio, it is a very good thing to talk out whatever it is that bothers you, and I am very glad you communicated these concerns to Diane. She is a wonderful sister, and is concerned about your concerns, just as I am sure you care about hers. Much more important to us than your marks, is your attitude toward yourself, toward the school and toward the world.

You are certainly aware by now that we do not press you for communication, although we certainly wish you would write us a little note now and then. Speaking for myself, you know without my telling you, that any time you have anything on your mind, anything that bothers you, you are free to write or telephone me collect—and the same, of course, goes for Mom. But if it is too much trouble to do either, then I am glad you tell Diane. She is by no means the giggly girl that laughs through long telephone calls to her friends—she also has quite a little mature wisdom for one so young. But still there are matters you should take up with older people, and you should convince yourself of the helpfulness of going to someone for advice—or even just talking out what's on your mind. That has helped me through many a rough time. And that's what friends—and teachers—and parents are FOR. It is never an imposition on them, and you need never feel embarrassed. In fact, most people look upon a request for advice as flattering, because it means that you like them well enough to confide in them and unburden your troubles.

Diane tells us you have had some unhappy moments over your girl. That too is the course of young love very often. But it helps to talk out THOSE problems too. Secrecy—or keeping things to yourself too much—is like a boil or a blister. It's better if it can open up, and let out what is inside. The very act of release is beneficial, and is the start of the healing process....

I wish you would make time to drop me a line—and you know how happy it would make your mother. It is such a small investment for such a big return. You don't have to tell us everything or *anything* that is on your mind, if you don't want to, but it would be very nice to get a note—or a letter—just telling us how you feel, what movies you have seen, what you've turned out in art class—anything. Or send us one of your drawings. As you know, your art is proudly exhibited back here among the natives.

We all send love. Daddio

TO ERIK BARNOUW / February 18, 1968

Dear Erik:

The Golden Web is so great, and for so many reasons, that I can only sputter my enthusiasm. [Barnouw had sent Corwin page proofs of the second volume of a trilogy on the history of broadcasting in America.] It is far more than a history of broadcasting—it catches the country and the world in its skein. Figures and issues that were shadows and blurs in the general landscape are made vivid and clear; again you have unraveled complicated intestines of broadcasting, and laid them out like a master medical examiner. People I knew only vaguely, I know now in their salient contexts; people I knew well, I know better.

Once again I am in awe of the skill with which you go to the heart of a matter, the economy with which you extract its significance, and the depth to which you penetrate in short, swift strokes.

I hope I am not being gratuitous in offering a few suggestions, all minor and trivial.

[Thirty-two large and small notes follow alluding to specific passages and covering six single-spaced pages. Several allude to Corwin's own part in the history.]

p. 369: Unfortunately there has been a little confusion respecting the quote on this page. Chou En-Lai did indeed say those words to me [when interviewed during the One World visit to China] but this was in his small house on the edge of Nanking some days earlier. The "communist spokesman" to whom you refer was in Peking   he was General Yeh Chien-Ying, Commissioner in the tripartite Executive Headquarters. He actually made a far stronger statement than Chou's, and I looked it up for you in my transcript:

GENERAL YEH: Such one-sided help (will) cost the failure of General Marshall's mission. Now the American government is at the crossroads. Either withdraw its one-sided support to the Kuomintang, or drop its position as mediator.

He was in effect writing off the whole HQ operation as having been invalidated by American policy. The American Commissioner [Walter S.] Robertson (later No. 1 U.S. negotiator in the Korean War) snapped at General Yeh, "If you want to propagandize, you can issue that statement from Yenan, but it can't come from here." (Yenan was then Communist Headquarters.) Yeh looked silently at Robertson for a moment, then continued into my microphone: "We hope the American government will change its present double-edged policy—so that the Chinese people will have a chance to exert their own pressure to bring about peace. This will enable the American representatives to restore their position as fair and just mediators who will then be able to use their good offices to influence China to take the road of peace and democracy."

The rest was just as you described it. But I have always thought of that incident as an accidental stumbling-in-upon-the-scene at the precise moment, and place, where the situation respecting China (hence all

Asia) and the United States, passed from hopefulness to hostility. The reverberations are being felt even now in Vietnam, and will continue to rattle for longer than we care to think....

In your section on radio's earliest short-wave broadcasts, you may want to mention that in 1934, the General Electric Company arranged for a series of weekly short-wave broadcasts, co-sponsored by newspapers in key American cities, to Admiral Byrd and his second expedition to the Antarctic. The programs were heard simultaneously in the U.S. over the NBC-Red network, the short-wave transmission going out from GE's transmitter W2XAF in Schenectady. I know because I was called upon to be master-of-ceremonies of a program originating in Springfield, Massachusetts, on the night of April 8, 1934. Governor Joseph B. Ely of Massachusetts spoke, and so did the mother of one of Byrd's men—the supply officer. From nearby Pittsfield, we picked up the sound of artificial lightning in GE's laboratory—they had just invented the apparatus. Byrd's main party was perched on forty feet of ice at the South Pole; Byrd himself was alone in a shack 123 miles south of his base of operations. For myself, it was my first network performance. The series was not two-way: There was no back talk from the Antarctic.

The only detail I miss in this canvas, is the operation of United Nations Radio between the years 1948 and 1952. It is true that the unit was extra-territorial, but its interaction with U.S. broadcasters, and particularly the networks, was not small. For a time it represented the high ground to which responsible radio drama retreated when TV inundated the once fertile plains of radio. Several writers—myself, Allen Sloane, Lawrence & Lee—wrote for them. I produced and wrote several big network shows under my portfolio as Chief of Special Projects: *Citizen of the World*, July 10, 1949, over CBS, narrated by Lee Cobb; *Could Be*, over NBC (twice) in September, 1949 (this is the one Admiral Nimitz got excited about); *Document A/777*, on the Universal Declaration of Human Rights, over MBS in March, 1950. This had an all-star cast even bigger in voltage than the show I'd done earlier on the American Bill of Rights. But the fact that it was carried only on MBS kept its impact down, although Jack Gould [in the *New York Times*] gave it big huzzahs, and the English press liked it.

The log shows a disentanglement by the networks from UN radio, as their emphasis on commercialism stepped up and their public service stepped down. At first the networks, as I recall, would contribute their time, studios and technical personnel. Then they started to charge for the studios and personnel.

UN Radio was one of the few outfits—probably the last on American radio—to commission a work by a serious composer. It was Aaron Copland, whom I got to do a setting for the preamble to the Declaration of Human Rights (for $500 and all rights reverting to himself). The Boston Symphony under Leonard Bernstein performed it at Carnegie Hall. Laurence Olivier, freshly knighted, flew over from England expressly to do a three-minute bit against Copland's score, and flew right back after the concert. We don't do nuttin like that no more.

TO STAN FREBERG, Satirist, Producer / April 29, 1969

Dear Stan:

Your Westwood 90024 correspondent begs to report the following telephone conversation with John J. (Judge) Anthony:

A: Would you do me a great favor?

C: Gladly, if I am able.

A: Are you a friend of Stan Freberg?

C: Define friend.

A: You know him?

C: Yes. Friend, yes; but not privy councilor. I worship him from afar, and two or three times a year, I worship him from anear.

A: Well, you know, he does those great commercials.

C: Great.

A: I would like to be in some of them.

C: Ah?

A: Yes. I'm no longer doing my radio show. The station changed management, and they've gone to an all-music policy.

C: That's life.

A: I've done some work in movies too.

C: I saw you. I am happy to say without perjuring myself, that you were between very good and superb.

A: Well, thanks. Thanks. Now about Freberg—

C: I dare not telephone him. I will be glad to put in a good word for you, but it will have to be a written good word. He is hostile to the telephone, both company and customers.

A: *Would* you write him?

C: Today.

A: Awfully good of you.

C: I caution you that I have no influence.

A: I understand.

C: But I will tell him of your interest. I'm sure he's heard of you. Maybe if he has a commercial that can use Judge Anthony—

A: That's the idea.

C: What's your phone number?

A: 652-1013.

C: 652-1013. Will do.

(noises of appreciation, and amenities of farewell)

Best,

TO ALEXANDER SEMMLER, Composer / May 8, 1968

Dear Alex:

It is an unconscionably long time since I got your last letter, but I did not want any more time to pass without telling you how moved and impressed I was, and am, by your statement of esthetic principle. Nowhere have I seen a more striking comment on the dilemma of the serious composer who stands in the middle ground between the dogged avant garde and the equally intrenched traditionalists. I took the liberty of showing your letter to some friends, and they agreed with me that it is a statement of extraordinary clarity and force.

I listen often to the Trio, and with increasing pleasure. Since I liked it from my first exposure to it, I have invested it with a warm patina— or perhaps it is more accurate to say that it has done this for me.

Kate joins me in sending love to you and Eleanore.

TO SAMUEL BRONSTON, Film Producer [Based in Madrid]
June 8, 1968

Dear Sam:

Together with millions, we have just watched Bobby Kennedy buried near his brother, and our hearts are heavy. One lunatic Arab kid, and a whole nation is jarred, its future altered, eleven children of an immediate family made fatherless, and who knows what the consequences may be in ultimate world destinies?

I have heard reports that you lost the studio. It is only a studio. There is still Sam Bronston....

Apparently you did not get my message upon my return from Sacramento. No matter. Give my love to Dorothea, both princesses, and the Dauphin. And come back and commiserate with your fellow Americans in their sadness.

TO JAMES BELLOWS, Editor, *Los Angeles Times* / June 23, 1968

Dear Jim:

Thanks first for the lunch—always a joy—and then for sending on Alan Sharp's piece in the May 26 *West*....

It is a gem: poetic, penetrating, and most of it true with great bongs of insight. Better writing than anything I have seen in *The New Yorker* for two years. Great God, where do you find these wonderful people? It is good to find Sharp corroborating my own hunch about people as creatures of their countryside, but I disagree with his too-easy assumption that the Apache country "could only breed a stony malevolence, a cruelty as unremitting as it was functional." No landscape could be more cruel or bleak than the Arctic or Greenland fastnesses, yet the Eskimos are the gentlest people on earth; and out of the same glorious countryside that inspired Beethoven and Goethe came the monumental cruelties of Nazism. No, in my opinion that continental hugeness creates a certain breadth of national character, I was not making any local stops. The generality will not hold up for parishes in Mississippi, or the Shakers of Pennsylvania. Proof again that all generalities are false....

Best to you and Maggie,

TO SALLY FLY CONNELL, Writer / July 7, 1968

Dear Sally:

...Congratulations on *The Nation* publication! I'm so glad I put that bee in your pretty bonnet. Doesn't it look beautiful in print? I love the dignity of print—my favorite medium still, notwithstanding my debt to space communications. And there is a certain satisfaction about being published in *The Nation*: unlike some of the slick, rich periodicals, it has staying power, and will be researched by students and historians for as long as there are libraries. *The Nation* has always been lean, brave, poor, and on the side of Man. I am very pleased that you are in it, forever....

Take encouragement from *The Nation* acceptance, and keep at your typewriter. I must obey this injunction myself.

TO RODERICK MacLEISH, Writer, Radio and Television Commentator / July 12, 1968

Dear Rod MacLeish:

I was delighted to learn from Jeff Hayden that I am no more a stranger to you, than you to me. I have been listening to you on Group W out here, and thinking that there is life in the old gal yet—some life, dignity, poetry and integrity, all of which I feared had forever fled American radio.

Two hours after Jeff told me of your recent visit, I got a call from Arnold Grant in New York. He is an old friend, a corporation lawyer, a big wheel in interlocking directorates (Fox, Continental, Hertz, you name it) and the kind of man who donates buildings to universities and countries, and sends a seventeen-volume set of *The Papers of Thomas Jefferson* to a man he knows who reveres TJ. Well, Arnold carried on for fifteen minutes about *The Sun Stood Still*, reading me passage after passage from it. "Hold!" I said. "All right already. I'll rush out and buy it."

I did. (Incidentally, only one of eight bookstores I telephoned had it in stock—Campbell's in Westwood—and it was their last copy. You must complain to Atheneum.) The book is as I expected. Marvelous. Grant and I agree on all points, especially on the greatness of the very opening paragraph in your Preface.

Please include me in your next California stop. And when you are next in New York, do telephone Arnold Grant and meet him for a drink.

In the meantime, I will be listening.

TO TANA DE GAMEZ / August 3, 1968

Dear Tana:

...[T]he problem of translation is always difficult....The late Lion Feuchtwanger, who wrote in German and depended on an interpreter for translation into English, once complained to me of the despair and frustration that faces an author who is primarily published in a language not his own. He had a skilled translator who did all his early novels. But the translator died untimely, and Feuchtwanger had reason to mourn him with special feeling. He was never adequately replaced.

I was grateful for the excerpts from Lorca poems—I have read too little of this great poet. It is a pity that, aside from *The House of Bernarda Alba*, Lorca is practically unknown to the general public in America.

It was good to hear your voice on the air. You sounded a little tired in spots—the result of dropping your projection. Remember that your prose has great energy, and when you read that prose you must never sound tentative. Above all you must avoid sounding academic, even though you are speaking on a literary plane of literary matters. Just be the vigorous and charming Tana of the salon and living room: Be yourself.

I am glad you are broadcasting. It is a medium I have never stopped loving, though it abandoned me long ago. But just as well, since whatever good work may lie ahead of me, will be done on paper and not writ in air.

TO NORMAN CORWIN / August 18, 1968

Dear Norman Corwin:

It was good to hear from still another Norman Corwin. We should form a club—there are two I have met in the east and two I know about on this coast, none of us related. We could field a basketball team with one man to spare.

I wish I could help you in some important way, but alas, there are very few open sesames in writing, and except for elementary rudiments, which you long ago mastered, I do not believe writing can be taught. At least talent cannot. Technique is important up to a point, but we have all seen masters who seemed to ignore the rules, and flourish—not because they had contempt for the rules but because they had something to say, and the individuality with which to say it.

I suppose the best advice I could give would be to keep on writing, whatever happens. Judging from your letter, you express yourself very well indeed, and vastly better than most men your age. I think it is important to learn, to read, to inquire, to keep fresh one's sense of curiosity, to be compassionate and understanding about the so-called human condition, to have convictions and stand for them and live by them. See movies and plays and read books and expose yourself to art and music. Sustain yourself by writing, if you can. I was a newspaperman at seventeen, and remained one for eleven years before I got into radio.

You may find your name a problem, if there are any people with memories who may confuse you with me. Do you have a middle initial, or a middle name, that might be added? Or maybe I should change *my* name. Do you think America can stand *two* writing Norman Corwins? I have taken stands in the past which may not have endeared me to certain editors, and I hope you don't run into that problem through mistaken identity.

I wish you the best of everything in life, including a successful literary career.

TO BESS MYERSON GRANT / August 19, 1968

Bess Myerson, Miss America in 1945, was living with her husband in Elberon, New Jersey

---

Dear Bess:

I have it from an unimpeachable source that you improved the morale of the medical profession by undergoing an operation recently. There is nothing that perks up a hospital more than to have a glamorous patient for ten days—unless it is the thrill they get from charging $1.50 for an aspirin—and I am sure they were as reluctant to see you leave as you were reluctant to stay.

All who love you, and that takes in everybody except the present regime in Algeria, rejoice that the operation was no more than cautionary, and that the findings were nice and negative. Arnie tells me you have been fidgety about being inactive during your recuperation, but you must remember that even a scratch on an elbow or a bruise on the elberon must be given a chance to heal properly, and that stitches in the skin ain't exactly like quick-drying Duco cement on china....

TO ROSS MARTIN, Actor / August 31, 1968

Dear Ross:

Just got back to town, and I learn that you've been laid up. I tried to call the hospital, but they did not like my accent on the switchboard.

There are very few compensations, ever, in being hospitalized, but one of them is that you missed watching the Democratic Convention on TV.

Please, for all our sakes, get well soon and take good care of that superb person who is you. And please charge dear Olivie to let me know when visitors are permitted. If indeed you should see voluble Jewish writers at all until you are back to playing tennis and flaying agents.

TO GEORGE MOVSHON, Producer, United Nations Radio
September 19, 1968

Dear George:

I now unmask myself as a Difficult Author. Up to the receipt of your letter of 17 September, I have been hoping that the Committee would, in its majesty and on its own, agree that we should have a human title for the human rights cantata. This hope has now been dashed by your selection of "Human Rights Cantata."

I agree with you that it has "a certain cleanness and strength" and also that it has little pizazz; but on top of these qualifications it is pompous. And cold.

Consider the titles of my shows for the UN, all of them accepted and broadcast without letting of blood: *Windows on the World; Could Be; Fear Itself; Document A/777; The Charter in the Saucer.* Of them only *Document A/777* sounded formal, and that had enough mystery in it to flavor the pudding.

Two cantatas were brought to me when I was producing for CBS. One was entitled *Ballad of Uncle Sam.* I thought that was too square, and changed it to *Ballad for Americans.* The change of preposition gave it a certain special interest, and saved it from pompousness. Next a work entitled *Lincoln Cantata* was submitted to me. I changed that to *The Lonesome Train....*

Arthur Miller told us he was under great pressure by his producer and backers, to change the title of *Death of a Salesman.* As the world knows, he did not. Now that I am face to face with a Committee decision, I am suddenly stubborn. The Committee also has a right to be stubborn, and withdraw the work from production. But I feel strongly about the one element of coldness, in a text that works up considerable passion. I was very deliberate—and I assume our friend Halffter has also been deliberate—about reaching a high plateau of emotion from which to launch the sublime language and sentiment of the Declaration itself. I would rather not have the work turned to marble by a marmoreal title. [Cristobal Halffter was the composer.]

Do you remember a vintage soap opera written by William Saroyan for a movie? It was called *The Human Comedy,* thus setting itself off against Dante. Unfortunately Mr. Saroyan is not Homer, and the bathos of his script made the title arrogant. I instinctively shrink from grandiose titles. To me *Human Rights Cantata* is almost, though not quite, as bad as *Constitutional Cantata,* or *Hammurabic Code Cantata....*

I like the drive and authority of *Yes Speak Out Yes.* It is young, in a world of the young. I am sure you and your colleagues agree that the cantata is being produced for people, and not cantata-hunters, or even primarily for delegates in the Assembly Hall on 10 December. The Declaration of Human Rights is meaningless and void unless it is for people.

By the way, "Si Habla Afuera Si" sounds beautiful to me. How does it go in the other three official languages?...

I wish we could all sit around a conference table—you, d'Arcy, Ritchie, Cisek, Holton, Halffter, Scrowaczewski, Dante and J.S. Bach—and all have a go at the issue. But in the meantime, and lacking this option, I have wedged myself into a suit of armor rarely worn by me, especially in this climate: Adamant.

Yours from the outhouse just behind the moat.

The title used was Corwin's: *Yes Speak Out Yes.*

TO STAN FREBERG / September 22, 1968

Dear Stan:

I have been trying to reach you. I got the usual strombazzata from your secretary about how you don't accept incoming calls of any kind, and I wonder whether this awesome and enviable antisepsis applies to incoming mail as well.

The point of my trying to get your hairy ear, is to broach the possibility of engaging you and Orville in a film at Four Star of which I am executive producer. It is a chance to say some of the very things you have been fighting so admirably to get across in your records and various appearances. This would be for theatrical film, not TV....

A very good wish to you, wherever you are inside your defense perimeter.

The film was not made.

TO RALPH SCHOENSTEIN / September 25, 1968

Arrested briefly at the 1968 Democratic Convention in Chicago for broadcasting criticism of Mayor Richard Daley, Schoenstein had been booked as "Bernstein."

Dear Ralph:

I am very sorry that our friendship should end this way. Please understand it is nothing personal, but I cannot in clear conscience associate with a criminal. How could I explain to my children that I exchanged letters and books with a convict? One must be realistic. Suppose I should run for alderman in Sherman Oaks one day, and it is disclosed by the opposition that I was once on close terms with a jail-bird?

My friends and associates number among them some of the finest people: several rabbis, Norman Vincent Peale, Charles F. Spearmint of Moral Rearmament, and Sandy Koufax. Law-abiders, all. Not a traffic citation against the lot of them.

Lest you think I am the kind of man who abandons a friend just because he gets into a scrape with the authorities, please understand that all my friends serve a kind of unwritten probationary period. I wait to see if, over a period of years, they exhibit or develop any anti-social, activist or criminal tendencies. If so, I try to correct them, as any good friend should do. In your case, I confess I was not shrewd enough to guess that you were a latent scofflaw, although I should have known by your frequent visits to Las Vegas, which is not exactly notorious for higher education, or as a place where a man is encouraged to live a moral life.

I am not blaming you: I am blaming myself. Some men are perceptive; I am not. Had I recognized this trait in time, I would have remonstrated with you, as a friend may try to dissuade another from smoking. But it is too late.

Still, I have enough regard for your poor wife and children to try, even though it is past midnight in your character-forming development, to alter your course. Ralph, please study the stamp on the outside of this envelope. It says LAW AND ORDER. That does not mean just law and order for me and the next man, but for YOU too. Do you see the cop pictured on the stamp? He is the guardian of order, the upholder of law, in Chicago as elsewhere. Do you see the trust that little boy has in him? I know you will scoff, and argue that the boy has a copy of *The Free Press* under his arm, and the cop is taking him quietly to the station because the boy has been trained in nonviolence and transcendental meditation. That is just the kind of poison pumped out by the peaceniks.

I cannot begin to understand why you broadcast an attack on Mayor Daley. I watched him all through the Convention and thought he was lovable. Indeed I felt he used great restraint. After all, he could have moved artillery pieces inside the Convention Hall, and used machine guns instead of billy clubs on those obstreperous young people. As for the three a.m. raid on McCarthy workers in the Conrad Hilton, is it not true that some hours earlier, one of them had dropped a wad of chewing gum from a window, on a police officer in the street below? *Wet* chewing gum? *Used?* How would *you* like a germ-laden gob of gum to land on your hat? I mean, if that sort of thing goes unchallenged, there would be no end of anarchy and spit in our street. The police is not a great spittoon, sir.

I believe in constitutional law, and in obedience to the ordinances of any city, incorporated on American soil and blessed with our heritage of democracy. Your open defiance of the appointed guardians and defenders of public safety, was like blowing marijuana smoke into the face of George Washington, the Father of our Country.

Well, I have gone on at greater length than I intended, Mr. Schoenstein (alias Bernstein) and I apologize, especially since I know that my friendly admonition will have been wasted—in one eyeglass and out the other. I only hope that out of your experience in prison will come a fresh understanding and appreciation of the American Way of Life. But frankly, from the tone of your piece in the *New York* Magazine, I doubt it.

My heart aches for Judy and the children. I would offer them the shelter of my home in case you get in trouble with the police again, but it would ease matters a good deal if they adopted a pseudonym. I mean the neighbors, and all.

I would appreciate it if further communication were addressed in care of my agent.

With frail but still lingering hope in your ultimate regeneration, so that you may be of service to God and country, I am, believe me, your good though disappointed friend.

TO GEORGE MOVSHON / September 27, 1968

Dear George:

Western Union, both the downtown and West Los Angeles offices, swears on a stack of siddurs [prayer books] that it never received your great wire. The implication was made that the foulup (native: fuckup) took place on the New York end. I thought you might like to know of this, so that you may proceed to torture the personnel of your communications department until you get a confession. Perhaps the cruelest torture would be requiring them to listen all the way through, to our cantata. But it is too early to make this boast.

I have composed the perfect epitaph for a man named Georges, fifth of that name in his family, who went down on the *Titanic*: GEORGES CINQ.

Among the sins of my youth, did I tell you my epitaph for Oscar Dystel, former editor of *Coronet*? —"Lay That Dystel Down." Also one for Carl Czerny, teacher-composer: CZERNY'S END.

I am now listening to the Nonesuch recording of Rossini's *Sins of My Old Age* (Stereo H-71089). For the quintessence of a long bygone charm, it is without rival.

Aloha from Smog Center.

TO R. LeROY BANNERMAN, Professor, Indiana University
October 4, 1968

Dear LeRoy:

I am sorry if I sounded rough on young Reemes in my estimate of *The Last Summer*. On a second hearing I liked it better, but I still have a passel of reservations. Since you ask for specifics:

First of all it's just *too* reminiscent of *Milk Wood* in its approach. Then—its cardinal sin—it is overblown with metaphor, most of them pushing too hard for effect:

..armed with an arsenal of energy...
..they exact a daily and matutinal vengeance
    on the comatose guardians of household lore...
..aubade of damp diapers
..he fries the graded ovum of a hen
..out into the caper-halting heat
..the flywheels cog away in his brainpan...
..the squirrels pelt each other with congratulations..

Then his construction of phrases is often strained, as though out of an anxiety to be original and striking. The use of nouns as verbs can be a wearisome business:

..they daschhund up
..he dragons down

and there is only awkwardness, not felicity, in a phrase like "the water dries from their two and tender skins," and "until his time is up and he can go uncommented home."

Reemes is not without talent, but I feel he is very young, perhaps not in years, but in style and taste. Every now and then he strikes a good image, "like the dormitory avenue of birds," "quiet as cancer," "others wear it (love) like a scar all the way to the grave," "the bondage of best clothes"—all good—but within a single phrase he can be very good and awful; thus "the afternoon collapses" (good) "and quits" (bad). And a phrase like "Unholy smoke!" belongs in a comic strip, not a verse play.

I may be unfair to Reemes in this next point, but I felt that in fastening upon Rev. Tready a fanaticism on the subject of smoking, and giving him a line like "The devil lies in wait for boys who smoke," he was equating a strong anti-smoking position with nutty fundamentalism. I happen to believe that the devil does indeed lie in wait for boys who smoke, and have been trying to impress this on my sixteen-year-old Tony, so I do not appreciate my position being assigned to a miserable flame-breathing bluenose.

Another serious reservation concerns a pivotal action in the play. The boy's revulsion on seeing the lady's bare breasts seems to me a gross overreaction, notwithstanding Reemes' brimstone bit about the deadly sin of consorting with creatures of the flesh. Most boys are only too delighted at a peek of those twin outposts of paradise (vide George Grosz's autobiography, in which he describes his sensation on first peeping at an undressed woman); and even if the boy was a little frightened, I cannot accept such emotional extremity as "horror and nausea and dread" and

swallows down the gray puke of fear and revulsion

or the teacher's stricken "What have I done? What have I done?" She done nothin' except get her bra caught on an obstruction that Mr. Reemes, not God, put in the script—unless of course you are speaking of the god out of the machine. I refuse to believe that this glimpse of anatomical goodies, even to a Canadian boy who says precocious lines like "...arrested my remark, so to speak, in the throes of birth," is so traumatic, so unsettling, as to mark the end of childhood and the beginning of morals, loneliness or privacy. Reemes forces everything: language, action and morality. In any normal situation, a boy to whom this happened would go home not to suffer torments and anguish, but to dream very pleasantly of Miss Teacher in particular, and of her sex in general.

Still, Reemes is talented, and once he learns to be simple and not facile, and makes room for a little humility, he should be a valuable member of the fraternity. Until then I would urge him to forget that *The Last Summer* was given an international award. That could hurt him more than a bad review if he takes it seriously and goes on writing in the same vein....

TO GEORGE MOVSHON / November 28, 1968

Dear George:

I attach a proof sheet of the Minneapolis text, on which I have underscored in red, those portions of Bob Hale's recitative which were obscured by the orchestra in each of the three readings we attended. It is no big matter for Cristobal [Halffter] and/or Scruffy Skrowaczewski [conductor of the Minneapolis Symphony Orchestra] to keep the orchestra down at these points....

If you will check the tape of Friday's performance, I believe you will find that in the line "proclaim it to the innocent ear and the innocent heart," Bob transposed ear and heart, which is the most curious heart transplant yet. But it does make a difference of accent. The line has been changed in the new version to "proclaim it to the innocent ear and heart," but I do not recommend any change in the sung line, which would be upsetting to all concerned. All I ask is that the ear precede the heart: I prefer that the line does not end on its ear.....

TO GEORGE MOVSHON / January 17, 1969

Dear Giorgio:

I have not yet received a check from the house of four thousand windows, which leads me to believe the bursar must have heard the cantata. Either that or he gave the check to Miss Van Buren, and she, taking one look at the address, automatically mailed it fourth class.

I can understand the accountants withholding payment until Halffter fills in his mysterious fermatas and mends his morendos; indeed, I consider ourselves lucky that we have not been sued for breach of peace; but all the same, the nations in concert should pay at least my expenses.

I shall wait a week and then write to Paraguay, which has a special fondness for me since the Lopez episode in *Document A/777....*

TO HOUSE JAMESON, Actor / January 27, 1969

Dear House:

Last night there was delivered to me a copy of a hard-bound, large-format volume carrying, in gold lettering, the crashing title of *An Empirical Analysis of Selected Radio Dramas of Norman Corwin, a Thesis Submitted in Partial Satisfaction of the Requirements for the Degree of Master of Arts in Theater Arts,* by Carolyne Malloy.

Mrs. Malloy's empirical analysis, with footnotes, bibliography and two appendices, comes to 161 pages, and I was naturally interested in all of them. I suppose it is unseemly to regard one's self in a mirror for longer than is necessary to shave, but when you are led into a house full of mirrors, each reflecting you as you are seen by others, then there need be no burden of narcissism: You may look at the reflected features fixedly and without shame. And so I did, staring unashamed, and unconvinced both by some of the kinder and less kind estimates of my work—but not unmoved. And what moved me—to tears—was a letter from you to Mrs. Malloy. It is included in Appendix A, under "Personal Letters from Corwin's Critics and Contemporaries." I regret only that four years have passed since your writing and my reading it, for by now you must have forgotten that you wrote it.

Nothing I have ever read, or written myself, captures those days as you do. The enthusiasm, the fun, the surprise, the joy of creating a living, yea, a national entity out of a half hour of radio time, where there was nothing but pages and intentions the day before; the not unwelcome pressure of An Opening, once every week, of an untried work owing nothing to last week or the next one. How were we to know we were working inside a Golden Age, the shortest on record, one that was soon to end untimely, and whose like we should not see again?

You were the closest of all people to my emergence. If I was the father of those break-through plays, you were the godfather. There might have been others who could have played Santa in The Plot as well as you, though I cannot for the life of me think who; but nobody—nobody—could have carried *They Fly* as you did. And that was the play that, by itself, made the biggest difference in my life. For that service alone, I would be eternally grateful to you. But it was, happily, not alone. There were other programs, uneven in quality and intensity, but all crowding under a magic umbrella of amity, good will, a kind of cultural derring-do and artistic insouciance—all bracketed and punctuated by Colby meals, or sandwiches and coffee sent up from a Madison Avenue drug store, coffee with traces of salt and B-coli in it.

You were a rock, House. Knowing your rich mind and the grace and power of your art, I was emboldened to write for you as a composer writes for an instrumentalist whose range and qualities broaden his own by giving him the confidence to reach high. One of the proudest of my trophies, the kind that do not hang on a wall but which echo in the ear and in the even more resonant chambers of the heart, was your Olympian irony in *They Fly*, an irony that at once masked and limned and contained both anger and compassion....

I could go on with other titles and titillations out of those days, but you are better at this than I: Your letter is the finest possible epitaph for radio and, I suppose, myself—

I am grateful to Mrs. Malloy for having elicited your letter and then for letting me see it, albeit after the lapse of a full Olympiad since it was written. Not all felicity has gone from life.

With esteem and love, as of old, I am

Yours faithfully,

TO ALEXANDER SEMMLER / February 1, 1968

Dear Alex:

...How singular it is, that of all the good men around CBS in what we must now look back at as the golden age, only you have gone on to write pure, personal, uncompromising music—only you have really worked at your art as an Art, not just a living. Herrmann, that poor dear curmudgeon, still firing all guns at friend and foe—especially friend—put his hand to an opera fifteen years ago, and has done nothing very distinguished since then; Lyn Murray told me in a melancholy confession the other day, that the work he did on my series at CBS, represented his best creative achievement; what has happened to Leith Stevens I have no idea; and the others have either disappeared, or are writing music for commercials, which is an even worse form of disappearance.

I congratulate you on the Trio. And I am going to take the liberty of calling it to the attention of two music critics—the only two—of my acquaintance: one in New York, the other in Washington. It is a good feeling to be able to feel and speak genuine enthusiasm for a friend's work. Too often one has to call upon affection and sentiment to compensate for lack of excitement, but that is entirely unnecessary in the work at hand....

TO BESS MYERSON GRANT / March 28, 1969

In early 1969, Mayor John Lindsay named her New York City's Commissioner of Consumer Affairs

Commissionaire la plus belle:

I have just returned from Boston, where I presided over the melting of snow, and I find your good letter of the 19th, with its escort of newspaper stories and the text of your speech to the BBB [Better Business Bureau] of New York.

Really, you are superb. Goddam! That is a marvelous speech; it lifts the heart. Clear, cogent, crisp, and studded with gold nuggets like "that dark corner of the economy where the payments last longer than the goods." Your warning that if dishonest operators go too far "the consumer may go too far, and in his anger, strike out against the honest and dishonest alike" was echoed grimly in the news from East Pakistan this week, where abused and hungry peasants and workers went berserk, and murdered and pillaged. Carl Rowan, commenting on the Pakistani disturbances over the Group W stations only this morning, said "It could happen here."

I like the sheer and dramatic fashion in which you have poised the warning: "... this may explode if we allow the poor to become poorer by not stopping those who give the poor less than a dollar's worth for their dollar." For their already devalued dollar, you might add. You are talking tough, Bess, and to an age fed up with Madison Avenue patois and old administration bilge, you sound like a chorus of avenging angels singing Handel....

TO GROUCHO MARX / April 12, 1969

Dear Groucho:

It was great to see you in the palace of culture last night. [Marx and Corwin had recently met again at the Motion Picture Academy.]

Don't forget your promise to send me a copy of that interview in the *New York Times*. In exchange, here is the text of a peculiar prayer that I wrote recently and which, even more peculiarly, was read on the Ed Sullivan Show by Eddie Albert. [Corwin had lately written *Prayer for the 70s*.]

I may find myself under investigation by Billy Graham.

Fond best wishes, as always,

TO EMIL CORWIN / May 16, 1969

Dear Em:

The Sullivan people tell me they have received thousands of requests for a copy of the Prayer, and indeed I have seen a few hundred letters myself. They are 99.5 percent adoring, but there are the usual nuts who write twenty-nine longhand pages full of Biblical allusions, and a few who peremptorily demand eight copies, and fast; and the kind who enclose a self-addressed (but not stamped) envelope. Mostly, however, real fine pipples, ministers, rabbis, nuns, and old Corwin fans, some who write on ruled paper, in pencil, and with touching misspellings....

News from Madrid is that *Yes Speak Out Yes* (*Si, Dilo Alto, Si*) was given three performances at the Teatro Real. The last of the three concerts was before an 80 percent student audience, and according to a letter from Halffter "the bravos and applause lasted twenty minutes. There has never been such a prolonged and enthusiastic reaction to the premiere performance of a work in Madrid in the last thirty years." —I find this especially touching and gratifying, since the students were obviously cheering a text which defied the government, and spoke those things for which they have been striking. The text, it should be said for the authorities, was printed in full—both in English and Spanish. Also the newspaper *Arriba* carried it in full, along with a big article about the poete norteamericano....

TO CRISTOBAL HALFFTER, Composer / May 24, 1969

Dear Cristobal:

My heartiest congratulations on the Madrid concerts [of the UN cantata]. The word TRIUMFO is always exciting, but never so much as when it is attached to one's own work, and I was delighted for both of us, that it was used in more than one review of the proceedings in the Teatro Real.

It is also good news that the cantata will be performed in Vienna next December. I would like to be there for many reasons, one of which is that I have never been to that city. But that reason is of course far behind the reason that it would give me a chance to meet you and Marita again, and perhaps even your children.

Have a happy and productive summer, and do keep me informed as to the career of the cantata as well as your own distinguished one.

TO DOUGLAS M. KNIGHT / July 22, 1969

A poet and past President of Duke University, he left the university to work on an educational program at RCA headquarters in Camden, New Jersey.

Dear Doug:

A poet at RCA is even rarer than a poet in the office of University President; and although one must be sorry for Duke, I am very glad for Mr. Sarnoff. My friend Sandburg once wrote, "Will it be a cold day when the poets and engineers get together?" Yet here it is hot summer, and the engineers have gone to the moon, and poets write about it in *Life* and on Page 1 of the *New York Times*. I have not yet seen MacLeish's piece; as for Dickey, he has done and will do better.

Congratulations on the forthcoming book [of poems] out of Texas. I look forward to reading it. For myself, I have barely kept the tip of my oar wet, with the attached brash verse [*Prayer for the 70s*]. Doubleday is bringing it out as a micro-mini-hardback in the fall, with design and art by Saul Bass. It was written at the behest of Eddie Albert, actor, who read it on—of all programs—the Ed Sullivan Show, on—of all days—Easter Sunday. I expected a storm of complaints; instead there were six thousand requests for a copy, which is what interested Doubleday perhaps more than the intrinsic qualities of the poem itself....

TO ELWYN AMBROSE, Puppeteer / August 2, 1969

Dear El:

I was stunned to get the bulletin on your hospitalization, but heartened—if I may use that term—by Day's report of very satisfactory progress and a good prognosis. That you were able to beat off a pneumonia infection while coping with the heart kickup, says something very encouraging about your basic constitution.

I hope that when you get back on your feet, you will honor those feet by moving them in some form of regular exercise. From all quarters I hear nothing but praise for the benefits of walking/jogging/swimming/fucking in combination, and while the latter has deservedly come in for the greatest attention and the best reviews, I have found that walking and jogging have their own delights. Anything that Thoreau did with regularity cannot be all bad. Swimming of course requires a body of water; and the body of a female in the pool at the same time adds a certain piquancy and interest, especially if she believes in nude swimming. But for day-in-day-out exercise there is nothing that beats the open road, and I hope your doctors will prescribe such a regimen, and that you will stick to it, and that a year from now you will join me as guest jogger in my daily ambit....

TO DR. WILLIAM B. OBER / August 3, 1969

Dear Bill:

I refuse to bore you with the reasons for my lateness in thanking you for the Boswell and Lawrence reprints. I was sorely delayed in getting to them, but now they are read; and once again, as so many times before, I both praise and scold. Praise for the extraordinary merits of the writing, admonishment for your seemingly stony indifference toward the very idea of a broader audience.

With all due respect to the Academies of Medicine of New York and New Jersey, they are not literary societies, and their Bulletins do not circulate among readers discriminating enough to appreciate what they've got in your papers. The Boswell thesis alone would entitle you to a Ph.D. in the most fastidious of academic degree mills. At the risk of insulting the brethren of your profession, I find them mainly a pack of boors when it comes to literature and art in general, and politics in particular—conservative to right-wing in their social and economic posture, venal in all important respects, cry-babies when it comes to the faintest suggestion of regulation and decent reform.

You may think that because of the scientific and medical centricity of your pieces—medical professor speaking to other medical professors—they have no broader appeal. If so, you are deluding yourself. Good writing is good writing, and one does not have to be a cetologist to be entertained by Melville's chapter on cetology in *Moby Dick*. Or a practicing naturalist to enjoy Thoreau or the journals of Von Humboldt.

I say that the wit, charm, cogency, scholarship and urbanity of your papers is largely lost on your *Bulletin* publics. Perhaps you have tokens of response to disprove this, in which case I gladly revise this estimation. In your "Lady Chatterley's What?" you mention Noah Fabricant. I knew Noah; had correspondence with him; he wanted me to adapt his essays for a series of TV shows. I met him both here and in Chicago, and liked him very much. But his "Famous Patients" essays, intelligent though they were, could not begin to touch your papers. His are informative; yours are that *and* entertaining.

Take the Boswell. It has every reason to be disagreeable reading, considering the morbidity of its subject, and its inexorable denouement of pustulence, vomiting, sepsis and stricture. The fact that Boswell shares the billing with GONORRHEA would be enough to turn most—nay, all—squeamish readers away; you are not writing "Boswell of Sunnybrook Farm." Yet one reads the paper with total fascination, with awe at its scholarship, admiration for its network of inferences, and the highest respect for the extra-gonorrheal pages touching on the WHY of Boswell's behavior patterns. Add to this the ecumenical thrust of your thinking, your gymnastic vocabulary, and your always diverting erudition (which you indulge with a snob's proper delight), and it comes out as something far beyond the ambits of even the best medical journals....

I speak—as I have before—of your snobbism. Nobody since Eliot flaunts his knowledge of languages as you do

one can reply *tu quoque*
voi sapote que; che fa,
desonsus Averno
in Italia son gia mille e tre
much of the *res gestae*

and how important is it to quote Ovid in his language, and be obliged to give both translation and footnoted source?

But don't get me wrong: I enjoy your snobbisms as I do your puns and word play, and I would not change them except perhaps in the degree to which you may struggle with temptation before punctuating a perfectly engrossing passage with a slug out of Dante, in Umbrian dialect yet.

P.S. I forgot to make this point about Fabricant: He sought, and got, his wider audience through book publication. At the time of his death he was seeking a still wider audience, through TV. There is nothing crass about reaching more and more people. Otherwise novelists and essayists would just write letters to each other, and Horowitz would play only in living rooms.

After Ober placed *Boswell's Clap* with Southern Illinois Press, that book and his subsequent writing won an enthusiastic readership.

TO GEORGE MOVSHON / September 1, 1969

Giorgio:

I am later than usual attending to our correspondence, because Tony and I went on a great tour of the eastern and northern Sierras—Yosemite, Tahoe, Lassen and Mount Shasta. All superb, shading upward to glorious, except for the overcrowding of the Yosemite Valley floor and the commercialization of the south shore of Tahoe. But there are still hundreds of miles of road in northern California where you pass another car once or twice in an hour; and winey air; and murmuring forests; and vistas to lift the heart if not the soul. Incidentally I didn't know Jo had her gall bladder lifted. I hope she is recovered fully, and that food tastes better than ever....

Halffter has managed thus far to keep secret from me the designs of Dusseldorf on the cantata—I have had no word from him since the excitement in Madrid. And lively thanks for the translation of the interview with Halffter; I had meant the long piece in the *other* newspaper, but no matter—my niece, Al's older daughter, translated this very expertly and propelled so much energy doing it that she is now back in Spain.

You are much traveled to the east of you, Movsh, but how about usns? This is, after all, the state of Nixon, Reagan and Murphy, and we need you.

I am listening to a lovely oboe passage in a Stamitz concertante as I write this, and I wish the same to you....

Love to Jo, Tony, Ann, and U Thant

TO LEO MISHKIN / September 9, 1969

He had written suggesting that Corwin had been influenced by James Branch Cabell.

Dear Leo:

I get a letter from my favorite critic, joshing me for having turned critic, and imputing that I cribbed and rewrote a passage from another critic, J.B. Cabell. You have forgotten those little gems of biography that you used to write about me when we both worked at the world's most prosperous whorehouse, CBS—I *was* a critic before I became a pompous documentarian and director and lecturer: How do you think I learned all my bad manners? I used to review films for *The Greenfield Daily Recorder* at age eighteen; also painting, music and theater. The most jejune commentary on the arts in their long history—but criticism nevertheless.

Now never in *my* long history, though I am ashamed to say it, have I read James Branch Cabell. Every so often a really cultured person like yourself speaks of Cabell familiarly, and one of these days I am going to do something about finding out what they are talking about, so that I will not feel inferior when his name comes up. Until then, however, I am going to run for office on the claim that, between the two quotes you selected—his and mine—I like mine better. Auctorial is such a stuffy word; "distinction" is so relative and vague in the particular context; so are "symmetry" and "tenderness." Does he mean by the latter, humans? J. Branch would have done better to have plagiarized or paraphrased from *me*. How is that for humility.

But all thanks, Leo, for your kind words about the review of *The Golden Web*. It is really a splendid work, this history; Erik [Barnouw] is one of the Good People, like Mishkin....

I keep hearing ominous rainfall statistics over the radio as I write..., and I am beginning to think it may be necessary for this letter to be delivered to you on an ark, but I am going to post it anyway.

Kate demands that I include her love as I send mine, and she has that right.

TO DR. WILLIAM B. OBER / December 26, 1969

Dear Bill:

...Congratulations on the move downtown: Every man should have a bigger and better lab to do his thing, and you have deserved the biggest and best. This means extra commuting miles for you, but I am sure they will be worth it, every rod and furlong....

Thanks for your limerick. The other day, in response to a story told me by a San Diego State professor about a Norwegian lady who broke off her engagement with a young man because she committed an audible fart while climbing a ladder in his presence, I wrote this one:

A skillful young lady of Norway
To love-making added one *more* way:
> The height of her art
> Was to let a loud fart
When she welcomed a swain in her doorway.

[Spiro] Agnew's speeches are, to be sure, written in the original German, but Mrs. [Martha] Mitchell's are writ in piss.

From that I make a rapid transit to a flourish of good wishes and love to you all,

TO ARCH OBOLER, Radio Writer, Director / January 12, 1970

Corwin and Oboler had each written articles for an issue of the Directors Guild journal, *Action*.

Dear Arch:

Our little excursion into nostalgia is rounded out by your generous and warming comment on the Channel 28 show, and by our side-by-side pieces in the current issue of Action magazine. I greatly enjoyed your article, and had pleasure invoking your distinguished name in my own piece.

They may have killed radio dead, but it rises to haunt 'em every now and then, and we two are among the best qualified spooks.

Every good wish for a hale and fulfilling decade, and others beyond.

TO DR. WILLIAM B. OBER / January 14, 1970

He had written the first and last couplets for a sonnet on Byron but said he was too lazy to fill in the rest. The middle ten lines are Corwin's contribution.

Dear Bill:

All right, here's your completed Byron sonnet:

> Your clubfoot didn't stop your chasing girls;
> You also had affairs with lots of boys.
> You had the best of two worlds, swine and pearls,

And sorrows sailors find, as well their joys.*
—Oedipus also had a deformed foot
With which he tried to kick against the pricks,
And a big mouth in which he firmly put
His other foot. For when Greek mates Greek
It is no simple thing, to be enjoyed.—
O Byron, when you made a willing freak
Of Sister, you were heading straight for Freud.
Arise from Sigmund's couch purged free of sin:
A touch of incest makes the whole world kin.

* A gesture in honor of the lines from *Childe Harold* reading
    The joys and sorrows sailors find
    Coop'd in their winged sea-girt citadel.
Any time. Love to all,

TO ROD SERLING / February 8, 1970

Dear Rod:

You are the winner and still champ. *A Storm in Summer* was memorable on every level: as drama, art, humanism and polemics. It was by far the bluntest facing-up to black anti-semitism I have yet seen in any medium, yet it was done with restraint, humor and compassion.

I kept thinking, as I watched, how important it was for this show to be seen by middle-class America—by the silent and, all too often, fatheaded and bigoted majority. You cannily put together representatives of the two leading national and international scapegoats—an old Jew and a young black—and yet the play you spun around them was not, if you'll pardon the expression, all black and white. The nephew, while entertaining, was no pride to the children of Israel; the switchblade and the readiness to use it, was no compliment to the youth of Harlem; old Shaddick did not have all the answers—he was told off very crisply by the pretty girl. A great set of balances, and not installed to please Hallmark.

I had made up my mind at the start, not to be moved or persuaded by [Peter] Ustinov, for the ungenerous reason that I felt he had for some time become increasingly smart-ass in his acting and public appearances (specifically I had been annoyed by a long and gratuitously unflattering anecdote he told about a Jewish soldier on the David Frost show recently); but you—and he—demolished that resolve, and I found myself shedding tears, along with Kate, in that beautiful last scene.

Summer Storm is another triumph for you, Rod. You should sleep better than ever—although, considering your fantastically prodigious output, I wonder that you get any sleep at all....

TO TOM SMOTHERS / February 25, 1970

Dear Tom Smothers:

It was grand to meet up with you at that USC coffee-and-cake conference last night, and to be able to tell you in person how greatly I have admired your work. You have been good for the medium, good for that dwindling portion of the audience that can still think, and good for America. The very nature and tactics of your adversaries is a form of sincere tribute to you: You have been effective. There is an old saying that people throw stones only at fruit-bearing trees.

I was impressed by your comment that sometimes mistakes are the most creative thing about a program; it took me back to a treasured meeting I once had with Sir Alexander Fleming, who discovered penicillin. The discovery resulted directly from a mistake in a laboratory, as you no doubt know—and it was nice to have this principle confirmed by your experience....

If you are free for lunch one day I would like to stake you to a steak; there are many world problems to be solved, and a half hour should do it.

With every good wish,

TO HAZEL COOLEY SPILLER / March 19, 1970

Dear Hazel:

It is always a joy to hear from you.

...For the past few years I have been writing what I blush to call Memoirs, but they are that, in a way—oriented to the history of broadcasting, with politics and the great globe itself present in quantity—and in the Springfield pages I had occasion to think of you many times. Of course you know that our collaboration on *So Say the Wise* was a thinly transparent device on my part to be *near* you. I sighed every time the street car passed your house. What interesting kids we must have been—for our time and its world. On another planet from the kids of today—meaning both good and bad.

Thank you for thinking of me in connection with Judge Heller's book,...but I am sticking to a resolve I made some time ago, to concentrate on original work rather than to adapt. It is enormously tempting to translate a work from one medium to another, especially if you respect the source; but as I get older I feel I must resist what I now consider a happy indulgence of my youth, and stay off adaptations as one stays off cigarettes and animal fats....

TO TONY AND JERRY COBB [the children of Lee J. Cobb, the actor, and his wife Mary] / March 27, 1970

Dear Tony and Jerry:

Thank you very much for your welcome comments on *Dog in the Sky*, which I freely confess that I wrote. I am most pleased that you liked it well enough to read all the way through, and are interested enough to ask me questions about it.

Jerry wonders if all those characters in the book lived, and I must answer that they did indeed live, but only in my imagination, which has a pretty good population, now that I think of it. Of course I never take a census of the people in my imagination, mostly because they could not be bothered to fill out the forms.

Tony, you ask what happened at the end. Well, Runyon and his dog Pootzy were reunited, and it can be assumed that they lived reasonably happy ever after, perhaps bothered only by the smog which is said to have reached even Curgatory, but not nearly as bad as it gets on the average summer morning in downtown Los Angeles.

Yes, I too was sorry about poor 345-B122 [a robot], but if you feel strongly about having him back, he can always be reconstructed from the original parts. Perhaps you might like to do that in a story of your own.

Please give my affectionate regards to your mother and father, and save two jumbo portions for yourselves.

TO RODERICK MacLEISH / May 30, 1970

Dear Rod:

After news of slaughter on the roads, in the Middle East, in the Far East, after the neurotic undulations of the market and the latest vomit from Agnew and the definitive un-Separation of Church and State at the Right Rev. Billy Graham's circus in Tennessee, comes your broadcast on this Memorial Day. What a beautifully wrought, lyrical, wise and moving piece—and how tonic to the dragging spirit!

You are one of the few friends of language left to us, and a glory to broadcasting. What you have to say is said with poise, dignity and cadence, elevated but never beyond reach, and down to gravel-bed when you need to be, for emphasis and earthy truth. Thus, the "trumped-up causes" of war, for which so many are lying today beyond reach of all transmissions....

Lately I have come to know Gordon Davis, Exec VP of the Group W station out here. Had lunch with him not long ago, and have exchanged reading matter and notes. He is an R. MacLeish fan; in fact he sent me the text of a piece of yours that I had missed. It is good to know that lightning strikes twice in a group as compact as W's....

TO RODERICK MacLEISH / October 14, 1970

Dear Rod:

...It was a triple-decker privilege to see you not once but three times in your short stay, and I enjoyed every moment of it.

Put that notion of a trip to Death Valley on a back burner, and cook slowly until ready to travel. Bring your wife and I'll coax Kate to come along so we can have a foursome on the Devil's Golf Course. There's a scenic area within the valley bearing that name, but it is a lake of halite formations having nothing to do with tees and greens....

TO CARL HAVERLIN, President, Broadcast Music, Inc.
November 25, 1970

He was a friend of Bruce Catton, the historian.

Dear Carl:

In honor of Bruce Catton, and also as a tribute to the legend of Leda and the Swan (the two being exquisitely unrelated), I composed the following limerick:

> An unbalanced lecher named Bruce
> Has a notion that he, just like Zeus,
> > Could change into a fawn
> > Or fuck like a swan
> Or at least offer Leda a goose.

May I suggest that if this is printed in the *Christian Science Monitor*, the phrase
> Or fuck like a swan
be altered to read
> Or screw like a swan.

I send you, and through you to Bruce Catton, my warmest regards.

> Fraternally,
> (dirty old man of Sherman Oaks)

Mr. Carl Haverlin
Dirty old man of Northridge, CA

TO DR. WILLIAM B. OBER / December 27, 1970

Dear Bill:

...I agree with you entirely about the Prado. Magnificent treasure, but it could do with a lighting expert. When I was there a couple of years ago, the room with the great Breughel allegories was as dark as a Third Avenue bar—and it happened to be a sunny day. Shmucks, the whole Cortes, from Franco up. I say up, because one can get no lower, except in Alabama and Mississippi, with the White House bearing down hard in the sweepstakes.

Yes, I have been to Toledo. You must certainly have taken that trip around the city, with the view from across the river. But I hope you saw that incredible porthole in the ceiling of the Cathedral. The set designers for Judgment Day need look no further. A shaft of sunlight was playing through that skylight the day I saw it, and I was ready for the Messiah.

From the sacred to the profane in one easy hop, I hope you have by now received the Felicien Rops volume. The mails have fucked up two gift packages to the east that I know about; yours would make it three....

Thank you for inquiring about what to send Tony and Diane. I didn't answer that because I didn't want you to bother your generous head about additional gifts for our household. The kids are big now—Tony big enough to be living in his own apartment, with his heart's choice, and Diane old enough to make very telling and acute critical comments on art, music, films and her old man. If you insist on sending a present to Diane next Christmas, make it a grand piano. She has outgrown her old standing Steinway. Only trouble with a grand is that I would have to buy a new house to set around it.

Did you know that Irving Belkowitz, Beulah's husband, is down with a stroke? His whole left side. Poor man—one of the most considerate men in the history of the race, and easily the world's finest brother-in-law....

I spoke with my father on the phone today, and he tells me he had a good long talk with your father just the other day. I hope the New Year is good to you all and us all, and that means, first and most and best, good health across the generations.

TO MEMBERS OF THE DOCUMENTARY COMMITTEE
February 5, 1971

> As Chairman of the Documentary Awards Committee of the Motion Picture Academy, Corwin wrote pseudonymous letters to Committee members at the end of each year's screenings.

Dear Sirs:

Regarding *Sexual Freedom in Denmark*, if by any chance this picture does not qualify as a "Documentary," I should like to ask whether, since I bore almost the entire weight of some of the cast in an important action sequence, I could be considered for nomination as best supporting actress.

Yours truly,

Jo-Ann Betty Lou Feldspar

TO GEORGE MOVSHON / April 24, 1971

Dear Giorgio:

The other day Darius Milhaud gave a farewell concert here at UCLA. He is quitting Mills College and going back to Paris to live out his years. It came to me with a terrible shock that at the time you invited me to write the H.R. cantata, I plumb forgot that some years earlier, Milhaud had expressed interest in writing music to a text on a socially important theme, to be set down by myself. We had been brought together by a mutual friend; indeed, as an outgrowth of that meeting, I had the pleasure of introducing Milhaud to a big audience at Royce Hall during one of the International Music Festivals held there during the last years of Franz Waxman. Now, then: You will improve my disposition by enabling me to chuck at least *that* nagging guilt, if you can tell me without perjuring yourself, that, even if I *had* proposed Milhaud at that hour, instead of our friend in Madrid, he would have been regionally, geographically, politically and idiomatically wrong for the occasion....

TO EMIL AND FREDA CORWIN / June 10, 1971

Dear Em and Babe:

The *Weekly Variety* of next Wednesday (June 16) will, I am told, carry a full page ad on the *NC Presents* upcoming series. [Westinghouse Broadcasting had commissioned Corwin to write, direct, produce and host a dramatic series for television called *Norman Corwin Presents*.] I saw a proof today—it has a caricature by Hirshfeld, in which I look like an Idaho potato with eyebrows and a moustache. But my hands, manipulating puppets (actors, get it?) are very graceferl. It's a cliche idea for a cartoon—I've seen similar ones by Hirshfeld—but after all he didn't have much to go by. Anyway, they spell my name right.

On Friday next (18) I fly to Toronto for a stay of about sixteen days, and the filming of the first two shows in the series. Not cast yet. I'll hop down to Boston for an overnight stay before returning to L.A....

I'm up to my ass in work. Not only the Westinghouse, but a twenty-six-show series on historical interviews (all American Revolutionary period), a musical based on Runyon Jones (book & lyrics & music almost at final draft stage—music by Ray Evans & Jay Livingston, who wrote "Buttons and Bows" and "Que Sera Sera" and "Mona Lisa," among other great hits); and a ninety-minute special for CBS on the Zola Trial. The latter two have less certainty of production than the first two, which are already moving, but the material is strong and I am sure that, with any kind of luck, it will be done by someone sometime somewhere.

This letter sounds like an ego trip, whereas it is meant to be only a news bulletin. We all send love,

---

All projects mentioned in the letter, except for the Zola, were realized.

TO BARNET RUDER / November 13, 1971

Dear Barney:

Many thanks for sending me the column on [T.S.] Eliot by John Barkham. Yes, I was aware of that streak in Eliot, who ranks among my least favorite intellectuals. In fact I once wrote a piece on Eliot's anti-Semitism, in which I cited expressions of it in (I believe) "Notes Toward a Definition of Culture." In the same piece I alluded to a fatuous review by Auden in *The New Yorker*, in which he tried to cover up for Eliot by saying that the master was only kidding. I sent the piece off to the *Atlantic*, where it was accepted and then, three weeks later, declined by [Edward] Weeks (who had been away in Europe or something) on the grounds that who was Corwin to knock Eliot....

How are you, Barney? It's always a joy to hear from you. As you may gather from the above letterhead, I am at it again. TV this time—a series bankrolled by Westinghouse. Thirteen have been finished, and I return to Toronto in two weeks, to tape another thirteen. No New York outlet yet for this syndicated series; so far we are carried only in San Fran, Boston, Phila, Baltimore and Pittsburgh. But the Canadian network has just bought the series.

Brother, is this a sick world! And we have [William] Rehnquist to look forward to....

TO MRS. HAROLD SIMMS GOODWIN / November 17, 1971

Sally Goodwin and her husband, an editor of the *Baltimore Sun*, were friends of Emil Corwin.

Dear Sally:

...I am delighted that you have been watching the series, and like it so far. I hope you caught *The Undecided Molecule*, which is one of my own favorites. Another, less successful but reasonably imaginative, is called *Soliloquy for Television*. I am going to write fewer original shows for the next thirteen, simply because I find this too taxing within the limited time available to produce the shows.

Many thanks for sending me Cedrone's column. It is good to have, and I add it to the growing press book—not all of which is filled with kind words. There was a lady critic in Boston who was outraged because I had the Vice President of the United States eating a banana while in quarantine with the Martian in the opening show of the series. Actually, it was a spontaneous piece of business by the actor—he had eaten an apple in earlier takes. But the lady, a spinster, may have some unhappy association with bananas. The kindest suspicion is that she may have slipped on a peel....

TO DAVID McCALLUM, Actor / From Toronto, Ontario, January 22, 1972

Dear Dave:

Well, you are the toast of Southern Ontario. By unanimous vote, acclamation and standing ovation, your performance as the most shlepperdik king since Farouk has been hailed as the finest stroke of acting in the entire series. We thank you individually and in chorus.

I now pass on to Phase II of this encomium, which is an invitation to star in a script which I will write expressly for you, and which will probably close the series. I well understand that it is not usual for you to accept a role script-unseen, but I flatter myself in believing that the enclosed script, which was done as one of the first thirteen, will give you some idea of the texture of what I have in mind—except that this would not be, like the enclosed, a soliloquy....

The reason I make bold enough to invite you to take this script on faith is twofold:

(1) to tailor it for you;

(2) to grab you before you are whisked off by your agent to some richer, more glamorous enterprise....

Write soon accepting this project for March 4th through the 8th, if only in order to avoid carrying a burden of guilt with you for the rest of your life. In the meantime I am having coins bearing your profile struck in your honor.

McCallum starred in two episodes of *Norman Corwin Presents—Crown of Rags* and *The Pursuit.*

TO RAY BRADBURY / From Sutton Place Hotel, 955 Bay Street, Toronto 5, Ontario, Canada, February 8, 1972

Dear Ray:

Wonderful to get your letter here in the frozen north. How frozen, I am in a position to testify as an expert witness. Yesterday it took ten men, three shovels and a bag of sand, to extricate my car from a snow-drift a little way up from the studio. A gust of bitter wind, straight from Greenland, spun my car around on the icy road, and *THUNK!* I was trapped like Amundsen in the Arctic Sea. That never happened to me on the way home from a Documentary screening, in all the years of attending those sessions.

I sorely miss having a Bradbury show on these 26, but I yield to *Dandelion Wine* and *Leviathan 99.* They are and will continue to be more enduring than any twenty-four-minute reel of TV tape can be, and I am delighted that you are bringing both to fruition on the stage. I am touched and delighted that you want Kate and me to be at the opening in Fullerton—something we eagerly look forward to. But I won't be back until after the 10th, because the final mix on the last show of the 26, takes place on the 11th and it will be the 12th or 13th before I can get back to L.A. So I am glad the play is running for nine performances....

Did you know that a crater in the moon has been named DANDE-LION for your *Dandelion Wine*? I came across the item in a news article, just before I left for Canada, and intended to send it to you, but it got away from me at the last minute. The clipping is sitting on my desk in the Westwood apartment. But surely you know about this. Next, a mountain peak on Mars named BRADBURY. It's only fitting—you have done so much for Mars.

I miss the Doc[umentary] screenings more than they miss me, and not the least of this deprivation is the chance to see you and daughter twice a week, and to hear your clarion check-off count as you vote to stop some dog in its sprockets.

I send you love, and the warm and devoted regards of all here who respond with Pavlovian alertness whenever your name is mentioned. For Canada is among your many provinces, like all four quadrants of the moon.

TO ROD SERLING / A Cold Boston Spring, April 9, 1972

Dear Rod:

Your magnificent letter was read to me from the coast.

If the Davies Award had brought me no other pleasure than your message, it would stand as one of the proudest moments of my life. The felicity of your letter is heightened by the fact that I had long rejoiced in your protean talents, in your massive accomplishments, and in your way of scrapping for all that is decent and good—but most of all, and this is selfish of me—I rejoice in your warm regard, which I treasure, and which I reciprocate with an esteem and affection of the most durable stamp.

Please let's get together for a drink when we are both on the same side of the Los Angeles River.

The Valentine Davies Award was given by the Writers Guild of America to the writer whose work reflected honor on all writers. Corwin was also a recipient.

TO DANIEL TARADASH, Screenwriter; President, Motion Picture
Academy / 10401 Wellworth, Los Angeles 90024, April 20, 1972

Dear Dan:

I was in the east on the night of the awards, and I watched from afar,
like the rest of the millions. One thing struck me with force: that the
entire corps of actors could take lessons from you in delivery. You spoke
with such ease and command, in contrast to actors who groped, hesitated, misfired, seemed a little lost. It is a natural hazard for most actors
when they appear before a huge audience in an alien role—that of
public speaker. But it was refreshing to see and hear a man who speaks
as gracefully and coherently as you do; and the crowning felicity lay in
the fact that as President of the Academy you symbolized the dignity
and importance that are proper to it.

So I congratulate you, and send my best wishes to you and
Madeleine.

TO KAREN HAZZARD, Actors Agent, Toronto
September 15, 1972

Corwin wrote on the letterhead of a television series that
was aborted.

Caro Karen:

Don't blame me, I didn't design the letterhead. I just designed the
series. It never came off, because the producer was sick sick sick. In the
head, I mean....We all have our obsolete letterheads. Just remember
what Rudyard Kipling wrote: "If you can keep your letterhead when all
about you..." etc....

What a small world—you and Pam [Barney] producing a show by
[Nehemiah] Persoff. He is one of my favorite actors and men. I see him
all too little out here, but like and admire him enormously....

Right now I am negotiating for a full-length production, in a vast
theatre-in-the-round (seats 2,800) in Woodland Hills nearby, of *The
Odyssey of Runyon Jones*. You will remember its TV incarnation as
Odyssey in Progress, in which your devoted fan played Father Time, and

Jay Livingston and Ray Evans—and Steve Franken—performed. It would run for two weeks around Christmas, if present plans mature. And then we'd have to see how it does and where.

You ask about my play [*The Rivalry*] in August. It was scheduled for Ford's Theatre in Washington, D.C., and full preparations were made—news and circular announcements, casting, and the rest. But the management of that theatre decided that it was making too much money from an extended run of *Godspell*, and blithely canceled not only our production, but a Comden & Green production which was to have followed. So now everybody is suing that theatre. What a fucking bore....

Are you in your new apartment yet? Where is it, and why is not a portrait of me hanging in a strategic place?

I send you hugs and kisses and wish you both a happy Jewish and Christian New Year, with the Moslems coming in third.

TO ROBIN LEVY / September 30, 1972

At fourteen, she had audited Corwin's class at Idyllwild.

Dear Robin:

Congratulations on your blue ribbon at the county fair.

I commiserate with you on having left your fourteenth year, which you describe as feeling like a calamity. But take cheer—as a member of your own faith, I am glad to advise you that there are several fine Jewish Old Women's Homes, and that as a people we tend to respect our elders. So that even the advanced ages of fifteen, sixteen and seventeen should not cause you apprehension.

I thank you for your Rosh Hashanah wishes, which I heartily reciprocate. So far the New Year has been blighted for me by the bleak showing of [George] McGovern [Democratic Presidential candidate] in the polls. I met him last week and found him to be warm, sincere and trust-inspiring. I'm sorry you're not old enough to vote in November—I would try to proselytize you. But then again, you're such a glorious girl that one shouldn't try to change a thing.

Blessings on every last curl, and on you.

TO KENNETH REXROTH, Poet / October 6, 1972

Dear Kenneth Rexroth:

You were right: I did get the letter sent to you.

As a longtime Rexroth fan, it is a pleasure to be mistaken for you. Anytime. Except for tax bills and traffic tickets. Warmest regards,

TO R. LeROY BANNERMAN / October 15, 1972

In 1972 Bannerman undertook a biography of Corwin, which was published in 1986. A research trip had taken him to New England to interview Corwin's relatives.

Dear LeRoy:

What a glorious account of your travels in New England! You are a marvelous reporter, and thanks to that I was well able to visualize your itinerary, your delays, your encounters. And I can tell you from triangulations in letters to me from the east, that your visit was much enjoyed by all of the family who had the pleasure of meeting you. I call my father every week, and each time since your visit he spoke of you in the warmest terms.

I was glad you were able to meet the New England family, because I think your meeting has confirmed the feeling I mentioned to you in Toronto, of unusually warm family ties. Of course time and distance, the exigencies of work, and the responsibilities attached to raising one's own family, have the tendency, universally, to weaken the bonds between families, but in my own case I feel fortunate in having been able to maintain over the years a loving regard—mutual, I am sure—between not only members of my original family, but some of the outer branches like Aunt Mildred and Uncle Harry. I have also, for years, had a lively correspondence with Harry's son Bill—an outstanding pathologist with wide-ranging interests that include medical biography (he has written scores of them for leading medical journals) and musicology. Many an LP bears Dr. William B. Ober's commentary on the back of the jacket. There may be some in your own classical LP library. Bill is a fierce iconoclast, a wit, and something of a maverick in many directions, but a very nice and humane guy. If you ever follow up your New England journey with one to New York, Bill might be a good guy to see.

It is seventy-five degrees and bright here today—one of the beautiful days of the year. Oakland, my pick, is ahead in the World Series; I wish I could say my candidates were ahead in the election polls. But one can't win 'em all. If only the November 7 contest were not so desperately crucial for the next four years, and beyond! But here, here, no electioneering in a letter to the great and good LeRoy.

TO RALPH SCHOENSTEIN / February 21, 1973

Corwin wrote on a United Nations letterhead.

Dear Member State:

I want to welcome you to this organization. It was wise of you to change the name of your country from Schoenstein to Curaculiambro, since Schoenstein would, I am afraid, be constantly confused with Lichtenstein, a state already confused enough with *Roy* Lichtenstein.

I want also to declare under oath that your latest piece for *The New Yorker* is smashing. It is polished like space hardware, and represents you at top form....

Your kindness in sending me copies of your pieces is not practiced without some hazard—the danger, always present, that I may send you some of mine....

Enclosed, a sort of state ode written upon merciless urging, for the opening of a ten-day flankenbake (no clambakes permissible under the dietary laws) called JERUSALEM FAIR, presented by the state of Israel, one of your fellow members. I delivered it myself before an audience of 3,000 at the Convention Center, and when I finished and got down from the platform, Teddy Kollek, the Mayor of Jerusalem who was sitting in the front row, rose, strode over to me, and flung his arms around me. I still think it's a decent piece.

As soon as you have Judy design a flag, let us have it so it can go up with the rest, down there on First Avenue. It is wonderful to have you in the General Assembly to help us continue to fuck up the world.

TO SARI GELMAN, Painter / March 12, 1973

They had met briefly in Israel.

Dear Sari:

Your letter moved me very much. It is so much like you and your painting—luminous, searching, sensitive, aware, rich in every grace, on good terms with the universe.

What a coincidence that you should have written to me while floating airborne among the clouds you love so much—a coincidence because, after seeing the glorious skies of your paintings, I thought of you instantly when, a few days later, I stood at my window and watched huge battlements of startlingly white cumulus, towering higher than Everest over lesser ranges of blue-black storm clouds, swollen with rain, snow and hail. To give credit where it is due, God of course makes the most daring and original of all landscapes and skyscapes, does She not?—but when we are gifted or lucky enough to be able to capture on canvas or paper or in photographic emulsion, some scintilla of that beauty, we become to that extent little fractional gods ourselves....

Keep painting, writing, thinking, feeling, living. It is a various and awesome world; and while its crud is continental in weight and extent, there are still enough people who feel as you and I do about clouds and poems and trees and light and color and music, and the man-made abstractions of peace and justice, to make you feel far from lonely, ever....

TO ELLIOTT SANGER / March 18, 1973

Dear Elliott:

Congratulations on *Rebel in Radio*, and great thanks for your kindness in sending me a copy, for the warm inscription, and for the lively recollection of my emergence from chrysalis.

I read the book with pleasure and instruction, and from time to time was bathed in a sunny glow of nostalgia. It takes its place on a rare shelf of treasurable histories of the medium, alongside Erik Barnouw's trilogy. It is more than a memoir, rich as that element is in your writing. The station, *The Times*, alumni like myself, and listeners in general are in your debt.

I had no idea [WQXR's] beginnings were so humble—$5 for a spot announcement, and a gross monthly income (in the year you took me on) of less than $200 for two summer months. Of course, I was paid nothing for *Poetic License*, but it seemed to me then that the price was right; and in terms of the good it did me, I might have paid *you* for the privilege.

I see by the photograph on the dust jacket that you are as handsome as ever, and I gather from your dedication that the honeymoon with Eleanor is still on. I send you both my most affectionate regards, escorted by unswerving best wishes, whose constancy over the years is one of the few consistent things in the checkered career that you launched there on 5th and 57th.

TO R. LEROY BANNERMAN / November 26, 1973

Dear LeRoy:

Your piece for the *TV Quarterly* is damn fine thinking and writing. I have nothing but praise for the way you packed much into little, clearly and cleanly and crisply....

The quote from Max Wylie on page 8 was of particular interest to me, because I either never ran across it, or forgot it. Max's was not the only comment of that kind, and they are all rooted firmly in a common misconception: that I was (or am) incapable of writing of "*people*" (Wylie's underscoring) or of showing more than a glimpse of "human interaction." Misapprehension is the polite term, bullshit the impolite. The fact is that the huge documentaries like *We Hold These Truths* and *On a Note of Triumph* could not have been the shows they were had I written a sort of Mr. Smith Goes to World War II, or The Virginia Boys Go to Philadelphia. What Wylie chose to ignore, in following the line he expressed, were plays like *My Client Curley*, which in small compass has *people* (the Agent and Curley) and a good deal of interaction; and *Untitled*, which has people and interaction, but certainly not in any Chekhovian or Millerian sense; and *Old Salt*, and the comedy people of *Murder in Studio One* and *Double Concerto* and *Mary and the Fairy*. Are

Zaragosa and Poganyi and poor Twombly of *Double Concerto* not people? And wasn't Hank Peters a *person*, and his mother and teacher and the editor? Platonic individuals? Remote?

Is Runyon Jones a rubric? Is Gunner Marshall of *To Tim at Twenty* a real person, for all that we meet him only a few minutes? Max, of whom I have always been fond, and still am, just did not do his homework. And I submit that in my TV scripts, movies and plays, I have written and continue to write about real people. Charles and Elsa Gumpert of *The One Man Group*, the psychiatrist and scientist and, yes, especially The Fairy of *The Hyphen* are as real in their way as Max or you or me in ours. [*Scandal at Scourie*], a modest little picture starring Greer Garson and Walter Pidgeon, is full of people and interaction, and the people were my total invention, superimposed on the barest skeleton of a synopsis. It must be seen before any judgment is passed on my capacity or incapacity to write about people. That I have not chosen to do so very often was controlled at first by the demand made upon me during the war, to write murals and polemics of the order of *Note of Triumph*, and later by a sort of type-casting in the TV and film industries. But I will match my Stephen Douglas and his wife Adele with any other historical figures populating plays on American historical themes, as to whether they were human and visceral characters.

Even in *Lust for Life*, I submit that Gauguin and Van Gogh and Theo did not write themselves. If I did not create those characters on the screen, who else did? No record exists of their dialogue; the fact that I mined the Letters does not mean that the characters were prefabricated for me in a dramatic context.

Enough of this silly rebuttal. I only wanted to disabuse whoever may be interested, of the notion incubated by those who knew me only for "symbolic representation." I know the difference between a rubric and a vignette and a soap opera and a symbol and a person and a dog.

Your piece is admirable the way it stands—I suggest no alteration unless you care to note my exception in the record, as they say in law. P.S. Enclosed, a review from *The Denver Post*, on *Cervantes*. The greater the distance from the poisonous reviews in the East, the more appreciative the reviews. Another good one came in from Portland, Oregon. Culture has moved west, maybe.

TO EMIL CORWIN / November 27, 1973

Dear Em:

Those are great notes, and they fill out some of the lacunae in my own hurried and far from exhaustive reportage. Many many thanks.

Your recollections are so much sharper than mine—you were already into the age of comprehension when I was still playing with buttons on the living room carpet. The Scenic Temple, for example, is beyond my memory; The Gem is barely over the threshold. The movie house was called The Central, I believe. My first recollections are of Pearl White serials. And there was a feature film in which some evil character had the magic power of making people disappear by simply pointing at them. The character just faded into the woodwork. Somehow this sickened me—to a point of nausea—although of course I wasn't going to leave my seat, because I had paid ten cents for it. More than that, I had come deliberately late to the first showing, which meant I was given a card that entitled me to sit in for the second show—and see it all through again. I closed my eyes every time the monster repeated his disappearance act.

Your memory of sitting on a curb while Pa went in for a snorter en route to Bremen Street, reminds me that not much has changed. I once took him to the airport here to catch a plane for Boston. He had about fifteen minutes to wait, but he made those pass pleasantly by seeking out a bar which served sherry. I did not think LAX had such, but they do—a restaurant bar apparently. I would say that Pa has ingested enough sherry in his time to float the Sherry Netherlands.

I am delighted by your notes on the Rotary Club loan—details I never knew. I remember your assiduousness in finding work to help you through the Amherst days. There was some waiter service in Atlantic City, as I remember. That name had the ring to me of distant Araby; I thought you were a model adventurer. I remember visiting you in your Woronoco period—the countryside was beautiful, if memory serves. You lived in a company hotel. I remember your giving me a guided tour of the paper plant. Strathmore. Also, for some reason, there crosses my mind a breakfast we had at a diner in Springfield one morning, when a waitress was rude. You put her in her place with some judicious comment, and left her no tip. It was one of my early lessons in how to cope....

TO ARNOLD M. GRANT / December 7, 1973

Dear Arnie:

I am joined herewith by two favorites of ours, Th. Jefferson and Jas. Madison, in extending to you best wishes for the present season, for the New Year, and for the years beyond. [Corwin gave Grant a document signed by both Thomas Jefferson and James Madison.]

The authenticity of the document and the signatures is sworn to by the American Library Service, a copy of whose covering letter I enclose.

What attracted me to this fragment was the unusual combination of the signatures of *two* giants within an inch-and-a-quarter of each other. Not even on the Declaration of Independence are their names that close, for the very good reason that Madison was not a delegate to the occasion, and wasn't around.

It would be interesting to find out just how many documents T and M signed in common. If there were very few, or if—God cooperating— this is the only one, its value might be far in excess of what The American Library Service wot.

But even if Tom and Jim signed a hundred documents jointly, it is comforting to have access to one of them, and even more comforting to know that it is now in your possession.

TO RAY BRADBURY / January 26, 1974

Dear Ray:

What a rich brace of gifts, your book and its inscription!

It is one thing to be great, as you long have been, and another to be growing in your greatness. *When Elephants Last in the Dooryard* is now high ground in Bradbury country. At your best moments, which crowd together so profusely as to be almost continuous, I think you have gone beyond even those high bench marks of your previous works, and even [Robert] Kirsch's rave notice seems modest.

The delights and surprises come so thick it is hard to single them out, much less comment on them, without doing a term paper. Where have you been keeping your felicity with rhyme all these years? And from what hidden pockets in your wardrobe of many suits, come those subtle cadences that sing sweeter and stronger even than the famous measures of your prose?

An incredible feast, movable and moving. The epauletted bees, the harvesters who lie harvested by grass, the Lincoln poem, the wit and charm of your valentine to Lavoisier, the epitaph, the gentle-sweet-sad-funny poignance and truth of Bradburys, father and daughter, being sent to the showers in that perfect marvel of a poem.

Jesus, what zest and taste and feeling for life! Now more than ever it has come out in public that language is a girl who skips rope for you and also tumbles in the sack with you. Thank God she is at the same time beautiful and rich, comes from a long line of poets, and is so cheerfully your obedient servant.

Kate and I thank you beyond my power to say it, and rejoice for you and art. Love,

TO THE DOCUMENTARY COMMITTEE, MOTION PICTURE ACADEMY

Another spurious letter.

ZOOLOGICAL ASSOCIATION OF AMERICA

February 4, 1974

Gentlemen:

Acting solely in the capacity of amicus curiae, we wish to call your attention to a scene in the documentary film *Up from the Ape*, in which a male pig is clubbed to death before the camera. We believe this scene to be the perfect example of a bloody boar.

Fraternally,
Martha Mitchell

TO MARY Y. MUNFORD / February 23, 1974

Dearest Mary:

The letters came, and I read them with nostalgia, a sense of warmly reliving some of the moments preserved, and an occasional surprise. [She had written recalling Corwin's reporting days in Springfield, Massachusetts.] What surprised me was that curious young man. Sometimes I think a man sheds his skin like a snake, not once but several times. I recognize myself of course, but the years do warp the mirror—or maybe they straighten it, I'm not sure. The one thing I *am* sure of, is that I have adored you with no small constancy, and with good reason. For you are you.

Thank you for your thoughtfulness in letting me see these again. I send you, always, my love.

TO R. LeROY BANNERMAN / April 25, 1974

Dear LeRoy:

You ask about the Yamashita script. It has already been taped, and will be on the air over ABC-TV on June 11. I went out to the studio for a few of the taping sessions, and watched mostly from the control room. Stanley Kramer uses the camera very fluidly, but his technique was almost stubbornly filmic rather than streamlined for tape. He had three cameras at his disposal, and mostly used two. Many stops for new setups and lighting changes; big overtime sessions to run up the budget. There were some very good things in what I saw, and also some poor ones. Certain readings by his actors drove me right out of the control room—I am not by nature a masochist. Kramer tells me that he had to cut ten minutes from an already very tight script, in the editing. God knows what it will look and sound like. I was distressed by the fact that Kramer, on the grounds that he would be speaking the narration (he is on-camera host and narrator throughout), made changes in the narration I had written for him. One such change was to insert the phrase, "Emotion ruled the day," which I would not write if Paul Getty offered me half his holdings. "Let's not commit a cliche," I said to Stanley. He kept it in. It's better to run your own show, a la Toronto, even at the hazard of falling into a pit. [Corwin had fallen into an uncovered pit in a studio at CFTO, Toronto, during production of the last program in the *Norman Corwin Presents* series. He broke a rib in the fall.]

TO RODERICK MacLEISH / July 14, 1974

Dear Rod:

Your good letter was forwarded to me here on a flank of Mount Jacinto, where I am teaching for the month of July. There are very few things I miss among the pines at five thousand feet, but one of them is your voice on KFWB.

Right you are about [John Gregory] Dunne and [Joan] Didion, and well said, too. I saw a movie based on one of her books [*Play It As It Lays*], with screenplay I think by hubby. About Hollywood people. Full of pus and pellagra: grisly, nasty, and awash in the hate you speak of. The only halfway likable character was a waspish homosexual who showed a few pale traces of humanity. He, of course, committed suicide.

I am delighted that you are writing that novel. The rest of us talk about writing novels—you do it. All the while giving us the best commentary on any air: best written, best conceived, best delivered. Enjoy the distinction, and take pleasure from the pleasure you give.

TO SALLY GOODWIN / October 3, 1974

Dear Sally:

How kind you are to write us such a warm and witty account of the occasion at the Hopkins Club. Your testimony on the state of Tony's [his son's] beard is of special interest to us because that adornment is undoubtedly more advanced than it was when we last saw him. Beard, moustache and long hair are obviously the proper equipment for a young painter, and probably serve today's artist somewhat as Paris served the painters and sculptors of a generation ago—the right ambience and decor.

And you must have inspired Tony to speak up, because he has been known to be silent as a clam in any gathering of more than two people—and sometimes with only another, such as myself. Anyway, you and Harold are very dear to have invited the Baltimore branch of the family to meet the Washington branch—something that might not have happened spontaneously for half a school year if left to Tony's initiative. But then he is a dedicated painter, and sticks to his easel.* So you once again have our thanks, along with our constant and most affectionate regards.

*"Manrise" is one of my own favorites, but he's done some quite striking things since then.

TO LYN MURRAY, Composer / November 16, 1974

> Murray was among several speakers at a luncheon in Corwin's honor given by the Pacific Pioneer Broadcasters but Corwin, in thanking the others, overlooked him.

Dear Lion:

I just got off the phone after crying on Bob Lee's shoulder about that miserable inadvertence which spoiled an otherwise magical day for me. It was not a fly in the ointment, it was worse: birdshit in the nectar, the birdshit being my own ineptitude in not having *all* my papers together when I went up to the podium. I called you immediately on discovering the lacuna, and you were understanding and forgiving, but I cannot forgive myself. It is not the first time this has happened to me on important functions: I gave a lecture up at USC-Isomata last summer, and I thought I was in good form until, when it was over, one of my faculty peers who was in the audience came up and said, "Do you know that you have two different shoes on?" There was also the time when I was introduced to a Mr. Threlkeld, and I had a lot of papers in my hand, and when the person introducing him said, "Mr. Threlkeld, I would like for you to meet Mr. Corwin," I responded to the stimulus of the last name I heard, and replied, "How do you do, Mr. Corwin." They were both startled, and yet said nothing, and went off to meet the next acquaintance. It was too late for me to run after them and say, "No—excuse me—I meant I'm happy to meet you, Mr. *Threlkeld*."

It's too late to reconvene the meeting to read what I had written to say about Murray, but I at least have the text of it, and it is as follows:

My very dear friend Lyn Murray is some of the best bad company I have ever kept. Besides being a superb composer, from which circumstance I have benefited (except for a certain discomfiture when his music was better than my words, which happened often), Lyn is a marvelous writer. He has just written a book of memoirs, and I recently had the privilege of reading it in manuscript. It is one of the wittiest and wickedest autobiographies ever written, and if there is a publishing house in the house, I urge you to option it before you leave the room. In its present form the book would keep an enterprising publisher entertained with libel suits for at least the first six editions, but I think it would be worth it, both to the publisher and to the posterity of music, broadcasting, and the general intercourse of human affairs. [Corwin recommended Murray's autobiography to Lyle Stuart, who published it as *Musician*. Corwin wrote the introduction.]

Please note the respectful billing I gave to intercourse....

The advocate within who lays consolation on me when I have disgraced myself by still another ineptitude, argues one main consolation: that, when I was asked in advance of the occasion, what friends of mine I would like to see at the luncheon, you were among the five I requested, and the only man from the world of music....Once again I thank you for being there, for the warm and characteristically witty things you said, and for a friendship which dates from before the Tonetti Woods, and which I shall treasure for all my days. Love,

TO WILLIAM S. PALEY / November 19, 1974

Dear Bill:

I was delighted to get your telegram at the Pioneer Broadcasters event, and I deeply appreciate the generosity of your comments. But of course nothing that I accomplished could even have been attempted had it not been for the impetus, the opportunity and the encouragement that came from CBS as an entity, and from you in particular.

There was an unforgettable aura about 485 Madison; to those of us who were lucky enough to work under its roof, it was known that the emanations began in your office and filtered down through the organization.

Again, Bill, as so many times before, my liveliest thanks, and, as ever, my warmest best wishes.

TO HERBERT BLOCK / November 20, 1974

Dear Herb:

Special Report [Herblock's collected cartoons] is very very special indeed. If, as Lincoln said, we cannot escape history, then history cannot escape Herblock. The very things I was thinking about the book as I devoured it, are all there on the back of the jacket, said by [Richard H.] Rovere, [William V.] Shannon, [Michael] Mok and [Paul] Szep.

Together with my liveliest thanks for the book and your inscription, go my congratulations. It is a work that will be cited, word and line, not only for those hundred years Shannon speaks of, but, I am sure, for as long as histories are written and illustrated.

I am sorry I missed you at the opening of the Cervantes play, but if your feeling was as negative as that of some of the critics present, you were spared some embarrassment. [Corwin's play, *Cervantes*, starring Richard Kiley, opened in Washington, D.C., to mostly bad reviews.] I am glad to say that the inadequacies of that premature opening were attended to subsequently, and it had a good run on a road tour that took it as far west as Hawaii.

I hope this letter finds you well and happy and as vigorous as your art.

TO THE TODAY SHOW / December 16, 1974

Corwin had heard a remark on the program that sending and receiving Christmas cards was a bore.

Gentlemen:

On the whole I think I like Christmas cards better than talk shows. They are brief, often colorful, sometimes witty; they don't plug books and records, they are not fragmented by a hundred interruptions, spun out on the pretext of "station identification"; they do not run down the amenities. Nor do they have a thousandth part of the commercial motivation of, let us say, the TODAY show.

I receive about three hundred cards a year. Except for two that I get from my car dealer and an oil company, toward neither of which I bear any particular good will at any season, I am delighted to hear from friends, old acquaintances, associates, children now grown, secretaries now married, trenchmates now retired, hale fellows and girls once well met in Australia and Scandinavia and Newark.

And what if there is now and then a little sediment of sentiment at the bottom of these cards? What's so bad about wishes for peace on earth and good will to men, for joy and content in this drab, dreggy, drecky, violence-prone world? Even if these sentiments are mass produced, they are good to have. So is the Bible mass produced. Repetition of a good thing does not make it tiresome or cliche. "Good morning," for example, is a greeting of which nobody ever tires, and so is Happy New Year.

Happy New Year.

Cordially,

TO LEW TRENNER, Chemist, of Denver / December 17, 1974

Dear Lew:

Your kind offer of shelter in the event of that balefully inevitable earthquake, is as warmly appreciated as it is soberly entertained....The pamphlet raised all the hackles that had not been used up by contemplation of the state of the world and the economy.

Interesting that you should call [Isaac] Asimov a horse's ass. I had only one exposure to him, when both of us were honored by the Boston University Library at a big bash. He spoke with a cockiness bordering on arrogance, but it escaped being offensive because it was laced with a kind of stand-up-comedian wit, and he had people laughing. One thing I have to respect in him is his incredible industry—every journal you pick up has an article by him; his horse's ass is very broad.

I have been thumpingly busy, working on three different projects simultaneously: two for TV, the third for the stage. I am hoping the latter, which is projected for a road tour, will stop off in Denver. If it does I will stop off with it, and you may find yourself having to make good that innocent tender of the spare bedroom....

It has been too long since I saw that handsome phiz. The bicentennial era is favorable for reunions of all kinds, and I go from here to consult the first oracle I can find in the yellow pages.

I hope you are enjoying Nixon's retirement as much as I am—although that dunce Ford can be just as damaging to the nation *without* the evil genius of his predecessor....

I enclose an affidavit of my loving best wishes to you and the missus.

TO BOARD OF GOVERNORS, ACADEMY OF MOTION PICTURES / December 31, 1974

I write to propose a candidate for a special award at the next Academy presentations.

I am sure there is not a member of the Board for whom Jean Renoir does not rank among the legendary figures of world cinema. Aside from the extraordinary esthetic and archival value of his contributions to the art of motion pictures, his entire body of work has been informed by a rich humanism that has made him beloved to co-workers and audiences alike.

Mr. Renoir is now in his eighty-first year. He has been ill, and for some time has been confined to a wheelchair. I believe it would do honor as much to the Academy as to Mr. Renoir, if he were to receive, while he is still among us, the highest award it is in your power to bestow.

The Board awarded Renoir the honor.

TO TONY CORWIN / June 27, 1975

Dear Tonio:

Okay. My first move is the same as your first; your second you have already given me, KKt to K2; my second is Kkt to KB3 [first two moves in chess by mail].

I would have moved sooner than this, but I am not many days back from the hospital after having my hernia repaired. The operation itself, done under local, was no more painful than a haircut, and the surgeon who did it has a policy of letting his patients get up off the operating table themselves and walk back to their room. Of course after the local wore off, it was clear to me that I was carrying around a sizable wound, and there were a few uncomfortable days and nights. But I was able to do without any of the codeine drugs that had been prescribed to allay pain. They tend to bind the bowels, and all a hernia patient needs in addition to post-surgical pain from the incision and the needlework, is gas pain and constipation.

While in hospital (the British never say in *the* hospital, but "in hospital"), I read two novels by Lawrence Durrell, *Justine* and *Balthazar*, and since I have been home I have extended this reading to include *Mountolive* and *Clea*. The four are combined as a tetralogy called *The Alexandria Quartet*, because they are set in Alexandria, Egypt. I have been late coming to Durrell (I haven't *yet* gotten to Dostoievsky, which will give you some idea of how badly under-read I am), but I find him positively brilliant. Enormous descriptive power, which you as a painter will I am sure find fascinating. A very curiously fractionated story structure, all the more interesting for being so—especially in the first two books. You might get them out of the library and give Durrell a whirl. The books are about fifteen or twenty years old; Durrell is alive and well, in southern France to the best of my knowledge....

TO SALLY AND HAROLD GOODWIN / From 1840 Fairburn Avenue, Los Angeles 90025, June 29, 1975

Dear Sally and Harold:

Part of the reason you have not heard from me earlier is reflected in the new address—a burdensome dislocation which gave me all kinds of trouble. After nearly ten years at the Wellworth address, and repeated assurances from a Dickensian landlord that they were NOT going to tear the building down, and if they did they would OF COURSE give us sixty or ninety days' notice, they gave all tenants thirty days to find a place and get out. It was a groan and a grunt, finding a place that could accommodate the incredible collection of books, manuscripts, files, paintings and objets de junk that I had collected—and which would have sufficient light, quiet and space. I finally found one, but it costs me close to three times what I had been paying.

My Baltimore representative, Tony, elected to stay on there for the summer. Whether the city or his girl has the stronger hold on him, I know not. We hear from him very little more than you do, and then it is usually when we phone him. You had the word for Tony: a private person. But lately he has proposed that we play chess by mail, and I have already received his first two moves and replied to them.

Moving and hernia created a work lull, but now the offing begins to fill up, thick with projects and negotiations. Including an invitation to go to South Africa for a bit of lecturing and seminaring. This I have to study. Long trip and all that.

Are you in touch with Emil and Freda? They love you too.

TO R. LEROY BANNERMAN / June 29, 1975

Dear LeRoy:

If the attached cassette has me sounding less energetic than my usual sleepy self, it is because I am still recovering from surgery, and also still not recovered from the shock of the death of Rod Serling. He was a good man in all ways, and if he had any bad spots I neither saw nor heard of them. His warmth and friendship, even though we saw little of each other, you can judge from that sweet letter he wrote (unknown to me) to Mrs. Malloy for her thesis. He was, to coin a phrase, on the side of the angels. The bright angels, not the dull ones who keep their wings waxed and polished.

TO JOHN HOUSEMAN, Director / July 2, 1975

Dear John:

A cartel consisting of [Producers] Lee Orgel, Norm Prescott, Lou Scheimer and myself met at a rooftop restaurant yesterday, mainly to discuss your reservations about the flash-forwards....[Corwin had asked Houseman to direct a play he had written about Jefferson, Hamilton and Burr.]

I understand you feel that it is disruptive to go from a progression in real time, into the future, and then back to real time. You particularly feel that the duel is kitsch, and you had the concern, on the telephone, that by the time we open, the duel will have been done on TV a hundred times.

Let me comment first on the last two points. The media have now been almost two years chipping away at bicentennial subjects. Not once yet has the duel been enacted. Nor is it likely to be, considering the complexity of the Burr-Hamilton story—a frowning complexity that has kept playwrights from tackling the area head on.

As for kitsch: In the hands of a tasteless director, anything can be kitsch. It could be argued that it was kitsch to show Van Gogh slicing off his ear, in our film. Well, it could have been but it wasn't. You are incapable of committing kitsch; never in your career has it reared its lumpy head. I am certain that the duel scene, which in its starkness and simplicity is the historical truth,...would in your hands take on power, dignity and tragedy....

You have expressed concern about our having filled the kitchen sink. It is indeed full, but with fine dishes. And of course one can always remove dishes. It will not be difficult to thin out, if there is need to do so.

On the time shifts: Once the audience has accepted the Asides—a device which you approve—then I believe it will readily accept a second step in which we make asides in time as well as in thought. Our flash-forwards are not arbitrary or antic. They have a deep organic relation to the rest.

I grant you that flash-forwards can be intrusive and disruptive, as for example in Joe Losey's *The Go-Between*, when suddenly without any local impetus we jump a whole generation. It got the audience nowhere and the trip was not necessary. The flash-forwards in our piece, on the other hand, take us to important destinations, and are neither arty in style nor egregious in substance....

Not only within the body of the areas at issue, but within the larger areas with which you are already content, there may well be need for adjustment, emphasis, pruning, enhancement. I will be there with my tools.

I send you as always my warmest regards.

When Houseman declined, Corwin directed the play, *Together Tonight: Hamilton, Jefferson, Burr.* It toured the country to good reviews.

TO LOU ASHWORTH / August 13, 1975

Dear Lou:

Yours was the first news I got of Bob Heller. A shock, as is the passing of any peer or junior, especially if he was part of the campaigning and barnstorming. We had been out of touch for years; even the Season's Greetings somehow slipped away. But our relations were always cordial, and I always believed he was a good man, a man of peace and reasonably good will toward the reasonably good. He seemed to me a strange bird at times, but then I supposed I seemed the same to him. Another jolt was losing Rod Serling, at an even earlier age. Our old friend Carl Sandburg once wrote a line about "the frail permits" by which we live. Too true, too true.

You ask me to describe the new apartment. Unlike the last place, which looked like a dorm occupied by a messy sophomore, the new one is staid, has two bedrooms, a large living room, big kitchen, two baths, two big walk-in closets, an ample balcony which looks out over a quasi parklike vista, and houses a small arboretum. The rent is higher than I ever thought I could get myself to pay, but the mail is delivered early, and there is a big garage in which I can park my '67 Cad cement mixer. It is an apartment, not a home, which means I can just lock it up when I go to South Africa (no kidding) at the end of September. Invited there to give seminars and lectures on communications, TV, radios, film and all that jazz.

Your roving uncle sends you love,

TO RODERICK MACLEISH / September 1, 1975

Dear Rod:

Like those masters who wrote symphonies when deaf and painted murals with brushes strapped to arthritic wrists, you perform as strongly under adversity as when the sun is out and all is in bloom. I would never have known from your recent broadcasts that you had been under painful stress. Indeed I was several times on the point of writing to say applauseapplauseapplause for some of your pieces—especially the one that ended with your comment that what Nixon wouldn't do for Congress and the Department of Justice, he will now do for David Frost's pay. But then as I have told you before, if I wrote you every time you hit a home run, I would soon be a bore, and put you in the uncomfortable strait of having to acknowledge repeated fan letters.

Kate and I are distressed by the loss of your father and the breakup at home and the scare of Diana's heart attack. Any one of those is traumatic, but the combination is enough to clobber a Job. Yet I am heartened by the knowledge that you have many friends who love you, and have kind words and thoughts for you; and I hope that the certainty of that will buoy you. I number myself among those friends who love you, and you are of course to call upon me for anything that I can do short of prayer, at which I am poor because I have no standing with the Authorities....

TO MAXWELL GEISMAR, Writer / January 27, 1976

Dear Max:

Well, the play [*Together Tonight*] is off and running. All right, limping. It opened to an audience of 3,500 in Bloomington on the campus of the University of Indiana, and the audience seemed to grab every point worth grabbing; it laughed, it applauded often. It was our first—very first—audience, except for a few friends who had come in to a small rehearsal hall in Century City, and seen a runthrough in which Jefferson wore a turtleneck, and Burr sneakers.

Notwithstanding many cuts and alterations I had made, profiting incidentally from your astute comments, the opening night's performance ran about eight minutes longer than I would have liked. [Geismar had offered suggestions after reading the script.] I did some cosmetic surgery on the thing, and by its third performance two nights later in South Bend, it was down to size.

I wish I could say the same about the cast. The man playing Burr, Monte Markham, is superb. So is the moderator, Lenox, the only actor

[Alan Manson] I cast myself; but [Dana] Andrews is a little too old and lukewarm for Jefferson, and [Howard] Duff blunders too much for anybody's comfort. He is an effective Hamilton, although at times a little too much like an Irish cop; but he has power, and his acting, when he remembers his lines, is good.

Myself, I have been steaming around the hemisphere—the steamy Amazon jungle, the high Andes, and the cold Midwest. And in four weeks I am scheduled to be off for a month in South Africa. A hard month of work.

This letter is disgracefully all about me and *Together Tonight*. How about Maxwell Geismar?

In February, 1975, Corwin had gone to Whitewater, Wisconsin, where the temperature was ten degrees below zero, to confer on a television adaptation of The Rivalry. The program went on the air as part of the Hallmark Hall of Fame series.

TO EMIL CORWIN / February 26, 1976

Dear Em:

Thanks for your wonderfully rich letter, in which I learn new facts about East Boston, and bask in your approval of my *Westways* piece. Why is it that I have no memory whatsoever of the house on Eutaw Street? Was I not born then? My earliest recollections are of 218 (or was it 242?) Bremen Street. Life to me then was bounded by Bremen, Marion, Brooks and Chelsea Streets—that one big block in which lived the Merchants, Obers, Lynns, LaFargues, and Yossi Borofsky.

I think you are right about the bird streets—I recall Condor and Falcon, although Eagle seems a little hazy. And I'm sure you're right about Apple Island being devoured. But as one New England historian to another, I am happy to confirm that it *is* Bumpkin, not Pumpkin Island. My source for this is a fascinating book called *The Romance of Boston Bay*, by Edward Rowe Snow, published by Yankee (what else?) Publishing Co. of Boston. Bumpkin is in Hull Bay, near good old Nantasket.

I don't recall Leverett Street; the only flat of our paternal grands that I remember was the one on a side street, off Blue Hill Avenue—a walkup of two flights.

Many many thanks for the clippings. Everything you send is unfailingly of interest, and this time I enjoyed both the article on statues in which you are honored by citation, and the Alistair Cook interview. I know Cook and like him greatly. He was principal speaker at the last Guild Awards dinner at which I presided as Chairman, and I had the pleasure of introducing him. I met him twice before—once at a party at Romanoff's yars and yars ago, and again at George Movshon's flat in Tudor City, about six or seven years back.

As of this writing, the South Africa trip is iffy. Though I applied for a visa on February 2, it has not yet come through, and I am scheduled to leave on March 3. I am, believe it or not, about 60 percent hoping that it will *not* come through, because I am apprehensive of the punishing pressure of the long, long flight (ten time-zones) and the very heavy agenda that has been worked out for me once I reach Jo[hannes]berg. There would be many exciting and rewarding features of such a trip, I am sure, but I find that as I grow older I am less patient and comfortable in pressure situations, and find it very hard to relax and get proper sleep. I would like nothing so much right now as a couple of weeks in the desert or the mountains, just idling in neutral. But the next few days will determine whether I go rolling down to Rio, or sit on my commodious porch here and enjoy the sun. Whichever way, I send love, as always, to you and Freda.

TO DOCUMENTARY AWARDS COMMITTEE, MOTION PICTURE ACADEMY / Undated, 1976

> Another Corwin phony letter on a letterhead of "Tit for Tat, A Gulf & Western Company."

Dear Sirs:

As the world's leading manufacturer and distributor of tattoo acupuncture needles, and a company which rewards the tattoo as a valuable adjunct of our culture, we are aware that during the current season you turned off, before it was half finished, a short documentary on the subject of tattoos.

We would like you to know what you missed. In the last reel there is a scene featuring the world's most completely tattooed man, Millard Throggs, Jr., on whose body are not only depicted beautiful landscapes, seascapes and portraits, but trademarks, mottos, inscriptions and place names. Every inch of his body is covered, including a section of his abdomen which reads, "BATTLE OF THE BULGE," and there are similar clever sayings relating to various anatomical parts. An out- standing example is a tattooed word on his male member, which reads TINY. As the camera alludes to this feature, a beautiful model enters the frame, and as she crosses the room, the adjective TINY becomes, before your eyes, TICONDEROGA, N.Y., which of course is a noun.

By turning off this film when you did, you missed the impressive calligraphy of the word Ticonderoga, and you also missed reacquainting yourselves with the memory of an outstanding American historical shrine.

The Tit For Tat Company feels that you overlooked a fine short, and hope you will change your mind and schedule another projection.

Sincerely,

Charles Scrotius

In March, Corwin flew to South Africa at the invitation of the Oxford Institute to conduct seminars on radio and television. Held in Johannesburg, they included a lecture at the University of Wittswatterand. In November, he would travel to Lima, Cuzco and Iquitos, Peru, as a member of a press party making the inaugural flight of Aero Peru's service between Los Angeles and Lima.

TO KATHERINE AND DIANE CORWIN / From Johannesburg, March 26, 1976

Dear Kate and Dianchik:

That I am still in reasonably good condition after the hard, hard work of the past three weeks and the hard travel that preceded it is, I suppose, a sign that maybe I am not so fragile as I had thought. I certainly have more hours of lecturing and seminar-conducting logged in these past weeks, than in the sum total of all such activity in the past. And when I have not been performing, I have been preparing—more like intense homework than anything else.

I have not yet had a chance to see much countryside, although I did manage to spend a day traveling to the capital, Pretoria (only an hour away) and looking around; and another day on a trip to what they call the low veldt—bush country, leading to an attractive dam by the doughty Afrikaans name of Hartebeestpoortdam. But now I am on the downhill side of the schedule, and next week I figure on flying down to Cape Town, which is at the southern tip of this huge continent....And after that, if there is time, I may go on a trip to a national park—a game reserve which more nearly resembles the true, unspoiled Africa-as-it-was, than most places. All fine, except you have to take anti-malarial pills before you go. And they say that sometimes the sounds of roaring lions and cries of other beasts keeps one awake at night. Still, much rather that than cars without mufflers and noisy neighbors.

Much, much to tell you about the country and the society—very complex, contradictory, fascinating. All this must wait....

TO FRANCES RING / From Sunnyside Park Hotel, Johannesburg, March 29, 1976

Dear Editress-in-Chiefess:

...I gather that neither of the postcards I sent you (one from Rio, the other from here) reached you by the time you posted your letter, otherwise you would have thanked me for their wit and pungency.

I have worked my ass off here, and only intermittently have I felt it was worth the trip....

Diamonds are not cheaper here, I am sorry to report. Only booze is cheaper, and I don't drink it.

I am going to try to stop in Athens on the way back. For no other reason than that it will be all Greek to me.

Now for a nap. As you can tell from this letter, I need it.

TO GEORGE MOVSHON / April 15, 1976

A South African himself, Movshon had sent letters to
Helen Suzman, liberal member of the South African
Parliament, and to friends named Jaffee, alerting them to
Corwin's imminent arrival in South Africa.

Dear Giorgio:

...I had no luck reaching Mrs. Suzman on the telephone, let alone
getting to see her. On receipt of your letter she kindly telephoned me
from Cape Town, I was out; she left a message; I returned the call; she
was out; I left a message; I tried four times subsequently to reach her
from Joberg, but got a domestic once and no-answers the rest of the
time. Then I went to Cape Town, rang several times, got through to
another maid with whom I left a message that I was staying at a number
in Sea Point; there was no word of a returned call (which could easily
have been a delinquency by the message operator at the hotel); I tried
twice more. Then it was time to start back for Joberg and Los Angeles.

The missed connection with Mrs. Suzman was a keen disappointment to me, since I have long admired her from afar, and would have
enjoyed expressing that admiration from anear.

Of your country I have nothing but the liveliest appreciation of
places and people—the beauty of the first, and the warmth and hospitality of most of the second. To which I add an equally deep apprehension and sadness for what the next ten years must bring in the way of
trial and hard re-configurations.

I worked hard—too hard—for both my pleasure and health, and
was so exhausted by the time I wrapped up my last seminar, that my
holiday to Cape Town almost had to be canceled because of a strange
virus that damn near turned my legs to jello. But I defied myself and
flew down to that glorious city and took the bus trip down to Cape
Point via Constantia Neck and Kommetjie, and back along
Simonstown, Fish Hoek, Chapman's Peak, and Hout Bay. Loved every
minute and tea/pee stop. Next day I did the tourist ritual to Table and
by night to Signal Hill, saw the Malay quarter in the good company of

Lee Marcus's sister (Mora?) and her husband, who is actually named Gesundheit. Julian Gesundheit.

I failed with Kruger Park. The report was that so much rain had fallen that the grass in the reserve was elephant-high, and that I would get to see no animals, only other tourists; also that it had turned hellishly hot there. That was all I needed for my Andromedan virus. I decided that if I were going to be stricken by a baffling disease, I had better collapse closer to home; so at the point when I began to be a worry and a drag to friends in your homeland, I booked myself on that long flight to London....

TO GERRY AND GLENNA KEAN / May 24, 1976

On the loss of their son.

Dear Gerry:

I am deeply saddened by your letter and the news which represents such unutterable anguish for Glenna and yourself and for that poor boy. What a tragic world, when within hours of receiving such heartrending word from you, comes the ghastly report of twenty-six high school kids, in the very bud of life, being killed in that bus accident in California. And to think that people in good health and allegedly sound mind kill each other for political reasons in Dublin and on the west bank of the Jordan! Gerry, Glenna, I pour out my sympathy to you, and can only hope that time, thief and miscreant in so many ways, can be best friend to the bereaved, the best of anodynes. That, and the love of friends, which you have, including ours.

TO ANNA NEETHLING-POHL, Actress in South Africa
From Los Angeles 90025, June 7, 1976

Dear Anna:

Your wonderful letter took two weeks to reach me (I sometimes wonder whether jets carrying airmail fly backward at intervals, or stop for weeklong refueling). But it is here, and brightens the spring overcast.

I am sorry I missed you at the dedication ceremony of the new TV complex, but I never received an invitation. If one was sent, it never reached me. Perhaps it was sent out late, and delivered to the Sunnyside Park Hotel after I had left for Cape Town. I believe I had already started the long trip back to the States on the day of the ceremony. I don't know where our good friend Hein Toorien got the impression that I had decided not to attend; I think that had I still been in Johannesburg I would have enjoyed the occasion—nay, if you were there I *know* I would have enjoyed it—but it also would have given me occasion to say hello again to de Bryn and de Villiers, whom I liked immensely.

How marvelous that you have a fortnightly poetry program on the air! It saddens me that here, in this country of two hundred millions, there is not, to my knowledge, a single regular poetry program on any of the major or minor networks! I speak feelingly about this because it was through poetry that I first established myself in radio. When poetry goes out of a people, it has lost part of its soul. Much that is wrong with the world today is that poets are no longer what Shelley called them—the unacknowledged legislators of the world. Instead they are unacknowledged, period. Except, I am glad to say, in S.A....

You are kind to ask about my family life. My wife was, like yourself, an eminent actress—mainly on Broadway, but also, to a lesser extent, in films. She has not acted in some time, having been preoccupied in raising our two children—Tony, who is now going to art school in Baltimore all the way across the country; and Diane, who is going to UCLA and majoring in the arts. Kate is blue-eyed and beautiful, like you. My birthday? May 3, Taurus, if you believe in the planets.

We share much, you and I, including our experience with portraitists. Years ago a sculptor asked me to sit for him. I, like you, told the artist I could not buy his work, but he went ahead. It took him many weeks—sittings were not exactly "sittings"—I could not spare the time from my work, but he sculpted as I was busy at my desk, and his portrait did not suffer from this method. I was with him at the foundry when it was cast in bronze—fascinating to watch. And when it was all finished, he presented it to me. That was thirty years ago. Today the head is on exhibition in Santo Domingo—on loan. And I wrote the introduction to the catalogue of this retrospective show. So a long friendship was built around that head.

Around your head, dear Anna, laurels and garlands, and among them, interwoven, my love.

TO ALAN MANSON, Actor / July 7, 1976

Dear Alan:

You are four of the best actors it has ever been my privilege to know and pleasure to work with. To have enacted four distinct roles in *Together Tonight* and carried off each with distinction is no small achievement, and I am happy that the critics in all thirty-seven cities where you played, agreed.

From a grateful director, to say nothing of playwright (I hate to say nothing of playwrights), please accept my liveliest thanks.

TO LOU ASHWORTH / July 31, 1976

Dear Lou:

No, Sam [Corwin] was sending you those cards because he likes you, and not because he was raising funds for anything. It is his one great foible, this business of assuming everybody can make use of greeting cards. I have tried to explain to him over the years that card selection is a very personal thing, like picking out a necktie, but he persists in sending them anyway, to a select circle of people for whom he has special fondness.

I spoke to Sam on the telephone today, and he was mortified to think that you thought he had sent you the cards to raise money. "But I've sent her cards before," he said, "and I thought she knew they were just friendly greetings, to use or not as she saw fit." Anyway, Lulu, they have to be the only box of cards you ever got from a ninety-nine-year-old man! We all hope we will be as bright and alert on his hundredth birthday celebration (scheduled for October 31st) as he is deep into his ninety-ninth year. Voice firm, still writes without a tremor, still puts away a half-pint of sherry every day.

I enclose f.y.i. a page from the *L.A. Times* of July 4th, which carries a piece by Sam Corwin's youngest son, who ain't so young any longer.

This is sent you with my compliments also, and not to raise money, but if you feel like making a contribution to the campaign of Ronald Reagan—Personally, I'm voting for that fourteen-year-old Rumanian girl gymnast.

TO DAVID AND ALBERT MAYSLES / August 4, 1976

Dear Dave and Al:

I am back from South Africa, and so are the prints of "The Salesman" and "Cristo's Valley Curtain" that you so generously loaned me. They were the hits of two seminars in Johannesburg, but that is about all the good I can say for that sad country and its film people. I had been misled by stories of the country's great wealth (diamonds and gold, etc.) but however rich DeBeers and Oppenheim may be, the film industry there is indigent, and fees for all creative aspects of film-making are ridiculously low. Their product looks it. As you have gathered from the news, the country is sitting firmly on top of an active volcano; it is safer to be in Peking with all its earthquakes.

Anyway, you are both princely to have let me borrow those beautiful films....

TO GENE KIRBY, Vice-President of the Boston Red Sox
August 21, 1976

Dear Gene:

A thousand thanks for your kindness in sending me the literature on the club. And multiple thanks too for those grand seats to the game. It was the first time I have ever been that close to the action, to say nothing of it being my first visit to the Anaheim stadium....

I have rooted for the Sox since I first heard their name (I was born and brought up in Boston), but now I have added reason. It is not every fan who knows a Vice-President of a major club, and I count myself lucky.

I join you in looking to '77. My crystal ball has just come back from the cleaner, and is nicely calibrated. It says Lynn will bat .346, Rice will hit twenty-six home runs, and Lee and Wise will win forty-one games between them. There is no charge for this prophecy. It's the least I could do for the cause. [Corwin noted afterward that he had sent his crystal ball back for repairs.]

TO TONY CORWIN / September 14, 1976

Dear Tonio:

Funny story about that Britannica entry. When I went to Peru last November I met a Brazilian named Martins who said to me in the fashion of polite people on such occasions, "If you are ever in Rio, please let us know and we will show you something of the city." But he meant it; and when my route to South Africa passed through Rio, I wrote and told him I would be coming through. So we met; he invited me to his home where I met his wife, and after that we were to go to dinner at a restaurant. One of the first things he brought up was that he found me in the new Britannica. I had not known of it, and he took the volume off the shelf and showed it to me. He said he had been so excited, he telephoned his mother in the interior of Brazil to communicate the news—HE KNEW SOMEBODY WHO WAS IN THE BRITANNICA!

So we went out to dinner. It was a very posh restaurant, the kind I have seen only in movies about the rich set. And although there was a reservation in his name, the room looked full, and the maitre said there would be a twenty-minute wait. Whereupon my host addressed the captain in a cascade of Portuguese. All I could understand of what he said was, "Britannica...Britannica...." The captain's mouth opened in awed amazement, and he made a table available immediately....

I enclose a few art subjects that may be of interest to you. Love,

TO DOCUMENTARY COMMITTEE, MOTION PICTURE ACADEMY / February 5, 1977

Corwin signed this letter "Japeth McFedries, Chairman, Friends of Noah's Ark."

Gentlemen:

You may think that the proceedings of your committee are privileged and confidential, and that nobody outside of your group knows which pictures you keep on and turn off. But sometimes parties on the outside know what is going on before you finish your count. That's what bugging is all about.

Now when you disqualify a dog of a film, that is understandable. But when a classic comes along, like the film on Noah's Ark, it is impossible to reconcile any kind of mature judgment with the action of your committee.

Even your chairman was obviously aghast when he saw fifteen hands raised. He was so astonished that he had to take the count three separate times before he would believe it; and he even made an unprecedented trip down the aisle to see if anybody was holding up two hands or possibly even three. And may I add that a three-handed member would not be at all surprising, considering the number of freaks and agnostics there must be among you. Because anybody who would laugh out loud at Noah's line, "Look, it stopped raining!" has no ear for the beauty of Biblical language, and no respect for a heavy rain....

If any of you had been on an ark for forty days and nights, without any distinction between first class and steerage, and the whole place smelling to high heaven, and the rain coming down like cats and dogs, of which there were already four on board, you too would have been exalted and thrilled when you opened the window and there was the golden sun and blue sky of Ararat, just like the travel agency promised, and you too would have cried, "Look, it stopped raining!"

TO STAN MARGULIES, Television Producer, *Roots*
February 25, 1977

Dear Stan:

I have waited until the blizzard has begun to abate, so that my congratulations would have a better chance of being noticed.

How does it feel to make history? Wow! It will be difficult to top, but if anybody can do it, you can.

Have a nice decade. Warmest best,

TO FRANCES RING / March 22, 1977

This note to *Westway*'s editor accompanied a manuscript that had given Corwin trouble.

Phew!*
Love,
  * Many interjections are called, but phew is chosen.

TO TONY CORWIN / April 17, 1977

Dear Tonio:

...Mom tells me you got a telegram from Arnold Grant. I hope you follow it up. Arnold is a good man, even though he talks a lot and speaks so quietly sometimes that I feel I need a hearing aid. Any apprehension you might feel about meeting him should be quieted by the fact that he likes to talk so much (always interestingly, I should add) that all you have to do is listen and agree with him (with now and then an observation of your own to meet the minimum requirement of conversation). You will like him, I'm sure, as he will you. And he enormously respects your talent. Whenever he speaks of you, or asks about you, he always refers to you as Rembrandt. "How is Rembrandt?" he'll say to me. The tone is not ironic but affectionate and interested....

Have you ever thought of doing sculpture? The two or three small things you've done have been very impressive, and I have a feeling you could be happy in that medium. But then you are great at whatever you do do—photography, for instance. You have made it ancillary to your painting, and maybe you are right to do so, but there is much power and beauty to your photographic composition....

TO TONY CORWIN / May 4, 1977

Dear Tonio:

In our telephone conversation last night, you commented that Mom and I should not have expectations that are too high. I want to add to what we said at the moment, that "expectations" is not the word for what we feel—somehow it has a quantitative implication, as though one might "expect" commercial acceptance, or a certain tangible result by a certain date. What we have for you begins with love, but beyond that there is a realistic confidence, based on your proven talent. We know what you have in you because we have seen it time and again in your work, and we are confident that you will succeed in your artistic goal because you have what our old friend Carl Sandburg called "rich wanting." You *want* to paint, and want to do it richly and you *do* do it, oftener than not.

We just hope you will give deep study to what you think is best for your future, in terms of location. It is not out of selfish considerations—the comfort of having you back here and seeing you oftener than once or twice a year—that makes us hope you will return to this coast. It is because the opportunities for the kind of cultural, artistic, professional and social stimulation are so much greater here. You will be within phone call or short ride from many people who love you—not that they would get in your hair or encroach upon you—but it would be comforting, I should think, to have the security blanket of people to whom you could turn for any number of things, including Grandma's borscht and cookies. More than that, the options for meeting new and interesting people—including girls—are greater here than there.

This is not pressure. I bring it up only because it is in the context of some of the discussion we had last night. If school ends in six or eight weeks, and you are not satisfied with the way things are going, it might be a good idea to make a list of alternative plans. California may be seventh or eighth on the list, but at least you would have some checkpoints, and you could shuffle them at will....

TO R. LEROY BANNERMAN / October 26, 1977

Dear LeRoy:

At last I have a few minutes to respond to your questionnaire of August, 1899. Sorry to be so late. Here goes:

Q. Is radio drama a viable programmatic feature of the future?

A. The future is so general, so hidden in fogs on the other side of the mountain, that I hesitate to speak for or about it. You may recall that the good gray poet in *Soliloquy* [*Soliloquy to Balance the Budget*, an early

Corwin play], has a passage to the effect that the future belongs to the future...that what our descendants decide to do is as far beyond prediction, as the world of today would have been beyond the prediction of people living in 1877. So the conditions under which radio drama might become viable programmatic matter would depend, I should think, upon a return to something of the sort of atmosphere and cultural configurations that made possible the so-called Golden Age of Radio. That turned out to be not so wild a dream. There was no Buck Rogers to it.

Q. In broadcasting, can commercialism be compatible with art?

A. It was once, and can be again. It certainly has been that way in motion pictures; in the best of hours of TV it is that way; so, although as currently practiced, such compatibility is not high or frequent, neither is it impossible. I think the greatest single deterrent to the happy marriage of art and commercialism, has been the rating system. It has even affected public broadcasting. I read a critique recently saying that KCET, along with other stations of its ilk and bulk, shies away from anything which does not, in the short or long run, produce satisfying numbers.

Q. Is there anything about the old days you might long for?

A. Yes; the camaraderie; the pride CBS took in its cultural accomplishments...when *Invitation to Learning* was thought to look as handsome in the boutonniere of the network as *Beverly Hillbillies*. The sense of eagerness to do good work, to expand artistic frontiers, to rush in where fools and NBC feared to tread.

Q. How necessary do you feel art is for the future significance of broadcasting?

A. I believe art is necessary for the future significance and development of *any* medium. I think it would be a drab, anaemic world, perhaps even asphyxiating to anything resembling significance, if art were to be neglected and all were sacrificed to formula drama, news summaries, sitcoms, game shows and exercises in violence. Look at the current season.

Q. What about poetry in broadcasting? How can poetry revive its interest?

A. Poetry definitely has a place. It is still called upon for ceremonious occasions; witness my commission to write an Ode for the CBS 50th Anniversary. Of course creating and sustaining interest in poetry is the function and responsibility of the entire cultural community, especially education, and not simply that of broadcasting. The latter can certainly help it, however. I think *Words Without Music*, according to mail in my files, was a good demonstration of the abiding latent interest in poetry. There were perhaps hundreds of thousands, if not millions of people who had never taken the slightest interest in poetry, but who, stimulated by what they heard in that series, became curious about poetry and began to read it, or at least to listen to it. I like to think that I contributed something to public awareness and acceptance of poetry. Some of the poets around the country, and many teachers, thanked me for what I suppose could be called a kind of midwifery. Broadcasting can do a great deal for poetry, and vice versa. *On a Note of Triumph*, though I disclaimed it as a poem in my foreword to the S & S edition, was nevertheless of poetic texture and thrust, and it did not hurt CBS or broadcasting one bit....

Q. What legacy do you feel that you and your kind of an earlier era, left to broadcasting?

A. Respect for the potentials of art in the medium. Respect for the intelligence of the audience....

TO LEO MISHKIN / January 3, 1978

Dear Leo:

In response to your question, I was asked by some outfit making an Oral History archive, to interview [Armand] Hammer shortly after he had presented the Island of Campobello (Roosevelt's home) to the U.S. Government. The gift was a princely gesture by Hammer, and he seemed then like an enlightened and decent fellow for an oil magnate. Ours was a pleasant interview which ran for about an hour, but I'll be damned if I can remember for whom I did it, and where the tape is archiving....

TO WALTER CRONKITE / January 17, 1978

Cronkite had delivered Corwin's poem, "Network at Fifty," at the end of CBS' 50th anniversary celebration.

Dear Walter:

I have been thinking about your conversation just after you delivered your message to Andromeda.

TV suffers, as you said, from poverty of language. But there are occasions when heightened language is not only acceptable, but called for—chiefly commemorative or celebrational occasions like the end of a war, a big anniversary, a dedication, Pericles at that funeral in Athens, Webster at Bunker Hill, Lincoln at Gettysburg, Cronkite in Studio 43.

But we need not wait for wars to end, for monuments to be raised, for CBS to reach its one hundredth. There are solidly built into the calendar, a series of choice occasions: the birthdays of Washington and Lincoln, July 4th, Memorial Day, Labor Day, Columbus Day, Veterans Day, Christmas Day, New Year's Day. Even, for that matter, St. Valentine's Day, April Fool's Day, and Hallowe'en—for there is no mandate that says good language must necessarily be solemn.

How would it be if, across the year at these comfortably spaced intervals, I wrote pieces which you could do in five-, ten-, or fifteen-minute special segments? Or longer, if needed or wanted. I'm pretty sure there hasn't been anything quite like this on any network here or abroad, and it might be both fun and stimulating.

What do you think?

CBS did not act on Corwin's suggestion. But five years later, National Public Radio broadcast a Corwin series on six of the subjects he proposed in this letter.

TO ANNA NEETHLING-POHL / March 29, 1978

Dear Anna:

Your letter makes me feel pridefully avuncular when you tell me that long before you walked in beauty through the portals of that tavern near the monument outside of Pretoria, we had met through my work. Nothing could make me preen with greater pleasure than your account of having been stimulated toward an interest in broadcasting through my work.

And I am happy to learn at the same time that you have been reading over some of the early stuff. I am only sorry that you have at hand nothing later than *13 by Corwin*. It is young and suffers from brashness and unevenness. The later books are more mature, for whatever that is worth to them; but they all share the melancholy distinction of being out of print, and are to be found only in libraries. Even I have to advertise for copies, and the few that turn up in rare-book shops sell for ridiculously high prices. A new book, however, will be off the press in a few weeks—a collection of essays that I think are pretty lively—and I am going to send you one. It's called *Holes in a Stained Glass Window*—and I leave you to guess the meaning of that title. [This was a collection of the essays Corwin had been writing each month for *Westways*, a magazine published by the Automobile Club of Southern California but given a literary and historical flavor by its editor, Frances Ring.]

Off I go to give another lecture. If I keep at this long enough, I could become pompous. But then you would scold me, and I must spare you that.

Have fun with the Strindberg role, and *do* do more TV!

TO WILLIAM N. ROBSON [the leading Drama Director at CBS when Corwin joined the staff in 1938] / April 7, 1978

Dear Bill:

I am as moved by your letter as you were by the "Network at Fifty" piece. From that first day we met at 485 [Madison Avenue] your approbation has meant a very great deal to me. You were of enormous encouragement always. I remember your telephoning from Chicago after *Seems Radio* went off the air; and you walked into the studio on the 22nd floor before Harry Marble [announcer] was even finished with the System announcement, to greet me after *They Fly Through the Air*, and to say it was better than *Air Raid*. It was a thunderclap to me, since you had with historic distinction directed *Air Raid* [by Archibald MacLeish] and here you were praising a kid who had just been around for a few months.

I have always felt that if it weren't for the pioneering of radio drama started by Irving [Reis] but carried forward mainly by yourself, it would have been impossible for me to have been handed the freedom to express myself in the control room and over the transmitter. You created the climate. You gave panache to the Workshop. If I had freedom to run with the ball, it was you who threw the key block, all the more wonderfully because you did some pretty terrific running yourself.

Do you think I could ever forget those receptions at your digs? I had never circulated among the kind of people I met there—Pare Lorentz, and good guys and gals of that kind. It was dazzling enough for me to have a great beauty—Betsy [Tuthill] as my assistant at a time when I properly should have been her assistant—but for her to be the sister-in-law of the No. 1 director of the network as well!—Holy Cow, as I might have said in those days.

And now again I have kind words from you about a work of mine. I do not take them lightly. You and I are among the few survivors of that great planned wreck called Radio. There are not many left.

The Word, that stately bark, has been beached, and it lies in the shallows. Language and ideas on TV are so impoverished that when something faintly aspiring comes along, both the medium and the critics don't know what to make of it....

There has been a good reaction to the Ode, including some outrage by partisans who resented the fact that the introduction was cut and Cronkite went into it cold (Mary Tyler Moore had taped an introduction crediting me—I saw it at a press preview of the show, but as you know, on the air this was excised and the only credit was in the fast-moving crawl at the very end). The definitive stroke was a phone call I got from a friend who said, "My mother called right after the show to ask me whether [I] thought Cronkite had written the piece himself, or whether Eric Sevareid had written it for him."

Never mind. You liked it, and with characteristic generosity wrote to tell me....

TO JANET MURROW / April 16, 1978

Dear Janet:

...Your kind comment about my poem more than makes up for Walter's too-fast reading of it. Ah, the things that happen backstage! I was in the control room when Walter first taped it. It was good, though a little flattened out in parts. I made a few suggestions to him, he redid it, and it was beautiful—the requisite mellowness and persuasiveness and intelligent authority. I went home greatly relieved, because the producers had earlier tried cutting up the poem to be read, a snippet at a time, by eight (8) *stars* (!), one after the other. These worthies were actually taped: Mary Tyler Moore, tentative as a schoolgirl reciting in class; Lauren Bacall, resembling nothing so much as a pancake wired for sound; Cicely Tyson, with a splendid hairdo but little sense of the text; and Alan Alda and Carroll O'Connor and Eric Sevareid and Walter. It came out hamburger. But to Alex Cohen's credit, when I urged him to drop the all-star approach and go only with Cronkite, he agreed. [Alexander Cohen produced the week-long CBS celebration.]

Anyway, as I say, I was happy with Walter's reading and congratulated myself on having rescued the piece from being atomized. But while I was away from the city subsequently, Walter was recalled, ostensibly because of some technical problem with the earlier tape, and the ode was done all over again. I may be a bit paranoid in this suspicion, but I wondered whether someone Up There wanted Walter to speed up because he was afraid an audience would not sit still for eight minutes of *words*.

I do not fault Walter, who has been very friendly both to me and the poem...I just think it a pity that a network in all its majesty does not know what to do with a piece of original work that tries to fly. And if I were Leonard Bernstein, I would feel very put out over the way the musical backing was suppressed. Earlier I had been concerned that the score might overpower the words in sheer volume, but on the air the music was almost imperceptible.

Anyway it's past, and there will not be a chance to take that flight again for another fifty years, by which time people will probably be communicating only by numbers....

TO FRANCES RING, Editor, *Westways* / May 14, 1978

Dear Francesca:

Attached, what I believe to be one of my better pieces, although I am stoned on lemonade as I say this.

I think this column will endure. (Until the August issue.) But if this premature summer heat keeps up, I may not.

TO ROY MADSEN / July 1, 1978

> Professor Madsen was on the faculty of the San Diego State University, where Corwin had been Distinguished Visiting Lecturer the previous year.

Dear Roy:

First of all let me tell you how happy I was to show you my minerals, Tony's paintings, the onyx eggs of Senor Pico [a restaurant], the Bridge that arches Century City's main champs, and the wrong way to cross over to the Hotel from the arcade on the upper level. Your visit spoiled me for good talk and bonhomie—I wish you had casting to do every weekend, or that you lived fifteen minutes away. Encore, encore....

Tomorrow I don the black robe and make a commencement speech at a small college here in town, incidental to picking up a degree. [The honorary degree was from Columbia College of Communications.] I have invited Tony and Diane, in the hope that they will listen to me for all of twenty minutes, which is well in excess of any previous records.

TO RON HOBIN, Chicago Broadcast Executive / July 8, 1978

Dear Ron:

Many thanks for your generous comment on the CBS anniversary show. Your eye and ear were sharper than most—I got a letter from Walter Cronkite only a couple of weeks ago, in which he wryly confessed to some ego strain in getting letters from people asking him for copies of the ode *he* had written. He sent me a batch of photocopies of the letters. I guess nobody watches the credits on a long crawl—not at midnight, anyway....

TO WALTER CRONKITE / From Idyllwild, California,
August 20, 1978

Dear Walter:

Many thanks for your letter and for sending on those copies of congratulations from listeners who thought you had written the Ode. I'm glad your reflex was not to say, "Look, I'm innocent—I didn't do it!" There have been a couple of times in my lurid past when I asked to have my name taken off movies because by the time the director and the producer and the star and the star's agent and the wives of all four had gotten through with it, one could find only traces of my intention.

I hope you have had a good summer. Mine has been spent among the tall pines up here on Mt. Jacinto, where I am teaching at a USC campus which compensates for that cold urban complex they have down in Smog Center.

I return to the lowlands in a week's time, and will be back at my usual digs in case you are suddenly struck by a vision on the road from Tarsus, or Great Neck, and the Voice in the vision says, "Get thee back to thinking about that idea for Cronkite Reads Corwin at Midnight, because thou art getting older every day, and Corwin is older to begin with, and TV needeth inspiration more than ever, yea, verily, and the time at the tone will be 2:45."...

TO FRANK BRESEE, President, Pacific Pioneer Broadcasters
January 14, 1979

The organization was honoring Arch Oboler.

Dear Frank:

I will be in cold Boston when Arch is being honored by our colleagues, and I shall miss not only the warm ambience of the occasion, but the pleasure of greeting him and paying tribute to him in person.

Arch and I share many things, including the memory of having participated in and contributed to the shortest Golden Age in history. We shared an abiding concern for the medium of broadcasting, and a respect for it, and I think we both brought something of the world into our productions. At one time our names were linked in the minds of listeners, and every now and then we would be mistaken for each other. More than once I was complimented for a program that Arch had written, and it was all I could do to resist the impulse to let the mistake pass.

But Arch and I shared other things, too—certain outlooks and pro-clivities, many mutual friends, certain enthusiasms for actors and actresses—especially actresses—and there was a period when we were both mineral buffs—he a big league collector, and I the kind who picks up a pebble on a beach and mis-identifies it.

One of the many things I admire about Arch is his steadfast passion for hippopotami, of all things—not the living beast in his garden, but the esthetics of its great gross bulk. I appreciate that passion, and for years I have been on the lookout, trying to spot a hippo figure that would make a gift for Arch's collection, but I have never found one that came anywhere close to the magnificent sculptures in his studio in the Valley. So if any of you at Sportsmen's Lodge on Arch Oboler Day, ever come across a well-turned hippo carved in jade or onyx, or even prop-erly mixed cement, please let me know.

And now, Frank, will you kindly turn on the dais, in the direction of Arch, and say hello for me at close range, and give him my affectionate greetings, and tell him that I wish him many happy returns and reruns of the high honor he is receiving from the hands and hearts of our fellow pioneers today, in the form of the Carbon Mike Award.

God bless you, Arch, and keep you in good health and spirits and working form.

TO JANET MURROW / March 10, 1979

In 1979, Corwin was appearing as host of *Academy Leaders*, a Public Broadcasting System television series.

Dear Janet:

I am delighted to know that you like *Academy Leaders*, and that you find my services to it not objectionable. The response to date has been mildly whelming, not overwhelming; I doubt if your forecast that I will no longer be able to move about unrecognized, will be confirmed—the series is half over, and so far *one* person has come up to me (in a supermarket) to comment on the program. But mail has been good—crowned by your note. A man named Hamilton in Beverly Hills, writing on a magnificent parchment-like letterhead, concludes with the arresting phrase that the programs are "a service and a grace and a delight." The grace note is "grace"—so much more pleasant than disgrace.

Please keep watching. And please come back to this reformed desert.

TO LEE MARCUS, Playwright / August 4, 1979

Dear Lee:

Your letter arrived while I was away in Alaska, filling my eye and camera lens with mountains, fjords and glaciers. And it is arresting to find in your letter an allusion to "glacier-wrapped silence," and your comment that you "want to go somewhere beautiful and in touch with nature...." That is where to go for spaces and silences, although the silences are sometimes thunderous, as in the cannonading sounds that come from within a tidewater glacier as it grinds along. "White thunder," they call it....

I am glad you are at last emerging from the depths, and I am awed by the steepness of the ground that you and Monte had to cover. Such a blow is so staggering that one hardly knows how to speak one's sorrow; at such times I worry that an expression of sympathy can have no more effect than a gas jet on the face of glacier. [Corwin had met Lee and Monte Marcus during his trip to Johannesburg. Their young daughter had recently died.]

Your postscript mentions having been banned by SATV [South African Television Service]. *Banned?* Why indeed? Have you entertained a liberal thought? Or friend? Is SATV so rich with talent, has it such a big pool of experienced and gifted writers, that it can afford to proscribe anybody with your credits? But then American TV is not much better, really. They keep tags on writers, directors, actors, producers, who are "bankable"; if you have been associated with a production or a series which has perhaps won honors and critical acclaim, but which has earned only a low rating in those damn monitoring systems, then your name appears in a "C" or "D" list, which means Untouchable. So the days of the blacklist are not over, they have only moved into a new phase.

Anyway screw them all! What counts is to be well and to do the best one can, to create and to cope, and to never run dry of love.

I send you and Monte great quantities of it.

TO MELL LAZARUS, Creator of "Momma" and "Miss Peach" Comics / August 21, 1979

Dear Mell:

The other day I went with some friends on a trip to Black Mountain [in the San Bernardino, California range], a formidable massif whose peak is so high that it was selected for one of the National Forest Service lookouts. This lookout is manned night and day by a ranger, and for those intrepid climbers who have the energy to make the climb, and are not bothered by acrophobia, there are government regulations which permit them to visit the tower between certain hours. Inside it is like a control room—walls of glass, radio equipment (no telephone—too deep in the wilderness for that) and sparse living facilities.

There is very little wall space in this lookout, since most of the area is taken up with windows. The visitor must climb steep metal stairs—a great many of them. But under the rules there can be no more than four visitors at any time.

I was one of three—my friends and I. And I was delighted to find, out here at this lonely outpost, that the *one* item pinned to the meager wall, was a strip of "Miss Peach"! In it the ranger had whitened out the smaller of two balloons, and substituted his own legend. I had my camera with me, and got permission to take a picture of the strip. The slide of it is enclosed; it will have to be projected to read it properly, although a small magnifying glass might do the same.

I thought you would like to know that you are everywhere. Including, I hope, in good health and spirits....

TO SAM WEISBORD, President, William Morris Agency
Circa Chanukah, '79

The Agency then represented Corwin.

Dear Sam:

You are a very hard man to shop for.

—Dried fruit? Tasty, but gone too soon.

—A Rodin Sculpture? You already have the best.

—A Rolls Royce? You have a fleet of two, one of which you use for shopping.

—The QE2? Impossible to find space for her at the Marina, and the upkeep would be enormously expensive.

—A book on Constable? Corot? Vlaminck? They were long ago added to your library.

But maybe there is one painter you haven't yet added to your shelf. Mr. Fuchs. He is mysterious and sensual and powerful and slightly mad—and besides, he's Jewish, so he can't be all bad.

Have a happy holiday, Sam, and a glorious New Year.

Corwin's gift was a book on the works of the fantasist Ernst Fuchs.

TO PAUL SELVIN, Chief Counsel, Writers Guild of America
January 2, 1980

Dear Paul:

Many thanks for the literature on the fine art of swearing....The old Romans could take lessons from the Yiddish as far as curses go. "May he own ten shiploads of gold," goes one of them, "and may all of it be spent on sickness." There is even a paired curse, which translates to, "May you turn into a blintz, and then into a cat, and may he eat you up and choke to death on you, so that we would be rid of both of you." That's an economy-size curse, and Latin offers nothing that can come near it.

Not curses, but blessings I heap on you. *Naches fun kinder* is one of the favorites of our people, but you already have that. To which I add, Everything good that you could wish for yourself. That cannot be topped in any language.

TO NORMAN COUSINS

Dear Norman:

I had heard nothing but praise for *Anatomy [of an Illness]*, and intended to get it when I had discharged the heavy reading demands of a series of projects in progress, but your kindness in sending me a copy, inscribed in your own generous hand, switched me onto it immediately. Only grudgingly did I put it down to keep an appointment, and I picked it up again the minute I got back. I now understand the praise, and join in it....

I thank you and congratulate you in equally hearty measure, and pray (not with my head down, like the golfing priest), that you will continue to be a glowing advertisement for laughter, ascorbic acid, and creative concern for one's fellow man.

Also an inspiration to fellow writers, including this longtime admirer and near-namesake.

TO SAM WEISBORD / From Aspen, Colorado, January 30, 1980

Corwin is discussing a contract with NBC for *The Odyssey of Runyon Jones*. "Jerry" is a William Morris agent whom Corwin considered "C-minus."

Dear Sam:

I have given much thought to your and Jerry's opinions of the first draft, and I want to make some observations which may serve to clarify my position and modify your own.

First, I must quote an estimate of Runyon which was made by *The Manchester Guardian* in England years ago:

The story of a small boy in search of his dog through the celestial system and among the powers above, presents a

hundred pitfalls if it falls into the wrong hands. Neither
sentiment nor humor could be anything but exasperating
if the treatment of this theme were unskillful. Fortunately
Norman Corwin brings it off brilliantly. The humor and
the pity are both expressed with such a light, dry touch
that it is all perfectly effective.

I quote this at the start because we are dealing with a type of material that is very delicate. I have seen fantasies butchered and laid waste
by heavy hands. Here is more evidence of that danger, in a review of the
book *Dog in the Sky* by *The Milwaukee Journal*:

This sort of interplanetary fantasy could make difficult
travel, or worse, in less expert hands, but Norman Corwin
imparts a sympathy and warmth that make the story come
off smoothly.

Just a couple of more reviews which point to the nature of the story.
The Hollywood Citizen-News:

This story is humorous, pathetic, whimsical, philosophical, science-fictional. It is highly dramatic, and is told
mostly in dialogue.

I submit that what is "highly dramatic" in a book, does not suddenly
become un-dramatic when drafted into a screenplay. That is the reason
why books are bought in the first place—for their characters and plot
and situations and dialogue. Here is another review of our property, not
from a provincial weekly, but the *New York Post*:

Corwin's characters from first to last represent with hilarious precision the complex of modern society. This wonderful, gentle satire shows little Runyon Jones making an
odyssey that is at least as sensible as the ten-year detour of
Ulysses, and much more moving....You may shed, as we
did, a few unmanly tears.

This uses the phrase "hilarious precision," which ties in with those
earlier comments about avoiding pitfalls, the light touch, and the

danger of inexpert hands. I especially commend to you and Jerry the word "precision." I believe that of the three of us, the ranking expert on precision in the matter of this subject is myself.

You made the comment, Sam, that this could have been written for a white boy. I disagree deeply with the basis of your opinion. Runyon could be played by a white, black, yellow, brown or red boy. What I did not do, and will not do, is to put a strain on the boy's blackness, or make flip ethnic jokes. One of the strengths of this play is that nobody on Earth or in space cares particularly whether Runyon is black or green, and the only allusion to his color is when Miss Summer says, "Hello, short, dark and handsome." I think it is an insult to the concept—even though a comic concept—of Time, Nature, and the Magic of life, for Runyon's race to be the subject of comment or even notice, by any of the characters. That in itself says something, subtly but surely, about race relations. They are most harmonious when not noticed. This picture is not *Different Strokes*, fine as that is. It is a different animal entirely.

You also spoke of a lack of "confrontations." That is formula talk, but *Dog in the Sky* is not formula. The air is jammed every day of the week with confrontations—action, violence, trading of blows and shots. Much of it is trash, indistinguishable one from the other; and what part of it is good, hardly aspires to be classic. You yourself have said that *Dog* has the chance of becoming a classic—and you are not alone in thinking so. I quote again from the statements in which *Runyon* is compared with some classics of its kind of literature:

> *Washington Post*: "It is a better piece of writing than Mark Twain's *Captain Stormfield's Visit to Heaven*...superb, gentle, effective, unostentatious fantasy."
>
> *Hollywood Citizen-News*: "If Jonathan Swift were writing *Gulliver's Travels* today, it might turn out something like *Dog in the Sky*. It's an amazing trip."
>
> *Denver Post*: "*Dog in the Sky* has the subtle charm, and is similar in many ways, to The Little Prince."
>
> *Cleveland Plain-Dealer*: "Corwin's conclusion should go far toward securing the book's place beside such contemporary classic fantasies as *Wind in the Rain* and *Peter Pan*."

Now as to particulars:

You have said that Runyon is pale; that he listens too much and is not assertive or aggressive. Let's see:

He gets into a fight with Bubb and has to be stopped by an officer.

He makes an aggressive and successful pitch to the Chief of Admissions.

He berates the Stationmaster, and retrieves the tickets that the Stationmaster has thrown away.

He scolds Father Time for dressing in a manner unbecoming to a Commander.

He gives what-for to the Mean Clock for turning its hands back.

He takes on the Giant even before he knows that the Giant is only a pigmy. And when the Giant takes a swipe at him, he knocks the Giant flat.

He resists the big build-up of the P.R. Man, tells him he does not like the song, and why; and then he confronts a whole plane-load of passengers and tactfully admonishes them not to make fun of a man's name. When the P.R. Man tells Runyon he is never going to find Pootzy so he might as well go home, Runyon replies, "Not in a thousand years."

He takes on the striking pilot, foxes him into getting aboard the Clipper, and then, faced with the challenge of flying the space-ship by himself, he does.

He refuses to be put off by warnings to stay out of Sorcerola, and marches up to the sign which reads, "Last Chance to Turn Back," and declares, "In case you're wired for sound, I am NOT turning back!"

When Runyon reaches the Sorcerer, he bawls him out for being uncooperative: "What, are you made of *iron* or something? You're not making any sense. Mr. Sorcerer, I have some news for you—." When Bubb arrives on the scene and threatens to make Runyon a prisoner, R saves the situation by the resourceful action of slipping the charm to the Sorcerer so that he can work his magic.

In Curgatory, Runyon spiritedly defends Pootzy against all seven charges brought against him, and when the decision goes against him, he still makes a big last-minute pitch for the dog's release. He fights right to the end.

So what do you mean, Sam, by saying this kid is not spunky? Did we read the same script? When a little kid takes on everybody in God's heaven, and stands up to them, all for the love of a dog and the faith that he will recover it? That's not spunky?

You seem to have some preconceived idea of what Runyon should be, based on the things Gary [Coleman, actor] has done successfully on the tube. But *Dog in the Sky* is not, I repeat, *Different Strokes*. I do not write stand-up comedian jokes, or highly sophisticated patter for boys. I thought that you, Sam, wanted to see a new Gary, a different one. Although he has done many fine things, I don't think he has yet had a chance to extend his range to the fullest—to be lonesome, pained, afraid, baffled (as with the Cat Lady), frustrated, pleading—*in addition* to his laughing, jolly, whimsical, sly, aggressive and sharp qualities.

Whenever Gary is himself, as in the interview with Tom Snyder, he is marvelous. There was a moment when he damn near broke my heart. Tom had asked him if he considered himself lucky, and you could see in Gary's hesitation before answering, a poignant realization that his kidney problem (about which he had spoken earlier) made him so vulnerable that it obscured the far future for him. He was just not going to answer flat out, "Yes, I am lucky." You saw in those great expressive eyes a flicker that made him knowing, compelling and precious.

Now how does this relate to the character I've written for him? Well, I show a boy in *love*—with a dog, it so happens, but still in love. And he is ready to die for that love, which he did do before the play begins. And if you will carefully read the business in this script, you will see that I have several times called for extreme closeups so that we may see the shifting expressions on that marvelously expressive face. Why do you think I have Runyon tasting experimental foods for Mother Nature? Simply to watch that face during his momentary role as a connoisseur. I say that time spent on a face like Gary's is more important than time spent on a stand-up joke.

You quoted someone as saying that the play reads like a radio script. Whoever that was, had better go back and read it again, and this time open both eyes. Does a radio script have milling crowds, and a crowded elevator full of dogs and people, and a Dog Hall of Fame? Does it have an Interheaven Junction, and costumes, and starry spaces, and tumbling asteroids, and gas masks in a plane half full of purple smoke, a Giant whose head is in the clouds, and a great shoe which zips open to reveal a dwarf? Does a radio show have a vast, spooky Domain of Time, a fantastic Pendulum, a huge cogwheel that can snare a demon and lift him off his feet?

Does a radio script show us a bizarre setting of clocks, or dancing space-ship passengers, or steam shooting out of a demon's ears, or flame spurting from a telephone receiver? Or the lush floral setting at Mother Nature's place? Or the mad cockpit of the Clipper that Runyon pilots himself (a takeoff on the controls of *2001*, including the On-Board Computer)? Does a radio script have laser beams, or talking appliances, or a loxodrome, or an Arch of Triumph with a mirror across its archway?

Does a radio script show a table full of magic-making implements, and a magician to make magic with them? Does a radio script show the transformation, before your eyes, of a demon into a Frog? Or a skjellerup tree with pretzel-like limbs? Does it show the customs inspection of Curgatory, and the strange round table of the Curgatory Council, with a witness chair in the middle, that revolves with every fresh question? Or the other-worldly types, and their fantastic forms and clothes, on the intergalactic Board? Or the long, long corridors where delinquent dogs are kept in cells?

This is a VISUAL script, and I am astonished that you do not see what is there.

I think it would be helpful if it were understood by your associates, including whoever it was that made the allusion to "radio," that I damn well know the difference between radio and film and video. I am not a kid out of film school. I have won an Oscar nomination, an Emmy, and a Golden Globe; I wrote, directed and produced much of the two-million-dollar Westinghouse TV series *Norman Corwin Presents*; I have written specials that were broadcast over NBC, ABC, PBS and CBS-TV. Perhaps this background is not known in all of the offices on El Camino. If not, it should be.

I have stated my position. I hope you will study it as carefully, and bring to it the same respectful consideration, as I did to your opinions. But now, after having gone to some length to answer your objections, I come to a very basic and important point.

At no time was it understood, either by NBC, Perillo or myself, that you and Jerry would exercise creative control of this project. In my long career, which is as long or longer than your own, never has my representative interposed himself squarely between me and a producer. I don't want this to happen now.

I know that your intentions are above reproach, and that you and Jerry have the welfare and prosperity of the script at heart. I appreciate this every bit as much as your brilliant generalship in getting the project to where it is now. But I am going to ask you to carry your commitment one step further—to have faith in my judgment and talent. That jury of eight far-flung critics cited above, testified in print, over their signatures, to the quality of that judgment. The same judgment has been exercised in the nature, the elements, the proportions and the structure of the present draft.

Of course revisions and adjustments will be made—that is what a first draft is for—but they must not be dictated.

It is vital that we all work together to prove that you were right in fighting so hard and resourcefully for this to be done—and not try to prove you are right about *how* it should be done. Many people will contribute to that result—producer, director, designer, photographer, wardrobe, special effects. Your opinions are always more than welcome, but they must not be mandatory or controlling.

Let us by all means avoid the one big confrontation that this script can do without.

This film was not made, but later television and stage musicals based on the same story were produced.

TO RALPH NELSON, Film Director / July 2, 1980

Dear Ralph:

I was elated to get your letter, but my elation lasted only until your report on the surgery undergone by your wife. What a damn cruel disease is diabetes!...But then what major affliction *isn't* cruel? Cancer, cardiac, arteriosclerosis, and that great stroke-maker, high blood pressure....

You are missed on the scene and on the screen. Everywhere the crud thickens. For the first time in my life, I will go to the voting booth in November knowing nobody worth winning will win. I name what passes for success these days: Ms. Krantz, Fred Silverman, *Dallas*, Laverne & Shirley, and Oral Roberts. Everything today is a Special Effect.

So enjoy Los Altos Hills, dear Ralph. The quiet and the green and the air. And let me know, please, when you come down—we must have a meal together.

My warmest best wishes to you and your wife, and my heartiest thanks for your kind words about the *Westways* pieces.

TO SYLVIE DRAKE, Theater Critic, *Los Angeles Times*
From Idyllwild, California, August 18, 1980

Dear Sylvie:

Your letter enclosing the column on puns crossed the ocean twice and was then forwarded to me up here on the mountain....

The pun patrol will no longer operate behind enemy lines in my sector. Starting with the December issue, *Westways* is changing over to a kind of house organ for the Auto Club—no more columns on the theater, films, music, books, media and restaurants. Instead there will be departments on auto repair, fashions, amateur photography, and travel. Onward and downward with the arts....

TO DON FREEMAN, Entertainment Editor, *San Diego Union*
January 28, 1981

Dear Don:

Once again I am in your debt. But for your thoughtfulness, I would never know that Kuralt had ever heard of me, let alone that he counts me among the worthies. I am warmed by his estimate, as well as by your report of it, and I thank you from here to the farthest satellite and back.

And thanks too for sending me your marvelous column on the events of the inauguration. Nobody in the land, writing fact or fiction, has ever written a better sentence about the character of a face than your

...this wise, grand, venerable face, this pol's face, this road
map of South Boston, this face and a half, lived in, voted
for, a neighborhood face; if a backroom caucus had a face,
it would look like Thomas (Tip) O'Neil.

I wish I'd written it. I saw an hour-long film documentary on Tip
O'Neil at the Academy last year, and it did not say as much, or so well.

TO THE REVEREND STEPHEN FRITCHMAN, Minister, First
Unitarian Church, Los Angeles / February 1, 1981

Dear Steve:

I am heartened to learn that you have recovered from a severe case of
sciatica, and am in a position to sympathize more actively than I might
have otherwise, because my wife Kate has just come down with it.

About *Westways*, they took a "survey" for which they paid $25,000,
to find out from their 450,000 readers what they would like more of in
the magazine. The sampling was two hundred people. From this they
deduced that people on their list wanted more fashions, articles on auto
repair, travel, and amateur photography. So out went the monthly
columns on films (Arthur Knight), theater (Leonard Gross), media
(Corwin) and other contributors like Jack Smith and John Weaver.
There have been many protests and cancellations. Art Arthur of
Rubidoux sent me a carbon of his note to the editor, Nicholas Kockler,
in which he took Kockler to task for bragging about the "improvements"
as a result of the survey, and asked for his subscription to be canceled: "If
decisions like that are the results of 'months of exacting research' you
should ask for your money back. Please allow me to do the same."

Anyway, it was a good run—seven years—and fun to do. Please stay
well, and give my love to Frances.

TO ANN SUTHERLAND, Mother of an Idyllwild Student
February 21, 1981

Dear Ann:

Many thanks for your greetings, and I reciprocate them heartily.

...What is the Panhellenic group you mention? If you think I should be a guest speaker, that's good enough for me, but I really should know something about them. Do they sit around and pan Helen? But that was so *long* ago, the war with Troy over that dumb beauty queen! Still, at least the armies on both sides knew what they were fighting for, which cannot always be said of modern wars....

TO LYNN ROTH, Screenwriter / August 8, 1981

Dear Lynn:

One day during the last triennial Guild walkathon [pickering by Writers Guild of America members against the Hollywood studios], you asked me why I had not written you a letter. The answer is as simple as it is melancholy.

Because when I held your pale hand beside the Shalimar, and kissed you progressively up to the elbow, you slapped me with the other pale hand for unseemly aggressiveness.

Because when I was sitting underneath the bough, with thou beside me, singing in the Wilderness, and you suddenly noticed that, instead of a jug of wine and a loaf of bread and a book of verses, I had brought a can of 7-Up and some rye krispies and a copy of *Penthouse*, you rose silently and glided off in the direction of Barstow, and it was five years before I saw you again. And then you were on the arm of John Houseman.

And finally there was that time in that tavern in San Juan Moribundo when, joy of joys, you drank to me only with thine eyes, and I, thrilled, pledged with mine, whereupon I implored you, "Leave a kiss but in the cup and I'll not look for wine," and you put down your cup and said, "What kind of a deal is that?"; and before I could reply, Mell Lazarus walked in, and in your haste to greet him you knocked over the cup you were supposed to leave but a kiss in, and I was drenched in seltzer water.

And that is why, O divine Lynn, I have not written. I am not a sore loser, but there are some hurts that never go away.

TO HELGA SANDBURG, Carl Sandburg's daughter
September 5, 1981

Dear Sister Helga:

[Corwin called Helga "sister" after she mentioned that her father looked upon him as the son he never had.]

I have made known to the publisher of the mini-book (to be called *A Date with Sandburg*) after the poem which concludes my attack on the attacker) that you would like copies for Sascha, Tristan, Sky, Birch and Marcel Andreas (what marvelous names!) and I hope he has the good sense to expand the very limited edition by that many copies. Much of it has been pre-sold, but I don't think there will be any problem.

I am just winding up three weeks of teaching a course in creative writing at the mountain campus of USC in Idyllwild—a setting of which Carl would have heartily approved. I have done this for a few weeks every summer for the last seven or eight years, and it is always hard to get down off this magic mountain, where the air is winey, the water pure, and the only noise pollution is from crickets, birds, and the wind.

Corwin's small book (twenty two-inch by three-inch pages and published by the Santa Susana Press in an edition of one hundred) was his response to an attack on Sandburg's poetry by a California Professor of English. He offered copies to children in Helga Sandburg's extended family.

TO HELGA SANDBURG / February 18, 1982

Dear Sister Helga:

I am much moved by the generosity of your suggestion that, if needed, Barney [Crile, Helga's husband, an eminent physician] would give me fighter escort to the Cleveland Clinic, and that I might break bread (low sodium) with you on Kent Road, on the same visit. But so far (knock, knock) I seem to be responding well to a cardiac rehab program that is ancillary to the UCLA CC Unit, and except for a fancy new flu mutant that knocked the hell out of me last week, I have felt better than before. [Corwin had suffered a mild heart attack late in 1981 and spent ten days in the UCLA Medical Center.]

They tell me the heart damage was minor, and the diagnosis would have probably been missed had it come along seven or eight years earlier, before the special blood enzyme test was developed. Anyway it is well to treat with respect *any* cardiovascular episode, and that's what I intend to keep on doing.

The mini-mini *A Date with Sandburg* is at last off the press....The printer decided that "Carl Sandburg" should be on the spine, and that Carl's signature should be on the front cover. That suggests *A Date with Sandburg* was actually written *by* Carl, when of course it is about him. When I asked the editor about the proprieties and amenities involved, he responded with the Not-to-Worry bit. Well, I won't if nobody else does.

Anyway whatever else it may be, it is little, and would fit in Marcel Andreas' vest pocket. Not so my love, which is family size.

TO STUDS TERKEL / June 8, 1982

Dear Studs:

I was moved to tears more than once by your *Born to Live*. It compounds so many of the things that make it possible to keep on hoping in spite of the Ravensbrucks and Hiroshimas and Falklands and Reagans.

Those beautiful people! Sloane Coffin and Georgia Turner and [John] Ciardi and [Pete] Seeger and Lillian Smith and our old friend Carl! And the protean Terkel! Man, count your blessings, to have met and drawn wisdom of heart and mind from these people, and then to have put them together in this rhapsodic and deeply human document!

Your little Japanese girl who hid her face on the ground and then jumped into the river, made me think of my own *Overkill and Megalove*, and especially of the poem *Killing with Kindness* in it. One of the most moving moments ever recorded is that agonizing "I don't think I can say it," from both Myoko and her interpreter....

It was glorious seeing you west of the divide, and I hope another decade doesn't pass before our next meeting, because I am running out of decades. As for you, Studs, you will live forever. I have arranged for it to be that way.

TO LOUISE KERZ, Documentary Writer and Researcher
Undated, 1983

Dear Louise:

It's good news that your work on Columbia's 60th will bring you back to this reclaimed desert in time to welcome officially the season of spring, which has been here five times already. Indeed the yoyo character of the local winter contributed to the worst siege of flu-related nuisances I have ever had in one calendar year.

Thanks for that photo, in which for once I look passably intelligent. That is the osmotic effect of propinquity. (If a student of mine wrote that last sentence, I'd send it back to be redone under the cloud of a D grade.)

Is Alex Cohen heading up the 60th? I have a few choice reminiscences of the 50th which I think may entertain you, although at the time I didn't find them particularly enchanting.

Have a good undelayed flight.

CBS canceled its 60th Anniversary celebration because of a Writers Guild strike.

TO DR. E.W. BILLARD, a New York Physician
October 26, 1983

Dear Manny:

At seventy-three I am active as you continue to be at eighty-five! [Dr. Billard had treated Corwin forty years earlier.] And that activity sometimes results in my falling behind in the amenities, such as replying swiftly to an old friend for whom I have always had the warmest affection.

Yes, it's great that my father is going strong at one hundred and seven. I spoke to him this very morning, and he asked, as usual, whether I was keeping my "time and mind occupied." That is the credo by which he has lived all his life and he has done well by it, and it by him. He's always been vain about his youthful appearance, and there is a true story about his 100th birthday which I think you'll appreciate. There was a big party for him on this occasion at the local shul, and a woman came up to him and said, "You know, Sam, you don't look a day over seventy!" My father thanked her and she went off; he then turned to my sister and asked, in all seriousness, "Do I really look that old?"...

I send you every good wish for health and happiness, and the wish that you too will take bows at your 100th!

TO ART SEIDENBAUM, Book Editor, *Los Angeles Times*
December 24, 1983

Dear Art:

...The new compendium I was telling you about, but was foggy on credits, is *The Travellers' Dictionary of Quotation*, subtitled, "Who Said What, About Where." It was edited by one Peter Yapp and published by Routledge and Paul of London, Boston, Melbourne and Henley—all unknown to me.

The title of the book and name of the editor could, I think, be improved; but the volume itself has extraordinary range and felicities of arrangement, style and substance. It runs to 1,022 pages and sells for thirty clams.

A happy, healthy, non-Orwellian 1984 to you.

TO TED KOPPEL, ABC Television Reporter / February 17, 1984

Dear Ted:

No, the jacket photo isn't all that old. [Corwin had recently published his book *Trivializing America*.] It's just *I* who am. It was taken three years ago while I was hosting a program for PBS in the Academy Theater out here; I benefited from makeup, ambience and distance. I guess I can fool some of the cameras some of the time.

As on so many earlier occasions, congratulations are due—overdue this time—on your superb handling of the postscript to *The Day After*. Nobody, repeat nobody, has your style and class when it comes to keeping order and preventing nabobs from beating their panjandrums too loudly.

You wear your greatness lightly. A hundred more like you, and I would not have had to write that book.

TO HERB ALPERT, Musician / March 17, 1984

Dear Herb:

Great thanks for your kindness in sending me your "Fandango," and for your inscription. I listened to it with the same relish as to the entire body of your work that has been an active part of my disc library for so many years.

Under separate cover I am sending you my own latest release, an item called *Trivializing America.* I'm afraid it does not have the entertaining power of any of your oeuvres, but then few things do....

TO ANNA NEETHLING-POHL / May 23, 1984

Dear Anna:

Your greetings are always treasurable, and more: The art that you bring to the stage, you also bring to the page.

Anna, I was seventy-four on my last birthday. While my father is living in Boston at a hundred and seven, and I hypothetically inherit his genes, he was never a writer, and never took himself and the world as personally and grouchily as I do. But I am rejuvenated by every passing wisp and chord and brushstroke and metaphor and image of fine art, and am in no hurry to bring down the curtain. Along with the grief and the anger and frustration that is so abundant in this world, there is also love and beauty, and the perception of them, not to say the creation of them, is as close as we need come to immortality.

O rare Anna! Thank you. And say hello for me to the cosmos blooms and the doves of Pretoria. Love,

TO CARL FOREMAN, Film Director / June 18, 1984

Dear Carl:

There is an old Jewish adage from the Talmud or Mishnah or some such exalted source, which goes, "Whoever visits the ill, takes away a sixtieth part of the illness."

I have known visitors who *added* sixty parts, so that's not a reliable method. Nor is there any formula for how much illness is alleviated by a letter. Depends on the letter, of course. But one sure means is the contemplation by the patient of how many people he has edified, enthralled and enriched by his work and his person. If each such beneficiary accounted for taking away only a millionth part of an illness, you would be competing in the Olympics....

TO BARBARA TOURTELOT, a former student at San Diego State
July 2, 1984

Dear Barbara:

I have changed my opinion of the world. It *is* a nice place. If a woman as beautiful and talented as you can also be a happy wife and mother, it means that the fates are not as grudging as I suspected. Too often those who are richly endowed seem penalized in some other way—Beethoven by deafness, Milton by blindness, Utrillo by poverty, Dylan Thomas by alcoholism, Keats by TB, Liz Taylor by sixteen husbands and recurrent pneumonias, the Kennedy family by half the griefs visited on Job.

I am delighted to learn of the felicities that have come your way, with still another scheduled for September. My God, a handsome, kind and loving officer who enjoys good music, springtime in Paris, three acres of Virginia countryside, three cats and a horse. Few of us can match that, including the undersigned, who has no acres in the country, not a single cat, only an obstreperous mockingbird which makes territorial claims all night long on a public address system.

Myself, I've been busy as always, too busy, and have to my recent credit or discredit, depending on the reader's viewpoint, a new book entitled *Trivializing America*. It has gotten some good press and letters, but any reader enchanted by Reagan will throw it to the floor and stamp on it.

TO LEW TRENNER / July 25, 1984

Dear Lew:

The photo you request is attached. I am older and grayer than when it was taken a few years ago, but it is still legitimate. The circles under my eyes are deeper, there are forty-five more wrinkles, and there is far more salt in my moustache, but I am still recognizable as the party pictured.

...A *second* paragraph is not the proper place to thank you for the munificent gift of the Tagore inscription and his GITANJALI. I tell you, amigo, my digs here are mighty proud of the Trenner trophies that have come to it over the years—that glorious bowl and platter from your potter's wheel, with "Prayer for the 70s" [inscribed on the rim] and a shelf full of chemical glass, which has given me pleasure every time I have passed it, fifty times daily, for the past dozen or more years. And now the hand of that glowing old man Tagore, facing a page inscribed by yourself. Thanks to the 10th power!

I agree with you about that week-long commercial celebrating the Statue. Vulgar, all except for the tall ships, the fireworks, and the Lady herself. How about our Leader [Ronald Reagan] alluding to EMMET Lazarus, poet? I would call him a numbskull, except that I know a few sweet and inoffensive numbskulls, and I don't want to offend the phylum....

TO ROY MADSEN / October 22, 1984

> Queen Elizabeth II, during a visit to San Diego, had unveiled Madsen's sculpture of Shakespeare.

Dear Roy:

I am distressed to learn of Barbara's condition. I revert to a kind of primitivism when I get news like that, especially when it concerns dear friends. I want to punch the gods on the nose, or noses, all the way around the pantheon. If pain and distress are inexorably to be handed out, why to the *good* people? Why not to the crooks and knaves and killers, why not to the arrogant and the heartless? Herman Melville once made the comment that if Emerson had been around when God created the earth, he would have offered some valuable suggestions. It doesn't need an Emerson to suggest that next time around, there be a better shuffling of the chromosomal deck, and, among other things, an improved correlation between the theory of justice and its practice.

Only my pouting about the unfairness to Barbara could delay my congratulations to her spouse on the splendid achievement of the Shakespeare bronze. The presence of Her Majesty at its unveiling is, to a confirmed anti-royalist out of revolutionary Boston, the least of the felicities that make me, once more, proud to know you and happy for the public recognition of your genius. You have given Will an aspect altogether lacking in traditional portraiture of him—he's *happy*, b'god— the script was great, the rehearsals went smoothly, and the opening was a smash. Why *not* a joyful genius?

Of *course* you may interview me for your book. How could you even ask? I am leaving at the end of this week to lecture for four days at the University of Michigan, but I will be back to cast my ballot in a lost cause, and expect to be here at Smog Center for the balance of the semester. A session over a hot tape recorder, followed by dinner, would be great, and I already look forward to a reunion far too long delayed.

TO DAVID DOUGLAS DUNCAN, Photographer
December 1, 1984

Dear David:

Well, if any added proof were needed to establish that you are great in every way, *New York/New York* would give it.

Your discovery of George Forss is of a piece with Emerson's discovery of Whitman—a master recognizing a master. [George Forss photographed New York City and its residents.] But more than recognizing him, you did something for the man and his art and, by extension, for all of us.

One would have to be made of carborundum not to be moved by those photographs—or by your account of the way they came to your notice. Jesus, the irony of the man getting fined for more than he made from a dozen of his street sales! The law can be a pig. And the touch of his doubling his price to $10 because the prints had been seen on the *Today* show! Made me want to cry.

Live forever.

TO HADLEY JENSEN / February 12, 1985

Hadley, three months old, was the child of Paul Jensen, who worked for the Democratic Party in Washington, D.C., and his wife, Carolyn, Corwin's production assistant for a series of radio programs he wrote and directed from the National Public Radio headquarters.

Dear Hadley:

How lucky can a girl be? To be the daughter of not one, but two, superior parents, to be born a Democrat, to be blissfully unaware of the existence of the first true muttonhead in the White House until long after he will have departed that address, to hear Mozart and Schubert for the first time on the highest fidelity instruments that electronics can produce, to grow up in a world where whales have at last been recognized as a species worth preserving, to celebrate your birthday on or around election day, which means that when you are elected to high office, the confetti will *really* fly and the champagne bubble—all this is in store for you, plus many other happy things that you will learn about as you go along.

Please give my fondest regards and felicitations to Carolyn and Paul, who had a lot to do with this, and exercise faithfully with your rattles and teething rings so you can grow up strong and independent. Love,

TO ZAN THOMPSON, Columnist, *Los Angeles Times*
February 18, 1985

Dear Zan Thompson:

I was charmed and moved by your tribute to Chuchulain. He made me nostalgic for all the cats in my long log—ranging from imperious to lunatic. There was a black-and-white one with a Hitler moustache, and a calico who was faintly strabismic with no excuse for it, like being Siamese, and an all-white alley cat who kneaded bread on my bread basket whenever I was horizontal in his presence, and several all-black ones with the grace of panthers, and a kitten who skittered sideways to avoid ghosts, and a Tom who brought me a live gopher almost as big as he was (and I, like a fool, freed it, and was repaid by a major gopher infestation of my lawn).

I ask you to remember me to Chuchulain in whatever converse you have with him, and I send you the warm best wishes of a fan of both cats and your columns.

TO MARY ANN WATSON, Professor, University of Michigan
March 2, 1985

Dear Mary Ann:

It was good to get your card from New York, where I have not been for so long that I risk forgetting how to spell it. There was a time when I thought I could not possibly stay away from the city for longer than three months at a time; and more than once, when I was first in California to work on a film at RKO, I drove my car to the top of a ridge overlooking the Burbank Airport (then the *only* airport in the area) in order to watch the 5 p.m. plane take off for LaGuardia.

And thanks too for sending me the crossword puzzle with my name spelled correctly. But most of all thank you for your verse. You have joined the club of versifiers, the dues of which are a poem each quarter, and the rewards of which, I'm afraid, are a quarter each poem.

I think of you often, and each time with lively appreciation of your grand generalship and indomitable hospitality during my rounds on your campus. I don't think I have yet adequately thanked you for your generosity in giving me a copy of your superb thesis, and to that I add still more thanks for having sent me the text of your introduction at the Stasheff lecture. I feel a sense of guilt for having put you to trouble in each instance.

I gather from the weather reports that winter's back is broken in your part of the republic. It just arrived here today with some cold winds out of Manitoba, but even with that it's toasty at midday.

Little new to report from here, except that a USC film unit has been busy making a documentary film about me, of all unlikely subjects— and that a broadcaster I much admire, Bill Moyers, is coming out here in a couple of weeks to tape an interview with me for a show to be aired in May. Wish me luck....

TO LYN MURRAY / March 31, 1985

Dear Lyn:

Don't ever apologize for your raunchy prose. It has vigor and color and humor, and it belongs on your writing palette just as legitimately as do your powers of narration, description and characterization. I am sufficiently a student of the bawdy, erotic and pornographic (see my chapter on Sex in *Trivializing America*) to appreciate that a good lusty appetite, and its satisfaction, are not necessarily the work of the devil.

I am disappointed that you felt the *National Geographic* scores were a drag for you. I did not catch them all, but what I did hear seemed to me quite worthy of the standard you set early on.

You speak of the aged Jeff Alexander. Is he as aged as the aged Norman Corwin, who will be seventy-five in four weeks? The USC School of Journalism, at which I am a visiting perfesser, is planning a big party for my 75th, but has been keeping secret from me the cast, the invitees, the program (if there is to be a program) and all but the number seventy-five.

TO REDA GETTY, former secretary / April 22, 1985

Dear Reda:

When you describe "feelings of shame at having been so lazy and undisciplined" at your writing, you are simply affirming that you are a member of the Club. All writers, including this one, have the same problem. The great catalyst is a stated and defined goal, a deadline, preferably one that is commissioned. If you can trick yourself into playing the *role* of a writer who has received an assignment which must be completed by a certain time, you will have a good chance of licking the problem. Try it.

TO STUDS TERKEL / April 25, 1985

Dear Studs:

Congratulations from here to both poles and around the equator! All the past sins of the Pulitzer Award juries have been atoned and purged in a single stroke, as in a great judgmental Yom Kippur.

I must tell you something that indicates in an odd way the joy I felt at the news. I heard about the award on an 11 p.m. newscast, just before going to bed. After I had been asleep for about four hours, I had a dream which awakened me. I was in a large room, crowded with pleasant people—a party. You were sitting at the head of a table with about twenty of us around you—I among them—while fifty or sixty others moved about the room. There was general conversation which I do not remember, but suddenly I became aware that you had not heard of your award. I felt a rush of the kind of pleasure one has when there is good news to announce, and I rapped on a glass object to get everybody's attention. "I have some news for Studs and the rest of us!" I shouted, and watched your face as I told of the Pulitzer. You broke into the famous Terkel smile, and the crowd cheered—at which point the dream ended.

It is not usual for me to dream about items in the news like that, or even about people I know, so I construe it as a tribute from my subconscious mind matching the esteem and affection of my conscious one.

A double set of cheers, then—amplified thousandfold—and my fondest and warmest regards, as always.

TO PAUL CONRAD / May 8, 1985

Conrad, the *Los Angeles Times'* cartoonist, had been master of ceremonies for the dinner given by USC to mark Corwin's 75th birthday.

Dear Paul:

Not only did you do me ineffable honor by your masterful mastering of ceremonies, but you spoiled me rotten by asking for a copy of the sober portion of my speech. It is attached, along with my allusion to the great Conrad.

I swear you are the only artist in any field, whose work is so consistently brilliant that I feel like writing a fan letter every morning. You would soon tire of that, especially since I am sure that your love/hate mail must form a great mound if you let it pile up for longer than ten days.

The word-of-mouth that has reached me concerning our evening, has been all warm, and invariably dwells on your superb performance as chief dispatcher and master of revels. There are not enough words in Roget, Webster or the Oxford, to express my thanks to you on all scores.

TO ERIC SEVAREID / May 9, 1985

Sevareid had called his memoir *Not so Wild a Dream*, from a line near the end of Corwin's *On a Note of Triumph*. He informed Corwin that lately a pornographic paperback had appropriated the title.

Dear Eric:

Your note helped make No. 75 my birthday of birthdays. A USC crowd—350 strong—gave me a bash, and among the props was a sky-scraper of a birthday cake with 75 candles ablaze, enough to warm up the Astrodome on a chilly evening. Lots of speeches including Norman Lear and Charles Kuralt, but no word of greeting was more welcome than yours. After all we go far back together.

The sex-violence paperback that swiped our title showed little imagination. They could at least have called it *Not So Wild a Wet Dream*.

It's good to see your hand, but it would be even better to see your face. Your appearance on the tube is always an event for me, but my first choice is Sevareid in person. Come on out.

Great thanks, Eric, and fondest best,

TO TOM BRADLEY, Mayor of Los Angeles / May 14, 1985

Dear Tom:

Everyone has dreams of glory, I suppose, starting at an early age. Mine progressed from the dream of being a baseball star, to composing symphonies, to writing the great American novel—none of which has yet been realized (it's getting late for baseball); but I never dreamed of having a Norman Corwin Day proclaimed.

Besides being a thing of beauty which my as-yet unborn grandchildren will admire, the Proclamation accurately lists my credits, which means my descendants won't have to look them up to find out what I did for a living.

The only thing missing from the banquet at the Beverly Hilton was Your Honor—a big lack, and one for which I blame the Japanese who were reluctant to let you get away. To me that is a far keener grievance against Japan than our trade imbalance.

TO GERALD KEAN / May 17, 1985

Dear Gerry:

...I had no idea I was all over the dial on May 8. You are only the second person to tell me about Charles Osgood, but you are first with the news that Mutual and ABC had allusions to me also. [Charles Osgood had quoted from *On a Note of Triumph* on CBS during the 40th anniversary of V-E (Victory in Europe) Day.] I hope I'm around and listening on the *50th* anniversary of V-E Day, but that's asking a lot. I'm seventy-five, and still a writer, and both make demands.

I'm glad you're in touch with Allen Sloane. We're all alumni of that crazy and wonderful time—a dwindling band, but, I hope, still with ample reserves of feistiness.

TO ERIK BARNOUW / Undated, c. May, 1985

Dear Erik:

Many, many thanks for your grand contribution to the [*Thirteen for Corwin*] volume. I trust you've received your copy of the book by now. As you may know, production of it was kept secret from me until the night of the dinner, and it was first put in my hands by Kuralt when he got up to speak. I was, and am, overwhelmed. How could I be otherwise? Along the lines of the old joke, had I known that seventy-five would be so much fun and decked with such honor, I would have reached that age long ago.

The dinner itself was something from which I will never willingly recover. Upwards of three hundred and sixty chickens were sacrificed; Paul Conrad mc'd with the same verve and elan that goes into his cartoons; Norman Lear and Kuralt and Chuck Champlin spoke; a skyscraper of a birthday cake appeared, ablaze with seventy-five candles—enough to warm the Sports Arena on a chilly night; there was a mini-documentary film about me, projected on a wall of the room (all that lacked to give it Biblical tone was handwriting on the wall and Belshazzar looking on); Tom Bradley, in absentia (detained in Japan), presented a richly illuminated and calligraphed Proclamation of Corwin Day (I apologized for the inconvenience of the banks closing); there was a cassette of *On a Note of Triumph* at each plate, courtesy of a recording company, and each guest got a copy of the book with you in it. Jesus! There was not a point in the evening when I didn't feel like asking, Who, ME?...

LeRoy Bannerman is properly excited by your having agreed to do the Introduction to his biography of me. As well he should be. The only thing I worry about is your getting awfully tired of Corwin.

Fondest best to you and Dotty,

TO FRANK STANTON / May 29, 1985

Dear Frank:

Many thanks for sending on Lou Dorfman's comment. It broke through an overcast. [Stanton had relayed a comment by Dorfman, the graphic designer, that if he could write like Corwin "I'd be the happiest guy in town."]

A careful search of this envelope will disclose a volume [*A Date with Sandburg*] that won't take up much room in your library. Indeed there can be very few volumes with less volume. It's a remembrance of Carl Sandburg, who once stayed in my house for a month. For me it was like having a royal box in a Circus Maximum where the poets eat the lions.

TO PHILIP DUNNE, Screenwriter and Director / June 5, 1985

Dear Phil:

Thanks for your letter and that marvelous piece you wrote for *Harvard Magazine*. From the title forward it makes superb reading, and gives lessons even to Carl Sagan, in the art of communicating. Indeed I could not help thinking as I went from concept to concept enjoying both substance and style, that it was a great pity you could not have written and *narrated* the *Cosmos* series. In addition to the wit and charm you'd have given it, America would have been spared those hundred closeups of Sagan looking raptly at the heavens. I respect Sagan and am glad he is on the right side of the big issues, but he was too often a pain in the astronomy of the series....

TO R. LEROY BANNERMAN / July 28, 1985

Dear LeRoy:

Not since my virginity was successfully attacked by sixteen starlets swarming all over me on a bare sound stage at 20th Century-Fox (not the only thing that was bare, as you can imagine), has my honor been so assailed as by your attempt to bribe me with a $20 check. I return it herewith, with the admonition that I cannot be bought for less than $28.50, plus tax.

Thank you for sending the Barnouw intro after I twisted your arm both clockwise and counterclockwise. I think it is very good indeed—brisk, clean and economical, like all of Erik's writing. Do you think it proper for me to write him about it, or am I not supposed to see it until the book arrives from Alabama with a banjo on its dust jacket?

I found an 8 x 10 of Ma and Pa, in which they are both speaking into an *NBC* microphone—a photo apparently arranged as a joke by Emil in the days when Emil was working for NBC's press department, and Sam and Rose were visiting New York. They both look well and in good humor. I am not in the shot, which is a great boon to its esthetics, but this may rule it out for you, since you have a quaint visionary notion that the subject of your biography should be in every picture of the book. I am sure that the reader of your book will get as tired of my face as you, Rita, Kate, and a cast of thousands have become over the years.

Please don't be offended by my return of the check. I have never yet taken umbrage at a check in the mail, the nearest to that being an occasion when I took Ursula Umbrage, an unchecked female, behind the bushes. To discuss Keats, you filthy-minded Hoosier.

TO BILL MOYERS / August 30, 1985

Dear Bill:

Godspeed (which I always figure is the speed of light) on the new series. I can't wait for it, and neither can your legion of constituents....

As a proven friend of *Trivializing America*, I think you will be pleased to learn that its hardback edition has sold out, and that the publisher is bringing out a quality paperback. But not before I make a few revisions to bring it up to date, to extend and confirm premises and arguments. Nothing wholesale, just some piping and trimming here and there....

I listened with emotion and gratitude to your great pieces from Ethiopia, and your commentary on Tutu and Falwell. I'm not sure whose America it is right now, but what I *am* sure of is that whatever the findings and conclusions of your series, this country is richer for your presence and voice in it.

TO GARSON KANIN / September 1, 1985

On the death of his wife, actress Ruth Gordon.

Dear Gar:

I am old enough to believe that a life as rich and productive as Ruth's should be celebrated and not mourned, and that those who knew and loved her—a legion in which I was conscripted long ago—may take pleasure and pride in the knowledge that hers was a rare and wonderful trip. That you were with her for such a great part of it was, I am sure, a privileged felicity for both of you.

As always, my warmest and fondest regards.

TO GERALD KEAN / February 6, 1986

Dear Gerry:

Your wonderfully newsy letter was worth waiting for. I am, first of all, delighted to learn that you and Glenna are landlords of a lighthouse. On the latter, I'm glad you went into detail about the history of your interest, the purchase, the rehabilitation, and the logistics of getting furniture, refrigeration, and yourselves installed, because you anticipated my questions. I find it fascinating, having been a lighthouse buff from my childhood. I grew up on the North Shore, and from my attic bedroom I could see the beams of two lighthouses—one, Graves Light, whose light was so powerful it played on the wall behind my bed. It was a constant companion. The other, Boston Light, still in service, is the oldest lighthouse in America....

Sad about [Jeff] Sparks. His name was fitting—he had a spark, and I enjoyed its light. I had heard that Hans Van Stuwe had gone to his reward, so I'm heartened by your story of having seen him not long ago in Paris. Carlos [Garcia-Palacios], after some happy years in Tahiti, left this world some time ago. I last saw him out here when he was subsidized for needed medical attention by his friend and fellow Tahitian Marlon Brando. Indeed it was at Brando's home up in the hills here that we met.

The hardest loss for me was that of George Movshon, who died after a long and agonizing struggle with emphysema. Goddam miserable shitty weed! I've lost more friends to it than I care to count, the first of them being Ed Murrow....

TO HOWARD WHETSEL, Physicist, of Oak Ridge, Tennessee
March 21, 1986

Dear Mr. Whetsel:

I only wish I had read your *Trouble in the Ivory Tower* while I was writing my book. There would have been a chapter on the trivialization of physics, and it would have been built around your position, just as my chapter on law was built around the position of Ann Strick against the adversary system. But then I would never have had a chance to read your paper if you had not already read my book, so causality is at work right there.

Unfortunately, as far as the lay reader is concerned, your case, though brilliantly stated, may be too abstract for even the run of readers who went to the trouble of finishing my book. You are quite right when you say that most of the public, including students of the social sciences, are unaware of the conflict between causality and acausality. I belonged (no longer, thanks to you) to the horde of the unaware. So I am greatly indebted to you for explaining the spread of quantum babble, and its influence on "the fleshy tablets of our minds."

I find fascinating your scoring of Heisenberg, having had not the faintest idea of the genesis of his theory of indeterminacy, nor of its political and philosophical ramifications. Neither was I aware of the smugness of the acausalists. How can they argue that Nature's laws are all argle-bargle when a thousand species of fish, fowl and insect have, strictly through causal routes, arrived at magnificent states of mimicry? Or when the spiral form is common to the chambered nautilus, the cochlea of your ear, the tendrils of a passion flower, and vast galaxies?

Indeed, as I write this I recall a column I turned out a little while back, that dealt with nature's laws as exemplars for the artist and toolmaker.

What to do about getting your message out? That's a hard one. Maybe there are still a few publishers of quality who might be interested. Or some university press. There are still gamblers in that field. (One such is bringing out a biography of *me*, this year, God help 'em.) I'm afraid the subject is a bit steep for Johnny Carson; but you write damn well, and if you are half as good a speaker, there ought to be some lecture opportunities.

As for your pushing seventy-five, you are my junior. I will be seventy-six in May. But maybe we both can take heart: My father, living in Boston, is in his hundred and tenth year, and has all his marbles except for the usual diminution, at that age, of short-term memory. But ask him what happened ninety-eight or a hundred and two years ago, and he will respond in great detail.

I am glad you liked my book. A paperback edition, same format as the hardback, is coming out in April or May. I took advantage of the new edition to extend certain areas (new beginning, new end, and eighty or ninety pages altered in big and little respects), because events of the two years since the book was published have, alas, confirmed much of what I wrote, and added new fuel.

I hope you have good luck harpooning the Heisenbergonians, and spreading the good word of causalism. You sure as hell have good allies in Galileo, Newton, Franklin, Jefferson, Planck and Orwell. And you have my admiration for the vigor and clarity of your stand.

TO SALLY BEDELL SMITH, Writer / April 16, 1986

Her biography of William S. Paley was published as *In All His Glory*.

Dear Sally:

Congratulations on the Gannett Fellowship. Make that two-way congratulations, because it does the Gannett Center honor as well, to have chosen you.

Of course you may quote from the pages I sent you. They are part of a five-hundred-page pack of memoirs commissioned ten years ago by a publisher. I worked very hard on it and I think it has good stuff, but I just got tired of writing about myself, and I put it aside intending to take it up again some day. That day has not yet come, and the pages just sit on a shelf.

I am halfway through the [A.M.] Sperber book [*Murrow: His Life and Times*], which so far I've been able to read only in fits, being locked in a chokehold of overlapping deadlines. It *is* marvelous, as you say, and has a good deal of stuff not touched on in Kendrick's massive biography. When I found I was mentioned by Sperber several times in a favorable context, I called the *L.A. Times* and said maybe I should be disqualified as reviewer for that reason, but they wouldn't hear of it.

TO ARLENE FRANCIS / June 19, 1986

On the death of her husband, Martin Gabel.

Dear Arlene:

A measure of the impact of Martin's loss on this household, is the fact that several people including Joe Wershba of *Sixty Minutes*, phoned to console *me*. Indeed I first learned the sad news from Joe. These good people—there have been six so far—apparently felt that Martin's and my association, even though it occurred so long ago, was unique; that my work had found its most eloquent expression through Martin.

I felt that too. And it gives me comfort to know that Martin told others that *On a Note of Triumph*, and *The Rivalry*, were his most fulfilling experiences.

Kate, too, is greatly saddened, for she shared my enormous esteem and abiding love for you both. Not idly did we give our only daughter your name. [The Corwins had named their daughter Diane Arlene.]

We send you and Peter our heartfelt condolences, and hope that we will see you on one coast or other before too long.

TO A.J. LANGGUTH, Writer, then in Rio de Janeiro
June 23, 1986

Dear Jack:

I am not at all sure about Washington, notwithstanding his strike across the Delaware. Anybody with any imagination could capture a bunch of drunken Hessians. There is something arch about him, something vain and ambitious—the sort of man who probably aspires to be King, to have his picture on postage stamps, who would want a capital city named after him, and possibly a cream pie, and who would encourage darkies to name pickaninnies in his honor. I simply do not trust him. He never acted in a B picture in his life, so what would he know about running anything more complicated than a military drill?

I am delighted that the book [*Patriots*] is going well. Your theory that I phoned at 4:30 a.m. my time in order to be sure I wouldn't interrupt your work, is nearly but not quite correct. I phoned that early in order to reach you before you left for the beach to continue your researches into whether the Minsky G-string is wider at the perineum than the Ipanema bikini.

Thanks for sending me the *Washington Post*'s review of the Murrow bio. My own review, which I enclose, ran yesterday. As for TRVZING AMER, whose most striking feature appears right after the title page, it drew the attached good notice from the *Chicago Tribune* (reprinted by the *Sacramento Union*); a nice plug, cum thumbnail picture, by [Alex] Raksin in the *L.A. Times* book section; and a two-page spread with text by Shirley Hatten, in the *Santa Monica Outlook*—a double truck, ornamented by a 6 x 11 (!) picture of me, in color yet. I'm sorry to report that I look as though I'm in urgent need of a laxative. I don't want to spoil your next meal by sending it to you. It can wait.

I spoke at the Santa Barbara Writers Conference last night, and was approached afterward by Charles Schulz, who turns out to be a very nice and warm guy. He asked me to send him something and gave me his address—1 Snoopy Lane, Santa Rosa. He said it with a modest chuckle.

Enjoy Rio for me.

TO CHARLES SCHULZ, Creator of the "Peanuts" Cartoon
June 29, 1986

Dear Charles:

It was grand to meet you and Mrs. Schulz at the Writers Conference, and to see for myself that a giant can be of average height and weight.

This accompanies the tape I said I would send, in which there is a section about three-quarters of the way through, in which I deal with What Have We Learned?

I certainly never expected the program [*On a Note of Triumph*] to be around forty-one years later, and at the rate I was going at that time, I wasn't sure I'd be around either. But one of the rewards of staying in the race was the constant pleasure of reading PEANUTS—crowned, last Sunday, by the pleasure of meeting its creator.

TO CHARLES KURALT / August 2, 1986

Dear Charles:

I knew Whitman sounded better in your custody, but I didn't think anyone could put meat on the bare bones of my Statue of Liberty piece. You did, and once again, for the 246th time, I am beholden to you. Garabedian sent me a cassette without any prior notice or description, and so I heard it with the freshness of listeners who caught you in real time. I was impressed by Adler's score, and the use of it as backing nicely covered the rawness of my narration. Altogether your treatment of the subject was compact, salient and civilized—solid virtues which, I'm afraid, were not conspicuous in most of the Liberty Week-End coverage that I was able to hear and see.

I was one of the millions privileged to catch our Leader as he spoke of Emmet Lazarus. Yes sir, good old Emmet. I grew up reading him along with Amory Lowell, Edmund St. Vincent Millay, Emil Dickinson, Will Cather, Sylvester ("Sy") Plath, Andrew Sexton, and John Didion....

My thanks—again, yea again—and my warmest best, as always.

TO BILL MOYERS / August 16, 1986

Dear Bill:

The USC jury which gives out Distinguished Journalism Awards tells me it has been after you for years to accept one, but that each time you have been too busy to come west for it.

They stubbornly nominated you again this year, and have pressed *me* to tender the invitation, on the bare grounds that (a) I have met you; (b) I am known as a loud fan of yours; (c) I am once again going to m.c. the presentations.

I told these people that none of that matters; that with the Constitution series coming up, you'll no doubt be even busier than before. They asked me to ask you nonetheless, on the same chance that business on this coast might bring you out around the time of the banquet (November 19) and so put minimal strain on your agenda.

I make no dramatic pitch, for I know how busy you are, and I am reluctant even to bother you about it. The only element that might have peripheral appeal to you is that *Sunday Morning* has accepted one of the four awards, so if you were batting in the cleanup spot, it would do that much more honor to the kind of programming that, God knows, the country sorely needs.

I thought you were absolutely smashing in the double-standard piece about Nicaragua/South Africa, and so did everybody else around here who heard it.

TO ERIC SEVAREID / September 13, 1986

Dear Eric:

It's always a holiday hearing from you.

By all means tell Michael [Sevareid's son] to get in touch with me. I'm not sure I can offer him expertise or sound advice relating to academia, since my experience in it has been channeled into a kind of free-wheeling lectureship. I have been teaching by invitation only, since my academic credits (never went beyond high school) are nil. The only degrees I have are honorary—two—and I am sure you have three times as many, all better deserved. I have always been, and am now, a Visiting

Professor, not interested in tenure or any other of the accustomed accouterments of serious teaching.

Nevertheless I have been in the company of enough resident professors, and in and out of enough classrooms and auditoria to have *some* notion of what goes on, and to the extent of that exposure, I hope there just might be something of modest value that I can relate to Michael.

In any case, I look forward to meeting him, and will send through him to you, more of what I now dispatch by the unreliable mails; which is

Warmest greetings and boundless best everything.

TO ROBERT NORTHSHIELD / February 19, 1987

> The CBS Producer who originated the *Sunday Morning* series had been dropped during a management reshuffling. He had remembered the line "a hunk of rainbow around your helmet" from *On a Note of Triumph* and quoted it back to Corwin.

Dear Shad:

I sat up very straight when I heard the announcement on Sunday. At first I was angry—an instant suspicion of foul play. But Kuralt's encomium was so warm that I put my indignation on hold. And then came that magnificent closing credit. I didn't think it was possible for a mere credit to be moving, but that one sure as hell was. It lingered gloriously, displacing the regiment of good people usually in the crawl. I'm certain I was far from alone in construing it to represent a tribute from every last member of the crew who waived the accustomed bow.

I know nothing of the circumstances, beyond what I read in a Sunday *NYTimes* story. I should like to think it was not part of the network's assholistic approach to its recent problems....

Shad, you ain't got just a hunk of rainbow around your helmet. You've got the whole thing.

TO LYLE STUART / February 23, 1987

Stuart had recently returned from Paris, where a taxi driver who spoke English asked him if he had ever heard of *Trivializing America*. A friend had sent him a copy, the driver said, and added, "I think it's terrific." Stuart then identified himself as its publisher.

Dear Lyle:

Thank you for that marvelous Paris story. It's an astonisher. The chances of that happening the way it did must be around a billion to one—of all the drivers who meet all flights, of all the passengers they carry, of all the conceivable subjects for conversation! It's very little short of incredible.

I have told the story a dozen times since I got your letter, and each time it produced a kind of awed amazement. Naturally the first one I told it to was Kate—in fact I read her your letter over the phone—and what made it even more remarkable was that it followed by only a week, a similar but considerably less exotic instance involving Kate herself.

It seems Kate took a bus back from local shopping, and got into a conversation with a the woman sitting next to her, a total stranger. They passed an area designated as Dart Square, and the woman remarked that she loathed the memory of the person [Justin Dart] for whom it was named. "I just finished reading a terrific book," she said, "and in it there's a chapter which tells just what kind of a creep Dart was." "What was the book?" Kate asked. *Trivializing America*, by Norman Corwin," she answered, upon which Kate introduced herself as my wife. You can imagine the rest.

Here again, what are the odds against that conversation taking place between two strangers? And the odds increase exponentially when one takes into account the fact that our book is not a big best-seller like a Sidney Sheldon title.

I hope the rest of your trip to Paris was as titillating as the ride in from the airport. Lucky you and Carole, traveling as often as you do. It's been nearly thirty years since I was last in Paris. In the interim I've been to far islands and Peru and Rio and South Africa and the Amazon jungle and Alaska—but Paris is Paris, and there ain't nothing like it on this earth.

TO W. ANN REYNOLDS, Chancellor, California State Universities
March 7, 1987

Dear Ann:

Great thanks for your kind note about the *Times* article on my father and me.

I was astonished by the volume of comment it drew—far more than any previous matter by or about me in the local prints. Apparently people who have parents of advanced years, take heart from proof that entering the seventies, eighties or even nineties does not necessarily mean the end. I also think many of the nearly hundred from whom I've heard, including strangers, are sensitive to degrees of communication between children and parents, and I suspect some of them took C. pere et fils as a kind of freaky model.

I am delighted that you are arranging a Long Beach nostalgia evening, and that Jack Smith, Paul Conrad and I will be meeting with you on April 20. I look forward to that; and in the meantime I abide by my father's prescription to keep my mind and time occupied, and to stay away from pool rooms, saloons, and fried food.

TO ELIZABETH MEHREN, Feature Writer, *Los Angeles Times*
April 18, 1987

Dear Elizabeth:

Beulah sent me the enclosed recent interview with the patriarch. I suspect some of it is sheer moonshine, because although Sam did chew tobacco in his brawny youth, I think he gave it up before I was born. And he does not speak as a representative Corwin male when he says that what attracted him at the Howard burlesque was "the beautiful clothes" worn by the girls. But then at 110+, I figure he's entitled to a filigree of malarkey every once in a while. For the rest, I offer five to one that he was speaking the truth, the whole truth, and nothing but....

TO DIANE AND DAVID OKARSKI / May 31, 1987

Corwin wrote this letter for the wedding of his daughter.

Dear Diane and David:

Epithalamium is a perfectly dreadful $2.50 word which may have been music to the Greek who invented it, but which to the American ear sounds like a medical term—"What you have is an inflammation of the epithalamium. Take two aspirins and call me in the morning."

But actually it means a poem, or any writing, in celebration of a wedding. So in the role of your friendly neighborhood epithalamiumist, I offer you a little epithalamium which has a reading time of three minutes and twelve seconds, although it may seem like four:

It happened that one summer night or, if you will, one enchanted evening, in Tarzana, a town named for a friend of jungle apes, two young people, one named for a goddess and the other for an ancient king, met in the foyer of a theater between acts of a play whose intermission was its only coherent feature.

It was a classic Boy Meets Girl. (The intermission, that is, not the play.)

The Girl, as freely admitted by her family, her friends and herself, is beautiful. Indeed that evening she walked in beauty—right past the Boy.

But the Boy noticed. And the Girl noticed that the Boy noticed. She inherits the gift of notice from her mother, who got great notices from acting in plays that were invariably superior to their intermissions.

The Girl knew instantly that she was in the presence of a Presence— a most presentable Presence, inheritor of very special quantities from very special parents, not the least of which qualities is Charisma.

Now Charisma is a Yiddish term meaning charm, talent, wit, warmth, and a host of ancillary goodies including but not limited to attractiveness, handsomeness, well-spokenness, outgoingness, and a willingness to drive a prospective father-in-law to the airport. This extraordinary act, rare in members of his generation, is a matter of record, and is also ahead of our story.

The Boy in no time flat perceived that the Girl matched him Charisma for Charisma. (It could even be said that together they enjoyed many Merry Charismas, but that will not be said because a pun, even a hit pun, is too base for an epithalamium—and of course a too-base hit is certainly beneath us all.)

So much for historical research and commentary. Which brings us to a genuine epithalamium:

> May the years, David, Diane, bring you every good thing you could wish for yourselves, increased by unexpected bounties.
>
> May you nourish the arts and be nourished by them.
>
> May you find joy in those pleasures that go by plain names but are more precious than treasure
>
> Such as kindness—pure and flowing, as in the justly famous Milk of Human Kindness.
>
> Such as the miracle-working touchtones of tenderness and tact.
>
> The quietly magical achievements of consideration
> Shared laughter
> Strolls together in the uplands of literature
> Appointments with music and other cherishable mysteries
>
> Attunement to nature, with an eye and a heart for green, for bloom, for growing.
>
> For skiey things, for sun and clouds and rain and storm, for fair winds, for Las Ventas
>
> For sparkling waters, for the pride of mountains, for deserts of yucca and saguaro, for roses, even for scallions, for rainbows even in the spray of a garden hose, for the dew of morning, which is the best of the brandies
>
> For cheerful reciprocities, paired like the eyelets in the figure eight.
>
> Reciprocities of trust and sharing.
>
> Of presents and pranks and pixilations and twinkles of surprise.

Of understanding in its many conjugations—
Reciprocities of doing, of giving and receiving, of
mutual faith and high heart
But especially, above all transactions, sovereign and settled in sacred orbits like twin stars that revolve around
each other,
The reciprocity of love.

TO HOWARD ROSENBERG, Television Critic, *Los Angeles Times*
June 17, 1987

Dear Mr. Rosenberg:
If the Pulitzer were awarded monthly, at the speed you are going
you'd have a dozen of them by the end of the year.
Your piece on Kuralt this morning is pure gold. My only complaint,
as I told K. himself, is that I wish I had written it.
Cheers.

TO W. ANN REYNOLDS / June 20, 1987

Dear Ann:
Your beautifully produced *Proceedings of the Second Distinguished
Artists Forum* is stunning in many ways, but it is much too late for me
to change my sex, which is what I'd have to do to justify the allusion to
me as *Norma Corwin*, in the list of Forum members on page 2.
While I would like to accommodate the editors in any way I can, the
prospect of altering my entire hormonal structure, revising my stationery, throwing out my present wardrobe, and applying for membership in The League of Women Voters, is forbidding. I hope you will
explain to the editors that any attempt by me to live up to their listing
would be awkward at best, and widely misunderstood.
Warmest best to you and Tom.

TO MARK WAXMAN / July 1, 1987

Corwin's former student, he had become a television
producer.

Dear Mark:

...Thank you, amigo, for your words of consolation on the death of my father. Even at his great age, it was hard to let him go, so young was his outlook, and so much did he enjoy living.

I guess you and I are in the minority of children who care about and keep in constant touch with their parents. The fact that you call Stan every day—every *day*!—is a tribute to you both. And that you are able to call him your best friend in the world, is a glowing jewel in the family crown.

TO U.S. SENATOR LEE H. HAMILTON / July 20, 1987

> The U.S. Congress was conducting hearings into the Iran-Contra affair.

Dear Mr. Hamilton:

Congratulations and gratitude are due for the dignity, eloquence and efficiency with which you have chaired the House Committee in the current hearings....

A small item of postscript status: We are beholden to you for advising Mr. Poindexter's counsel at one point, to let the witness answer in his own words. It seems that each time a sharp or momentous question is asked, the response is, in effect, made by his lawyer and not by the witness. In baseball terms this is tantamount to a pinch-hitter taking over when the count is three and two and the bases are full, and then restoring the original batter. Perhaps nothing can be done to avoid this under procedural rules, but it was refreshing to have this reproof from you. I hope it is invoked as often as the need arises.

TO DR. WILLIAM B. OBER / July 28, 1987

Dear Bill:

Many thanks for *The Trial of Spencer Cowper*. It is my least favorite of your monographs, only because it is so heavily technical and particularizes in drowning, which I rate low among spectator sports, and whose graphic descriptions are not for my coward's stomach. The case itself strikes me as a refractory subject for medical literature, especially when its central figure is such a cold pill. I'm sure it's a damn good read for pathologists, but your papers usually have far more appeal to the lay reader, among whom I perhaps rank layest. I much prefer Ober in the vein of Keats and the drowse of poppies.

I too have been watching and am disgusted by the Iran-Contra hearings. All the President's men seem to me worthy of a description once ad-libbed by Carl Sandburg in my living room: "Snakes fucking in a barrel of snot." [Oliver] North is a genuinely dangerous zealot. Poindexter's vaunted photographic memory he generously retouched. Elliott Abrams is my candidate for Asshole of the Eighties. Meese is half crap and half lard. I write this before hearing from Donald Regan and Cap Weinberger, but they are scooped out of the same swill. Thank God for [U.S. Senators] Inouye, Mitchell, Brooks, Cohen, Stokes, and Hamilton. The other day I put aside my work and sat down and wrote them letters of support.

TO MICHAEL KANIN, Screenwriter / From Idyllwild 92349, August 12, 1987

Garson Kanin's brother, and married to Fay Kanin, he wanted Corwin to write lyrics for a musical to be based on the Western film *Destry Rides Again*.

Dear Mike:

Greetings from the upper slopes of Mt. San Jacinto, where I am doing my annual August thing on this bracing campus. Personally, I prefer the upper slopes of Sophia Loren, but she is not available.

I have at last pulled together on one blueprint, a sort of three-year plan accommodating various unfinished projects, and two long-range objectives that I had promised myself to reach, including another book. And sorely as I was tempted by your invitation to slip back on my head the hat of librettist, I think I had better desist out of respect for both of us. By this I mean that unless, in the finest Jewish tradition of worrying, I can help to worry through an enterprise (conferences, drafts, rewrites, more meetings, more rewrites—all legitimate requirements) then it would not be fair to either of us. Many bruises have taught me that riding several horses at the same time can be injurious to the health of both horses and rider.

I was very pleased that you thought of me as a member of a backfield that included your esteemed self. That indeed was the highest attraction for me. It goes without saying, but I'll say it anyway, that I wish you nothing but the best, including what even agnostics call godspeed, on the musical. And I combine with these good wishes, my love to you and Fay.

TO WILLIAM F. NOLAN, Screenwriter, Anthologist
November 26, 1987

Dear Bill:

It's always tonic to hear from you. I only wish we met oftener than has been recorded by historians.

Speaking of historians, I am not sending out any copies of my biography, because the book is not by me but about me, and it would be like my passing around copies of feature articles or interviews in which I was the subject. To the extent that the book is generous to me—and it is, I guess—my distribution of it would rank as an exercise in vanity, and who wants that? I have not even mentioned the bio to good friends like yourself—and Ray and Stan Freberg and Marty Halperin, because among other things, the publishers have set an intimidating price on it—$28.50. For that dough you can buy a book for your coffee table, if not the table itself. If in spite of that bleak statistic you are still rash enough to want to buy it, the best way is to order it from the publishers, The University of Alabama Press, in the town of University, Alabama, 34586.

I missed you at Ray's [Bradbury's] Hallowe'en party, just as I miss those occasional meetings of the Vic and Sadists. You and I are among the founding fathers of that good society, and we should do something about restoring it to good standing in a culture that needs us.

Professor R. LeRoy Bannerman's biography of Corwin, *Norman Corwin and Radio: The Golden Years* (University of Alabama Press, 1986) was subsequently released as a trade paperback, *On a Note of Triumph: Norman Corwin and the Golden Years of Radio.* Corwin objected to the title but approved of the price—$8.95.

TO CHARLES KURALT / March 28, 1988

Dear Charles:

A great moving segment on Woody Guthrie.

I have some awesome letters from Woody, which I would be glad to donate to the archivist of his memorabilia who was on your program yesterday. Would *Sunday Morning* have an address for him?...

I promise not to write you twice in one week again, if I live to be a hundred and seventy-five. You have enough things to do without opening mail from me, and you do them superbly.

TO HOWARD WHETSEL / July 17, 1988

Dear Howard:

Congratulations on finding a publisher for your book, which ain't so easy these days, since oil and soap companies have taken over the likes of Knopf and Random House, and General Electric owns a major network.

And the fact that your publisher is willing to start all over because his printer made so many errors in the galley proofs, is a good sign. Another good sign would be if he changed printers.

Your question about who might be interested in a high-quality documentary on UFOs is a rough one simply because there have been so many passes made at the subject. I have seen two or three attempts over the years, and was never impressed by the way they were handled. Even if you have wonderful new material based on hitherto neglected or undiscovered scientific evidence, you would have a hard time getting a hearing. I'm afraid it would take a major event, some Bermuda Triangle sort of hard *news*, to revive interest. Once it hit the headlines, you'd have no trouble—the *Enquirer* and *National Geographic* would answer your letters, and you *could* make a deal. But my guess is that it won't happen unless and until.

Please keep me apprised on the new book, because I want to order it as soon as it's off the press.

TO ED LINN, Writer / July 20, 1988

Dear Ed:

Long time no correspondence.

I just finished reading a borrowed copy of one of those limited editions of a classic, this one put out by the Lord John Press of Northridge, CA, 1977, three hundred copies printed on Curtis Rag, and signed by the author, who happened to be John Updike. It's a reprint of his famous "Hub Fans Bid Kid Adieu" piece originally written for the *New Yorker*, but with the added flourish of a Preface and two and a half pages of Notes. I was delighted to find that in Notes 2 and 3, Updike pays tribute to your TED WILLIAMS book, and in case this is the first you've heard about it (very unlikely, I should think), I have photocopied the allusions and enclose them.

I trust you have kept up with the writings of our mutual cousin William [Ober] of Tenafly, whose latest book drew notices that I would be proud to have buried with me. [Ed Linn, Norman Ober, and Dr. William B. Ober were first cousins.] One of the pleasanter reflections of my old age, which is older than your old age by a long chalk, is that somehow the Ober genes produced writers of fairly conspicuous quality. I think if the other Norman, who calls himself Norman East in his letters to me, had kept at it, he would have been fourth man in the regular infield. As it is, he has at least one book to his credit, and it's of a type I never had the temerity to attempt—a novel....

TO ED LINN / August 10, 1988

...Your admonition not to abandon the idea of writing a novel, has me rethinking that decision. Lyle Stuart, who publishes me these days, wants me to do one. But every time I go to a bookstore like Crown, I am dismayed by the endless shelves of remaindered novels, $18.95 books selling for $1.98. Each started with high hopes, involved hard labor, and went through the usual assembly grind. Fully half of them, it seems to me, are decently written; some are of high quality. So I ask myself why anybody should want to part with $20 to read a novel by Corwin, who no longer has the national profile afforded by extensive and continuous propagation over a network for upwards of ten years. Still, I realize this is the sort of negative head-scratching that would have aborted all kinds of missions and projects. Age is a factor, of course. I have already exceeded the actuarial figure for life expectancy, and so has my Apple McIntosh.

It's good news that you expect to be in Kashmir shortly. By all means save some time for a meal and an evening of talk.

TO RAY BENDINER / September 4, 1988

Dear Ray:

...The summer has whisked past. Where are the pollens of yester-year? (All in West Los Angeles, I suspect.)

When last we met, in the Bread Basket Restaurant, Idyllwild 92345, you spoke of the possibility of my coming to Claremont to speechify. [Bendiner was a student at Idyllwild.] And later you slipped me a slip of paper with the address of Jill Stark, Director of the Atheneum, and the suggestion that I send her my vita. Only trouble is, I never solicit a speaking engagement. My agenda is so heavy that I never go looking for a booking. I'm spoiled, to be sure, but I speak only when invited, and then not always.

I hope this finds you thriving, and that you are fecund, as always, with puns.

TO DR. E.W. BILLARD / September 4, 1988

Dear Mannie:

Ninety doesn't seem so old to me these days, since in another nineteen months I'll be eighty. But both of us should make note of my own father, who left us only a year ago last May, at the age of 110-plus. And up until the last week of his life, he was on his feet and enjoying everything that came his way, especially bourbon and sherry.

Those forty years have zinged past like a supersonic jet in full throttle. I wish to hell those decades could have given people like you and me more to cheer about in the way of national politics. Just think of that array of stumblebums—Nixon, Agnew, Ford, Reagan, Meese, and now Bush and Quayle! This just ain't the America we knew in the days of FDR, or even JFK.

Anyway, we're still in harness, you and I, and I note with pleasure that you have a girl friend whom you see regularly. That does not surprise me, since you were always handsome, deeply knowledgeable, and engaging, and I suspect nothing has changed.

TO JOHN SANFORD, Writer / September 9, 1988

Dear John:

Thank you for *Gods of Another Olympus*, and your warming inscription.

I can now brag that we are kinsmen, because your piece is in some respects the identical twin of one I wrote in *Overkill and Megalove*. I called it "Killing with Kindness," based on a quote from the unspeakable Dr. Teller, and it comes along on page 47.

We both were stung by the same swarm of bees in *Hiroshima Diary*, though we seem to differ on the name of the man who was standing at the Itsukaishi station. I have him down as Dr. Hachiya, not Mr. Hashimoto, but I have only my text to support me here. Doesn't matter, really. What matters is that we've both been furious about it for a long time, and thank God we're both still snarling.

I hope Maggie is fully recovered. Give her a hug for me when next you hug her for yourself.

TO DR. MAXIMILIAN EDEL, Physician, Sculptor
October 11, 1988

Dear Max:

The sculpture arrived today. [Edel had asked Corwin to sit for a portrait and then presented him with the result.]

How can I begin to thank you? The head is of a better man than I am. I am uniquely in a position to know that for certain, and I intend to keep it a closely guarded secret, but you are entitled to this knowledge because you are the creator.

I am indebted to you three-, four-, fivefold, not only for this rich token of your art, but for the privilege and pleasure of the sittings, for the opportunity to enjoy hours of discussions with you, for the educational experience of watching you build the portrait from a loaf of shapeless, inert clay into something that the first three friends to see it, believe to have been made with rare and uncanny insight. I am too close to the subject to know whether I have been caught like a fly in amber, but I suspect that you have captured a quality in me that other portraits, photographic (or as it happens, twice in paint), have never done.

I leave in a few days for a trip to the east, featuring a stop in Asheville, North Carolina, to deliver the keynote speech at a Carl Sandburg commemoration. But when I return, I hope we can get together so that I may thank you vis a vis, buy you a celebratory meal and, between us, settle the politics of America.

TO CHARLES SCHLEIN, California Painter and Sculptor
November 15, 1988

Dear Charlie:

Man, you have fought the good fight.

We look around, this late in what has been a remarkably cruel century, and we see crud everywhere but in a few small islands and scattered archipelagos. The things we have written and painted and sculpted and urged and defended, seem to have lost out through such forces and agencies as the elevation, time after time, of gnats to high office; the General Electric-ization of media; the scourging and ghettoizing of liberals; the jamming of decency into solitary confinement; integrity shot down as in a gang war; even some of our most cherished ideals, the Judaic Ethic carved so powerfully into so many of your sculptures, now corrupted by fanatics in the Land of the Book.

But nothing of this negates or cancels out your or my labors, or those of the small cadre whose hearts and minds and work we respect— a cadre, indeed, of which we are a part. I don't think it is wishful or airy to believe that by our stand—whether taken in the exercise of our art, or in dinner conversation, or in meetings, or whenever and wherever— we delayed the ascendancy of the Toads, and hastened, by however small increments, what I choose to think will be the inevitable return of sanity and good order—the only alternative to chaos and a kind of perpetual nuclear winter.

In my already long trip through this time, I have known and met all too few men and women whom I esteem highly for themselves and their work. You are one of them—one of the gifted who nourish and inspire, and whom it's good to be around. You have *counted*, and even though the count right now seems to be against us, we have made some noise and knocked a few dents for causes that persist, and will continue to persist, long after us. We have asked a lot of ourselves, and more than that no one can ask.

TO RAY BRADBURY / November 22, 1988

Dear Ray:

There we were, in a cavernous banquet hall at the Viscount Hotel, four hundred aficionados of old-time radio. And blind John Gassman, who sees more without sight than most of us see with eyes and glasses to support them, introduced my old and dear friend Ray Bradbury.

And there was your voice, filling the room, clear and crystalline, like FDR when he was in good fettle. And what you had to say warmed everybody in the room, especially and profoundly myself. Once more you were generous beyond the deserts of the subject, and once more I worked myself up to a pitch of believing maybe you were right.

And though a lot was going on, and I was about to be called on to perform a half-radio-half-stage version of *The Undecided Molecule*, there flashed through my mind a happy sense of symmetry in our long relationship.

We both enjoy and indulge in fantasy, although you have exclusive rights to Mars, naturally.

We both believe in the sovereignty of the word, and love our language.

We have dedicated books to each other.

We are both listed in the main vocabulary of the Random House Unabridged Dictionary, just an alphabetical unit apart.

We like the same composers, living and daid.

We have on many occasions introduced each other to gatherings.

We share some of the same awards.

We also share literary heroes—from the man in Stratford, to and through Melville, Dickens, Dickinson, Hopkins, and Stan Freberg.

There could be no greater symmetry between two people unless they were twins, or were named Yo Yo Ma and Yo Yo Pa.

Let me add that I'm a candidate for President (denied that, I'll go for the post of Corresponding Secretary) of the Bradbury Society, whose motto is YEA YEA RAY.

I tried to reach you after the Sperdvac evening to thank you viva voce, but the machinery of GTE told me 839-9874 is no longer current.

My love, current and future, to you, Maggie, and your shining descendants.

TO HOWARD WHETSEL / November 26, 1988

Dear Howard:

Here I am nearing seventy-nine, which is also nearing eighty, and I still have an agenda that refuses to shrink. This gives me the illusion of being younger, and although there is much to be said for preoccupation as against idleness and boredom, there are prices to pay. One is that I miss out on a good many of the amenities that seniority is supposed to enjoy—leisure, travel, contemplation of the whorls in one's navel, but mostly the pleasures of being with or communicating with people one likes and respects.

I am vexed with myself, for example, that I had not responded to your good letter of last July (!!!), when, with better discipline of time and activity, it would have been fun to reply in three days or three weeks, not three months. But I have so many damn pro bono interests, like being 1st V-P of the Academy of Motion Pictures, and letting myself get drafted to make the keynote speech at a Carl Sandburg commemoration in Asheville, North Carolina, two weeks ago (Subject: Poetry and Politics), and teaching at USC, and doing this and that and the other, that the days slide by like greased pigs or greased geese or greased grease.

I enjoyed both your letter and "Modern Theoretical Physics: Did Orwell See It Coming"? You deal in profound matters, and do it with a touch that makes it assimilable to mathematic illiterates like me. By the way, do you know the writing of my good friend Tim Ferris, whose latest is *Coming of Age in the Milky Way*?

Recently I was asked to stage a production of an old radio play of mine, called *The Undecided Molecule*. I wrote it in 1945 for CBS, as part of a series called *Columbia Presents Corwin*, and it had a lulu of a cast—Groucho Marx played the Judge, Vincent Price the prosecuting attorney, Keenan Wynn was attorney for the defense, and Sylvia Sidney was Miss Anima. It was published in a collection of my plays, now long out of print, and because I thought it might amuse you, I am sending a crude photocopy of the script.

I hope this finds you well, and in good spirits. The two go together, of course. When I look around at the thinning ranks of our generation, I get a good impression of the ability simply to get up in the morning, walk on one's own two feet, do a fair day's work, put away meals, and down a drink. The rest is gravy.

TO CHARLES KURALT / December 17, 1988

Dear Charles:

I would not have known about the Acrostic in Harper's but for your having solved it and alerted me. I went out and got a copy. Since I have a talent for not remembering my writing, it was not much easier for me than other crostics I have tackled.

It's fun, especially if you don't know you're working on your own text. That happened twice to me—once in an Elizabeth Kingsley puzzle (*Saturday Review*) and a second time in a Wortman. I also had the experience in another puzzle, of stumbling on a six-letter word listed as "American writer, director, actor." The only six-letter hyphenate I knew who fitted that description was Orson, so I filled in "Welles." In ink, yet. It hung me up for a half hour, until I realized it was "Corwin." The hitch was that I was never an actor, hence the miscue threw me off.

You are princely, as always, in consenting to be interviewed by a USC filmmaker. The whole enterprise does me too much honor, and makes me suspect I may have fooled a lot of listeners a lot of the time. But what the hell, if a monument can be raised to a race horse, like the one at Sandringham Palace, I guess maybe it's all right for a guy who spells correctly to be the subject of a documentary. [Broadcasting students at the USC School of Journalism were preparing, under the direction of Professor Joe Saltzman, a documentary television biography of Corwin.]

You, Chas, have been going great, and that ain't hyperbole. I have to restrain myself from writing every time you hit for extra bases. It happens every time you come up, and is one of the few glories left to CBS.

I send you greetings of the season.

And deep thanks for all seasons.

TO EMIL CORWIN / December 19, 1988

Dear Em:

...Enclosed, a *painting* of Fenway Park, one of the historic graveyards of old Boston.

Also enclosed, a Chanukah endowment for a supply of Matlomeal, to which you introduced me in Washington during one of your cigar walks when we stopped in at the People's Grocery.

Also enclosed, one of the few snapshots taken of me in which I don't look like a Hallowe'en mask. Circa last June in Idyllwild.

TO DIANE CHANDLER / January 3, 1989

One of Corwin's students at Idyllwild, living in Las Vegas.

Dear Diane:

I was delighted to learn that you gave yourself a holiday in the Caymans, where seldom is heard a discouraging word and the skies are not cloudy all day. That's about 180 degrees removed from Vegas, where, even though the skies likewise tend to be clear, discouraging words do get spoken, and there is more gravel than sand....

I seldom get to Vegas, since I am not by instinct a gambler except in the sense that every piece of writing is a gamble. The only times I've been there have been on my way to visit the Dam, or when invited to speak before a conference. That has happened twice. Even less frequently do I get to the Caribbean—once to Havana before it became off limits, and once to Jamaica. It's an enchanting part of the world, and I like it more than the South Seas, where I've also been (both Samoas, a plane stop in Fiji, and another in New Caledonia). But have you tried Hawaii? Not Honolulu, which is too much like L.A. to soothe me, but Kauai, and parts of the big island....

Enough about geography. You sound vital, in control of your life, awake and aware. I wish for you Joy in the New Year, and always.

TO SALLY COHEN, Writer Living in New Hampshire
March 5, 1989

Dear Sally:

...I read *Armageddon*, and I'm afraid I have to report that your comment, "I don't know what the hell I'm doing" is accurate in the case of this screenplay. You write with great wit and you have the power to be vivid—even, at moments, moving; you have an excellent ear for dialogue; there is a bold freshness to your insouciance. But as a movie or TV script it is shapeless, it has no structure, it would be utterly impossible to shoot. Moreover the characters are not clearly defined. The Narrator, while frequently amusing, is cumbersome and superfluous, and he violates one of the first laws of writing for a visual medium: *Show, don't tell.*

Dear Sally, how in God's name is anybody going to film the four wolves, the dog dismembering a poodle, the donkeys, coyotes, the tiger, the grand black horse, and the earthquake? And as your Narrator says on page 91, "I'm sorry there are so many characters in the movie." So am I.

Writing is hard under any circumstances, but it is hardest when you are writing for a medium of which you know little. If you are attracted to drama, then you must first of all *steep* yourself in it—read, watch TV and movies (even bad stuff, to study why it is bad). And simplify your first objectives—don't try to get the world into 120 pages. Write about things you know, or about which you have strong feelings.

There is a surrealist quality about *Armageddon* which I like, but it would make a long and diverting poem, not a movie.

Keep writing, but try something that does not run berserk. Find Sally Cohen first; when you do, she will light the path for your work.

TO HARRY JACKSON, Wyoming Sculptor and Painter
April 8, 1989

Dear Harry:

Phew! Being first Vice-President of the Motion Picture Academy sounds nice and honorary, but I had no idea of the amount of work involved. No sooner was the Awards ceremony over, than the Disney people huffed and puffed and threatened to sue because the opening number used Snow White, the little dear, in an expansive production number. Violation of copyright, sez they. Big flap, lots of meetings and conference phone calls, and it's settled....

Congratulations are in order for your concept of "The Strip Miner." It has uniqueness and quality written and sculpted all over it. The concept of a limited edition of an art work this huge, this commanding, and bearing the imprimatur of Jackson, is breathtaking. And with it, the added excitement of a movie written around it!

Your vision has always been big. This is one of the biggest.

Before Jackson became an artist, Corwin had known him as a soldier during World War II and cast him as the narrator of a radio special, *Word From the People*. More recently, Jackson had created an equestrian statue of the actor John Wayne, which is displayed in Los Angeles outside a Wilshire Boulevard bank building.

TO ROBERT SAUDEK, Custodian of Recorded Materials, Library of Congress / April 16, 1989

As an executive at NBC in 1939, Saudek had written to William B. Lewis at CBS, praising Corwin's production of *John Brown's Body*. Corwin had recently found a carbon copy of the letter fifty years later and sent it to Saudek.

Dear Mr. Saudek:

It is not often one preserves a carbon copy of a letter for fifty years, and finds it as good to read now as when it was received. Thanks again—jubilee style.

Considering the perils of the planet, the span has been good to both of us.

I wish you many more years as fulfilling as I know the past has been for you.

TO GREGORY PECK, Actor, Former President of Motion Picture Academy / May 20, 1989

Dear Greg:

...You are generous to suggest that, since I hold the office of First VP, I am in line to be the next Prez. That has never been my ambition, but it's academic anyway, because in a few weeks I will reach the end of my ninth consecutive year on the Board, and the statute of limitations takes over. I'm sorry I won't be around to press for needed reforms, but there are a lot of good people on the Board, and judging from the voices raised (along with my own, I must add) at the post-mortem session, the chances are good that the '90 show will not reprise the calamity of '89. Let's hope so.

Warmest best as always.

TO MARY ANN WATSON / June 28, 1989

Dear Mary Ann:

I love your idea of putting together a compendium on Presidents and Poetry. It's a fresh notion. I'm sure nobody has come up with the idea, let alone the research. It would be fascinating to know whether Lincoln heard of Whitman, whether Woodrow Wilson, who after all had been President of Princeton, had a favorite poem or poet; whether Reagan ever got beyond Jack & Jill, or maybe Edgar Guest. What the presidents *didn't* read would be almost as interesting as what they did, so it could be fascinating either way.

It's good you've hired a research assistant. I wish I could find a good one. I tried it—but it was like hiring a turtle to run errands for me.

TO JOHN SANFORD, Writer / July 21, 1989

Dear John:

A Walk in the Fire is full-strength Sanford, and there can be no higher praise than that.

Your fortitude! To be able to work as you did through the pain of Maggie's illness, and to be able to continue working after the terrible blow of her loss, makes me think once again of the miracle of those great artists and writers and composers who carried on against cruel adversities—deafness, blindness, chronic illness, the deaths of loved ones—and somehow they infused such high spirit in what they did that one never suspected it was done against fierce odds. We had to find that out in album liners, program notes and biographies.

Re *Walk*: You have captured, as on a crystal-clear x-ray plate, a diseased Hollywood in the time of the McCarthy-McCarran Plague. The power of the book is amplified for me by the fact that I knew many of the characters in it—Mannix, Schary, Deutsch (once a Schary Democrat, later a staunch supporter of Reagan), Saul Marks (Plantin published one of my things), Maltz, Beecher, MacKenna, etc.

Tremendous. All of it. And all of you too. Congratulations.

Edward Mannix, Dore Schary, Milton Beecher and Kenneth MacKenna were MGM executives, Albert Maltz a screenwriter and Armand Deutsch a producer.

TO PAUL DICKSON / October 20, 1989

An author of compendia, he had published, *A Collector's Compendium of Rare and Unusual, Bold and Beautiful, Odd and Whimsical Names.*

Dear Paul:

...I have some new names for you: a professor at the University of Chicago named Mihaly Csikzentmihalyi. A writer for the *L.A. Times* named Thomas Bonk. A Mr. Edward John Timmw of El Cajon, CA. An accountant in the Virgin Isles named Ray Sewer. A design consultant who improved on the Biblical name, thus: Zsuzsanna. A policeman (policewoman?) named Josie Moneymaker.

Keep going.

TO FRANCES RING / December 1, 1989

Dear Miss Ring:

After much thought, and even mental turmoil, I have reached a decision respecting the release you seek for use of "At Home with Captain Bligh" in your anthology *Analecta*, which sounds like a disease.

The problem is that you did not enclose a self-addressed stamped envelope. I wanted to make sure that my affront over this was justifiable, and so I made a daytime person-to-person call to the President of the Authors League of America, who happened to be vacationing in Cape Town, South Africa. He was out but I spoke to his manservant, who put me on hold while he called the South African cell of the Authors League, but everybody was out to lunch, and the janitor, who answered the phone, said he would have to think about it, that he did not want to make a snap judgment, and that if I called back on Wednesday he would give me his answer.

I then called Jack Langguth, who said you certainly *should* have enclosed an SASE, and that he considered it uneditor-like conduct on your part, but he hedged by saying that you probably *meant* to do it, but were distracted. He suggested that I get a second opinion, so I called my doctor, an internist, who said he does not handle such cases.

I then asked a Catholic friend of mine if I could borrow his confessor, and after mass last Sunday I confessed to him that I was confused about this issue. Was I making too much of it? Was there some lack of charity in my heart, since after all a first-class stamp costs only 25 cents (which of course carries no guarantee of delivery). Was I wrong to make a *tsimmis* of this (prune salad)? Yet was not a principle involved? The priest listened in silence for ten minutes and then said quietly, "Say three hail Marys and don't eat fish on Friday, especially haddock."

I realized I was getting nowhere. I put in another long distance call to PEN headquarters in New York. An answering machine advised me the entire staff was away and would not be back until after the holidays.

I did not want to put this over until 1990, so I finally decided that, since expenses were piling up, I had better reach a decision and reach it soon. So I tossed a coin, figuring if it came up tails I would drop my resistance, invite my soul to be calm, and waive the prepaid self-addressed envelope. It came up tail. So I made it three out of five, and it came up tail twice more. Three out of three.

That, and only that, is the reason you have my signed release, which is enclosed.   Yours very truly,

TO CHARLES KURALT / January 30, 1990

Dear Charles:

...When I'm weary of reading about the zoos and nuthouses of government and commerce, I soothe myself by looking at these world-scapes, and reading what travelers on that high road had to say about it. [With the letter, Corwin sent a large-format book, *The Home Planet*, by Kevin W. Kelley.] It's better than taking warm milk before going to bed; sort of neutralizes my generally persecutorial dreams. You know the kind—you can't find your car, or don't know what you're doing in a strange city, or you've foolishly agreed to fight a light heavyweight contender—you, Norman Corwin, who have angina. I actually had such a dream, in which I was terribly embarrassed by the prospect of having to wear a big nitro patch visible to the whole arena, and getting chest pains forty-five seconds into the match. Mercifully I woke up just before the bell sounded for the start of Round One.

Happily Panama and Nicaragua and Azerbaijan are indistinguishable in these photos, and so is George Bush. I hope you like all five pounds of your coffee-table spread, and that every morning is Sunday morning.

TO LOUISE KERZ / February 16, 1990

Dear Louise:

...You do get to work on fascinating and colorful projects, and I think highly of Smith/Hemion for thinking highly of you. [A documentary film maker, she was working on a program on the Bush White House.] I hope you enjoy beating around the Bushes in the White House; myself, I think she'd make a far better President than he. As for Quayle, if you bump into him, bump hard and don't bother to say Excuse Me.

Isn't there enough illiteracy in California to bring you out here for research? Think of that boob Congressman Dornan alone.

TO LOU ASHWORTH / March 10, 1990

Dear Lou:

Seventy! That's just as unthinkable on you as eighty is on me, and that number comes up in just six weeks! But except for a tendency to sag a bit in the afternoon, remediable by getting off my feet for thirty consecutive minutes, I don't feel much different from when I was in my forties. Not even much wiser, alas.

About the Museum of Broadcasting: They are more interested in promoting themselves and getting big corporate endowments, than in creating a serious archive to live up to the promise of their name. I've had some dealings with them, and they strike me as 50 percent drowsy and 100 percent opportunistic. In the case of your generous offer to them, they were damn rude not to acknowledge. No excuse for that whatsoever.

I understand there was an expose of the BOM (fitting acronym) in a magazine named *Spy*. I've not seen it, but hope to catch up with the issue one day, after I catch up with myself. I continue to behave as though I were a committee of four, which means overcommitted as usual.

You are very kind to offer the *Stars in the Afternoon* and *God and Uranium* relics to me. I would love to have both items, which happen to be lacking in my own collection. Ultimately they will go to some library, along with my intact correspondence with Lou Sawyer Ashworth (unless you object, of course)....

In the parlance of mining operations, the schist hits the fan every now and then, and one occasion was recently when a drunk young lady, uninsured, from my home state, ran a red light at 70 mph and sideswiped a car in which Kate was riding. Kate went to the hospital for a while; the lady should have gone to jail for a while, but of course did not.

Enjoy your septuagenarian estate, and I'll try to do the same with my octogenarian.

To JAN WAHL, San Francisco Radio Commentator
March 14, 1990

Arthur Nadel had been Corwin's successor as Chairman of
the Motion Picture Academy Documentary Awards
Committee.

Dear Jan:

I was much moved by your letter, for I had no idea Arthur suffered
from negativity, was melancholy, or as you put it so vividly, there was in
him "film noir...more shadows than light." I realize now that he must
have called upon great reserves of spirit to present to me, as he invariably did, the aspect of a man in good control of his psyche, vexed no
more than the rest of us by the follies and crud of this crazy world.

I suspect that the demise of Filmation, a nasty and heartless episode,
must have been a greater blow to him than I was ready to believe. I
think it killed him. I had confidence in his ability to rebound, simply
because there was so much warmth and wit in his makeup, and so
much sheer intelligence that I figured he would be far more sought after
than seeking, when it came to jobs.

It comforts me to know that you were close to him in his last year
and especially his last days. It would have been unspeakably awful if this
wonderful, sensitive man, who had much in him that I felt to be noble,
had been alone through that difficult passage.

You speak of his idealization of me. I was warmed and touched and
grateful that he not only felt that way about me, but expressed it to you
and others. My only trouble with this was that I felt he overrated me,
that I did not merit nearly as high an estimate as he placed on me. But
if it was all a misapprehension on his part, at least we both enjoyed it,
and I was not about to try to persuade him that I really have one foot of
clay and the other rests on a banana peel....

TO PHILIP ROTH, Writer / March 27, 1990

In *Portnoy's Complaint* (1969), Roth's narrator says, "I have written a radio play, inspired by my master, Norman Corwin, and his celebration of V-E Day, *On a Note of Triumph*."

Dear Philip Roth:

One day twenty-two years ago a friend put in my hand a copy of *New American Review #3*, and directed me to read *Civilization and Its Discontents*, right away. Since I was already late on a deadline, I asked why I should drop everything to read eighty-one pages of small print unrelated to what I was writing. "You'll see," he said, and went off.

I was hooked before I finished page one, and forgot about my script, and it was not until Morty presented his birthday gift on page 71, that I saw why my friend, the actor Byron Kane, had insisted I read your story without delay. He knew I was the type who would put something away to read later, and never get to it.

I wanted to write you a fan letter then and there, but I was by now even deeper in my own end zone for time, and I figured I'd do it on Monday. A quarter century of Mondays has passed since then. And now, soon, in five weeks, I will reach eighty—eight zero!—Jesus! and out of respect for actuarial projections, and even though my father died at one hundred and ten (not long after seeing a ball game at Fenway Park), I am telling you now, on this Monday in the spring of 1990, that you have given the author of Morty's recommended text immense pleasure over the decades; that my esteem for your work has steadily compounded; that on my scorecard you are one of the all-time greats; and that you have my warmest best wishes right up through the end of the twentieth and into the twenty-first.

Sincerely,

Roth's response began, "Well, I'm glad you got around to it...."

TO HAROLD SCHONBERG, Music Critic Emeritus,
The New York Times / June 18, 1990

Dear Harold:

Marvelous.

The Great Pianists is a delight. It's a phenomenon of a book, really; it's like taking a trip on a luxury train that rides on rails so smooth you don't hear the wheels click, and passing through a fascinating series of landscapes.

I have never read a book based on whole polymer chains of research—biographic, aural, photographic—that I enjoyed half so much. Your eye and ear, your range-finder and spectroscope, and, commanding them, your style, must be thanked for that. I thought I knew something about the big guns—Chopin, Liszt, Mozart, Mendelssohn, Beethoven, but I feel now as though I've just begun to know them. And through your crash course in the pianism of composers I've long loved—especially Hummel, Field, Busoni, Clementi and Schumann, my enjoyment of their work is expanded.

What a romp when you deal with genuine eccentrics like dear old daft de Pachmann, like Hummel and Von Bulow, and, in his youth, Albeniz. You have a fix on the *mot juste*, the definitive anecdote, the illuminating detail, not only with birds of that feather, but all the way through.

You may gather by this time that I like the book....

Kate joins me in sending fondest best wishes to you and Helene.

TO BURGESS MEREDITH, Actor / August 5, 1990

Dear Boigess:

I really can*not* thank you for sending me your "Rap and Roll" tape, because it has thoroughly debauched and corrupted me. And just as I was preparing to enter the ministry, too. Bad timing! Now I will have to work for a living.

You have given a saucy reading to impudent lyrics, and the combination is, well, devastating. I had to look up the meaning of copulation and consummation, and I couldn't believe my eyes! Why, they are worse than smoking!

And to think that all these years, I thought you were a friend.

With great sorrow,

TO ALLEN SLOANE, Writer Living in Connecticut
August 13, 1990

Dear Allen:

I knew a lot of people read the *NYTimes*, but had no idea so many worked on the daily crossword. I've heard from more good friends in a wide swath of the union, through the appearance of my name in the four by four box, than I have from my last three books combined. So I am beholden to the puzzle-maker, especially when his work draws a letter from a treasured General of the Old Guard, like you.

I'll thank you not to place me in the nineties. Not so fast. I turned eighty last May. You're only four years my junior, but that's enough to require you to respect your elder, notwithstanding that I'm no wiser at eighty plus than I was at thirty.

I'm not moved by your blast against the word processor. To a messy writer like myself, it's a godsend. I resisted getting one for a long while, but now I resent every day I delayed. Jesus, not to have to go back and white-out a mistake, or redo a page six times before even *I* could read it!

Yes I caught the latest Murrow doc on PBS. I care much less about whether or not the Shirer episode was accurately told, than I do about the reminder, to two later generations, that there was once a man high in network broadcasting who had the integrity to stand up against that asshole McCarthy, and who fought for people like Radulovich. I read Shirer's autobio, and I thought he went on at too great length, and was unnecessarily starchy about the falling out with Murrow. Ed was no saint, but by God when he volunteered to help a blacklisted [John Henry] Faulk and went to court to testify for a relatively obscure actor in the person of Joe Julian, he insured himself a place in the American pantheon for all time.

I get to New York far too little, alas....But the continent between us does not diminish my regard and affection for you, decade in and decade out. May you flourish, and may your little deaf girl prosper gloriously. I send my loudest best to you both.

TO ROBERT KAISER / August 25, 1990

Then in his late teens, Kaiser was Corwin's nephew and an aspiring physicist.

Dear Robbie:

Our letters crossed in the mail. Thank you for your latest, which I read with special interest because it bears on a matter to which I've given some thought in the past.

I happen to agree with your Dad about orthodox Judaism—indeed about orthodox anything. Alas, most of the greatest atrocities of history have been either initiated or fueled by orthodoxies—the Inquisition, the Crusades, the Jihads of Muslim fanatics, the shameless things that are being done by far-out ritualists in Israel today.

Some of the thinkers whom I'm sure you most admire, have expressed themselves forcibly on the subject. George Orwell, for example, in *1984*, wrote "Orthodoxy means not thinking—not needing to think. Orthodoxy is unconsciousness." And Benjamin Franklin, in a letter to his father, wrote: "I think vital religion has always suffered when orthodoxy is more regarded than virtue. The scriptures assure me that on Judgment Day we shall not be examined on what we thought but what we did."

You are a scientist by inclination and training. How do you feel when you read Galileo's recantation to the priests—this genius who advanced astronomy by the power of his mind? I can never forgive the tyrants of orthodoxy who made him beg for his life, and plead, "Having been admonished by the Holy Office entirely to abandon the false opinion that the Earth was not the center of the universe—with a sincere heart, I curse and detest the said errors and heresies, and all and every error contrary to the Holy Catholic Church."

What I'm saying has nothing to do with one's belief in God or faith in him. Indeed, I give Him higher marks than the traditionalists. For to me it is inconceivable that a majestic, omnipotent, omniscient God could be fooled by flattery or ritual, or hold against anyone transgressions of minor codes relating to diet, or punish anyone for going into a place of worship with an uncovered head. Nor can I believe that a God worthy of respect and worship, would discriminate against women—would insist that they sit in the back of the shul, and shave their heads, and soak in baths to purify themselves because they are inherently or recurrently unclean. Do you really want to believe in a male chauvinist God?

I have nothing but the profoundest respect for and admiration of ancient Judaic ethics. I try, not too successfully I'm afraid, to live by those ethics. I have always celebrated the grand poetry and wisdom and philosophy of the Psalms, of Isaiah, of Proverbs and Ecclesiastes and Job—but these monumental works have little or nothing to do with Ritual.

There is in the Himalayas a religion which uses prayer wheels. They are ardently spun—the faster the holier. The spinner may be a perfect asshole, a mean and vicious man, but so long as he spins vigorously he's supposed to be protected from bad gods, or demons, or a falling exchange rate, or ulcers. Again, orthodoxy. No thinking is involved.

I understand you have invested in some of the equipage of orthodoxy. Fine, if it makes you feel better or cleaner or purer. But to me what makes one feel better are essences of mind and heart, not anything worn—the great precious abstractions of truth, justice, compassion, and such questing as the search for peace and betterment for a world that badly needs it.

I urge you not to be beguiled by any system of thought which *demands* conformity. Even the dictionary acknowledges that conformism is the backbone of orthodoxy, for it defines *orthodox* as "pertaining to, or conforming to the approved form of any doctrine, philosophy or ideology—approved, conventional." I would be uncomfortable wearing those hats, and I have a hunch you too would be.

I place high value on the fellowship and warmth and good will that can be generated in company such as the Judaic study group you have been meeting with, and I would be the last one to suggest that you deny yourself this enrichment. The question is what proceeds from that ambiance in the way of basic attitude, of mindset, of life style. Even if you reject the argument advanced by me, and, I assume, by your Dad, there is still a consideration I think you should take seriously into account—and that is how you *manifest* this attitude. If you're going to do it overtly, by wearing garments or other tokens that advertise your beliefs, you must expect to be regarded as more or less parochial by many of your associates and other people, as you probably regard an East Indian who wears a spot of paint between the eyes, or an African with a ring in his nose, or a Sikh with an elaborate turban, or an American Indian who shows up at a conference wearing a feather bonnet. I am even uneasy about women wearing pendant crucifixes or Mogen Davids. To me this practice differs only in degree from wearing a sandwich board saying "I am a CHRISTIAN"; "I am JEWISH."

I apologize if this letter seems intrusive, or if you feel it's none of my business, and Who Asked You? I simply believe you have too fine and logical a mind, too rich a vein of curiosity, and too keen an imagination, for me to pass without remark, on the absorbing substance of your last letter....

TO RAY BRADBURY / November 7, 1990

Dear Ray:

A tsunami of thanks! I am proud and moved by your dedication, by the generosity of your preface, and by the fact that I am now linked, for as long as print endures, not only to R. Bradbury, maestro, but W. Bradbury, editor, as co-dedicatee of a classic. [Bradbury had co-dedicated the 40th Anniversary Edition of *The Martian Chronicles* to Corwin and the book's original editor, Walter I. Bradbury, who was not related.]

I now have a new, felicitous way of calculating my age—I'm twice as old as *The Martian Chronicles*. And what a forty years for you! A string of triumphs like a parade of ten-strikes in a glorious, protracted bowling match with the fates and their mafia.

I am happy to note that we are scheduled to meet in the company of media compatriots twice in the next week-and-a-half. By all means we must go on meeting like this—and go on celebrating the fact that we were born into the same century, planet, and language.

To you and Maggie, as ever,

love

TO CHARLES KURALT / November 23, 1990

Dear Charles:

I'd like to refresh the credentials of the word marvelous, by giving it rest and recreation so it may apply full strength to *A Life on the Road*....

I had no idea of the reach of your career, how long the road, how many the doglegs, how splendid the vistas, how hard the bumps, how deep the potholes, how ornery the anatomy and cogs of your four-wheeled casas, how sharp your ear, how encompassing your eye....

The book is sequined with little unintended poems:

> The sun came out and the wind came up and the bright foliage of the New Hampshire autumn shivered and began to fall. A shower of lemon and scarlet and gold washed across our windshield....

and

> ...the citizens feel the urge to inhale April while strolling the cobblestones of the riverfront, which is crowded with shops and ships, now as ever....

and

> I can hear the soft splash of the fountain outside the door, and beyond that the brassy staccato of a trumpet from a jazz joint on Bourbon Street, and beyond that the moan of a tugboat horn from away the other side of Jackson Square on the river.

In chapter after chapter there are resonances. The story of your harrowing ascent of a Peruvian Ande (singular of Andes, and why not?) is riveting, even without the poor Quechua who was trying to sell you a fish, and whom you roared past. "I could have gone back. I could have apologized...sometimes at night before sleeping, little regrets come back to me. The guy with the fish comes back," you write long years afterward—and it reminds me of Tom Jefferson's regrets at having driven past "a poor, wearied soldier with his pack on his back, who begged us to let him get up behind our chariot...[I] began to calculate that the road was full of soldiers, and that if all should be taken up, our horses would fail in their journey. We drove on therefore. But, soon becoming sensible that though I cannot relieve all the distressed, I should relieve as many as I can, I turned about to take up the soldier; but he had entered a by-path, and was no more to be found; and from that moment to this I could never find him out, to ask his forgiveness." As you probably knew before I did, this is from a letter Jefferson wrote in his Paris days, to a married woman named Maria Cosway on whom he had a crush.

Is there something about North Carolina that makes its sons the sweetest singers of country and countryside? Tom Wolfe was eloquent on rivers and railroads, but you sure as hell match his best with "Down by the Riverside," and though you shift into another gear in "Flight" and "The Aluminum Tube," your chapter on airplanes is every bit as rewarding in its way, as Wolfe on trains. Indeed the second, excerpted from the book, could—and should—stand on its own in travel magazines, and/or the travel sections of Sunday papers, especially the *NY Times*, *LATimes*, *W. Post* or *Boston Globe*.

I cannot begin to match your experience in flying, but I have at least one entry which belongs in the repertoire of stories told around a hot chili stew on a cold night. My very first flight, my first time off the ground, was in an armada of six hundred U.S. Army planes: fighters, bombers, interceptors. All biplanes. All open cockpit. I wore a helmet, goggles, and felt-lined boots, and sat on a folded parachute. I was then a kid reporter in Springfield, Mass. It was the Spring of 1931. The Air Force, courtesy of General Billy Mitchell, was out to familiarize America with its military flying machines, a PR ploy of some grandeur. The armada, called just that, toured the country, section by section, and chose for its New England base a big grassy airport outside Springfield. Hence my opportunity. I had to sign a quitclaim, forgiving the Army any damages if the plane should crash.

But this is your story I celebrate, not mine. Let me say at once that your "Luck" chapter is the greatest boost to religion since the episode of walking on water. When that six-pack of Budweiser materialized out of the watery wilderness of Okefenokee, you should have all prostrated yourselves, sprinkled holy swamp water on your heads, renounced all worldly goods, and with many a feverish incantation, emptied at least one bottle of beer into the lake as a sacrifice, especially as how it was warm beer. The miracle, for that is what it was by any reckoning, would have been stunning enough had the response to Cosgrove's profane wish been a pack of Michelob or Pabst, but when it was *just* what he had ordered—*Budweiser*—the phenomenon reached a pitch that makes apparitions of the Virgin at Lourdes little league.

I could go on with other praises of your book, selecting other plums and cakes and candies, but I trust the reviewers will take over where I leave off, if they haven't done so by now....

TO WALTER CRONKITE / November 26, 1990

Dear Walter:

No apologies necessary. I well know the time-squeeze syndrome, having grown up with it. Early on, I wrote a Deadline Song to which Lyn Murray set music—sort of a radio folk song.

> A deadline is the one thing I abhor
> Go away, deadline, and don't come back no more
> Go away and stay away because you are a pest
> There ought to be a law to put you under arrest
> A deadline is hungry, a deadline must be fed
> Some day I'm gonna get so mad I'll kill a deadline dead.

The *Encyclopedia of the 20th Century*, the autobiography, the Granada series, assorted speeches—an agenda that Hercules, in collaboration with Atlas, would think twice about taking on, and even then would probably ask for extensions. I envy and applaud you....

Of all your current commitments, the autobiography strikes me as the most important. I've just finished reading Kuralt's *Life On the Road*, in which you appear and reappear. Not only is it very well written, but I think it solves with considerable ingenuity, the problems of structure inherent in a work of modest proportions. Most autobios, at least those I've read, tend to run long, as though that were an obligation. It ain't. Yet in a career as crowded, eventful and luminous as yours, I would hate to see anything foreshortened for the sake of foreshortening....

TO PHILIP DUNNE / December 10, 1990

He had sent Corwin a limited edition of the screenplay of
How Green Was My Valley, which he had written for
Darryl Zanuck and 20th Century-Fox.

Dear Phil:

It's a gem. What screenplay has ever had so splendid a reincarnation? Facet by facet, the book glistens—script, printing, paper, typography, binding, photos, the cache of deleted scenes, the marvelous, strong, kind, wise face in the portrait, and above all, your introductory essay.

Every writer who has ever been part of an assembly line should read *No Fence Around Time* for pleasure and instruction. I shared your vexation with the changes made behind your back, identified with your suspicions of collusion between Zanuck and Ford, identified completely with the annoyances you felt when nuance, motivation, preparation, resolution—all those delicate linkages which are Swiss watch mechanisms, not kitchen plumbing, were swept aside like crumbs off a table, on the grounds that auteur knows best.

That you understood and forgave Z and F, and unhesitatingly praise what was praiseworthy in them, is solid Phil Dunne largess. You're more civilized than I, since I'm not sure I'd have neutralized my pique even after fifty years, feeling as I do that when a director truncates, bypasses or alters a text, the writer should be consulted, or at least advised beforehand, and not left to discover such enhancements on seeing the finished picture. I'm speaking of common courtesy, of professional ethics. As for *harmful* changes, I'm afraid I can never make peace with those who commit them, because the damage they do is repeated perpetually each time the picture is shown down the years, and there is, to me, a renewed sense of loss at every showing....

TO RALPH SCHOENSTEIN / December 11, 1990

Dear Ralph:

Pursuant to our conversation of the other day (lawyer lingo), I have to tell you that *You Can't Be Serious* rings more bells than are catalogued

by Poe. (There is, by the way, an infirmity in males called tintinnabula-
tion of the balls, occurring mostly in poe white trash.) You can see what
your book has done to me....

Gems and nifties are as copious as raisins and nuts in a Roumanian
fruit cake, and I play back some of them for your edification:

—it was like going into the Sistine chapel to gaze at the floor.

—just as a lawyer knows by instinct when to start his clock.

—my lawyer was asleep, dreaming of the income of another of his
clients.

—I marked my place in the wallet.

—a couplet that had tried, a la Emily Dickinson, to rhyme
"Humphrey backer" with "motherfucker."

—a promise to never again impersonate a Chicago policeman, a
restriction I felt I could live with.

—his place had been taken by a new man whose name and coast I
missed because I was concentrating on memorizing a defense of my
script.

—the shows on CBS were designed to reflect not life but ABC.

—You can wrap gift garbage, but the aroma still fills the air.

—the most momentous event since Emily Dickinson went out for
bread.

—Jackie's books seemed to go not just through editors but Elizabeth
Arden's too.

—Tote that cream and lift that face!

—"Hi!" I said with heartbreaking breeziness.

—I picked up the morning paper as if holding the obituary of the
world.

and so on and on. And while we're on the on's, on page 149 you have
Laurie discovering a holly Bible, which I assume is used only for
Christmas, just as matzos was invented to be used only for Pesach. And
on page 111, I am indebted to you for *organza*, which heretofore I
thought was a Mexican bean....

Keep firing, amigo.

TO JOHN RICH, Television Director / January 30, 1991

Dear John:

I don't know how much the average student benefits from going to UCLA, but I certainly benefited from being on its campus the other night, and meeting the man behind that fabulous string of fabulous programs [Corwin met Rich, Director of many of the *All in the Family* television series, at a UCLA symposium.]

I was happy to learn that my name is as familiar to you as yours has long been to me, and to discover, moreover, that you are a fellow Perelmanista. I though you might like to see a column I wrote shortly after Sid had the temerity to die. If nothing else, it testifies to the width and depth of my acquaintance with his works. He is up there on my best-dusted shelf with Keats, Thoreau, Twain, and the man from Avon.

TO GILBERT CATES, Producer, 1991 Academy Awards Show / February 14, 1991

Dear Gil:

Several stalwarts of the Documentary Committee, which I chair, think it would add to the zing and strength of the Awards show if the best known film documentarian of the day, Ken Burns, were to be a presenter on the program. His monumental Civil War film is already a classic by any measure of that term, and we believe it would reflect well on the Academy if he were invited to present the Oscar for best documentary feature.

Burns is handsome, warm, articulate to the point of eloquence, and has the respect of the entire film and television community. He is also a past nominee and Oscar winner.

There is precedence for a documentary film maker as presenter— David Wolper. In the case of Burns, he made what is acknowledged to be the greatest account, in any form, of the struggle that remains the central event of our history.

The actress Phoebe Cates presented the documentary award.

TO CHARLES KURALT / February 18, 1991

Dear Charles:

Another book for your planet shelf, this one distinguished not so much for its pictures or its writing, both of which are pleasantly agog, but for its engrossing and at times astounding facts about our favorite oxide. Watson strains at times, and gets a bit silly on 139, when he allows that maybe water likes to be serenaded (opens up a new aria of physics), but I thank him for all the good reading he's done on the subject.

Of the making of books there is no end, but of the making of a months-long best-seller out of a short autobiography that is at once literary, humane, rich and warm, there is no precedent—at least none I can remember. You didn't fly the Atlantic in a single-engine plane, you didn't resign from the presidency, you didn't stroke a guitar and sing from your pelvis, you didn't service Marilyn, Elizabeth or Zsa Zsa, you didn't offer a system for making millions in five easy lessons, yet your book sells and sells, and is negotiated in and out of libraries at a great rate, according to my librarian friends. Are you surprised? I'm not.

I am honored that you would like a photograph of the grizzled Chair of the Southern California Chapter of the Kuralt Society. But along with it you must accept as a package deal, photocopies of some shots taken at the 75th birthday bash which you so kindly graced. I'd send the originals, except that they're cemented to pages in a bound album presented to me by the university.

Also in this kit, a copy of *Network at Fifty*, printed recently by the Thousand Oaks Library Foundation for members of its Board....I wrote the piece back in '78 at the behest of CBS, to function as epilogue to its week-long 50th Anniversary Celebration. It was read on the air by Cronkite. I intend to update it for the 100th Anniversary, and will insist that you perform it, so please put it down in your calendar for 2028.

Heartiest, as always,

TO KEN BURNS, Documentary Film Maker / June 30, 1991

Dear Ken:

...To be as young as you are and *know* you have created something for the ages, should make life in Walpole sweeter, make you sleep sounder, make your steak and potaters taste better, and serve as an unending time-release vitamin supplement for all your days.

Eight honorary degrees in two weeks! That is at least four times more than the average distinguished person gathers in a lifetime. Incidentally I got in the mail this past week a felicitous little fallout from an honorary degree granted me twenty-five years ago in Chicago. I take the arrant liberty of enclosing a copy of a letter from the President of that college, whom I have not seen or heard from in the intervening quarter century. This should give you some idea of how assured, as though by government decree, is the longevity of your magnum opus. If a two-minute aria in a radio piece written in '45 can be printed in a commencement program here in '91, think of the power and sweep of your Civil War, and the myriad ways it will work its wonders in the years to come.

All of the best all of the time.

TO ROBERT ALTMAN, Film Director / August 14, 1991

Dear Bob:

Secret Honor is even greater on second viewing. [Altman had filmed Donald Freed's play about Richard Nixon.] There has never been anything like it. Neither the years that have passed since it was made, nor the procession of political events, nor the campaign to rehabilitate Nixon through apologists, forgivers and cozy interviews, nor the establishment of the ludicrous Nixon Library, nor the tangled mess of Irangate, nor the turkey shoot in Kuwait, nor the decline and fall of the Soviet Empire, nor the ascendancy of certified assholes to our two highest offices, have done anything to diminish the power of the film, to say nothing of its art and ingenuity. On the contrary, its strengths increase. Nothing will ever date or dim Philip Baker Hall's performance, or yours.

I have a strong feeling that *Secret Honor*, which up to now has been honored far too secretly in this country, will, after Nixon and Kissinger pass on to the great Bohemian Grove in the Sky, become a cult classic; that it will be studied by generations of scholars and film-makers, not only as a benchmark of originality and uniqueness in cinema, but as a commentary on a period of history, no less penetrating than the Philippics of Demosthenes or the satires of Jonathan Swift. Can you imagine what it might have meant, and might still mean, to cineasts, historians, scholars, politicos and electorates, if movies of like substance, quality and power would have been made about Hamilton, Burr, Lincoln, Teddy, Ike, JFK, LBJ, Reagan?

Renewed congratulations, and endless thanks. When you are finished with *The Player*, and can draw a free breath, let's have that lunch.

TO MS. ASHBY, Handwriting Expert / October 12, 1991

Dear Ms. Ashby:

Thank you for your kindness in sending me your analysis of my handwriting. I only hope I can live up to it.

And thanks too for the analysis of the writing of Norman Cousins. You ask if his and my paths crossed. Not only did our paths cross but so did our letters. People frequently confused us because, apparently, to them the names sounded alike, and I occasionally would get mail intended for him. Also compliments. After a while I got tired of explaining the mistakes of identity, and accepted the compliments for Cousins with good grace.

Speaking of compliments, please accept mine for the literary quality of your analyses. And with them go my best wishes.

TO U.S. SENATOR JOHN SEYMOUR / October 15, 1991

Dear Senator Seymour:

I ask you whether a great corporation would hire a top executive if there were as much controversy and lingering doubt about him as there are about Judge [Clarence] Thomas. Especially if several equally or better qualified candidates were immediately available.

If the vote today goes against Judge Thomas, passions on both sides will subside in a few days, or at most a few weeks, just as they did after Judge Bork was turned down. But if Judge Thomas is confirmed, the odds are very great that bitterness, resentment and controversy will surface for years and years, every time a sensitive issue comes before the Court.

I hope you will help to spare this wonderful country an additional judicial burden that it certainly does not need.

TO EMIL CORWIN / October 18, 1991

Dear Em:

When I was eight or ten years old (note that I have arbitrarily skipped nine), you took me to Symphony Hall to hear my first symphony orchestra. You paid $2.50 for the ticket, and I just remembered that I never reimbursed you for it. Well, $2.50 in 1936 is worth $50 today, and the interest compounded over sixty plus years comes to exactly $501.87. This explains the enclosed paper....

TO TIMOTHY FERRIS, Writer, Producer / January 29, 1992

Dear Tim:

Thank you, thank you, for *The Mind's Sky*.

There just ain't nobody like you. No other writer dealing with the cosms—micro and macro—animates the reader so consistently page after page, concept after concept, book after book, with such felicity, style, wit, poetic sensibility, substance to marvel at, and even more rare in such a combination, a kind of nobility. Science is one thing and philosophy another, but to be able to make them both unfailingly provocative is like being able to throw a curve, fastball, forkball, sinker, spitball and changeup, and also hit like Ted Williams and run like Brock.

I wanted to write you after reading *Coming of Age in the Milky Way*, but I was afraid it would be a long letter, and there is a tendency to groan on receiving a fat envelope stuffed with a half dozen pages of single-spaced text and accompanied by various exhibits. But now I have double the compulsion to write, and if this be plethora, make the least of it, and I'll understand.

First, I was much taken by your pages on symmetry in *Coming of Age*. To me one of the most staggering mysteries in all creation is the sweeping, powerful symmetry of the physical *squaring* of quantities, as in $E = MC^2$, the equation that seems to me the father and mother of us all, being that it stokes the fires of the sun. And then all those ancillary phenomena such as gravitational force being diminished by the *square* of distance; the Fibonacci series, and all the vast rest. It's E = MC *squared*, dammit, not E = MC x 3.141592, but *squared!* Am I a bumpkin, to be so boggled by that?

Can there be any symmetry slicker than a square? The sphere is symmetrical too, but in your line of business don't spheres get misshapen oftener than not—don't they bulge at the equator? Don't they tend to be fat-assed? The circle can be coaxed into an ellipse, a sphere can acquire bumps and warts like the earth and moon, and still be called a sphere, but if a square suffers the slightest deflection, takes on the mildest accent, it's already another form, it takes another name, it turns into a rhomboid or some other geometrical boid.

I take the liberty—you're allowed a groan for each enclosure—of attaching an item titled *For example* that I wrote some years ago, on symmetry and natural models. And a second piece—Groan II—on the subject of extraterrestrial species, with which you deal so brilliantly in *Mind's Sky*. I have never subscribed to the notion that extraterrestrials would necessarily be technologically or in any other way superior to us. They might sooner be slobs or dullards than monsters. How could any species generate worse specimens than Adolf, Joe, Idi, Imelda, Ronnie, George, Danny and the majority of our high court? My feelings about intelligent life afield are ventilated in *Look Homely, Alien*, which ran in the *L.A. Times Magazine* after you left town.

I am bothered only by your concept of an intragalactic network creating linkages of intelligence. The time factor bugs me. If it would take ten times the interval between Moses and Alan Dershowits to say *Hello, Can You Make This Out?* and another such span to respond *Garbled Message Received Please Repeat*, so many things could happen at both ends as to string out any communication so long that whole civilizations could perish, as ours certainly will, along with all their codes and transcripts. And speaking of codes, I worry that you give too little shrift to the required decoding and cryptography. If we can't interpret the conversation of whales and dolphins, who also represent intelligent life on our planet and are no farther away from us than Sea World, how can we expect to figure out glyphs received from a planet of Eridani?

But then, I'm the guy who was sure we would never land a man on the moon, let alone take pictures of erupting volcanos on a satellite of Jupiter or Uranus or wherever the hell, or heaven, it was and is.

One last thing about *The Mind's Sky*, and I'll let you get back to your family. I was mightily impressed by your chapter on the unity of the universe and the human mind, because of something I experienced in my twenties. I had a tooth extracted one day, with gas used as anaesthesia. Under the influence of the gas (nitrous oxide?) I had the most astonishing dream of my entire life. COSMIC is the only word I have ever found to express it. It was as though the absolute inner essence of all consolidated mind and matter was *revealed* to me, compressed and refined and reduced to an entity the size of a grain of sand. It burst upon me, in my dream, as a disclosure of the greatest truth that could possibly be extracted from all the eons behind and ahead, from all matter, living and insensate. I awoke with an exhilaration impossible to describe. The dentist was apparently struck by my aspect, because he asked if I had had a strange dream. The effect did not soon pass. There was an unsubstantiality about everything around me, including the dentist and his office, and even though I was clamping my teeth down on a wad of cotton over a bleeding socket, the power of the vision still gripped me.

I took a bus home to my apartment on Riverside Drive (this was in Manhattan), and all along the way, everything seemed to be more than half unreal—passengers, bus, streets, traffic, buildings. I was at that time sharing an apartment with two brothers, and they had invited some friends to dinner, so when I arrived there were a dozen people in animated conversation, drinking, laughing. I withdrew to a room by myself and tried desperately to find my way back to that profound revelation, but it slipped from me almost palpably, like trying to hold onto something smoother than the slickest oil, something delicate and yet of great weight. And I lost it; yet it was another twenty minutes or so before the walls around me no longer seemed to be loose lattices of matter. And I left my retreat and joined the group, but I was in a haze for the rest of the night.

At the height of this hallucination, for that is what I believed it to be, I had the sense of a responsibility ordained by some vast universal force, a sense of having been commanded to devote the rest of my life to seeking and finding my way back to the awesome Truth that I'd been permitted to glimpse, as though a portal to the Ark, to the holy of holies, had been opened a little way, and I was permitted to see the glowing jewel inside it; and the jewel was no bigger than a mote.

So when I came upon your quote of Dogen's "grain of dust," and William Blake's "To See a World in a Grain of Sand," both of them on your page 92, it twanged deep chords in me. I suppose if the gas dream had happened to me in the days of Saul of Tarsus, maybe after chewing on a pinch of hash, I'd have become a visionary, and ended up losing my head, as Paul did.

Anyway, it was great reading your book, and I salute you once again. Your puissance is the good news. The bad news, which I got just this afternoon from Jack Langguth, is that [Irwin C.] Chet Lieb is in hospital with what appears to be a malignancy in a lung, and liver complications. One of the mysteries is why it seems to happen to good guys more often than to bad guys. I guess the answer is that we *know* more good than bad guys.

TO RAY BRADBURY / June 10, 1992

Dear Ray:

One night in the fall of '89 a young nephew of mine, a student of physics and ravenous fan of Ray Bradbury, asked me if I could get the great man's autograph. I mentioned this to you while we were riding in my car to or from a dinner, and you made me stop the car while you dashed into a bookstore and came out with a pocket Bradbury, signed and ready to ship off.

My nephew responded by sending you a work of his own, on the romance of measuring protein hydration shells by using a quartz microbalance, a subject with which we are both so familiar that it is like reading the alphabet. He sent it c/o me, since he did not have your address. I put the paper aside with the intention of sending it on, but naturally and routinely it was misplaced by my cleaning woman and has just come to light. I enclose it, only two and a half years late.

Not nearly so late are some thoughts that occurred to me after seeing *Next in Line*. I was distressed that this, like your previous play at the

Ivar, closed so soon. And I want to make a suggestion about the marketing of your stage works. I think it is a mistake to open a Bradbury or a Corwin play in Los Angeles. We write, both of us, for a special audience, one that does not serve the Taper or the Doolittle. With one exception my plays have opened out of town—*far* out of town. Vancouver once, Bloomington, Indiana once (University of Indiana), and Portland, Maine; and each did not open before a series of bookings had been made for a national tour. Every one of these performances constituted a preview, although all were for paying audiences. It takes time to mold a play, to see what works and doesn't work; to take things out and put things in; to make little or big changes, which can then be absorbed gradually by the company while traveling by bus or train or plane from one city to the next.

The one time a play of mine [*Tonight: Jefferson, Hamilton, Burr*] opened in a big theater in a big city was in Washington, D.C., and over my protest. But the producer, a New York fat cat, wanted the glamour of some high-ranking politicos whom he had invited to the first night. The play (not directed by me, incidentally, but by Frank Corsaro) was soundly drubbed by both local and New York critics who had come down for it, and had not the production been previously booked for a tour that included Hawaii, it would have closed then and there at L'Enfant Plaza. But it went on, having learned from the Washington experience, and redeemed itself in the weeks and months that followed.

Now Ray Bradbury is a powerful name around the country, and there are hordes of Robert Kaisers in the provinces who will go to see a play from your hand. They don't demand the same polished production in Hartford, Eugene, Akron and Lubbock that they do in L.A. or New York or Washington. You have time to tinker and adjust, and are not rushed. You also pick up a body of favorable reviews than can be used in advance publicity further down the line, and all the while you are smoothing out the wrinkles and cranking up the power.

It would entail a whole new policy of presentation, but that is not a bad idea, since the losses in the past three starts must have been painful, especially since so much great talent and hard work went into them all. There is a place for live Bradbury theater in the nineties, but I'm not sure the place is at first the Ivar or Burbank or any other venue covered by the *Times* critics—not until your play has had the chance to mellow while taking in money at the box office, as happens on the road.

Just to give you some idea of the feel of a touring company I enclose a brief log I wrote at the invitation of *Theatre Arts Magazine* back in '69. Responses included both nectar and acid—but at least when you're on the road, good receptions neutralize the acid, cut the losses, and make a profit.

Kate and I send our love to you and Maggie and the extended family.

Flourish!

TO MORTON GOULD, Composer; President of American Society of Composers, Authors and Publishers / July 31, 1992

Dear Morton:

It was refreshing to be on a conference-call broadcast with you a few weeks ago, but also frustrating not to be able to talk with you directly. For it has been far too long since we met—half a century, at least—and in all that time I have relished your music, and taken pleasure in the knowledge that we are auld acquaintances.

From your earliest to your latest work, nothing of yours has dated—Interplay, Fall River Legend, both symphonettes, Spirituals for Orchestra—and Strings—Salute, Derivations Soundings, West Point, Sarajevo (alas, poor Sarajevo), Ballad, Jericho—the whole bag. They're all alive and well, and I listen to them across the years, always with a sense of reward.

At least three times since the archival Cresta Blanca days, I wanted to communicate with you, but was stopped by the crazy kind of deadline pressures that have always beset me, and still do, notwithstanding that I am now an octo. The first time was when I was invited by the United Nations people to produce the first of what has since become an annual concert on the anniversary of the signing of Universal Declaration of Human Rights. The Boston Symphony, then under [Serge] Koussevitzky, was elected to be the orchestra, so I went to Tanglewood, where it was summering, to make arrangements with K. First off, I proposed that the concert open with a new work by Morton

Gould, to be commissioned by the UN. K found the suggestion tempting, but explained that he was under doctor's orders to lay down his baton after the Tanglewood season, and do nothing extracurricular for a year or so. He said he was going to turn the orchestra over to a young man by the name of Leonard Bernstein, and that he, Leonard, would have to be consulted about the UN program. That was what happened. LB opted for his pal Copland, who wrote a fanfare; and for the Chorale of the 9th.

A few years later on, the UN asked me to write the text of an "oratorio" for orchestra, soloists and chorus. Once again I asked for Gould to be the composer, but this time the commissioning was obliged to be governed by protocol—the librettist and the composer could not be from the same country. So the invitation went to a Spanish composer named Cristobal Halffter—a nice enough fellow, but one of the wild Turks of the far-out dissonance school. The work was performed both in Minneapolis and in the General Assembly Hall of the UN, by the Minnesota under Skrowaczewski (chorus conducted by Halffter). All I need tell you is that one of the movements, the text for which I had labored hard to write, was played and sung under a *meshugina* license to anarchy provided by the composer's direction *aleatory*. The whole goddam movement sounded like a riot in downtown Teheran. I could not distinguish a single word, and I wrote it.

Occasion 3: I rejoiced in your election to the Presidency of ASCAP, and meant to congratulate both you and the Association; but that intention, along with others as good, was buried under feverish activity, and by the time I remembered how remiss I had been, it was awkwardly late.

Anyway, I am not going to let this fourth impulse get away from me. After all, I owe you a great deal, not only for the good times I've had listening to Gould, but for the fact that you sponsored my membership in ASCAP way back when. That I have not been a productive member of the club is only because the demise of Radio as we knew and practiced it, robbed me of the regular working company of composers.

So hello, friend Morton. Carry on, as you do so well, and stay vital and creative.

TO WILLIAM SHATNER, Actor / November 9, 1992

Dear Bill:

It was a lucky day for me when I phoned you at an athletic club somewhere out in the [San Fernando] Valley—and had you paged, and introduced myself as the author of a play about a scientist and a she-fairy, and asked if you might be interested in starring in it, and you responded with awesome cordiality. After one meeting and a reading of my script, you consented to appear in the role of scientist Ted Bigelow, an expedition that took us into darkest Utah for a month of what I recall as a good deal of hard work and clean fun. It was in that same Mormon country that you introduced me to the Moped and guided me over the washboard roads of the Wasatch foothills, where I tipped over only once.

Since then you have been a best friend to the best of my writing, and, beyond that, you have responded with unhesitating generosity to calls made upon you for services to various historical and biographical accountings of the aging though not yet decrepit Bostonian who answers to my name. The latest of your tokens of surpassing good will is Mary Beth Kirchner's *American Voices*, to which you added your justly famous Canadian voice as narrator and cicerone.

Nobody, just nobody, can match you for all-around impeccability, from the unflappable commander of star-trekking operations to the flappable scientist of *The Hyphen*, to the austere Hank Peters of *Untitled*, the diverse roles you've played in all the performing media, plus the vagaries and subtleties of narration, as in the freshly minted WETA production. May I add that this latest gave me added pleasure in that you and your esteemed father-in-law [Perry Lafferty] appeared together on the same program—and, even better, that you introduced him. All in the family.

So, as I say, I'm lucky to have had that renaissance man Bill Shatner, who acts and sings and writes and directs and God knows what else, as a treasured friend and redoubtable ally for all these years. And, as so many times before, I say thanks—thanks squared, quadrupled, and then, for good measure, septupled.

TO RAY BRADBURY / November 17, 1992

Dear Ray:

Another burst of thanks for your kindness in sending me Bradbury Chronicles III. [A series of comic strip versions of *Ray Bradbury Chronicles* had appeared.] They bear out what I was saying at your digs last week— that I would have no hesitation in rising and proclaiming before the General Assembly of the United Nations, or any other group of reasonably sophisticated anthropogi (which excludes Congress, I'm afraid) that no other writer, including those we both prize, has inspired and fueled so many adaptations, variations and incarnations of his/her work—plays, musicals, radio, movies, television, periodicals, the art of the late (late far too soon!) Joe Mugnaini—and now color cartoons seriatim.

I was unaware of the Chronicles series, and now will see to the filling-in of 1, 2 and 4 in my cabinet of Bradburyana. The work in 3 is compelling, especially Truman's *Veldt*. His are the meanest lions since the Roman revels where they dined on fresh Christians. The texts throughout the strips are unlike any others that have accompanied comics in the history of the medium, and no wonder considering the source.

TO ROBERT YOUNG, Writer, Sacramento / February 7, 1993

Dear Bob:

You're a princely fellow to have sent me *The Paris Edition*....You are absolutely right about it, further proof that you have a good eye. I am already well into this rare and rich memoir, and am enjoying it very much.

There is a tug of melancholy nostalgia for me in [Waverly] Root's Chapter "C'est Fini," about the Sacco-Vanzetti executions, in which a man from *l'Humanite* and several members of the French S-V Defense Committee asked for permission to come to the office of the *Herald* in order to get the cabled reports as they came in on the night of the executions. I, too, was in a newspaper office that night, waiting for telegraphed reports to come in. I was a kid reporter for the *Greenfield Daily Recorder*, circulation 25,000, and I was asked to work that night fielding telephone calls as they came in. It was before the day of up-to-the-minute radio news, so the people of Greenfield and its environs could learn the latest bulletins only through calling the *Recorder*.

Interest was at high pitch, even in this American backwoods. It was Massachusetts, after all, where the crimes against those poor men took place, and where popular sentiment was, like Waverly Root's, mostly against Judge Webster Thayer and the courts. I remember having to answer callers, "Yes Sacco has been executed. Yes. Four minutes ago. Vanzetti is now on his way to the chair."—*Ring*—"Yes, they have been executed."—*Ring*—"Yes both men are dead."—*Ring*—"Yes—yes—yes—yes—"

Things go reasonably well here of late, the atmosphere having been lightened by Clinton's win, but my personal agenda continues heavy as ever. I am toiling on the transfer of my papers, scripts, tapes, memorabilia, the whole shebang, to a library that has acquired them for valid American currency, and I am also teaching at USC, and squaring away on a new book. Some days I don't leave my digs.

TO DR. WILLIAM B. OBER / February 8, 1993

Dear Bill:

You have lost none of your powers. *Obstetrical Events* is up there with some of your best, notwithstanding its express audience of medics and its consequent reliance on terms like nuchal arms, hypovolemic shock, blood dyscrasia, and meconium-stained amniotic fluid—routine terms to your professional brudders and understandable even to me, but of course not the lingo you'd use, and have used, in your hard-cover writings.

It's a striking concept—the effect of obstetrical events in shaping history—and I insist it belongs in another volume to expand the Ober shelf. You consistently have a unique approach to your material—a high style that both complements and compliments the deep research underlying all your papers. In how many medical or scientific journals does one find sentences like *He played it by the book, but his library was small,* and *the Kaiser's carapace of self-confidence?*

What impressed me, among other things, was that back in the time of Henry VIII and even as late as Princess Charlotte, detailed and explicit medical records were kept of royal accouchements, citing millimetric dilation measurements, the position of placenta in various stages, and time logs. Poor Charlotte—a hellish event from start to finish. Considering the absence of asepsis and the chasms of medical ignorance until relatively recently, it's a wonder the race persisted.

Nice set of clerihews you concocted, especially the one of John Cage. It baffles me as to why clerihews are not called bentleys, since the inventor's full name was Edmund Clerihew Bentley. How many forms, artifacts, machines and continents are dubbed after middle or first names? But hold—there is America, named after one Vespucci.

Things go reasonably well here, and I am glad the same goes for Tenafly. I spoke yesterday to Ed Linn, who delivers the sad news that your and my aunt Gertie Linn died last week. At ninety-six. A good long ride, but I'm afraid the last decade or more did not have much in the way of quality. And of course you must know that Norman Ober has been both married and divorced (to Maggie Weisberg) since we last communicated. Too bad, because they are both good, warm people, and I rejoiced when I learned they had merged.

Kate is now living in a house in Thousand Oaks, forty miles from here—not expressly to be near our son Tony and his wife, who also live there, but to be away from the city and its smog and traffic and noise. I see her only occasionally, but we are in telephone touch almost daily. Diane as you know has been married for some time. Her husband is a television newscaster for a station in Yuma, Arizona, and we all hope he will be able before too long to graduate to some bigger and nearer venue, because right now they are apart except for breaks in his schedule, and he must commute expensively by plane.

So much for bulletins from this end. We send you, Rhoda, Elaine and Stephen our love as a united front.

TO EMIL CORWIN / February 27, 1994

Dear Em:

You will be ninety-one in a few weeks, and I'll be eighty-four six days later, and we are both able to say, with a ritual knock on wood, that we still enjoy the grace of women skaters in Lillehammer, and Hillary in the White House, and Doonesbury daily and Sunday, and the annual spring illusion that the Red Sox will make it this year—a baseless notion, to be sure, but we are from Boston, and it's in the blood.

I'm up to here as usual, and from what you told me last Sunday you are up to there, each of us with an agenda that stretches into the next century and invites us to do the same. After all we are Sam's sons, and I've long suspected that his combined creed and war cry, *Keep your time and mind occupied!* is as much inherited as the color of our eyes.

The *Letters* sure as hell have kept me occupied. The first hurdle was to convince myself that anybody would give a damn about letters I wrote as a young dog seeking to mark territory. Next I wondered whether correspondence relating to radio drama, then a nascent medium, could possibly engage any reader not old enough to have heard much of it, or my kind of it.

As I read the letters I was moved, vexed with myself, entertained, appalled, sometimes instructed, too often saddened by the loss of friends and loved ones, reminded of passages at arms, or encirclement by arms, even startled by things I had written. As for letters to amours and amourettes, I'm sure that by the standards of today's young lovers they were—are—hardly what you'd call mash notes or even billets-doux. I evidently squandered my native prurience on limericks and occasional japes like a letter I once wrote to Jack Goodman on the subject of sowing wild goats.

I was amazed to find in my groaning files about ten thousand letters. Don't gasp. Our friend Thos. Jefferson wrote upwards of fifty thousand, but he was a titan, and he didn't have to pay postage. It was not that I saved pieces of string and crumbs of spent erasers. Very early I realized that I didn't have the patience to keep a diary, and that whatever entries I made were grudging and barren. So I decided that copies of letters I wrote might partly make up for lacks and slacks in the log, since they would at least pinpoint dates, events, people, moods, speculations, wins, losses and no-decisions.

The idea of publishing a collection of letters with the author still around, worried me because I assumed posthumousness was a main requirement, and I was in no hurry to honor that convention. I even went to a library to see whether there were any *non*posthumous collections. After a tiring search I found only one. When I got home I discovered in my own shelves a great specimen—the letters of E.B. White. Since I rate White as one of the choicer glories of civilization, that took care of that.

But as with White and other collectees, an *editor* was needed for my collection, being as how it ain't seemly for a writer to present his own letters. Not only unseemly but unthinkable. So an approach was made to A.J. Langguth, my favorite chronicler after Gibbon (*Patriots*, the forthcoming *A Noise of War*, a bio of Saki, etc.). After some hesitation he accepted, and lucky for me he did. He consulted me at times for data and dissa and datta, but I importuned him to act as umpire with the power to order me off the field. Instead he persuaded me to admit whole generations of letters such as the early ones with all their gaucheries, and some bawdy ones, and he left in letters which made use of quaint terms like fuck and asshole. All this on grounds which made great good sense to me.

Several letters to you are in the mix, and I hope you will not be discomforted by any of them. You once sought my advice on marriage, which was like asking an Eskimo what brand of seersucker suit to buy, and I answered with my usual brashness, quoting counsel given by Rabelais to an undecided swain who asked the same question. The text was apt and funny but went on too long and was judiciously cut.

Enough about the letters. I found a crack in one of the walls of my apartment yesterday, a full month after the Northridge shivers, and I notified the building's manager. He said inspectors had checked the premises and posted a sign reading NO APPARENT STRUCTURAL HAZARD. Which doesn't exactly thrill me. No *apparent* hazard? Why, the earthquake itself was triggered by what geologists call a hidden fault, and Hidden means Not Apparent.—So which way New York?

Joy to the world, including Washington.

And love.

INDEX

The numbers in bold type indicate recipients of letters.

Kuralt, Charles, ix, 363, 378, 379,
387, 389, 394, **398**, **405**, **412**,
421, **427**
Kurnitz, Harry, 93

LaCossitt, Henry, 104
LaFayette, Marquis de, 236
Lafferty, Perry, **48**, 52, 437
LaGuardia, Mayor Fiorello, 91, 103
LaGuardia Memorial Commission,
118
Lake Success, 121
Lambert, Jeanne, **25**
Lancaster, Burt, 102
Lanchester, Elsa. *See* Laughton, Elsa
Lanchester
Langguth, A.J. (Jack), **386**, 411, 433
Last Summer, The, 284
Las Vegas, 406
LaTouche, John, 153-54
Laughton, Charles, ix, 46, 47, 49,
50, 58, 62, 75, 76, 108, 139
Laughton, Elsa Lanchester, 46, 47,
49, 50, **75**
Laurents, Arthur, 101
Lawless, The, 127
Lawrence, Jerome, 160, 272
Lawrence of Arabia, 235, 237
Lazarus, Mell, **354**, 365
League of Women Voters, 394
Lear, Norman, 378, 379
Leaves of Grass, 53
Lederer, Ann Shirley, **227**
Lederer, Charles, **227**
Lee, Robert E., 160, 272, 321
Lemmon, Jack, 197
Levant, Oscar, 93
Leviathan 99, 307
Levy, Robin, **310**
Lewis, Fulton, 111, 115
Lewis, William B., 39, 40, 42, **51**,
61, 409

Lexicon of Musical Invective, A, 201
Liberalism, 110-12, 134
liberty, concept of, 250-51
Librarian, Princeton University, **238**
Library of Congress, 72, 149
Lie, Trygve, 135
Lieb, Irwin C., 433
Life, 139, 181, 241, 292
Life on the Road, A, 421-23, 427
Limericks, 123, 191-93, 258, 297,
302
Lincoln, Abraham, xi, 153, 205,
248, 263, 409, 429
Lincoln casting, 153, 245
Lincoln-Douglas project, 153, 154,
162
Lindsay, Mayor John, 289
Lindsay, Vachel, 33, 157
Lindtner and Collins, 154-55
Linkroum, Richard, **195**
Linn, Ed, **399**, 440
Linn, Gertie, 440
Litvak, Anatole (Toler), 101
Living History, 39, 40
Livingston, Jay, 305, 310
Locke, Jenny, **142**
Locke, Katherine (Kate), **69**, **79**, 80,
91, **93**, **95**, 98, **99**. *See also*
Corwin, Katherine
Locke, Maurice, **142**, 146
Locke, Sam, 143
Lockhart, Gene, 153
Lockridge, Ross, Jr., 118
Loesser, Frank, 135, 224
Lonesome Train, The, 280
Look Homely, Alien, 431
Lorentz, Pare, 348
Los Angeles Times, 193, 338, 363,
369, 374, 377, 385, 386, 391,
431
Losey, Joseph, 108, 127, 328
Lost Weekend, The, 45